AN EMERGING
ENTERTAINMENT

The Drama of the American People to 1828

AN EMERGING ENTERTAINMENT:

The Drama of the American People to 1828

Walter J. Meserve

INDIANA UNIVERSITY PRESS
BLOOMINGTON / LONDON

Published in Canada by Fitzhenry & Whiteside Limited, Don Mills, Ontario

Manufactured in the United States of America

Library of Congress Cataloging in Publication Data
Meserve, Walter J
An emerging entertainment.
Bibliography: p.
Includes indexes.
1.   American drama—History and criticism.
I.   Title.
PS332.M39   812'.009   77–74444
ISBN 0–253–37007–8   1 2 3 4 5 81 80 79 78 77

For Edward Wagenknecht, one who has taught well

"The love of learning, the sequestered nooks,
And all the sweet serenity of books."
—Henry Wadsworth Longfellow,
"Morituri Salutamus"

CONTENTS

PREFACE

A few weeks ago Lanford Wilson gave a lecture at Indiana University. As the author of *The Hot L Baltimore* (winner of the Best American Play Award of the New York Critics Circle, the Outer Circle Critics Award, and the OBIE Award for the Best Play of 1973), Wilson would seem to represent the popularly accepted American playwright of the 1970s. Addressing his audience in a pleasingly informal fashion, he reminisced about his early trips to New York, where he was not overly impressed with the plays he saw until he visited the Caffe Cino. There he found an atmosphere where plays were produced with a verve and perhaps an audacity which created in him a singular excitement and deep satisfaction. People always, or nearly always, thoroughly enjoyed what they watched. They laughed and laughed with the enthusiasm of innocence and abandon. At last, Wilson confessed to his university audience, he "knew what theatre was all about."

As I listened to these words, I suddenly realized that two hundred years had not really brought more than superficial change either to American audiences or to American theatre—at least, to one segment of the American audience and to one facet of American theatre. Those early farces and melodramas which entertained some of our ancestors are not very different in structure and objective (and sometimes content) from some plays we watch today—from, for example, *The Hot L Baltimore*. Early or recent, they are the plays of the American people, each perhaps soon forgotten as art but worthy of remembrance as a "momentary stay against confusion," if I may adapt Robert Frost's attitude toward poetry to an evening in the theatre. Only a few plays in any period of history rise above the limitations of popular entertainment, and with them critics and historians trace the development of drama.

Tracing that development, recording and assessing the plays which entertained Americans during the early years of our country, has absorbed my interest for many years. But I have not worked alone. A substantial part of my research has been concentrated in the material reproduced in the American Periodical Series, and I owe lasting debts to several student research assistants at the University of Kansas who helped me roll through those innumerable reels of microfilm in search of comments on American drama. Both the University of Kansas and Indiana University have been generous with grants-in-aid for that research. I must also gratefully acknowledge the Senior Fellowship, 1974–75, from the National Endowment for the Humanities, which allowed me time to complete my research and write this volume.

For particular material I wish to acknowledge and thank the Houghton Library for permission to quote from John Howard Payne's letter to Stephen Kemble and from James Philip Puglia's *The Embargo*; the Huntington Library, San Marino, California, for permission to quote from letters of George Washington Parke Custis and of David Humphreys; the Pierpont-Morgan Library, New York City, for permission to quote from John Neal's letters to the Reverend John Pierpont;

and Professor Peter Coulson, Southwest Texas State University, to quote from John Howard Payne's letter to Robert W. Ellison.

It has been my experience that few scholars show much interest in American drama prior to World War I. That I set about to change opinion is my own fault because I was warned during my graduate-school days more than twenty-five years ago not to waste my time with American drama. Quite naturally, then, I have a particularly deep sense of gratitude toward those who have encouraged my efforts and commented on my work: Professor Emeritus Hubert Heffner, Indiana University; Professor Gerald Weales, University of Pennsylvania; and Professor A. C. Edwards, University of Kansas. And for the one person who knows all my idiosyncrasies and tolerates them, most of the time, and who can read my impossible scrawl and transcribe it, most of the time—for that person, my wife, Ruth, my thanks, always.

W.J.M.
February 1977

AN EMERGING
ENTERTAINMENT

The Drama of the American People to 1828

ONE

Introduction

THERE IS the drama, and there is the theatre. Each means something quite particular, and yet common usage confuses the two while the academic community
sometimes creates meaningless and stereotyped attitudes suggesting antagonism
rather than interdependence. For example, in a midwestern university there was
a course in American theatre for which the theatre department instructor was
not allowed to assign plays because they could be taught only in the English
department. And there are students who read plays only in terms of a lighting
plot, a particular acting role, or a series of images. The drama and the theatre
may best be explained, however, through the metaphor of ideal lovers, each
enjoying a distinctive individuality of heroic or charming proportions, yet each
finding greatest fulfillment only with the other.

There is, then, the drama and the theatre, the "imitation of an action" and
the "place" for that action. But the theatre is more than a place. It is an institution which has a history; it is a created effect which one becomes aware of and
reacts to. Theatre is that period of time during which a story or an idea is represented through sight and sound upon a stage. The drama, too, is more than
the imitation of an action as it unfolds plot, character, dialogue, theme, tension
and conflict, dramatic structure, and complications and resolutions. The drama
is first created as literature, and in its distinctive form it may exist for all who
can read and understand.

The point here is simple and straightforward, yet frequently misunder-
stood. The historian of the drama is not the historian of the theatre. Rather
than be concerned with theatrical effect, how it is created and by whom and
whether the techniques of the creation, shown both by mechanical means and
by human beings, are innovative or imitative, the historian of the drama is interested mainly in the story or idea and the way it structured the effect—that is,
in the dramatic composition which the artists of the theatre turned into an

3

evening's performance. Once in possession of that literary composition, the historian of the drama becomes both recorder and evaluator, whose obligation is to explain what the play is all about and to place it properly in the developing history of dramatic composition. In his *Annals of the New York Stage,* George C. D. Odell occasionally noted that he could give the plot of a particular play, but he did not because he was writing, as he explained, a history of the theatre, not a history of the drama. In the present instance I am writing a history of the drama, and, in addition to pertinent historical development, biographical material, and critical evaluation, I will provide the plots of many plays.

For this history, however, there is a more difficult problem than simply distinguishing the historian of the drama from the historian of the theatre. The problem centers on the word *American.* What is American drama? Who are the American dramatists? The historian of American theatre has an easier task here because once one has found a group of actors and actresses performing in a building they call a theatre, one can discuss anything and all that they do. One need not be concerned whether the play they perform is English, French, or Russian. They are in America and creating theatre; that is all one needs to know. The historian of American drama, on the other hand, has a more delicate decision to make. What are the conditions which make a drama American? The question is particularly sensitive when the historian is researching the writing of drama in a large area, described generally as North America, which was colonized by the French, the English, and the Spanish before a portion of that area fought for its independence and became the United States of America.

Can the drama of that general area be called American only after the political division was created by revolution? Or, because the unsettled country was called America, is there sufficient reason to catalogue all dramas written there as American? Historians of American literature in general have faced the same questions and concluded that the writings of John Smith, William Wigglesworth, Cotton Mather, and scores of others who were never citizens of the United States of America nonetheless contributed their part to American literature. If one were to be most particular on this point, of course, one might insist that only the writings of the American Indians—for example, such Harvard College–educated Indians as James Printer, who acted as John Eliot's interpreter and corresponded with the English during the captivity of Mary Rowlandson; or Caleb Chaesahteaumuk (class of 1665), who could write passable poetry in Latin and Greek—were truly American literature. But wisdom seems to align itself with a liberal point of view and, in the general manner accepted by historians of American literature, all recorded drama written in North America prior to the establishment of the United States of America will be described as American drama. There is not a great deal, but the plays of that period do constitute the beginnings for a history of American drama.

One people in America who did not object to theatre but incorporated it into their daily lives were the American Indians. Although their native rituals and ceremonies do not belong in a history of American drama, the refinements which the white man's interactions with the Indians imposed on certain ceremonies have been considered the first evidence of theatrical and dramatic activity in America.[1] These are the ceremonies accompanying the treaties which the Indians made with the intruding white man. In the course of events, the general procedure of the treaty ceremony had become established by the Six Nations of the Iroquois Nation and accepted by the white man. In each instance there were interpreters and scribes. The treaty ceremony involved dialogue, episodes resulting from disagreement, and the spectacle of dance and mimetic action as well as serious dramatic action revealing a dignity of character and a beauty of language. As recorded history the Indian treaties and the accompanying ceremonies became, as Benjamin Franklin described them, distinctive literary documents. They also record events of a dramatic nature, and they exist in number—about fifty printed in small editions of which five appeared in the seventeenth century.

A recorded treaty meeting, or event, between the English and the Mohawk Indians after the destruction of Schenectady on February 18, 1690, illustrates this early form of literature.[2] On the first day the Indian Sachems spoke. After some speeches they gave a "belt of wampum, according to their custom," and after others they gave a bearskin. One speech suggests both the attitude of the Indians and the distinctive beauty of their language:

> Brethren, do not be discouraged, this is but a beginning of the war. We are strong enough, the whole house have their eyes fixed upon you, and they only stay your motion, and will be ready to do whatever shall be resolved upon by our brethren. Our covenant is a firm covenant, it is a silver chain and cannot be broke, it must not be broke. We are resolute and will continue the war, we will not leave off; if there were but thirty men of us left, we will proceed; therefore pray take good heart, do not pack up and go away; if the enemy should hear that, it would much encourage them. We are of the race of the bear, and a bear doth not yield as long as there is a drop of blood in its body; we must all be so.

On the following day the mayor and others from Albany answered the Sachems and made specific recommendations for the Indians' action and for their own defense. At the end they also gave wampum in addition to tobacco and provisions. Thereupon the Sachems "gave a shout according to their custom" and thus agreed to continue the war.

Sometimes the treaty ceremony involved much more give-and-take dialogue such as in "A Conference of His Excellency the Governor with the Sachems and Chief Men of the Eastern Indians" at Georgetown on Arrousick Island on August 9–12, 1717. In that discussion about land and water rights, there was not always accord, and at one meeting "the Indians rose up at once and withdrew, in a hasty abrupt manner without taking leave." Finally, with all complaints satisfied, a treaty was accepted with the proper formality, the giving of gifts, and a dance.

Although these Indian treaties varied in minor ways, there was always an argument or discussion leading to a climax. In this process several elements of drama were satisfied in ways that have influenced some critics to consider Indian treaties as a most appealing and somewhat sentimental beginning for drama in America. The difficulty, of course, lies in the acknowledged purpose of the event and the record. The writing was preserved only as any treaty protocol or transcript of a trial might be preserved, and the event was an act rather than the representation of an action, intended neither for present entertainment nor future staged performance. Consequently, transcriptions of such activity—clearly dramatic in a general sense but lacking the artistry and imagination imposed by a dramatist—do not belong in a history of American drama.

The identification of particular individuals as American dramatists presents a more serious problem, one already marked by disagreements among the few historians of American drama and theatre. Thomas Pollock, writing about the Philadelphia theatre in the eighteenth century, finds a certain joy in determining *The Conquest of Canada* as the product of an English author, George Cockings, whereas Arthur H. Quinn readily accepts Cockings as an American dramatist. For the period prior to the American Revolution, of course, any argument is academic. However writers of this time have been subsequently identified by critics and historians, they were all settlers or immigrants in an English colony. Whatever their personal philosophy or political persuasion, they were, presumably, under the aegis of the King of England, on whose authority land had been parceled out to the developers of the individual colonies. It is hoped that those prerevolutionary and revolutionary writers do not present a problem, however academic, that cannot be resolved through a reasonably acceptable literary fiat. If all drama written in the colonies during the prerevolutionary periods can be considered American (as the literature of the time is), the authors of those works can legitimately be catalogued as Americans (as literary figures are). Perhaps those qualities, both social and cultural, which distinguish the colonies from England and in some instances from each other may be used as an argument for this conclusion.

The early years of the American republic present additional difficulties for identification, which are intensified by the very nature of drama and its dependence on the theatre for the ultimate vision of its creator. The theatrical reforms which permeated England during much of the eighteenth century were sufficiently severe that the actor, in his extremity, was sometimes allowed a modicum of pity in contrast to the contempt heaped upon him in the past. Pity notwithstanding, the actor considered places other than England to apply his art, and in the Western Hemisphere first Jamaica and then America appealed to him. Contending with religious prejudices in the English colonies, acting companies led by Lewis Hallam and David Douglass brought English plays to establish theatre in America. After the Revolution theatre managers in America yearly augmented their companies by recruiting actors and actresses from England. A number of those theatre artists spent the major part of their careers on American stages; others, mainly stars, simply toured in America on occasions. While they were here they needed plays as curtain raisers or afterpieces as well as for the evening's major entertainment. Whereas the main plays were, of course, English or perhaps adaptations from the German or French theatres, with the brief pieces they frequently tried to catch local interests. Because Puritan attitudes seriously discouraged either appearing on the stage or writing for it, plays written by Americans were in short supply. Consequently, actors and actresses frequently wrote plays, sometimes very shortly after their arrival in America. The question is, are their plays English or American? In as much as a historian of American theatre accepts such actors as John Henry, John Hodgkinson, or James Fennell—all of whom wrote plays—as American actors, surely their plays may also be accepted as part of American drama. Robert Merry, husband of Anne Brunton Merry, who established herself as a major American actress after achieving success on the London stage, perhaps represents the extreme of the group. He was in America only a short time before he died but long enough to write a play—English or American?

For some readers of early drama in America, the nationality of the individual dramatists seems insignificant. They see only the large number of late-eighteenth- and early-nineteenth-century plays which seem to be American only by the publisher's imprint. In those plays they see plot, character, scene, action, dialogue, and theme as completely English. For them the history of American drama begins with the work of Eugene O'Neill because he had the genius to invoke the unusual and the timeless through a temperament and artistry which sprang from an American identification. It is one obligation of the historian, however, to correct such views and draw equal attention to that American identity which distinguished many plays during this early period.

What makes a drama distinctively American? In the history of America, as a continent and as a nation, at what point can the literary historian start talking about an American literature? In the academic world students at Middlebury College heard lectures on English and American literature in 1848–49 although for the American part oratory was the major emphasis. Of 109 colleges and universities surveyed for the year 1870, only 24 mentioned American literature. After 1900 more teachers became interested in American literature, but special courses in American drama came only after World War I through the efforts at the University of Pennsylvania of Arthur H. Quinn, who also offered graduate work in the area in 1922. In 1926 only 19 of 148 leading colleges and universities offered graduate work in American literature. In fact, it was not until immediately after World War II that American literature became a truly respectable emphasis for graduate study, and a flood of new Ph.D.'s in American literature hit the expanding college market.

For the historian American literature becomes identifiable when writers show an awareness of America as a social, political, and psychological force as well as a physical entity. In the more basic steps of this awareness the dramatists were more alert than were the writers of poetry and fiction. The Yankee character with his peculiar dialect and odd habits appeared in the drama before the Revolution, and the American Negro appeared on the stage as a comic character during the same period. By the time Washington Irving became recognized as the American Goldsmith through his *Sketchbook* stories of Rip Van Winkle and Ichabod Crane in 1819 and William Cullen Bryant was explaining the beneficent relation between God and New England through poetic metaphors involving the waterfowl and the yellow violet, American dramatists had written a number of plays emphasizing the peculiarities of the Yankee, shown considerable interest in the American past through plays about Indians and America's wars (the Revolution, the Barbary Coast War, the War of 1812), introduced several character types (Negro, Irish, Dutch), and provided an abundance of satiric and comic comments on America's social and political institutions.

After those initial steps, however, American drama lagged behind other genres of American literature. The nature of drama makes an awareness of people, of their customs and speech peculiarities, an obvious requirement, but the fullest expression of America comes with the recognition and imaginative creation, not only of distinctive American qualities in scenery, people, and events, but of those ideas and perceptions which unite humanity. In this respect American poetry, short story, novel, and essay came into their own by the middle of the nineteenth century. For consistently comparable artistic genius and philosophical insight, readers had to wait—except for some brief moments on both page and stage—for American plays written after World War I.

American drama developed at a pace consistent with the demands and permissiveness of society. It could not have done otherwise. Because some colonial fathers (and city fathers into the nineteenth and twentieth centuries) saw all theatre as a gateway to hell, they tried to abolish it. Others took a different view and saw in the drama a vehicle for moral instruction. Against certain prejudices and in support of this or that social or political view or just as a means of thoughtless entertainment, theatre in America grew in proportion to potential audiences but at a moderate rate. American drama, on the other hand, for reasons already noted, developed much more slowly. Furthermore, it was impossible until late in the nineteenth century to make a living as a dramatist. That some early authors state frankly in the prefaces to their plays that they wish to realize some financial return is a comment on the times.

Historians, whether literary or otherwise, are usually bound by a chronological development of subject matter as they constantly search for significant points of demarcation. For the present volume the starting point depends on recorded history while the activity of dramatists during the colonial and revolutionary periods is sufficiently different to be easily distinguished. The next important date in the development of American drama—important also in the political and cultural history of America for changes stimulated by the election of Andrew Jackson as President—is 1828, which marks the beginning of Edwin Forrest's Prize Play Contests. For the first time American playwrights were asked to contribute their plays and to be recognized for their work. In a very real way, American drama received a necessary stimulus that would eventually bring about healthy changes in the life of the American dramatist. But those changes would be long in coming.

During the two score and odd years separating 1828 from the revolutionary war, the number of Americans writing plays increased while the number of American plays produced in the country's theatres was still embarrassingly small. It was a rare season in New York during those years that two or three American dramas were performed. There were other American cities with active theatres at this time, however, and American plays were performed by both professional and amateur groups outside of New York, which in the 1820s was just becoming recognized as the theatre center of America. More than a few plays were published without productions, some because they were obviously more for the closet than for the theatre, others for the numerous reasons that managers find when they must reject plays to ensure a profitable season. Even in a history of the drama, performed and unperformed dramas should be distinguished although at that early point in the history of American theatre the distinction is not as meaningful as it is later.

For the 230 years which this volume covers my purposes are (a) to provide a chronological study and critical evaluation of the plays written and published in America, (b) to explore the kinds of drama written during particular periods and the relationship of drama to the cultural and historical progress of the country, (c) to provide biographical material on important dramatists and historical information on relevant plays, and (d) to determine the development of American drama as a literary genre and its contribution to American theatre.

TWO

Colonial Attitudes and the Beginnings of Drama in America

THE HISTORY of drama is the history of people. Around the beginning of the sixteenth century, when European explorers were seeking new lands and new sea routes to the West, there were perhaps as many as 800,000 Indians living on the continent of North America. In their distinctive fashion these people faced each day contending with each other as well as with the unknown. The light and the dark, the warm and the cold, life and death in nature and among men—all were a part of their joy, their suffering, or their enduring. And as seasons changed or special events occurred, they celebrated with ritual and ceremony which may be described as theatre in a basic form. When the invading adventurers from Spain, Portugal, France, and England began to establish settlements on the new continent, they too found or remembered occasions worthy of celebration. Having the background of a more sophisticated culture, however, they presented, not a ritualistic ceremony, but an action representative of the event which excited their imaginations. In this manner the first dramas were enacted in America, and the records of those performances, along with an exciting manuscript in one instance, mark the beginning of American drama.

During the approximately 150 years that followed Columbus' extraordinary voyage, most of the settlements in America which would determine national interests were established. Spain created settlements both in Florida and in Central America, from which it penetrated north of the Rio Grande. France explored what is now eastern Canada and the shores of New England. By the end of the first quarter of the seventeenth century, the Netherlands had

11

established trading posts in the New York area, and England had started colonies at various points along the Atlantic seaboard. With strong traditions in drama and theatre, settlers from Spain, France, and England quite naturally tried to bring their own form of entertainment to their new country. Unfortunately, few examples were recorded. The history of drama and theatre during this period of settlement in America, however, is essentially the story of the entertainment these settlers devised to celebrate events or simply to lighten the burdens of daily life.

Perhaps no people in Europe had a more passionate love of the theatrical than did the Spanish. That they brought this passion with them, not only as a part of their religious tradition, but as a necessary embellishment of their explorations, conquests, and settlements is a historical fact. Consequently, some of their more conventional theatrical activity blends into the varied background of American drama. At the Spanish mission at Tequesta in Florida, for example, two comedies were performed on or about June 24, 1567. There is no way of knowing whether these were traditional church plays or simply ones written for the occasion by the person in charge of the mission, a lay brother named Francisco de Villareal. Brother Villareal's letter to his superior, January 29, 1568, does not clarify the issue: "We have put on two comedies one on the day of St. John when we were expecting the governor. This play had to do with the war between men & the world, the flesh & the devil. The soldiers enjoyed it very much."[1] Spanish fascination for theatrical entertainment is also clearly evident in Cortes' tales of Mexico as well as in the song-and-dance entertainment which was a part of his expedition into Yucatan. But that is material for the broader history of American literature.

The conquest and occupation in 1598–99 of the territory of New Mexico by Don Juan de Oñate for the King of Spain provides a story more relevant to American drama. The particulars concerning that military expedition and the play which was performed during it appear in the *History of Arizona and New Mexico (1530–1888)* by H. H. Bancroft, who in turn took most of his material from an epic poem published in 1610 by Captain Gaspar de Villagrá, one of Oñate's companion conquistadors. The expedition, it seems, started off poorly as the King of Spain, causing a sense of failure and anger among those involved, delayed the venture. But the order finally came, and the army of 400 men (130 of them with families), 83 wagons, and 7000 head of cattle started northward on January 20, 1598. Soon it was joined by a Captain Marcos Farfán de los Godos, who with a small party had escorted Padre Marquez. On April 30, 1598, just ten days after he reached the Rio Grande, Oñate took formal possession of New Mexico for God, the King of Spain, and himself. The impressive ceremony he devised to celebrate the occasion included a mass held in a chapel built especially for the event and a sermon. Then, as Bancroft states, there occurred "finally in the evening the performance of an original comedy written by Captain Farfán on a subject connected with the conquest of New Mexico" (p. 127). What a pity that nothing more is recorded of this quite momentous event—the first play known to be written and performed in North America.

The expedition continued, and in November Farfán was sent out with another captain and a squad of men in search of mines. Farfán was evidently a trusted and effective member of the expedition. At one of the more difficult points in the advance, he was one of several officers and seventy men sent by Oñate on January 12, 1599, to capture the Indian village of Acoma. Later, on March 2, 1599, when support for the expedition was needed, Farfán was again chosen to carry the necessary letter to the governor in Mexico. Happily, he was also one of those who survived the expedition which has established him in the history of American drama.

The fact that Farfán wrote in Spanish may disturb some who search for the beginnings of American drama. Nor are those searchers likely to be gratified by the next example of American drama, a play performed at Port Royal in the wilds of Nova Scotia in 1606. Although the French explorer Cartier first mentioned the name of Canada after his second voyage there in 1535, it was Marc Lescarbot (or L'Escarbot, as nineteenth-century historians called him) who applied the name to the entire northern region. Lescarbot (1570– or 1575– 1634?), born into French lesser nobility, as his seat as advocate in Parliament indicates, was a lawyer, historian, poet, essayist, playwright, Commissaire de Marine, traveler, and explorer. Today he is remembered mainly for *The History of New France*, which he wrote in 1608, but during his lifetime both the *History* and the *Muses* (his plays) appeared in five popular editions in France, and that portion of the history dealing with Port Royal was translated into English by Pierre Erondelle.

Of the people involved in the historical incident at Port Royal which Lescarbot described in his play, or masque as it is more properly termed, the most important were Samuel Champlain, founder of New France and associated with Canada from 1603 until his death in 1635; Jean de Biencourt, Sieur de Poutrincourt and a gentleman of family who sailed with Champlain and returned to France in 1605 to obtain the concession for Port Royal; and Robert Du Pont, son of Pontgrave the navigator. Although Champlain considered Port Royal the most fitting place for a settlement, life at the Stronghold, or the Habitation as it was called, was not easy. Unfriendly Indians were a constant danger, scurvy caused many deaths, and winters were particularly bad. When, on May 24, 1606, de Biencourt received a letter stating that his "privilege was revoked" and that he should bring the settlers back to France, the band at the Habitation was gravely depressed. At first de Biencourt did not comply, and during this time—the fall of 1606—Lescarbot added his masque to the devices by which the gallant little group helped keep up their spirits. Another diversion was "The Order of Good Cheer"—the first social club in North America—organized by Champlain.

De Biencourt had been on a voyage down the coast looking for a warmer place to settle. Champlain, who was with him, made this note in his *Voyages*: "Upon our arrival, Lescarbot, who had remained at the settlement along with the others who stayed there, welcomed us with sundry jollities for our entertainment." Among these was *The Theatre of Neptune in New France* (first entitled *Les Muses de la Nouvelle-France*), "presented upon the waves of Port Royal the fourteenth day of November, sixteen hundred and six, upon the return of Sieur de Poutrincourt from the Armouchiquois." As Sieur de Poutrincourt and his men approach the Habitation in their shallop, they are welcomed by Neptune, who, in a colorful chariot "drawn over the waves by six Tritons," swears to favor the exploits of Sieur de Poutrincourt and foretells a "prosperous domain . . . in this fair, new world." Then a trumpet sounds and the Tritons begin to praise Sieur de Poutrincourt in traditional laudatory sentiments which are happily interrupted by the humorous verses of the fifth Triton, who speaks in a Gascon dialect and who warns against "dat high flown God Neptune." Four "Indians," who had trailed Neptune's "chariot," then bring gifts to Sieur de Poutrincourt with more words of praise. The first Indian brings "a quarter of a moose or deer"; the second, the skins of beavers; and the third offers, with an appropriately courtly speech, a scarf and bracelet "made by the hand of his lady love." The fourth Indian suggests Lescarbot's imagination. Having been unsuccessful in hunting, this Indian brandishes his harpoon and explains that he is going fishing and will bring something for "monseigneur" if he is lucky. Sieur de Poutrincourt then thanks Neptune, the Tritons, and the Indians and invites them all to a great feast at Port Royal, whereupon the Neptune troupes sing a four-part song in which they pray to Neptune that they may all meet again in France. More trumpets sound; cannons break forth on all sides. As Sieur de Poutrincourt lands, he is addressed by "a companion in a merry mood"—most likely Lescarbot himself—who explains that "the days of loneliness are past" and who then describes the feast they are ready to enjoy: "Let each man drain his cup!"

The entire masque contains 242 rhymed lines, for which Lescarbot begged the reader's indulgence because "they were made in haste." All is quite staid, burdened with the formality of verse and enlivened only by the costumes and the words of the fifth Triton and the fourth Indian. The sentimental prayer at the end presents another contrasting mood. More pageant than drama, it has value mainly as a theatrical and literary curiosity. Not until 1927 did an English translation appear. On August 2, 1926, the Historical Association of Annapolis Royal (Port Royal), Nova Scotia, unveiled a tablet in honor of *The Theatre of Neptune* and the next year crowned its celebration with the publication of Harriette Tabler Richardson's translation of the first (1609) edition of the masque.

While the French were searching the northern coasts of America for appropriate sites for settlements, the English were conducting similar explorations farther south. In 1587 John White, under the authority of Sir Walter Raleigh, left a group of colonists on the coast of North Carolina, only to find no trace of this "Lost Colony" on his return in 1590. But the attraction of the New World was not diminished, and by 1660 New England, Virginia, and Maryland boasted full-fledged colonies. After years of controversy and conflict, the Dutch settlements in New Netherlands became a part of England by treaty in 1674. Next William Penn, receiving a slice of the Duke of York's land grant, came to America in 1682 to conduct his "Holy Experiment." As the population of the colonies in America multiplied (72,000 in Virginia by 1700, for example, and approximately 106,000 in New England), however, the usual human problems appeared. The process of government became a more complicated affair. In many places simple survival demanded a determined struggle, and, as a contrast to the serious work to be done, there had to be play and entertainment—a lighter side of life to be enjoyed.

This contrast between two facets in human nature—interpreted by many early colonial fathers as a conflict between the flesh and the devil—provided not only the background for much social commentary and legislative activity in the New World but also the matter for the beginnings of a drama. It all started in Virginia, where the early settlers were largely middle-class Englishmen, Puritan in manner, who had in their first Virginia Assembly (1619) quickly enacted a code of laws "Against Idleness, Gaming, drunkenness and excess in apparell." By the middle of the seventeenth century, however, the population had become less homogeneous; Puritan congregations had been outlawed since 1643, and the colony was governed by Sir William Berkeley, a strong royalist. Given the Englishman's traditional interest in the theatre along with the exuberance of many settlers and that natural conflict in human nature, it was reasonable that some form of dramatic entertainment would appear, that some indignantly pious individual would inform on the actors, and that a liberal court would make the appropriate decision.

A play, *Ye Bare and Ye Cubb*, was performed on August 27, 1665, on the Eastern Shore of Virginia by three citizens of Accomac County: Cornelius Watkinson, Philip Howard, and William Darby. For reasons not specified in the Accomac County Records (Vol. 1663–66, folio, p. 102), one Edward Martin informed the king's attorney, John Fawsett, of the event with the result that the three actors were summoned and cross-examined by justices of the court held in Accomac County on November 16, 1665. This exercise, however, was insufficient, and the trio were ordered to "appeare ye next court, in those habilemts that they then acted in, and give a draught of such verses, or other speeches and passages, which were then acted by them."

It is unfortunate that the play is not extant, but the judges seem to have been rather thorough in their examination. The sheriff detained Watkinson and Howard only until they "put in security" but was ordered to "arrest ye body of William Darby," who seems either to have been mainly responsible for the play or to have served as the spokesman of the group. At any rate, Darby was singled out "to answer at his mates suit, for acting or being actour of a play commonly called Ye Beare & Ye Cubb." On December 18, 1665, however, the judge must have been impressed with the defense, for Martin was ordered to appear at the next court to show why he should not pay charges. At this later date, January 17, 1666, "finding the said persons not guilty of fault," the judges "suspended ye payment of Court charges" and ordered Martin to pay all costs.

In that history of the drama which exists in the American courts of law, this case was a good beginning. Whereas this incident took place in Virginia, in other colonies where the so-called drama of life was frequently not only exciting but spectacular, American drama had an even more difficult time getting started. The concept of drama, however, and the institution of the theatre were frequently in the minds of the people. As many existing documents suggest, drama and theatre were significant issues in the records of colonial courts and in the church annals. But because no evidence appears about specific plays being written or performed, the history of American drama during the remainder of the seventeenth century is, in part, a history of reactions to drama.

That man may turn his back on his cultural heritage only with great difficulty is a commonplace observation. During the seventeenth century a number of those who came to America were men with classical educations and Puritan ideals. Their thought and action reflected the prevailing attitudes toward drama in England, where theatre doors were closed by the Puritans in 1642. To the modern mind, however, they developed an intolerance toward some of their assets. As Samuel Eliot Morison states in *The Intellectual Life of Colonial New England*, "Puritanism banned three forms [of art] in which the English excelled: the drama, religious music, and erotic poetry." Holding considerable power in America, the Puritan, the Quaker, and the Presbyterian solidly opposed drama; yet, each was concerned with the principles of classical education, which were traditional in England. Clearly, one part of a cultural inheritance warred against another.

The concern for religion and education which directed the energies of the Christian devines in the Plymouth and Massachusetts Bay colonies and even impelled them to teach their theology to the Indians was not only their response to the "voice of God" but also was clearly in keeping with the Letters Patent (1606) issued by the King of England for the colonization in America. According to a 1642 Massachusetts legislative act, children were to be taught "to read and understand the principles of religion and the capital lawes of the country." By 1672 all the settled territory of New England (with the exception of Rhode Island) had compulsory education. The creation of educational institutions in other colonies generally lagged behind New England, where Harvard College had been founded in 1636, and Virginia, where as early as 1619 Sir Edwin Sandys had proposed a college for Indian and English youths in common. In all of these early ventures the classical tradition was united with the study of religion.

With regard to dramatic literature, the compulsory readings in the schools together with the reading habits of the intellectuals foreshadow interests which many people in positions of authority at this time were trying to limit. In 1676, for example, a freshman at Harvard College would read the works of Sophocles, Euripides, and Aristophanes. He perhaps would also read satiric poetry and parodies. This interest in the classical tradition permeated many aspects of colonial life: education, church, literature, and statecraft. It was understood that educated people would know the classics although they might use their knowledge—As Samuel Sewall quoted Ovid against the theatre (*Diary*, III, p. 379)—to further their own particular views. Those of literary taste were generally inclined to collect books of history, theology, travel, and orations, but Increase Mather's library also had the works of Plautus, Seneca, and Sophocles.

When Samuel Lee brought his extensive library to New England in 1686, it included works by Seneca, Sophocles, Euripides, and Aristophanes. Books were important to cultural life in the colonies—even Miles Standish had almost fifty in his library—and a good education suggested breadth of character.

Generally, at least in New England, theology satisfied the average colonist's desire for reading matter. For the one person who read a play, there were hundreds who read theological tracts. Booksellers imported books from London at a surprising rate, and there was also a press in Cambridge which in 1670 recorded 157 publications, mainly on religious subjects and under rigid supervision. Thomas G. Wright (in *Literary Culture in Early New England, 1620–1730*) quotes from a letter in which a bookseller describes one of his customers: "The chief books she bought were Plays and Romances; which to set off the better, she wou'd ask for Books of Gallantry" (p. 120). Such books were available in Boston by the late seventeenth century. In 1692, for example, bookseller John Usher's order from Robert Boulter, a London bookseller, numbered nearly 800 volumes, including Reynolds on "Murther" and other "light reading." Among the gentry of Virginia, reading was of a more liberal nature. Governor William Berkeley, for example, having written *The Lost Lady* for a performance at the court of Charles I in 1637, had a small reputation as a dramatist before coming to Virginia.

In as much as any literature was created in seventeenth-century America, it was meagre. Little writing, particularly in belle lettres, was encouraged. When education demanded literary creativity, the classical tradition dominated. Even the few Indians educated at the Indian College built in Harvard Yard in 1656 were subjected to its rigors. Any number of sermons and trials were published, of course, and some poetic thought did find expression, but much of it was of a homiletic nature such as Michael Wigglesworth's *Day of Doom* (1662). Anne Bradstreet was mainly concerned with religion as personal experience in her poems but revealed also her delight in natural beauty. The best of the seventeenth-century poets was Edward Taylor. Perhaps the most exciting prose work of this general period, however, appears in the several Indian-captivity stories: Mary Rowlandson's *The Soveraignty & Goodness of God Together With the Faithfulness of His Promises Displayed: Being a Narrative of the Captivity and Restoration of Mrs. Mary Rowlandson* (1682); John Williams' *Redeemed Captive Returning to Zion* (1707); or Captain Benjamin Church's *Entertaining Passages Relating to Philip's War* (1716). Real, straightforward, even humorous on occasion, such works show dramatic material, which at this time, unfortunately, no one seemed willing to put into play form.

It is difficult to determine the power of the English prejudice which followed the Puritans to America or the influence of such works as J. Rainold's *The Overthrow of Stage Plays*, Burton's *Against Showing of Stage Plays*, or George Ridpath's *The Stage Condemn'd* (1698), in which he argued against such books as Denis' *The Usefulness of the Stage to the Happiness of Mankind, to Government and to Religion*. Ridpath's attempt to prove "that the corruption of the stage is in a great measure owing to the method of educating our youths in schools" was taken seriously by many colonists and noted ministers. A person daring to follow another drummer was generally in trouble.

Such a person was Thomas Morton, Gent., a trader, adventurer, and lawyer in Clifford's Inn, who was among the settlers landing at Passonagessit (now Quincy, Massachusetts) in 1625 with Captain Wollaston. When Wollaston went to Virginia, Morton took charge of the settlement, renamed the place Ma-re Mount (hence Merry Mount), gathered about him a group of epicureans who were of the Anglican faith, and openly expressed an interest in wine, woman, and the pleasures of a fur trading post. The best-known episode of his career in revelry was his celebration around a Maypole, which the Pilgrims termed a pagan rite. Presumably, Morton's major offense was his defiance of the law in selling liquor and firearms to the Indians, but he had also scandalized the Pilgrims, who had him arrested and sent to England in 1628. As persistent as he was original in his life-style, Morton returned to his fur trading in 1629 only to be expelled again the following year and then jailed in Boston in 1644–45 when he returned to New England. His own account of his adventures, *New England Canaan* (1637) is a lighthearted attempt to satirize his pursuers. Probably if Nathaniel Hawthorne had not exploited his experiences in *The Maypole at Merry Mount*, he would have been more easily forgotten. As it is, his experiment in entertainment was more of an episode at a fair than it was a theatrical happening. More important was the immediate and consistent reaction of the authorities, whose worst fears of anything even remotely related to theatre were realized in the carefree atmosphere of the Maypole celebration as well as in the social and moral rebellion of its prime mover.

Morton was certainly not the only one to try to lighten the gloom of the New England theocracy. But such activities are recorded almost entirely by those who were opposed to them, and references are understandably slight. Samuel Sewall (1652–1730) and Cotton Mather (1667–1728), author of *Magnalia Christi Americana: or, the Ecclesiastical History of New-England, from its first Planting in the year 1620, into the year of our Lord, 1698, in Seven Books*, are two available sources for information on daily activity during the seventeenth century. As Puritan moralists, they also had opinions and did not hesitate to draw conclusions from what they saw and heard. Early in his history of New England, Mather scourged bawdy houses and alehouses: "Don't contenance drunkenness, revelling and miss-spending of precious time in your houses." Fond of philosophy and argumentation, Mather provided questions and answers (book 5) which were to deter people from such activities as might lead them to a theatre if one were allowed to exist. Games of cards or dice were "diversions" which "*fascinate* the minds of those that practice them, at such a rate, that if ever those persons come to be converted unto God, they bitterly lament the *loss of time* in which that practice hath involved them."

> *Question*—Whether Instrumental Musick may lawfully be introduced into the Worship of God, in the Churches of the New Testament?
> *Answer*—If we admit instrumental musick in the worship of God, how can we resist the imposition of all the *instruments* used among the ancient Jews?
> —yea, *dancing* as well as *playing*, and several other Judaic actions?
> [Pp. 266–67.]

Cards, dancing, and theatre were aspects of English life which some people obviously wanted to bring to America, and their efforts were occasionally recorded. When Sewall noted in his diary for June 21, 1699, that someone had strewn a pack of cards in his front yard, he knew that he was being mocked for some stern action that he had taken. Some years earlier, in late April and May of 1687, Sewall had worried about Maypoles, dancing, and a staged fight after which the two antagonists went through town with naked swords, a drum, and an interested following. The first dancing master who came to Boston was investigated by the Court of Assistants on September 6, 1681 and ordered away as "a person very Insolent and of ill fame, that Raves and scoffes at Religion."² Increase Mather, Cotton's father, also recorded in his diary activities that wasted time and on April 27, 1687, complained that "sword playing was then openly practiced on a stage in Boston"; on May 1 he noted that "a Maypole was set up in Charlestown." Thomas Morton would undoubtedly have been highly amused had he still been alive, but it was a solemn affair for Mather, who, in his preface to *A Testimony Against several Prophane and Superstitious Customs Now Practiced by some in New England* (London, 1687), sadly admitted a serious step toward the downfall of the human race: "there is much discourse of beginning Stage-Plays in New England."

Central to the objections of the New England clergy toward entertainment in general and the theatre in particular was the concept of time: people must be meaningfully productive in the eyes of God and use their time wisely. Richard Mather, Cotton's grandfather and a minister, was determined "to strive aginst . . . excessive sleeping . . . vain jangling, and misspending precious time." The argument for the best use of time was presented again and again down through the years and centuries until it became the theme of the American businessman from Benjamin Franklin to Horatio Alger to the modern capitalist. In the seventeenth century, however, time was carefully related to a morality by which success meant going to heaven rather than getting rich. Becoming wealthy as a consequence of the hard work which Christianity demanded was to be avoided although not all did so. In that particular society, then, it was a basic obligation of the exponent of drama to defend the theatre as a moral and, therefore, valuable use of time.

It is interesting to look at the writings of those stern accusers of the drama and see how very dramatic they frequently were both in the kind of material they chose to discuss and in their mode of presentation. Many of the clergy were undoubtedly admirable actors if their sermons provide any indication of their style of pulpit oratory. The forms of some of their sermons, even their metaphors, were frequently truly dramatic. Cotton Mather, for example, clearly considered the pulpit as a stage and on numerous occasions in his many works explained that a member of the clergy had "come upon the stage." Certainly he was concerned with the drama of what he described. Read, for example, his "A Narrative of Hannah Swarton," an account of a woman who was captured by Indians in May, 1690, and taken to Canada to suffer trials with both the Indians and the French before being returned to Boston in November, 1695. It is a dramatic story, well told.

A term which Cotton Mather and other clergy of his time frequently used in their sermons and writings was *discourse*. A playwright might have substituted the word *dialogue* and dramatized the incident with little revision of the minister's text. Frequently there was drama inherent in the situation described, and, although a distinct plot was lacking, there was continuity, purpose, a theme, and a number of the elements of good drama, as in, for example, Mather's "The Discourse of the Minister with James Morgan, on the Way to His Execution" (vol. 2, book 6, pp. 410–13). As the two men walk along, it is clear that Morgan is a murderer, while something of his character is revealed in the minister's admonition and Morgan's confession, repentance, and acceptance of what follows. During their walk along the "plashy street," Mather does not always make things easy for Morgan but forces him to want, and plead for, his prayers. Finally they reach their destination, the gallows, and the convert leaves the minister with as dramatic a curtain line as would end most melodramas to be written over the next 150 years: "O Lord—I come, I come, I come."

Contrary to his reputation for dullness, quite adequately illustrated throughout most of his *Magnalia Christi Americana*, Mather occasionally dealt with exciting material which he described or narrated in a dramatic form. In addition to his discourses between minister and criminal—a man who slit his wife's throat, for example—on the road to the gallows, Mather also discussed preternatural occurrences in the invisible world. His ability to write about witches, devils, and Satan in an exciting manner should not be discounted, and his tales of the Indian Wars display the matter of drama which he seemed to envision in terms of theatre. Describing one of these "actions, whereof Plymouth was now the stage" (vol. 2, book 7), he tells of the return to Boston on July 22, 1676, of Massachusetts forces that had just killed 150 Indians and lost only one Englishman. Even Mather's theological arguments suggest his natural inclination toward the dramatic. In his long discourse between a Quaker and a minister (Mather's alter ego) the argument that the church commanded baptism with water revolves around a disagreement concerning the difference between *therefore* and *because*. Within this discourse is a good bit of dramatic dialogue in which a meaningful point is pursued with conflict and tension involved and with character revealed.

In none of these examples, of course, is there true drama although in some instances it would take rather little work to create a drama from the material. Yet the spirits of those seventeenth-century New England clergymen would undoubtedly consider any comparison of their works with the theatre an abomination beyond measure. They were writing of human experiences and the search for meaning through an understanding of the Christian way. They were not simply representing the human condition for entertainment purposes, and they were not writing for the theatre, which they considered a waste of time and, therefore, sinful. The argument that the theatre could be a moral force was not credited in seventeenth-century New England. Had it been and had the theatre's true potential for propaganda been recognized, men like Cotton Mather might have been extraordinary playwrights.

South of New England a planting ground for American drama appeared equally barren. The Dutch had been interested in trading posts, but their drawn-out disputes with the English consumed their energies during much of the century. When the Duke of York took over New Netherlands in 1654, the laws he created were much like those of New England. In that land between

Virginia and Spanish Florida, divided among eight people in a charter issued by Charles II on March 24, 1663, Charles Town became the seat of government by 1680. Not until after the turn of the century, however, would it become important in the history of American drama and theatre. Quite naturally the Quakers had found a home in Pennsylvania with Penn, a convert and a friend of George Fox, but, just as Penn's laws became restrictive, so the Quakers' concern for moral legislation restricted both artistic and cultural development. In 1682, for example, there were laws which provided penalties of hard labor for anyone who would introduce "into this province or frequent such rude and riotous sports and practices as prizes [prizefights], stage plays, [and] masques." In unsuspecting cooperation with the Puritans, the Quakers continued their fight against the theatre until almost the end of the eighteenth century.

Nor was all of the opposition to drama and theatre limited to what would become the United States of America. When, during the years from 1691 to 1695, Count Frontenac caused two plays to be acted in Quebec, there was a great storm of protest from the Jesuits. One man was sent to prison. Although the Quebec Jesuits had both written and acted plays as early as 1640 and 1658, Quebec became a divided city over the incident.

Thus during the seventeenth century the faint beginnings of an American drama and theatre remained victims of legal restrictions and religious prejudices. By the eighteenth century, however, a climate more hospitable to the drama very slowly and cautiously developed in the colonies as the necessary social forces gathered. Between the Treaty of Utrecht (1713) and the Treaty of Paris (1763) the character of the colonies in the New World was forged and molded by the disparate ideas of the colonists, the environment in which they lived, and the politics which affected them. During the last half of the seventeenth century, a great migration from various European countries had increased the population in the colonies to over 250,000. By 1776 there were ten times that number who would soon call themselves citizens of the United States of America. Scarcely a united people, they were, nevertheless, the people in America. What was there in their daily thoughts, their mode of living, and their personal or group ambitions which would encourage or reject the creation of drama? How does a diverse mass of people living in settlements remote from one another create an intellectual and emotional climate suitable for the nurturing and development of a distinctly American drama? Most forms of entertainment, drama included, tend to be hardy, but transplanting can be a problem, and there must be both determined and creative people as well as a receptive society.

Although the theocratic government in the Massachusetts Bay Colony came to an end in 1691, the strictures of Calvinism were not easily loosened. Most New Englanders, struggling against severe winters and hostile Indians, found little solace in Calvin's theory of "total depravity" and looked for an emotional outlet which Puritanism did not provide. Consequently, moral laxity and a disregard for the law were common. In the South people seemed freer to indulge an interest in entertainment. Citizens of Charles Town enjoyed balls and cotillions, and it was there in 1703 that Anthony Aston, an English actor, wrote and acted a play about America. One remarkable aspect is that he evidently found no opposition to his activity, which one might conclude was not new to the area. In Charles Town, where economic and social levels made its citizenry quite different from that of New England, drama would become not only tolerable but desirable.

Yet progress came slowly. Early in the century the developing mercantilism in the larger cities—Boston, New York, Philadelphia, and Charleston—fostered a strong attachment to England which was naturally increased as wealthy families sent their children to England or to the Continent to be educated. Although as the century progressed this cycle of influence tended to encourage the arts in America, throughout the colonies in general the mercantile aristocracy could ill afford to emphasize play over work.

By the time of the Revolution, however, the growth of a more distinctive social structure aided entrepreneurs interested in bringing theatre to America. In New England a secularization of life partially eliminated the aristocracy of the clergy, who, however, along with the merchants as the most highly educated of the colonists, continued a certain cultural as well as economic domination over the shopkeepers, fishermen, or workers of the lower freeman class. One reaction to the passionate but short-lived Great Awakening, during which Jonathan Edwards argued that New Englanders were abandoning a strict Christian morality for the code of the American businessman, was an eventual liberalization of cultural activities. In the South the landed gentry were the most highly educated and exerted a strong control over social and political affairs. In the middle colonies, Pennsylvania for example, the upper class was represented by the Quaker aristocracy, which demonstrated the dilemma of the times. On the one side was the Quakers' constant war against the theatre and "the reading of plays, romances, novels, and other pernicious books"; yet, as their wealth increased, even the Quakers began to take pleasure in living. Besides the aristocracy, the mercantile class, and lower freeman class, there was a servile class of indentured servants and slaves, but they had little effect on the question of drama in the colonies.

Although newly accumulated wealth in colonial America did not breed an immediate interest in the arts, the old wealth in the larger cities created an atmosphere of sophistication and culture. These were the people who read books, appreciated the arts, and helped to establish schools and colleges in America. William Byrd II, for example, the scholar and amateur historian from Virginia, who was educated in Holland and England, read five languages other than English, had a personal library of over 3600 volumes, and is said to have proposed to his second wife in Greek. Would that he had been a dramatist! Certainly he had the wit and courage. This classical point of reference would act as one force to move colonial society toward an acceptance of drama and theatre through a concern for great literature, traditional theatre, and education.

Among the colleges established in the eighteenth century—Yale, 1701; Pennsylvania, 1740; Princeton, 1746; Columbia, 1754; Brown, 1764; Rutgers, 1766; Dartmouth, 1769—some provided the early experiments in colonial drama. Libraries, booksellers, and printing presses also fostered potential interest in literature and the arts. Although the larger libraries were still private (Cotton Mather's library included approximately 4000 volumes), the Harvard Library catalogue of 1723 lists some 3100 titles, including the best of English literature from Shakespeare and Milton to Swift and several volumes of plays (even Wycherly). The library at Yale showed a comparable range of interest. Booksellers were most prevalent in New England, Pennsylvania, and Virginia. Printing presses had been slow in spreading throughout the New World, but by 1763 every colony had one. Mainly, their products were predictable. It is something of a surprise, however, to discover that Lillo's *George Barnwell* was reprinted in the *New England Weekly Journal*, beginning on February 14, 1732, the year after that domestic tragedy was produced in London. Almanacs appeared in America as early as 1639, but the first newspaper to last more than an issue was the Boston *News-Letter* (1704). Other periodicals which followed were the *New England Courant* (1721), which was modeled on the English *Spectator*; the New York *Gazette* (1725); the Maryland *Gazette* (1727); the South Carolina *Gazette* (1732); and the Virginia *Gazette* (1736). The *American Weekly Mercury* of Philadelphia was founded in 1719, and ten years later Benjamin Franklin acquired an interest in the Pennsylvania *Gazette*. These were the early journals in which people, readers as well as editors, expressed their candid opinions about the theatre in America and the plays being performed there.

Slowly an intellectual elite began to appear in America, including men of considerable learning and culture such as William Brattle, Zabdiel Boylston,

John Winthrop, and Cotton Mather, who were among the thirteen colonists elected Fellows of the Royal Society of London between 1713 and 1733. But a bias against literary creativity in America continued. There was neither fiction nor poetry worthy of mention during the eighteenth century until the first part of John Trumbull's *M'Fingal* appeared in 1775. Instead, there were sermons such as Cotton Mather's "The Whole World Lies in Wickedness" (1711) and Jonathan Edward's "Sinners in the Hands of an Angry God" (1741). Or there were diaries, journals, accounts, and autobiographies: Sarah Kemble Knight's *Journal* begun in 1704; John Woolman's *Journal* begun in 1756; and the *Autobiography* of Benjamin Franklin, for which he wrote the first part in 1771. William Byrd achieved some fame for the diary begun in 1728 which became his *History of the Dividing Line*. Cotton Mather's *Manductio ad Ministerium* (1726) and Jonathan Edward's *Freedom of Will* (1754) are among the best philosophical treatises of the century. A few controversial books and essays also appeared from the growing number of printing presses in the colonies: John Woolman's *Some Considerations on the Keeping of Negroes*, Part I (1753); Franklin's numerous essays; and John Dickinson's *Letters from a Farmer in Pennsylvania* (1767).

Such was the literary trend in the colonies prior to 1776—a commentary revealing the moral, political, and social tenor of the times. In terms of belles lettres, however, the drama received more serious attention during that period than did either poetry or fiction. And as religious, social, and, consequently, legislative prejudices made the drama a field of battle, the reactions of the colonists both to the drama itself and to the controversy it created become an essential part of the history of American drama.

In their efforts to protect all from the evils which they saw inherent in drama and theatre, the New England Puritans were joined by the Quakers and the Presbyterians.[3] Cotton Mather emphasized the authoritarian God in "A Cloud of Witnesses," where he expostulates against an issue in the "Larger Catechism":

> What are the sins forbidden in the Seventh Commandment? Light behavior
> —Unchaste Company—Dancing, Stageplayes, and all other Provocations to
> Uncleanness in our selves or others.

The repetition of this idea in eighteenth-century sermons and essays is incalculable, but it is not difficult to imagine the predicted fate of a youth who presented the following argument in Benjamin Keach's *War With the Devil* published in New York in 1707:

Conscience art though? why dids't not speak e'er now?
To mind what thou dost say I can't tell how.
Thou melancholy Fancy, fly from me,
My pleasure I'll not leave in spite of thee.

.   .   .   .

And that's the way to wear your Patience out,
I'll go to Plays and Games, and Dancing too,
And e'er a while, I shall be rid of you.

It was a common text to describe the theatre as a place of vice where one sold his soul for a laugh and risked the horrors of Divine Wrath.

Although the Mather dynasty ended in the 1720s and the revival power of the Great Awakening in New England was depleted by the time of Jonathan Edward's death in 1758, the basic religious intolerance against the theatre— a strong example of sin because it was so easily observed—continued. Sermons such as John Blair's *The New Creature Delineated in a Sermon, Delivered in Philadelphia, February 26, 1767. Published at the Request of a Number of Hearers* emphasized this opposition to theatre. In order to bring about a new world, the Reverend Blair advised his readers to "avoid the present public snare in the city, I mean entertainment of the Theatre. . . . God has not appointed the Stage as a means of the reformation of mankind, and therefore we have no reason to expect His blessing upon it, without which nothing will be effectual to that purpose." Theatre in Philadelphia, however, was going rather strong in 1767, and, had he waited two months, the Reverend Blair could have preached about the new American tragedy, Thomas Godfrey's *Prince of Parthia.*

Drama and theatre also suffered from the law during the prerevolutionary period, quite obviously because the law was established by people who either acted on their own prejudices or sought to influence others by their piety. Samuel Sewall, diarist and magistrate, was probably sincere in the indignation which his letter of 1714 to Isaac Addington reveals:

There is a Rumor, as if some design'd to have a Play acted in the Council-Chamber, next Monday; which much surprises me: and as much as in me lyes, I do forbid it. The Romans were very fond of their Plays: but I never heard they were so far set upon them, as to turn their Senate-House into a Play-House. Our Town-House was built at great Cost and Charge, for the sake of very serious and important Business. . . . Let it not be abused with Dances, or other Scenical divertisements. . . . Ovid himself offers invincible arguments against public Plays.

Although this rumored performance evidently never took place, arguments against the drama persisted among those prerevolutionary legislators and men of authority who saw fit to ban the drama at various intervals.

In Boston the effect of the clergy and of such outspoken moralists as Sewall seems to have succeeded in squelching any attempts at public dramatic productions until 1750, when a performance of Otway's *Orphan* brought such a protest that in March of that year the General Court of Massachusetts passed "An Act to Prevent Stage-Plays, and other Theatrical Entertainments." The Court's objective was to prevent and avoid the "many and great mischiefs" which result from "public stage-plays," which not only bring unnecessary expenses and "discourage industry and frugality" but tend to increase "immorality, impiety, and a contempt for religion." The consequences for allowing one's house to be used for playacting was a fine of twenty pounds. For the persons watching the play or acting in it, the fine was five pounds, one-half payable to his Majesty and the other to the informer—an interesting if unsubtle appeal to one side of human nature. Although there were some attempts to repeal the law, probably some circumvention by private groups and clear infringement by the English during the Revolution, it remained in force and was reenacted in 1784.

One interesting event in the history of drama and theatre in Boston occurred in 1767. The journal of the House of Representatives of Massachusetts for that year records a bill "for repealing an act for preventing stage plays and other theatrical entertainments, and for making more effectual provision therefor." The bill's failure to pass left the 1750 act intact, but the interesting event was the publication that year of Joseph Tisdale's speech against the bill.[4] Admitting that he had never seen plays acted but had only had the advantage of reading them, Tisdale argued that all free and civilized countries countenanced the drama as "of admirable use, by carrying corrections into the mind with irrefutable force and energy, as to engage the whole faculties and powers of the soul in the course of virtue." It was his opinion that the House should be careful not to drive youth from "such noble amusements," which in his own reading experiences had taught him to respect and favor religion, virtue, and honesty. Such a published argument suggested a healthy change developing in the public attitude toward the drama. Another publication that same year, an anonymous essay entitled *True Pleasure, Cheerfulness, and Happiness, The immediate Consequence of RELIGION. Fully and concisely proved. With some remarks on the THEATRE. Addressed to a Young Lady in Pennsylvania*, reinforces this conclusion.

The early official, or authoritarian, attitude of the Pennsylvania colony to the drama was adequately framed by William Penn in *No Cross, No Crown* (1699): "How many plays did Jesus Christ and his Apostles recreate themselves at? What poets, romances, comedies and the like did the apostles and the saints make or use to pass their time withal?" This doctrine became an integral part of the Great Law of Pennsylvania, and there began a kind of running argument between the colony and the English government. The act against "Stage-plays and revels" passed by the Assembly of Pennsylvania was repealed in England on February 7, 1705. A similar law passed by the Assembly in January, 1706, was disallowed by England on October 24, 1709. Another attempt in 1711 was vetoed in 1713. And there the matter of drama was allowed to rest until 1759 although the Quakers advised their membership against going to plays while other citizens could have enjoyed some traveling theatre as early as 1723.

In 1759 David Douglass, the actor-manager of the most successful theatre company before the Revolution, got permission "To build a Theatre and Act Without the bounds of the City." Immediately "An Act for the More Effectual Suppressing and Preventing Lotteries and Plays" was introduced to the Assembly at the request of certain churches (Quaker, Lutheran, Baptist, Presbyterian). At this time opposition to drama and theatre was as much social and economic as moral, and the Quakers who controlled the Assembly passed the act on June 20, 1759. Governor Denny, however, as one who disapproved of the act, was able to change its effective date to January 1, 1760. By then William Smith, a strong advocate of the drama, had returned from England, and Douglass' American Company of actors had had an opportunity to start their season. It is interesting that Benjamin Franklin, whose correspondence gives ample evidence that he thoroughly enjoyed the theatre despite his urging people not to waste time, was obliged to defend this act before the Council in Whitehall, London, on June 24, 1760. The Quaker-controlled Assembly, however, could not have been pleased with his argument. "We don't see any sufficient reason for an Absolute Prohibition of all Theatrical Representations in Pennsylvania," Franklin explained, but he was also aware of "the Mischiefs which might ensue." Essentially, he suggested that the Crown disallow this act while looking favorably in the future toward an act which would "by proper Limitations prevent the Inconvenience that may attend . . . Excess." The fact that Franklin would circumvent the intention of the Assembly in his argument may suggest that his knowledge of his constituency was broader than the Assembly's. Obviously, he felt secure in what he was doing, and the disallowance came on September 2, 1760.

Theatre continued in and around Philadelphia until the Continental Congress resolved on October 20, 1774, that "We will in our several stations, encourage frugality, economy and industry . . . and will discountenance and discourage every species of extravagance and disipation, especially all horse-racing, and all kinds of gaming, cock-fighting, exhibition of shews, plays, and other expensive diversions and entertainments." That resolution was followed by a more severe interdict on October 16, 1778, which threatened the jobs of government employees "who shall act, promote, encourage, or attend such plays." Then on March 30, 1779, Pennsylvania passed a law against theatres which remained in force until March 2, 1789—a law which was frequently evaded.

Other colonies in New England, Rhode Island and New Hampshire, enacted laws against public theatre. On May 6, 1709, the Governor's Council of New York passed a law forbidding "play-acting and prize fighting." Farther south, public opinion, stimulated by neither moral indignation nor legislative activity, was not so seriously aroused against drama and theatre. Virginia and Maryland never enacted legislation to oppose the theatre, and their citizens never allowed themselves to be intimidated by their northern neighbors' abhorrence of wasted time, however that might be defined. The South, obviously, was a place where theatre and drama might be encouraged.

The facts indicate that the first and continuing obligation of the early theatre manager was to defend his art in a positive manner. Having faced opposition in eighteenth-century England, Lewis Hallam, manager of the first theatre company to appear in Virginia, understood his opposition and decided to be optimistic. In a special prologue to that company's first performance in America—*The Merchant of Venice* in Williamsburg, Virginia, September 15, 1752— the actors expressed a faith and a hope:

> Haste, to Virginia's Plains, my sons, repair,
> The Goddess said, Go confident to find
> An audience sensible, polite and kind.

Considering the attitudes of colonists other than those in Virginia, it is clear that the company's expectations were not always fulfilled.

Later, in 1758, David Douglass, then a successful actor-manager of a company in the West Indies, reorganized the Hallam company, which had retired to Jamaica and disbanded, married Hallam's widow, and came to New York. The variety of managerial techniques which he was forced to practice suggests both continuing opposition and the necessity of an effective propaganda campaign. In his campaign Douglass showed his particular genius when, for example, in New York he respectfully disassociated himself from drama and declared his interest solely in "Dissertations on Subjects, *Moral, Instructive, and Entertaining.*" Then he opened his season with Nicholas Rowe's *Jane Shore*, certainly a carefully selected play. When in 1761 he performed *Othello* in Rhode Island, he advertised it as a "Series of Moral Dialogues in five parts depicting the evil effects of jealousy and other Sad Passions and Proving that Happiness can only spring from the Pursuit of Virtue."

Following Hallam's example, managers and actors continued to use prologues as a positive technique to influence people. The following excerpt is from a prologue given in New York in 1758:

> Much has been said at this unlucky time,
> To prove the treading of the stage a crime.
> Mistaken zeal, in terms oft not so civil,
> Consigns both play and players to the devil.
> Yet wise men own, a play well chose may teach
> Such useful moral truths as the parsons preach.[5]

The early actors and their managers also tried to present themselves in as acceptable a light as possible. For his 1761 tour into New England Douglass brought a letter of recommendation from Governor Dinwiddie of Virginia. Previously, Hallam had prepared for his visit to New York with a long ad in the New York *Mercury* (July 2, 1753): "The case of the London Company of Comedians, lately arrived from Virginia, humbly submitted to the Consideration of the Publick; whose Servants they are, and whose Protection they intreat." This early attempt at public relations provided a brief comment on the actors, their hard work and aspirations, and presented a plea to the "worthy Magistrates" that they be given the opportunity to show that "we were not cast in the same mould with our Theatrical Predecessors." For his part, David Douglass would seldom fail to thank the public for its generosity or applause.[6]

Off and on, depending on local opposition, David Douglass and his company of actors provided the colonies with theatrical entertainment for several years. Many colonists saw his productions, and some thought very highly of his work, as an excerpt from an anonymous letter in the Maryland *Gazette* (September 6, 1770) suggests:

> The merit of Mr. Douglass's company is, notoriously, in the opinion of every man of sense in America, whose opportunities give him a title to judge—take them for all in all—superior to that of any company in England, except those of the metropolis.

If all viewers did not agree with that gentleman, many must have enjoyed what they saw, and among that number were some influential men. Benjamin Franklin, by all reports, thoroughly enjoyed the theatre. George Washington was another who seems to have gone to the theatre whenever he could. On one trip to Williamsburg, for example, Washington attended plays on March 12, 16, 19, 25, 26 and April 3, 7, 1772. The next fall he was in Annapolis, where neither his interest in the drama nor his energy faltered as he saw plays on October 5, 7, 8, 9 and attended a ball on October 6. Presumably, his tastes were representative of the people of his social class.

Another fashionable person who appreciated the theatre was Anthony Wayne, a patriot general in the American Revolution. He was a constant member of the audience at the Southwark Theatre in Philadelphia, which Douglass had built in 1766. When in February, 1767, the Quakers circulated a petition asking the Assembly to close the theatre, Wayne was particularly indignant and applauded Governor John Penn for circumventing the request. This was the year Thomas Godfrey's *The Prince of Parthia,* which had been a second choice, was accepted for production when the originally scheduled comedy, Thomas Forrest's *The Disappointment,* was withdrawn because it contained "personal reflections." Wayne was one of a small number who protested angrily at the change of plays. Always opposed to censorship of any kind, he might also have known that *The Disappointment* was a far more entertaining play. At any rate, Wayne is reported to have found *The Prince of Parthia* a "tedious" play—an assessment with which many students of American drama will wholeheartedly agree.

By the time Douglass' American Company (the name he chose as anti-British feeling increased) was enjoying some success in cities throughout the South and the middle colonies and even into New England, there were a number of periodicals in existence which not only reported theatre activities but also recorded the views of those who opposed or defended the drama. Occasionally, there was commentary which might be termed the beginning of a dramatic criticism. Ever eager to express their personal opinions, especially on something controversial, theatre-conscious people provided numerous "letters to the editor" to supplement occasional editorials and essays concerned with drama and theatre. Sometimes the letters are humorous, sometimes overbearing in their piety; most are repetitious, as are the arguments that appeared for and against the drama for the next 150 years.

Probably very few writers converted their readers, but one writer who seems to have converted himself—and in a rather brief period—illustrates the controversy very well although his purpose might have been a finesse from the beginning. He called himself Philodemos, and, in a rather long essay published in the New York *Gazette* (December 7, 1761), he condemned the drama as being neither innocent nor lawful according to the principles of religion, common morality, or good policy. It was, consequently, neither useful nor instructive. Besides contradicting the life of self-denial which the scriptures demanded, plays debauched the minds and provided scenes of immodesty upon which no lady should look. From the "political view" Philodemos reasoned that maintaining "a set of vagrants that are of no use to society" is a waste of money that could be better spent relieving the miseries of the poor. Having argued that plays tend to make vice reputable, he then condemned all who frequented the theatre as interested in "criminal indulgences." A month later a letter on the front page of the *Gazette* (January 18, 1762) showed that Philademos had undergone a change of mind. "Fully convinced of the Absurdity of my former opinion," he cheerfully renounced his prejudices and thanked a benefactor "for raising me from the gloomy Abyss of Error, to the luminous Summit of irrefragable Verity." He went on to point out the value of the theatre, particularly as a means of teaching moral lessons.

That the argument over theatre was of particular interest to Philadelphians during the first half of 1767 is evident in the publicity in the weekly publications. A theatre had recently been erected in the environs, and the production of an American play added to the controversy. Writing letters "to the Printers" of the Pennsylvania *Journal* seemed to be the proper method for venting personal opinions, and the printers showed a fine impartiality. On February 12, 1767, a certain "Z" defended the theatre with a flourish. After a preamble of satiric comment on those who had the "indisputable power . . . to deal damnation round the land" and therefore praised Mr. Hallam over his fellow comedians while damning him in the hereafter, "Z" decided to consider the theatre simply as the "best school for *practical morality.*" Admitting that obscene comedies had been acted, "shall we," he asked, "because the powers of the Drama have once been prostituted, violently damn all Dramatic Performances?" He seemed to have a strong argument, but a blunt answer came in the next issue (February 19, 1767): Yes! According to this respondent, the drama, by concerning itself with fictions, imbues man with an indifference for truth, resulting in "an idle puerility that weakens our character, influences our talents, and by giving us a disgust for our duties, entirely ruins the reality of them."

Evidently, attacks on the theatre outnumbered letters defending it, and Douglass tried to enlighten the opposition with a letter to the Pennsylvania

Journal (February 19, 1767). Commenting on "the torrent of incomprehensible abuse," he confessed that he would "look forward with terror, if I thought myself engaged in a business that could be productive of the horrid consequences imputed to it." Then he appended an essay, written some five years previously by another person, which defended the stage "under proper regulations" while granting that there could be plays which should be suppressed. This was the moderate position that many readers would accept, and Douglass used it to launch the stronger view that no one group of people had the right "to *prescribe* or *proscribe* the amusements of others." It was an interesting point, one that too few people considered. A response appeared in the *Journal* (March 5, 1767) in the form of another essay condemning Douglass as "most openly against God": "Can pious persons who use the Stage, tell you of any *one* play for this forty or fifty years, that has been free from *wild* rant, *immodest* passions, and *profane* language?" In the mind of the writer the answer was clearly negative. But Douglass may have induced some people to think differently, and the *Journal* (March 12, 1767) carried a letter from one hard-headed individualist whom some like to imagine as typical in the colonies. The answer to the question "whether plays are pernicious to society" could be answered for this person only "at the bar of reason." "For God's sake then," he pleaded, "let every man judge for himself, in a case of this kind." Reasonable as he sounded, however, he had little effect on the letter writers. A letter in the Pennsylvania *Gazette* (April 30, 1767) condemned at some length the "impunity, falsehood, and impiety" which plays contain. Throughout the controversy the Pennsylvania *Gazette* advertised the current theatre productions along with the emotional complaints.

The several journals published in America at this time offered quite varied news and views of the theatre: prudish moral advice, satiric commentary for humorous ends, pretentious ramblings by exhibitionist letter writers, some public-relations work by people in the theatre, and perhaps even dramatic criticism. One has the impression, however, that much that appeared in print was an exercise in purgation or therapy and that it was allowed to continue as long as the editor found it interesting. The South Carolina *Gazette and Country Journal* provided extensive information on theatre activity and occasionally a letter to "Mr. Printer." The Virginia *Gazette* also printed letters of various persuasions such as the one which equated playhouses with drinking clubs (January 29, 1767). Or it might reprint the prologue to a play such as that spoken by Miss Osborne on her benefit night which encouraged sympathy for the actress' life (February 4, 1768).

Sometimes letters in journals excited responses that continued in several issues. The argument by "Dramaticus" (New York *Gazette*, December 7, 1767) insisting that the theatre adds "strength to the interest of virtue" was picked up quickly (December 31, 1767) by one who scoffed at the dangers of temptation and charged all people to put virtue to a test and to find religion "more lovely in your eyes." This discussion continued in the pages of the New York *Gazette* until, on February 1, 1768, a tradesman presented evidence condemning the theatre that probably found a sympathetic audience. He had finally succumbed to their emotional pleas and taken his wife and daughter to the theatre but was furious with the consequences of his rash act. He soon found that they did nothing but talk about their experience, borrow and read plays, and waste their time acting out parts from the plays they read. Righteously, or playfully indignant, he provided a forceful argument that those rich people who support the theatre would have much to answer for "as long as this cursed engine of pleasure, idleness, and extravagance remains."

An excerpt from an essay in the Maryland *Gazette* (March 6, 1760) may be the first printed theatrical criticism in America. It depends, however, on one's definition of criticism. The single important sentence in the essay reads as follows: "The principal characters both in the play and entertainment were performed with great justice, and the applause which attended the whole representation did less honor to the abilities of the actors than to the state of their auditors." With few exceptions essays condemned or extolled without reference to the plays produced. One quite lengthy evaluation of a particular performance which the anonymous writer of the letter neglected to identify also appeared in the Maryland *Gazette* (September 6, 1779). Specifically, the writer was quite overwhelmed by the performance of Miss Hallam: "Such delicacy of manner! Such classical strictness of expression! The music of her tongue! The *Vox Liquada*, how melting! Notwithstanding the injuries it received from the horrid *ruggedness* of the *roof*, and the untoward construction of the whole house, methought I heard once more the warbling of Cibber in my ear. How true and thorough her knowledge of the character she personated! Her whole *form* and *dimension* how happily convertible, and universally adapted to the *verity* of her *part*." Other comments in the letter reflected his opinion of the set, the costumes, and "the stillness and good order preserved behind the scenes." Maryland, according to the editor of the Maryland *Gazette* (October 4, 1771), had always encouraged "theatrical representations."

Evidence of scattered theatre activity from the various publications indicates that audiences for legitimate theatre were being formed among the colonists in America prior to the Revolution. It was a slow process, thwarted constantly by religious prejudice which frequently resulted in legal measures, but, as the colonies developed social and commercial centers, an atmosphere conducive to the drama generally appeared, particularly to the south of New England. Once the Revolution was over and a new nation had emerged pridefully concerned with itself at home and abroad, drama and theatre would be allowed to grow although the battle over the morality of the drama would still be waged with vigor. For the moment, however, groundwork was being completed for a substantive American drama and theatre. Actors had been allowed to perform. Theatres had been built. Innumerable people had written openly of their opinions concerning the theatre. A developing society had allowed and, in some areas, encouraged all these activities. The fact that the arguments pro and con had taken place showed growing awareness and tolerance. And plays were also being written, American plays!

THREE

Experiments with the Drama
in Colonial America

ACCOUNTS AND records of the early eighteenth century provide clear evidence that the drama in America was denounced and prohibited, but there was also legal encouragement. The first indication is a petition by Richard Hunter to be allowed to produce plays in New York:

> To the Hono^{ble} John Nanfan, Esqr his Maj^{ties} Governor and Commander in Chief of the province of New York and territories Depending thereon in America and Vice Admirall of the Same.
> The humble petition of Richard Hunter, Sheweth That your hono^{rs} Petitioner having been at great charge and expense in providing persons and necessary's in order to the acting of Play's in this citty;
> Humbly prays your Hono^r will please to grant him a Lycence for so doing.
> And your hono^{rs} petitioner shall ever pray.
>
> Richa^d Hunter.
>
> Indorsed,
> Petition of Richard Hunter
> License issued and recorded.[1]

Lieutenant Governor Nanfan served as acting governor during two periods— from May 16, 1699, to July 25, 1700, and from May 19, 1701, until May 3, 1702—but, as no further evidence exists, the precise date of the licensing must remain uncertain. Nor can one be certain that Hunter took advantage of the license and actually produced plays or, if he did, what plays—English works or plays newly created for him?

Another possibility of a play's having been written in America at this time appears in the adventures of Anthony Aston.[2] A buoyantly extroverted young man, Tony Aston (1682–after 1749) first studied law, then became interested in poetry in 1697, and finally sailed in late 1701 for Jamaica, where he hoped to make his fortune. This was not to be, however, and, although he did turn his hand to both law and soldiering in Jamaica, there is no evidence that he acted there. Chance took him to South Carolina, where he immediately joined Governor James Moore's unsuccessful expedition against St. Augustine. Returning to South Carolina with Moore, Aston made this note in his autobiographical sketch, which interests and frustrates historians of the drama: "Well, we arriv'd in Charles-Town, full of Lice, Shame, Poverty, Nakedness and Hunger: —I turn'd Player and Poet, and wrote one Play on the Subject of the Country." The time was January, 1703, but that is all that is known of Tony Aston's playwriting. According to his own account, he went on to New York, where he passed the winter of 1703–4 with old friends "acting, writing, courting." In the spring of 1704 he returned to Virginia, where he may have continued his acting before sailing for England later that year. As a restless but imaginative adventurer, his place in English theatre history is minor, but he might have fared much better in the history of American drama had he submitted his play for publication.

An invaluable record of American drama, Hill's *American Plays Printed 1714–1830* must nevertheless be subjected to some discriminating observations.[3] The compiler lists plays by "(1) American authors; (2) foreign authors living in America; and (3) American authors living abroad" but does not distinguish the authors under those three headings. Two of the dramatists for whom he lists eight plays before 1776 may be reasonably eliminated from this history. Although both were born in America, they left early in their lives to live and write in England. James Ralph (1705?–1762) was a friend of Benjamin Franklin, with whom he went to England, never to return to America, and there wrote and published plays which were performed in London theatres. Although Charlotte Ramsay Lennox (1720–1804) is listed in some sources as an American novelist and dramatist, at the age of fifteen she became a permanent resident of England. Her earliest plays did not appear in print until 1758, twenty-three years after she left New York. Hill also includes an anonymous play, *The Toy-Shop*,[4] a plagiarized copy of *The Toy-Shop* by the Englishman Robert Dodsley (1703–1764), which, Hill points out, was sent to the Virginia *Gazette* as an original play.

It is paradoxical that the first play printed in the United States be Robert Hunter's *Androboros* (1714).[5] Considering the efforts of many of the founding fathers to prescribe both morals and manners for the colonists, it is ironic that *Androboros* should be a rather intemperate farce complete with biting satire and excremental humor. But the play also has qualities which make it most characteristic of the country which America was to become. An independent and strong nature abounds in the play while the spirit of righteous attack is clear in the force of the satire. Its author was a man of wit and intelligence, conversant with the best literature of the Old World and able to use his learning and talents as a writer to defeat the small-minded intrigues of his self-centered and irascible enemies. By appealing to instincts within the comprehension of the common person, *Androboros* not only lampooned an imposed corruption seriously detrimental to the general population but also helped bring about change. Beyond those particular characteristics *Androboros* represents a distinctive genre in American drama—satiric comedy—which has grown in popularity and developed in style and form from this early beginning to the present moment.

Robert Hunter (d. 1734) is best known in history as the royal governor in New York and New Jersey (1710–1719) and as the governor of Jamaica from 1729 until his death, but he was also a writer of sufficient talent that Jonathan Swift ranked him with Addison, Halifax, Congreve, and Steele.[6] The political situation which Hunter found in New York was factional, corrupt, and sufficiently frustrating that he complained in a letter to his friend Dean Swift of the "torment and vexation" which followed his efforts to administer the colony. Foremost among his tormentors was the legislative assembly, which frequently opposed the instructions of the Crown, particularly in financial matters (even the governor's salary). Next came his problems with the Anglican ministry, which were focused on the Reverend William Vesey, rector of Trinity Church, whose narrow interpretation of eccleciastical affairs warred with Hunter's rational approach to the teachings of the Church of England. Hunter's difficulties reached a climax when General Francis Nicholson, the Royal Commissioner of Accounts, arrived in New York to investigate Hunter's administration. According to those who knew and wrote about him, Nicholson was a violent and foul-tempered individual. Associated with government in several colonies since 1688, Nicholson had shown interest in religious education and military expeditions before being given a royal commission in 1712 to look into provincial affairs. As his dislike of Hunter was public knowledge, his presence in New York became a rallying point for all of Hunter's enemies. But with a single act, showing both his literary ability as well as his political wisdom, Hunter silenced his opposition, turned the people to his point of view, and, aided by events in England, could report by 1717 a political harmony in New York.

That single act was the creation of *Androboros,* which "so humorously exposed [Hunter's enemies] that the laugh was turned upon them in all companies and from this laughing humor the people began to be in good humor with their governor and to despise the idol of the clergy."[7] Called "A Biographical Farce in Three Acts," *Androboros* has a cast of fifteen characters, all but three of whom have counterparts in real life. It is dedicated to "Don. Com. Fiz," evidently the Reverend William Vesey, called Fizle in the dramatis personae, who first is urged to read the play and then is broadly berated in language and fable reminiscent of Chaucer's Miller's Tale:

> And it was a most Masterly stroke of Art
> To give Fizle Room to Act his Part;
> For a Fizle restrain'd will bounce like a F——t.

The scene of the play is an asylum of sorts with a Keeper (Governor Robert Hunter), a Deputy (George Clark, secretary of the province of New York), and Tom of Bedlam, who acts as clerk to the senate which the inmates organize to receive Androboros (General Francis Nicholson), whom they consider a deliverer. Present in that body, which "disclaims all Powers, Preheminencies or Authoritys, except its own," are the Speaker (William Nichols, whom Hunter disliked but respected for his legal abilities), Coxcomb (Daniel Coxe, whom Hunter removed from the Council in 1713), Mulligrub (Samuel Mulford, Hunter's most active opponent), Doodlesack (Abraham Lakerman), who expresses himself by "Staring, Grinning and Grimacing," and Aesop (David Jamison, a close friend of Hunter), who throughout the play defends the Keeper with clever fables. When Androboros the "man-eater," a boastful, strutting creature, enters and declares himself off on another expedition, the senate resolves to defend him against "all Wardens, Directors, Keepers, and their Abettors."

Unsuccessful in their efforts as a senate to depose the Keeper, the inmates decide to become a consistory with Fizle as their leader: "This same Fizle is a Notable Fellow for the head of a Consistory, if he had but a Competent Doze of Brains; but These are so shallow that a Louse may suck 'em up without surfeiting, which renders that noble Portion of *Malice,* with which he is Liberally endow'd, of little use to the Publick" (II, i). It is their purpose to replace the Keeper with Lord Dinobaros (Edward Hyde, known for his venality and corrupt practices in colonial administration). Furious at having his vestment "beskirted and Bedaub'd with what I must not name," Fizle writes a letter, the major thrust of which rests in the wording of the insult he intends. Should it be ordure or, as Mulligrub insists, "Write it down so then, for a T—— is a T—— all the world over"? When word comes that Androboros has returned from his expedition, the Keeper suggests that they may "use the mighty Man according to his Deserts." In Act III, subtitled "The Apotheosis," Androboros is first ignored and then physically abused in good farcical tradition before Fizle and Flip (Adolphe Philepse)—"when Malice becomes a Moral Virtue, that Couple must be sainted"—attempt to help him by placing a chair over a trapdoor to catch the Keeper. The climax to the scene and the play comes when Androboros makes his awaited entrance, runs blindly into the chair, and sinks, Fizle and Flip falling with him, into the trap prepared for the Keeper.

Although the construction of *Androboros* is rough and unfinished, the play has both a theatrical quality and a literary pretense which lend it some distinction. Moreover, its satire is pungent and devastating while the action and the climax are consistent with the characters and thought. Obviously a slight play, it nevertheless has wit, particularly in the lines of Solemn and the fables of Aesop, and irony to complement the robust satire. Hunter relied heavily on invective and manipulated language to gain his desired end, but he was also adept at using standard farcical effects. If the personal situation which inspired Hunter's satiric comedy has led some to discount its significance, that is unfortunate, for it is considerably more than diatribe. Rather than of importance for historical interest only, as some have contended, it is a fair beginning for American drama.

The nature and preservation of *Androboros* are all the more significant because no play manuscripts written during the fifty years following Hunter's expression of outrage and frustration have been discovered. During those years, however, there was a steadily growing interest in theatrical productions. Before the middle of the eighteenth century, there was sporadic theatre activity in Williamsburg, Virginia; Charleston, South Carolina; Philadelphia; and New York. Theatres were being built, and professional theatre came to America in 1749 with a company of actors headed by Walter Murray and Thomas Kean. Lewis Hallam's more experienced Company of Comedians from London opened in Williamsburg on September 15, 1752. From this company, which disbanded in Jamaica the following year, David Douglass created a substantial company of actors and in 1758 set about to establish a tradition of theatre in America until the approaching revolution forced him to return to Jamaica. Although the plays that these actors performed were probably all English or adaptations of European drama, it is possible that curtain raisers or afterpieces were written by members of the company. Some prologues and epilogues which Douglass and others attached to plays have been preserved, but, unfortunately, no manuscripts of these early imagined farces are extant. Given the aggressiveness of various known colonial tempers and the wit of their owners, the unstable social and political conditions, and the growing popularity of theatrical entertainment, people other than Hunter may have expressed their indignation in the manner which he chose. The only real evidence, however, is *The Paxton Boys*, an anonymous satirical farce; and its date is 1764, fifty years after *Androboros*.

If colonists during the prerevolutionary years were not actively engaged in writing plays for entertainment, a number of them were at least becoming aware of the drama's potential for instruction. For some it was not the theatrical presentation which attracted as much as the dramatic confrontation. In keeping with a rich tradition in church history (yet one not readily accepted in Puritan America), these people served God by writing dramatic dialogues. One published anonymously in 1735 is entitled "Dialogue Between Christ, Youth and the Devil." Following the tradition of the English morality plays, this dialogue shows the Devil praising the Youth for going against his parents, abandoning "good," and following him. When Christ asks the Youth to "have sweet joy from me," the Youth refuses and says that he must have his "will." At this point the Calvinistic Christ declares, "In Hell thy *soul* shall burn." Immediately, the Youth repents and refuses the Devil's proposal to drink and be merry because he now believes God's word. But the Devil is clever; he will yield but also win: "There is a Heaven, but man can always repent." "Take heed!" replies Christ. "Don't reject my call!" But the Youth is confused; he wants his comforts now, and when he is old he will ask for God's mercy. Then to the Youth's plea—"spare me, and I'll make amends"—Christ turns a deaf ear; he will take vengeance and allow no more time on earth for one so prone to folly. Death comes for the Youth and takes his soul to Hell: "Thus ends the days of wofull Youth"—that is, those who will not follow the truth given by parents and preachers.

Dialogue Between a Minister and an Honest Country-Man, Concerning Election and Predestination by John Checkley, published in 1741 in Philadelphia for "the purpose of doing good," shows the Country-man coming "to be instructed and to know my duty." The idea that election and predestination take away his free will and make God the author of sin and himself a brute, arbitrarily punished, confuses the Country-man and makes him miserable. The Minister tries to explain. God, he says, only gives His grace to help man's infirmities. Although all of the Glory is in Him, "yet something is still left for us to do." It is all quite dull and sermonic with references to Edwards, Wesley, and Whitefield, but the Country-man is easily convinced and takes over his own instruction in a long monologue, enlivened only by references to farming and rural life. This kind of dialogue had a popularity which continued many years before it was absorbed into both fiction and drama of the mid-nineteenth century. Its writers, however, never mastered the problem of making the stated conflict anything more than a discussion, and their conclusions held no surprises.

For that person living in the eighteenth century who craved entertainment, there was cock fighting, horse racing, gambling, cards, musical concerts, theatre, balls, and cotillions. Religious-oriented dialogues were clearly not for entertainment purposes, and the eulogistic "exercises" staged during college commencements for nearly twenty years before the Revolution were more the poetic effusions of a literary elite than the efforts of budding dramatists. As theatre, these exercises held an esoteric appeal for a limited audience only. The man most responsible for initiating them was the Reverend Dr. William Smith, Provost of the College of Philadelphia, whose enthusiasm for the drama earned him the disdain of the Quaker-controlled Pennsylvania Assembly.[8] It was he who strongly supported Governor Denny's alteration of the 1759 petition against building a theatre, an alteration which essentially rendered the petition ineffectual.

Smith's first effort for the theatre was an adaptation of *The Masque of Alfred*, which he produced at the College during the Christmas recess of 1756–57.[9] The masque tells the story of Alfred the Great's rescue of England from the Danes. Presumably because his student actors were men, Smith felt obliged to eliminate all women from the work and let the pathos be drawn from Alfred's departure from his children in order to destroy the Danish forces. In consequence, Smith contributed in the stilted, metaphorical mode of his day some 200 new lines of blank verse plus a prologue with a properly moral point of view and an epilogue. Although he deserves credit for supporting native drama and theatre and for encouraging the work of Thomas Godfrey, Smith's own efforts in dramatic literature are limited, as were all those exercises, by the artificial eloquence of the blank verse and an overzealous interest in classical allusions and pastoral scenes and characters.

All college productions followed a certain pattern. They celebrated some event or person, contained dialogue in poetry, an ode and sometimes music, and involved two or three characters with such names as Horatio and Philander or Damon and Lorenzo. Generally, they are uninspired recitations, significant historically for showing the part which colleges and universities have played in the development of an American drama.

Occasionally, however, propaganda motifs crept into and enlivened these dramatic exercises. For the May 23, 1761, commencement at the College of Philadelphia, "An Exercise consisting of a Dialogue and Ode Sacred to the Memory of his late Gracious Majesty, George II" was presented. William Smith wrote the dialogue, and Francis Hopkinson, the first American poet-composer, the ode. Fourteen years later, for a similar event on May 17, 1775, Smith prepared "Exercise, containing a dialogue and two odes set to music," chiefly taken from previous exercises but made suitable for the "present occasion." During the spring following Smith's first exercise, Jacob Duché, who played the part of Alfred in Smith's masque, created "An Exercise containing a dialogue and ode on the accession of His Present Gracious Majesty, George III." This tribute to a "Thrice happy Monarch! skilled in every Art/ To win a Nation's smile and fix their love" was presented at the May 18, 1762, commencement. Later that year, on September 17, 1762, in Nassau Hall of the College of New Jersey, an anonymous musical entitled *The Military Glory of Great Britain* outlined Britain's power in five long speeches and concluded with a solemn wish for the continued prosperity of the British nation. The political bias was evidently recognized, and, for the commencement at the College of Philadelphia in 1763 (repeated in 1772), Nathaniel Evans returned to a safe and traditional topic to write "An Exercise containing a dialogue and ode on peace."

As years passed Patriot voices were also heard. For the May 20, 1766, commencement at the College of Philadelphia, Thomas Hopkinson wrote the traditional exercise with traditional characters and odes but managed to praise America's own cause while emphasizing liberty, the Patriot band, and "our infant strains." He hailed news of the repeal of the Stamp Act as "brighter than the Orb of Day." The following year, however, Thomas Coombe composed a less provocative "dialogue and two odes," in which he praised the late Reverend Nathaniel Evans and just about anything else that entered his mind: nature, science, Britain, and the New World.

The most significant—in form and in theme—of these college exercises was written by Philip Freneau and Hugh Henry Brackenridge, both of whom went on to achieve permanent places in the history of American letters: *A*

Poem on the Rising Glory of America being an Exercise delivered at the public Commencement at Nassau-Hall (September 25, 1771). The three speakers— Leander, Acasto, and Eugenio—narrate the discovery of America by Columbus, inquire into the origin of the natives, and discuss the uncultivated land and the people who migrated to America. They tell of those who died in settling the new land and of the potential of those who lived. They talk of agriculture and science and pay particular attention to commerce and its dangers. George Whitefield becomes the "holy messenger of peace," and America is "a thousand kingdoms rais'd" where "fair freedom shall forever reign." It is a "rising glory" which the authors envision. As Acasto says, " 'tis but the morning of the world." It is not, however, a drama. There is no real conversation, no conflict, no tension, no plot, and no character portrayal. As do all the other exercises, it simply acknowledges existence of a stage for which it may be acceptable to write plays and on which people may act without discrimination. It was a meagre but first step by a completely worthy institution, and in that step lies the importance of those productions.

Accepted by religious authorities and college administrators, dialogues became a significant and interesting aspect of dramatic ventures in eighteenth-century America. Their popularity as an act of celebration was established at the colleges in Pennsylvania and New Jersey, but their effect most certainly filtered into general community activity as indicated by such titles as "A Dialogue Spoken at Opening the Public Grammar School at Wilmington, on Tuesday October 26, 1773." The advantage of a dialogue for the purpose of propaganda, of course, was also quickly recognized. The church recognized it as did individuals who wanted to comment on political or community issues or perhaps argue in dramatic fashion a personal opinion. When the "Paxton Boys" caused some social upheaval in 1764, "A Dialogue, containing some reflections on the late declaration and remonstrance, of the back-inhabitants of the Province of Pennsylvania . . . By a member of that community" was printed in Philadelphia. Another dialogue, "The Substance of an Exercise, Had this Morning in Scurrility-Hall" (1765), probably by Isaac Hunt, employs a classroom situation with a professor and students through which the author showed his Tory bias. Classical tradition made the dialogue acceptable. There is also a compelling effect which a dialogue may have, whether actually spoken or simply printed, as many of these were, and the colonists took greater advantage of this type of writing as the Revolution approached.

During the years following David Douglass' appearance in America, attendance at the theatre became an acceptable activity, finally reaching that social level in which the fashionable world attached some snob value to being seen at a play. Douglass, of course, worked hard to achieve acceptance. He built theatres, tried to appeal to particular groups such as the Masons, and worded his programs carefully. The tragedy *Douglas,* for example, was carefully advertised as by "the Rev. Mr. Home, Minister of the Church of Scotland." Listings of performances appeared in the major newspapers, and new theatres such as the West Street, advertised in the Maryland *Gazette* in September, 1771, were described in glowing terms. Probably the controversy in the gazettes and other publications over the morality of the theatre increased its appeal, while local gentry added a fashionable touch by occasionally taking part in dramatic or musical productions. This was particularly true in Philadelphia, where in 1769 college students read or saw plays or operas in the Assembly Room in Lodge Alley for the "Lovers of Elocution." About this time the study of declamation and oratory became popular in private schools, thus helping to build potential audiences for legitimate theatre. Generally, the decade of the 1760s was a high point in the early development of American drama as public controversy, popular appeal, and institutional endorsement provided a focus for action.

It is a revealing comment on the nature of early American drama that *The Paxton Boys* (1765)[10] has a number of characteristics in common with *Androboros.* Like the earlier play it is a satirical farce inspired by a disrupting situation and created by a person, though unknown, whose sense of humor was fired by serious irritation and touched with a ridiculing irony. Unlike *Androboros* it has no bawdy elements, but certain lines suggest that real people were being lampooned. In the colonies and, later, in the new nation, the political and administrative control exercised by the eastern belt of settlements created a sectional antagonism which erupted in movements such as those involving the Paxton Boys, the Regulators, and Shays' Rebellion. One source of irritation was the border warfare with Indians. As the Pennsylvania Assembly provided inadequate military support, westerners bore the full burden for their defense; indeed, many felt that the westerners were responsible for creating the Indian difficulties. Bitter sectional rivalry occurred when a band of frontiersmen—the Paxton Boys—attacked and massacred a settlement of peaceful Christian Indians in retaliation for raids by Indians whom they had perhaps provoked. When the Paxton Boys marched on Philadelphia to demand support for their campaign, only the diplomacy of Benjamin Franklin prevented open conflict with the militia.

The situation was not widely understood, but a lack of understanding did

not prevent a considerable amount of fear and controversy among many Philadelphians. Although the dramatization of that near-conflict, *The Paxton Boys,*
is largely argument, it does have a certain amount of action and conflict. In
the first of its seven brief scenes, the citizens are called to arms by a messenger
who then proceeds to warn the governor of the approach of the Paxton Boys.
The skittish citizenry gathers, and an imminent confrontation turns out to be
a false alarm when a Dutch Company of Butchers appears. Night comes. Some
Presbyterians, meeting to discuss their religious cause, are interrupted and
verbally attacked by a Quaker and an Anglican churchman. At a climactic
point the Quaker denounces the Presbyterians for trying to destroy the best
of governments, the best of kings. The Paxtons finally approach, and the
Quaker dares them to attack him: "and if you make me mad enough I'll
change this farce into a tragy-comedy."

The play is written from the point of view of the Quakers, who regarded
themselves as socially superior to everyone else and more loyal to the King
than were the English. The common citizenry are ridiculed as cowards and in-
competents while the Presbyterian Scots-Irish are boisterously attacked for their
political and religious factionalism. Throughout, the Quaker (who could be
the author's spokesman or an object of ironic comment considering the author's
masquerade as a native of Donegall translating the play from the French) is
the authoritarian force who regards himself as in complete control of the
Paxton situation. The play lacks a unified approach, however, and even its
main satiric thrust remains confused and obscure.

The author of the other dramatic work concerned with the Paxton Boys,
"A Dialogue, containing some reflections on the late declaration and remonstrance, of the back-inhabitants of the Province of Pennsylvania" (1764), was
clearly concerned with a reading public rather than with a theatre audience.
In an argument embellished with classical references, Positive contends that
the Governor of the Assembly should do what the Boys ask whereas Zealot
sees their action as bordering on rebellion. But Lovell, the plain and honest
man, considers their declaration "a sophisticated piece of Irony, artfully" composed to control "the Minds of the Ignorant and Vulgar." After attacking
both Positive and Zealot, Lovell complains bitterly of the harm caused by the
"Protestant Dissenters called Presbyterians." "Why hate the Quakers?" he
cries. "Why destroy the government?" Emphasizing oratory more than drama,
the writer turns his dialogue into strong political and religious propaganda.

It was clear that the time was ripe for a full-length American play. The
first play written by an American and produced in an American theatre by

professional actors was *The Prince of Parthia* by Thomas Godfrey. It was only through a quirk of circumstances, however, that this "first" would be Godfrey's tragedy rather than Thomas Forrest's comedy, *The Disappointment*, which Douglass' company had put into rehearsal early in 1767.[11] Douglass had opened his New Theatre in Southwark in Philadelphia the previous November, and people like Provost William Smith and Anthony Wayne were bringing the theatre dignity and fashionable acceptance. For this particular production of an American play, Provost Smith may also have had some influence although there is no evidence beyond the fact that he was a recognized and powerful advocate of the theatre and that Godfrey was his protégé. In any event, *The Disappointment*, advertised for performance on April 20, 1767, was withdrawn on April 16 as "unfit for the stage," and on Friday, April 24, *The Prince of Parthia*, "a tragedy written by the late ingenious Mr. Thomas Godfrey of this city," was performed. It was given only one performance, however, and evidently did not appear on the stage a second time until produced by the Zelosophic Society of the University of Pennsylvania on March 26, 1915.

Godfrey never saw his play produced. Born December 4, 1736, into a family of modest circumstances, he was brought to the attention of Provost Smith and was not only well educated but introduced to influential people of his time—Francis Hopkinson and Benjamin West. Through the efforts of Smith, Godfrey was commissioned an ensign in the Pennsylvania militia in 1758. The following year he took a job in Wilmington, North Carolina, from which he sent to Smith in November, 1759, a copy of a tragedy which he had just finished. His desire was that Smith try to get it produced, but it was too late for that year. Douglass closed his Philadelphia season on December 28. Three years passed, and for unknown reasons the play remained in the background. Godfrey died of a fever in North Carolina on August 3, 1763. Two years later his friend, Nathaniel Evans, published Godfrey's *Juvenile Poems on Various Subjects with the Prince of Parthia, a Tragedy*. Another two years passed, and Douglass, having built up a theatre clientele and being faced with a sudden withdrawal of a rehearsed play, substituted *The Prince of Parthia*.

Although Godfrey was too young to have seen plays by the Murray and Kean company during their brief stay in Philadelphia in 1749, it is very likely that he witnessed performances of Hallam's company in 1754 and probably worked with Dr. Smith's production of *The Masque of Alfred* over the Christmas break of 1756–57. Poetry also interested Godfrey, and his first poems were published in issues of the *American Magazine* in January, August, September, and October, 1758, along with a short biographical sketch by Dr. Smith. Other poems followed, the most ambitious being "The Court of Fancy" (1762), which with "The Assembly of Birds" have occasioned comparison with Chaucer's *House of Fame* and *Parliament of Fowls*.

For the most part, Godfrey's verses are typical of the literary tradition of the eighteenth century—the usual personification, use of classical mythology, and irregular meter. He was not the "untutored genius" that some people have suggested but a man who, according to Evans, worked hard and read much to develop his techniques, which were, nevertheless, generally faulted by contemporary critics. Those unknown guardians of public taste praised his poetical imagination but commented on his "little learning" with regard to the classics and his neglect of the unities in dramatic construction. In the drama he was probably influenced by works of Nicholas Rowe and Ambrose Philips, which he had an opportunity to see on the stage, and most certainly by Shakespeare. He borrowed, as did all writers; yet, with all the weaknesses which his only play reveals, he must be considered an outstanding dramatist for his time with a potential denied only by his early death.

The play tells the story of a good but weak king, Artabanus, and his three sons: Arsaces, in whom "ev'ry virtue meets"; Vardanes, a man of pride, ambition, and "canker'd heart"; and Gotarzes, the youngest son, a "glorious youth." The first act establishes the characters of the sons and presents the sources of the play's conflicts: the jealousy and hatred Vardanes bears Arsaces; the vicious hate which the Queen, the King's second wife, has for Arsaces, who killed her treacherous son; the love which the captive Evanthe has for Arsaces. Then in great splendor the King and his attendants welcome Arsaces' triumphant return from the war in which he captured Bethas, who had opposed the King. As Vardanes plots Arsaces' death and the overthrow of the King, the gallant Arsaces decides to ask the King for Bethas' freedom when he learns that he is the father of Evanthe, the war prisoner Arsaces loves and wants as his just reward from the battle. Unfortunately, the King also loves Evanthe. Although badly shaken he grants Arsaces' request, but then becomes an easy dupe for Vardanes' villainous insinuations that Arsaces' love for Evanthe and his sympathy for Bethas are indications of treachery. In the climax to Act III, the weak King orders the arrest of Arsaces and gives Evanthe to Vardanes. Act IV opens with the news that the King had been murdered. Violence continues, but the Queen's attempt to kill Arsaces is prevented by the ghost of the King, whom Arsaces, having been made aware of Vardanes' treachery, rushes off to avenge. In the final act Arsaces kills Vardanes. Watching them fight, Evanthe's confidante mistakenly reports Arsaces' death. Immediately, Evanthe takes poison and lives only long enough to bid goodbye to Arsaces, who then kills himself, leaving Gotarzes to bring order to the city.

The popularity of classical education and the background of the author and his sponsor should have prepared the audience for *The Prince of Parthia*, but its unrelieved somber tone and unsubtle imitative qualities did not evoke a happy response. Perhaps a topical play would have been more appropriate and better appreciated at that point in colonial history. Only a concern for freedom from tyranny and the uncertainty of a monarch's rule even suggest Godfrey's society. Instead, in both construction and theme, the play is deeply indebted to Shakespeare and the conventions of Tudor and Stuart drama. Shakespeare is a rich source: the rescue of a man from drowning, dreams of destruction (*Julius Caesar*); the King's wish to retire, numerous storms (*King Lear*); the ghost, the revenge (*Hamlet*); the heroine's self-administered poison, the hero's suicide, the emphasis on fortune (*Romeo and Juliet*); and Vardanes' use of Iago's techniques (*Othello*). Sometimes the very words come from Shakespeare: the Queen asks the ghost, "Why dost thou shake thy horrid looks at me?" (*Macbeth*); Marullus in *Julius Caesar* cries "You blocks, you stones, you worse than senseless things!" (I, i), and Arsaces complains, "Ye figur'd Stones! Ye senseless, lifeless images of men" (II, vii). Much of what seems to be weak imitation, however, was simply characteristic of eighteenth-century heroic tragedy and the excessive sentiment and rhetoric of the period. The numerous references to gods, fates, and furies, the use of a confidante, a terrible villain, a gullible king, and a Marlovian hero of superhuman qualities are consistent with the time. So, too, is the theme of love and honor (filial duty) seen in Evanthe/Bethas and Arsaces/Artabanus along with the interest in politics as revealed in the villain's craving for an empire as well as for the heroine.

Despite an indebtedness which disturbs the modern reader and a generally uninspired poetry, *The Prince of Parthia* has some creditable qualities. The exposition is carefully handled, the plot is relatively simple, and the action, though not always clearly motivated because the characters are not fully developed and believable, at least proceeds speedily to a unified conclusion. Stage directions suggest that the altar scene at the close of the first act could have satisfied the audience's interest in spectacle while songs and a good juxtaposition of scenes provide an interesting change of pace. Whether intended or not, the lines of the villain are some of the most noteworthy in the play. Vardanes knew his villainy and accepted it. While Arsaces muses in his incredibly good

but naive fashion—"How dark, and hidden, are the terms of fate!" (II, iii)—
Vardanes explains:

> How easy 'tis
> To cheat this busy, tattling, censuring world!
> For fame still names our actions, good or bad,
> As introduc'd by chance, which ofttimes throws
> Wrong lights on objects; vice she dresses up
> In the bright form, and goodliness of virtue,
> While virtue languishes, and pines neglected,
> Rob'd of her lustre. . . .
>
> [II, iv.]

Arsaces is a man of action, absolute virtue, and sentiment; he could never have
understood this idea nor the brother who espoused it. "Let coward schoolmen
talk of Virtue's rules [says Vardanes],/ And preach the vain Philosophy of
fools;/ . . . But form'd for nobler purposes I come,/ To gain a crown, or else
a glorious tomb." And he died "Just as I wish, and daring for a crown." Even
with limited development Vardanes is an interesting villain and perhaps shows
some of that potential in the drama which Godfrey never lived to realize.

It is impossible to determine precisely the course of events which forced
the substitution of Godfrey's play for Forrest's. The only relevant information
appeared in the Pennsylvania *Gazette* (April 16, 1767): *"The Disappointment* (that was advertised for Monday) as it contains personal reflections is
unfit to be played." When first published in 1767, *The Disappointment; or,
The Force of Credulity* was described as "a new American comic-opera of two
acts. By Andrew Barton, Esq." As a farcical satire on numerous Philadelphians
—particularly a German printer, Anthony Ambruster, and Richard Swan,
Philadelphia's foremost hatter—who believed the tales of treasure hidden on
the banks of the Delaware River by the pirate Blackbeard, the play was a source
of great joy among those who read early copies. With its local setting and
broad burlesque of local personalities, this musical farce would have launched
acted American drama in quite a different manner, perhaps more appropriate
to the rugged individualism of America, than did the somber and stern *Prince
of Parthia*. With the opposition of those being burlesqued, particularly Swan,
however, a production was prevented.

The author of *The Disappointment* impresses the reader as a sensible young
man with wit, a sense of humor, and few literary pretensions. He wrote, he
confessed in a preface to the play, for "private purposes." Because there were
few plays in existence, he wished to contribute to entertainment in the arts, but

he was mainly interested in putting a stop to the foolish searching for buried treasure. He was also clearly aware of the social pressure of his time and perhaps of classical tradition. At any rate, his prologue included the accepted formula:

> Our artless muse, hath made her first essay
> T' instruct and please you with a modern play.
> Theatre-business was, and still shou'd be;
> To point out vice in its deformity;

But Forrest cannot be lightly dismissed as a man with no talent for the drama. His plot is simple but fitted with exuberant farcical action, and his characters are appropriate types for the action he describes and the satire in which he indulges. A raucous, fast-moving, occasionally bawdy, but always funny play, *The Disappointment* caused some to resent the substitution of Godfrey's tragedy. Certainly, it was as good as or better than many other comedies written and produced during the late eighteenth century.

The characters in *The Disappointment* include the Humorists (Hum, Parchment, Quadrant, Rattletrap), the Dupes (Raccoon, Washball the barber, Truehoop the cooper, and McSnip the taylor), and Moll Plackett, Raccoon's kept woman, plus assorted wives and servants. In a tavern the Humorists purposefully drop papers descriptive of buried treasure in order that Raccoon, a Negro who speaks in dialect, may find them. The other Dupes then become involved. By scene four the Humorists have produced a conjuror, Rattletrap, and the Dupes have revealed their greedy attitudes toward treasure. Finally, all meet, discuss money and courage, decide on a watchword—"canoe"—drink a lot and sing a little, and agree to meet again at the stone bridge at eleven that night. Act II opens with a riotous scene in which Moll Plackett and a sailor are interrupted by a suspicious Raccoon, whom Moll distracts with a story about spirits (her uncle could tell fortunes and detect lost maidenheads) while the sailor escapes. Near the stone bridge the Humorists rig "a figure representing the head and shoulders of Blackbeard" and bury an old chest with two or three pieces of silver in it. As the Dupes enter shouting "Canoe!" Rattletrap begins his hocus-pocus, complete with fireballs. The chest is then dug up, and all plan to meet at Washball's house to divide the treasure. When the chest is found to be empty and the Dupes begin to understand what has happened, the Humorists run off laughing and shouting "Canoe!" to return in an epilogue for further comment on the play and the audience.

In 1796 "Andrew Barton" published a three-act revision of *The Disap-*

pointment, "revised and corrected with large additions by the author." New characters are added; dialect is emphasized; Rattletrap explains his conjuring more thoroughly; Parchment provides more satirical comments on the government; and there are more details about the treasure. Three additional scenes, exploring the problems which the Irishman, Truehoop, has with his wife and servants, are added to the second act. In the final act the ghost plays a more important part, but the play ends at Washball's house with the same events and conclusion. In the epilogue the Humorists assert their purpose more distinctly to "reclaim the vicious," hoping the play "caus'd a reformation/ Amongs't the dupes of this our congregation" (look at audience through a glass).

The strength of the play lies in the farcical action, the songs, and the bawdy wit. With the passage of time the purpose of the satire has been lost although the "personal reflection" and the boisterous quality were obviously sufficient to remove it from the stage in 1767. The few distinctive characteristics of the play, however, should not be forgotten. It is generally accepted as the first American ballad-opera although the eighteen songs or airs were to be accompanied by popular tunes of the day such as "Yankee Doodle." The play may also present the first Negro in American drama—Raccoon, whom Truehoop calls a "black mout"—while the Negro, Irish, and Scottish dialects provide another prerevolutionary distinction which this play brings to the drama of colonial America.

A play of a more serious nature written during the same decade is Robert Rogers' (1731–1795) *Ponteach; or, The Savages of America* (1766), called a tragedy in five acts. Born in Massachusetts, Rogers moved with his family to the New Hampshire frontier. During the French and Indian War he began a military career which must truthfully be described as checkered. He served well on the expedition to defeat Fort Detroit, during which he met Ponteach, but he was soon disgraced for being involved in illicit trade with the Indians. Removing himself to England, he published his *Journal,* for which he received some praise. Although his later career in the American Northwest has been the subject of much speculation, Rogers was finally acquitted of charges that he plotted to sell out to foreign interests. Again he went back to England but in 1775 returned to America, where he was arrested as a Loyalist spy. After escaping from prison, he joined the Loyalists, went to England in 1780, and died there in obscurity in 1795. Allan Nevins, in his 1914 edition of *Ponteach,* suggests a dispute concerning its authorship, but Rogers seems to have been mainly responsible for, if not the sole author of, the work. London critics in 1766 accepted the play as Rogers' but had little good to say for it. They found the plot "weak and conventional," the diction "colloquial," the blank verse "rude," and the literary art "negligible."[12] Subsequent critics have seldom questioned these judgments but have found other qualities of both historical and dramatic interest.

Although Rogers' play is the first to treat a native subject at all seriously, it is not the first play dealing with Indians in America. That distinction belongs to Le Blanc de Villeneuve, an officer in the French colony of New Orleans who in 1753 wrote *Le Père-Indian*, which was then performed by amateurs. Taking his plot from a local event in 1753, recorded in Gagarre's *History of Louisiana*, de Villeneuve dramatized a story of Indian heroism and sense of justice. In a quarrel a Choctaw brave had taunted the Calaprissa Indians as being "humble dogs of the French" and was killed by a Calaprissa brave who was then captured by the French authorities. Seeking their own justice, the Choctaws petitioned the French for the murderer but were thwarted by his escape. In a dramatic climax the escaped Indian's father offers himself as a sacrifice for his son; his offer is accepted and he is beheaded. From the little that is known, the play might have had potential as a contribution to American drama by a French colonist. De Villeneuve presumably also wrote a tragedy, *Poucha-Houmma*, based on a story he heard among the Indians.

Robert Rogers is unquestionably a colonial American by birth. Nor can his personal experiences among the Indians be doubted. He knew the life he used as a background for his romantic tragedy and provided some social realism with comments on trading customs, the unchristian activities of French priests, and the degrading conditions in which the Indians were forced to live. He was also interested in language and interspersed his prose with passages in blank verse and rhyming couplets. Numerous references to nature and a concern for picturesque imagery are, however, weakened by amateurish polemics and the stilted manner of heroic tragedy. Combining history and art with sufficient incidents of human evil to dramatize the social problems of the time and also provide spectacle and sensation, Rogers created a hero whose nobility of spirit heightens the effect of his eventual defeat by the British.

The time of the play is the 1760s, and the scene is an area near Detroit. Both Moses Coit Tyler and Francis Parkman, American historians, regard the play as reliable source material, particularly the presentation of Indian-English relations in the opening scenes. Two trappers tell how they give the Indians rum and cheat them in weighing their furs; two English hunters blame the Indians when they cannot find game, shoot some of them down in cold blood, scalp them, and steal their packs. Yet the English officers callously dismiss Ponteach's complaints until Ponteach, an intelligent and sensitive man, warns them in calm and forceful speech that there must be war unless the Indians are treated fairly. In preparation for hostilities Ponteach enlists the advice and aid of his sons, Chekitan and Phillip, and learns that Hendrick, the Emperor of the Mohawks, wishes to remain a friend of the British. Chekitan also is reluctant to fight and urges caution, partly because his sweetheart, Monelia, is the daughter of Hendrick. Pretending to help Chekitan, Phillip, an ambitious and unprincipled man who hates his brother, plans to kill Monelia, make the murder look like an English act and, thereby, arouse both Hendrick and Chekitan to battle and eventually make himself the supreme leader of the Indians. Events progress, and the opening of Act III in a romantic forest setting, as Chekitan declares his love for Monelia, is well contrasted by the Indian chiefs' decision to fight and a highly theatrical war song. After a battle in which the English are defeated, their fort burned and the two villainous hunters treated to Indian justice, Phillip, as planned, kills Monelia and her brother, Thorax. At the funeral Chekitan swears revenge and is dramatically enlightened by Thorax, who regains consciousness long enough to accuse Phillip. As the brothers fight, Chekitan kills Phillip and then takes his own life. Left alone, Ponteach, deceived by the French priest who stole his battle plans, hears of the British victory and an Indian retreat. Yet he still maintains his personal dignity and a noble hope: "Britons may boast, the Gods may have their Will,/ Ponteach I am, and shall be Ponteach still."

Ponteach was never produced, and presumably Rogers did not imagine a performance. Viewed with the scores of other Indian plays that appeared on American stages before the mid-nineteenth century, however, it would not suffer by comparison. A superior hero, a variety of villains, well-motivated passions, a love episode, some highly spectacular scenes, and strong social protests enhance a melodramatic plot. But it would be well after the revolutionary war before an Indian play would be performed by professional actors on an American stage, and even then the author, Anne Kemble Hatton, would be English.

That distinctly American play—written by one born in America, concerned with American subject matter or ideas, and performed on an American stage —is thus difficult to find in colonial America. Generally, one or two factors are missing, and the following play illustrates this point. George Cockings (d. 1802) was an Englishman who for a number of years held a minor position in the British government at Boston. Although he spent his last thirty years in England as Registrar of the Society of Arts, Manufacturers and Commerce, during his years in America he was prompted to write some poems and at least one play, *The Conquest of Canada; or, The Siege of Quebec,* which was published in London in 1766. By means that are not clear, a Philadelphia printer published an edition in December, 1772, and David Douglass was persuaded to produce the play. By all reports it was a spectacular production, opening on February 17, 1773, and repeated on February 19 and 22. Suggesting the magnitude of the production, the management asked the audience to "dispense with a Farce; as the stage will be much crowded with the Artillery, Boats, and, etc. necessary for the representation of the piece; and with the Men from Both Corps, whose assistance the Commanding Officers are glad enough to indulge us with."[13]

Spectacle was clearly the major asset of the play, and Cockings had no pretense about his abilities as a dramatist. "Not being conversant with the stage" and "the rules of the drama," he stated in his preface, "I may have greatly erred" in composing the play. Events in America deeply interested him, and he had once planned to write a play of epic proportions and call it *The Matchless Era.* But he settled on the 1759 Siege of Quebec and, fascinated by people "fired by patriotic order," tried to stay as close to history as the drama would allow. Clearly, this was not overwhelmingly close, as the sentiment and patriotism of Acts I and V reveal. In these acts, too, his reverence for England is at its greatest, but he was, after all, an Englishman. His lack of feeling for language is less excusable. His prose-poetry is artificially sustained, and he resorts to elaborate and unnatural words and phrasing as well as to long, stiff speeches. He also pays little attention to character and relies mainly on a good change of pace and the music and spectacle that would increase the effect of martial scenes. Undoubtedly, the appearance of military personnel and equipment on stage were major factors in the play's success.

Called a "historical tragedy" in five acts, *The Conquest of Canada* is essentially a tribute to General Wolfe, the young English general who died on the Heights of Abraham while leading the English forces against Quebec. Taking leave of his mother and sweetheart, Wolfe sails from England eager for glory and adventure, which the playwright undercuts with long, dull, and unnecessary shipboard exposition on the historical events leading to the siege. In Quebec the French generals, Montcalm and Bougainville, discuss battle plans and the skill of the attacking British general. Act III is primarily a water spectacle as two men, using speaking trumpets at the front and rear of the stage, direct the British attack in boats, which were met with fire floats launched by the

French. Indians, along with a band of Scottish Highlanders, take part in the battle, which a sea captain describes. Act V opens on Montmorenci as Montcalm, always intelligent, dignified, and filled with respect for Wolfe, prepares for the decisive battle on the Heights of Abraham. There Wolfe is wounded —"My country bleeds!—my honor's lost!"—and dies. In London his mother and sweetheart receive the news in a long and sentimental scene which ends with a toast to "George, and liberty, and martial honor." Essentially imitative of heroic tragedy in concept and focus and using history in that traditionally loose manner of writers exploiting an actual event, *The Conquest of Canada* at least shows a wise choice of hero and history.

As the few plays written in colonial America reveal, audiences were expected to be interested in current events. Hunter, Forrest, Rogers, Cockings, the author of *The Paxton Boys*—even, to some degree, the writers of exercises and college dialogues—all concerned themselves with the world around them. The major exception is Godfrey, whose *Prince of Parthia* must remain an indifferent beginning for American drama in both resource material and construction. In general, however, awareness of events and strong opinions about them distinguish the writing of most early American plays, and the result was mainly satire.

As the Revolution began to fade into history, other approaches to dramaturgy would become popular, but satire persisted as a dominant part of American drama. David Everett noted in a preface to *Daranzel; or, The Persian Patriot* (1798) that "a playhouse is an ample field for satire," and numerous playwrights agreed with his conclusion as they attacked almost every aspect of government and society. As the nineteenth century progressed, the satire tended to become more benign and sought to exhibit the theatre as a corrective and moral influence on society. During the Revolution and prior to it, however, bawdy and boisterous satire was prominent. One has the impression that the early American playwrights, amateurs or theatre hacks as they obviously were, took great delight in their work. Artistry was perhaps the last thing that interested them. Instead, they had opinions which they delivered with a sense of humor and with some understanding of those human impulses, whether base or elevated, which prove attractive in theatrical productions.

One such writer was John Macpherson, a Philadelphian, who enjoyed Forrest's satire in *The Disappointment* and contributed some of his own to "A Pennsylvania Sailor's Letters, Alias the Farmer's Fall: With Extracts from a Tragic Comedy called *Hodge-Podge Improved; or, the Race Fairly Run*," published in 1771. The pamphlet suggests political satire, but the single excerpt (I, ii) from the play, which shows a farmer, alone on stage, concerned with proving something destructive about man, is too brief to be meaningful.

Another satirical dramatist was the anonymous author of *The Trial of Atticus, Before Justice Beau, for a Rape*, published in Boston "for the author" in 1771. Of the author—identifying himself as "the Compiler," who adds "nothing of his own" but only gives "a plain narration of facts"—nothing is known. As with most trial plays, this one could have been easily staged; but if it was, that performance has been lost to history. For the reader there is a minimum of theatrical inventiveness revealed, but the play achieves its main goal—a depiction of the pettiness of the local colonial courts—with force and good humor. It satirizes not only lawyers, judges, and the court system but also ministers, deacons, doctors, educators, innkeepers, gossips, and astrologers. In fact, in the rambling and episodic manner that a trial might assume, the author manages to ridicule an extremely broad segment of colonial society.

In a series of eight scenes which vary in length from a few lines to several pages, the author focuses his attack on the venality of the courts and the lawyers who not only countenance but support slander and hypocrisy in the community. Atticus, something of the modern antihero, is moderately dissolute and exceptionally stubborn. He is also a rather silent person, having only ten brief speeches in the entire play. Arrayed against him are a particularly debased group: a judge and a lawyer more interested in their fees than in due process and a number of unsavory witnesses with only petty and irrelevant grievances.

The play begins in Justice Beau's house as Mr. and Mrs. Chuckle report that "about two years" ago Atticus raped Mrs. Chuckle. In response to the Justice's threatening letter, Atticus declares that he knows nothing of the "pretended crime" and "shall make no private satisfaction." The circumstances surrounding the "event" are, in fact, rather hazy. "He led her to the bed," says Chuckle, "and both set down, and she verily believes he would have overcome her, if [her] child had not cried." Brought to court, Atticus pleads "Not guilty!" and hears the witnesses give their evidence. Lieutenant Scant, an innkeeper, did not see the act committed, but he hates Atticus, who has accused him publicly of watering his rum. Mrs. Prim, the gossip, testifies that Atticus once put his hand in her pocket to take some "loaf sugar" as she had directed, "but he did not feel for the sugar." Dr. Pip explains in ostentatious language that Atticus ridiculed his ability to cure the bite of a mad dog. One man's testimony about snow at the time of the incident confuses the season of the crime, which was accepted by Mrs. Chuckle as August. Such irrelevant and contradictory evidence gives Lawyer Rattle some problems in his summation, but he manages. Unfortunately, even after the Justice finds him guilty and sets the fine, Atticus refuses to pay, and nothing can be done but to send him "home about your business," by which action the "court is dissolved" and the play ends.

The work is more a satiric dialogue than a play although there is a central issue, a hero, a number of adversaries, and a resolution. Humor, the major goal of the author, is gained through a variety of slightly sketched characters whose peculiarities are burlesqued. Atticus turns out to be a rather admirable person —honest, forthright, witty, a good writer, suspicious of fraud and hypocrisy, and afraid of no one. It would be surprising if a group of stubborn New Englanders of the calibre of Giles Corey did not enjoy acting or watching this satirical farce.

During these years of experimentation with drama in colonial America, attitudes toward the theatre changed considerably. The Great Awakening in New England, which created an explosion of religious fervor and then disappeared, left many problems for acting companies which performed in the more liberal South before making their way through Maryland to New York and Pennsylvania, where controversies over the drama burst forth in publications and in the assemblies. Existing evidence proves, however, that by the 1760s colonial Americans were writing plays. Colleges were also showing an interest in the writing and production of stage exercises. By the early 1770s there was clearly a developing audience in America as well as a number of plays by American authors. Had there been no great social upheaval, no "continuation of politics" in the form of war, it is difficult to say how these attitudes and activities would have progressed. But war did come. David Douglass' company of actors left for Jamaica, and Americans, fighting for a new existence, decided that there should be no time for play, no time for theatre. Consequently, theatre activity and the writing of plays in America underwent a change as the drama began a new phase in its development.

FOUR

Drama and the
"War of Belles Lettres"

DURING THE Revolution a recognizable change occurred in the drama as it began to reflect the new and differing moods of the people. As the colonists found themselves caught up in the Revolution—some reluctantly and some with great enthusiasm—they began to express their ideas vigorously in the newspapers or in privately printed pamphlets, which were a major source of literature during the war.[1] In the emotional battle of words by which Loyalists and Patriots attempted to defend their social and political positions, the pamphlet play became a strong propaganda weapon. The "War of Belles Lettres," as Vernon Lewis Parrington described it, waged fiercely, and the drama, though unrecognized by Parrington, was an important feature of that "war." Previous playwrights, few and amateurish as they may have been, generally wrote about bothersome events in their daily lives and tried to burlesque them out of existence. Now, whatever their political persuasion, playwrights were absorbed by the Revolution. For the duration the drama naturally reflected that absorption but far more graphically, satirically, and vigorously than American dramatists reacted to any other American war prior to World War II.

During the decade of the explosive political events leading up to the shot heard 'round the world on April 19, 1775, and to the Declaration of Independence the following year, the American theatre had enjoyed some healthy progress thanks to David Douglass, whose efforts had set standards and promoted art and culture in America. Less than five months after it first played in London, for example, Douglass had brought Goldsmith's *She Stoops to Conquer* to the John Street Theatre in New York on August 2, 1773. Although his main interest was certainly not American drama, he was creating an appropriate millieu for future efforts. Then, as the political events became more numerous and intense, Douglass' career and the period of colonial American theatre came to an end with an announcement from the First Continental Congress. But that was in the fall of 1774, and American drama was already a worthy participant in the War of Belles Lettres.

On October 20, 1774, a report signed by the "Association" and included in the *Journals of the Continental Congress* declared "that the present unhappy situation of our affairs is occasioned by a ruinous system of colony administration." To obtain regress for their grievances, the delegates agreed on fourteen items. Number eight stated that "we will, in our several stations, encourage frugality, economy, and industry, and promote agriculture, arts, and the manufactures of this country, especially that of wood; and will discountenance and discourage every species of extravagance and dissipation, especially all horseracing, and all kinds of gaming, cock fighting, exhibitions of shews, plays, and other expensive diversions and entertainments." Clearly, the delegates felt that a program of austerity was in order, and their declaration, though completely without authority, was indicative of the seriousness of the situation. Although several of the colonies already had laws on their books banning theatrical shows and plays, the laws had been circumvented. Now there was necessity for cooperation, and as the years passed prohibitions were enacted. Edicts from the Continental Congress recommended (October 12, 1778) "effectual measures . . . for the suppressing of theatrical entertainments" and declared (October 16, 1778) that "any person holding an office under the United States" would be dismissed if he "shall act, promote, encourage, or attend such plays." A Pennsylvania act (1779) declared all theatrical performances illegal.

The limitations imposed by the Revolution tended, as in all wars, to stultify cultural, artistic, and intellectual advances. From 1774 until the Treaty of Paris in 1783, when the new nation was recognized, theatre and drama in America endured a period of relative stagnation that contradicted the progress which the preceding years seemed to anticipate. Despite the prohibition of plays in America for the duration of the war, there were two good reasons why the law was not always followed. In the first place, a significant number of people among the colonial aristocracy had come to enjoy theatre, and they did not abandon this pleasure easily. Next to jovial dinner companions, Anthony Wayne's favorite diversion was the theatre. (On the other hand, Polly, his wife, saw no virtue in acting and considered the boys in the balcony who threw orange skins on the people below as truly representative of the social tone in the theatre.) It is not likely that Wayne either discouraged or refused to attend the theatre during the Revolution. It is known that George Washington saw a play in New York with the British General Gage on May 28, 1773. In September of that year he saw three plays at Annapolis and, despite the interdict against plays, later attended *The Lying Valet* at the Southwark Theatre in Philadelphia.

Clearly, there were social sets in New York and Philadelphia for whom the theatre was agreeable entertainment. Someone had to attend the plays which the British produced during their occupation of Boston, New York, and Philadelphia—although those who did were presumably Loyalists for whom the congressional edict was not a serious document. The important point is that the audiences which Douglass had lured before the Revolution did not languish completely during the eight years of war and that as soon as the war seemed to be ending—the Yorktown campaign brought Cornwallis' surrender on October 17, 1781—many were eager for theatre to be legally operated once more. Their revived interest would serve to encourage Americans to write plays.

A second reason why the laws prohibiting plays were evaded rested on the sound principle that soldiers must either be busy fighting battles or be well entertained. It was a matter of morale. Mainly, the British amused themselves and their friends by producing plays during their periods of inactivity: in Boston's Faneuil Hall, in New York's John Street Theatre, which they renamed the Theatre Royal, and in Philadelphia's Southwark Theatre. The soldiers under General Washington had less time for theatrical performances, but there is evidence of occasional plays at Valley Forge during the spring of 1778. By 1782 plays which could be enjoyed by soldiers and civilians alike were being performed by professional actors in Philadelphia, in New York, and probably in Baltimore and Annapolis. Two years later a number of actors from the old American Company had returned to form the strongest acting company that had been gathered in America.

In terms also of a developing American literature, productivity during the American Revolution existed mainly within the limitations of war. Only the literature of persuasion—that of John Dickinson (1732–1808), Samuel Seaburg (1729–1796), and Tom Paine (1737–1809)—was outstanding. The poetry of the period, represented by Francis Hopkinson (1737–1791), John Trumbull (1750–1831), and Philip Freneau (1752–1832), was both meagre and propagandistic. Those who gained a reputation as Connecticut Wits and attempted to save their state from the corruption of democracy wrote mainly after the Revolution. Because fiction was still felt to provide a false notion of life for youthful readers, novels were not written in America until after the Revolution. The acceptable prose form was the essay, in which Franklin amused himself and others, while Hector St. Jean de Crèvecoeur (1735–1813) offered his memorable *Letters from an American Farmer* (1782). Meanwhile, the drama, as were the other literary forms, was reduced to the level of servitude in the War of Belles Lettres and was additionally hampered by the government's restrictions on stage productions. It did, however, provide some of the most exciting literature of the time as well as a respectable quantity, perhaps because some of those who created it also had respectable literary reputations: Mercy Warren, H. H. Brackenridge, Jonathan Sewall, and Robert Munford. Although judgments on the quality of their dramas have generally been severe, those views should be tempered by an understanding of the stress of the occasion and by an assessment of the propaganda effort of the plays, which was their major *raison d'être*.

The effect of drama as propaganda during that decade and a half prior to and throughout the revolutionary war can never be completely or accurately assessed, but some statistics can help one understand how plays fitted into the politics of the time and satisfied a certain constituency. Between 1770 and 1776 the Whigs published five dialogues and six plays. Prior to 1767 some six dialogues performed at the College of Philadelphia and subsequently published either praised Loyalist principles or attacked ideas favorable to democracy, independence, or revolution. After 1771 and through 1776 four plays which supported the Tory biases and ridiculed the Patriots were published. Throughout the Revolution at least seventeen partisan plays and dialogues were published. These constitute the drama in the War of Belles Lettres. Because most of them were already written by 1776, it is clear that Patriot fervor burned a bit low even among playwrights as the years and campaigns passed. But all of these plays, inasmuch as their authors are known, are American contributions, whether Patriot or Loyalist. Together they form one brief phase in the development in American drama which, however, must also be considered a major part of the contemporary literary activity in America.

As reflected by the division of drama into Whig and Tory plays, the Revolution was in a large measure a civil war. On the one hand, Sam Adams and his Sons of Liberty were a definite minority voice of idealists, frequently from among the working or small-business classes and opposed to a mercantile or landed aristocracy. On the other hand, Loyalists were strong in all the colonies, particularly in New York and New Jersey but also in Georgia, which did not send delegates to the First Continental Congress. The Loyalists were generally from the upper classes—the older, conservative, well-established families who opposed the Revolution—with the marked exception of Virginia planters and some New England merchants. Within the divided colonies, neighbors and even members of the same family embraced different political views and easily fell victim to the tyranny and fears which those views fostered. Soon their emotional reactions exploded, not only in the chaos of revolution, but in a torrent of published condemnations, explanations, and arguments.

The burst of printed emotions from both sides of the controversy appeared largely in pamphlet form—that small printed work which was generally stitched together and which boasted no cover and sometimes not even a title page. Frequently, the informal and hurried appearance of a pamphlet clearly reflected the thought within. But pamphlets held tremendous advantages for the kind of reporting and commentary that highly emotional situations demand; at such times they became the tool of the propagandist and an outlet for the indignant idealist. The size of the pamphlet, too, well fitted the requirements of the propagandist and polemicist: it was reasonably easy to prepare at the printers, and, sometimes costing only a few pennies, it was inexpensive to buy.

As one event after another led up to the Revolution, the number of pamphlets increased. People were interested in what was happening, and, if they did not read, there were other people who did and who enjoyed passing on views and news via tavern or sewing-circle gossip. From 1763 through 1783 some 1200 to 1500 pamphlets were printed in America. The number, though impossible to determine exactly, is large considering a population of only about 2.8 million in 1780 (up from less than 1.2 million in 1760) and does not include reprints or republications by different publishers. Among a variety of printers, James Rivington, the Tory owner of the New York *Gazette*, was a dominant force. Comparably effective for the Whigs was Isaiah Thomas, who edited and printed the Massachusetts *Spy*. They were men of some power whose pamphlets probably influenced a great number of people. But with power comes danger, and one man's satisfaction is another's irritation. Rivington's press was wrecked in 1775, and he had to run for his life. Those staunch advocates of certain political views, however, knew the value as well as the risks of their work. The stronger the phrasing, the more biting the attack; the more heroic the praise, the more effective the pamphlet would be for the morale of the people for whom it was being written.

Within the world of propaganda pamphlets, the drama held a unique position. Stirring events call for dramatic expression. Despite religious condemnation and legal prohibition, the drama seemed both a natural and a logical means of communication. And *communication* is the proper word. Writers of plays and dialogues during the Revolution had something to say, and their primary objective was to persuade others to their points of view. Because they were protesting attacks on their sense of freedom or their means of livelihood, they showed anger, indignation, and defiance in plays which mocked, ridiculed, and assaulted adversaries in bitter terms. For many years in the colonies, the social, religious, and political propagandists had realized the impact of dialogue on the listener or reader. Conversation was a valued part of daily life; a long speech did not provide the same appeal. Although the play form can be interpreted as another step toward the threatre beyond the printed dialogue, the pamphlets of protest drama were, as an analysis of their structure reveals, intended more for reading than for performance. It was the idea that was important—the dramatic representation of a historical event as filtered through a certain political or philosophical persuasion. Personal feelings and morale were what mattered. Plays were read and perhaps acted, while spokesmen of opposing factions condemned or praised.

One secret of effective propaganda is simplicity, and the drama of the Revolution followed this rule. Responsive to a particular event—the Boston Massacre or the Battle of Brooklyn, for example—the dramatist simply and quickly created a dialogue or play from his particular bias. He might present a variety of people, always in the simplest terms, while the dialogue seldom involved more than two people, and monologues were frequent. The local setting for the event or crisis would be noted, but more important was the self-interest of the author. Although three of the identifiable dramatists of this period—Mercy Warren, Hugh Henry Brackenridge, and Robert Munford—had backgrounds that included or were associated with classical education and enjoyed reading drama, most plays of the period suggest only slight knowledge of dramaturgy. In general, those who created plays for the War of Belles Lettres showed little interest in plot, no concern for character, and no knowledge of stage setting. They were writing emotionally biased protest plays, bitter satires for which they sought reactions as explosive as those generating their creations. The effect of their work is difficult to discover, but, in reading some of the plays two hundred years later, one can still feel their power.

Among those dramatists who championed the cause of the Patriots, none was more concerned with the events of the Revolution than was Mercy Otis Warren (1728–1814). Born into a sturdy Massachusetts family which traced its colonial activity back to 1635, Mercy was the third of thirteen children. With domestic duties demanding her attention as the oldest daughter, she was sixteen before she ever left her home in Barnstable. The event which occasioned her first trip was the Harvard graduation of her brother, James Otis, whose speeches and pamphlets during the 1760s did much to further the Patriot cause. At twenty-six she married James Warren, who became President of the Provincial Congress and a general in Washington's army. Always alert and both emotionally and intellectually close to the work of her brother and her husband, she was a strong-minded person who used her literary talents effectively to attack the Tory leaders and their activities during the early years of the Revolution when the pamphlet war was at its height.

Growing up in a small colonial Massachusetts town, young Mercy Otis had grasped every opportunity to enjoy reading and writing, both of which provided important outlets throughout her life. When early in 1779 her eyes gave her trouble and she experienced some of the emotional instability which plagued her brother, her husband suggested that she "write a satire on Villains, there are enough of them; if not, take in Fools, then I am sure you will have enough."[2] This activity, he felt certain, would be a successful remedy. Obviously, this was not the ordinary husbandly response to wifely complaints, but Mercy Warren was not an ordinary woman. Although her earliest reading was influenced by her minister and limited to certain books and the newspapers which came into her home, she was soon reading history and philosophy and writing poems, which she shared with her friends, on nature, friendship, and religion. As a poet she had no ambitions to be published, while her letter writing was simply part of her private life, revealing her intellectual affinity to such people as Samuel Adams, John and Abigail Adams, Jefferson, John Dickinson, and Washington as well as showing the interest in language, the wit, and the emotional power of a woman of intelligence and sensitivity. Yet her impressive letter writing and her personal poems helped start her career as a propagandist. John Adams early recognized her ability as a satirist who handled political situations with great wit and suggested—even providing a brief outline—a poem on the Boston Tea Party, which she eventually wrote as "The Squabble of Sea Nymphs." Other people also were aware of Mrs. Warren's talent. After Hannah Winthrop, the wife of the Harvard professor and staunch Patriot, John Winthrop, saw the massacre of Lexington, she begged her to depict "the moving scene" with her "poetic pencil."

Urged by friends and impelled by her own conscience and inexplicable impulses for creative activity, she entered the War of Belles Lettres. Perhaps the physical injury of her brother, who was so severely beaten for his opinions that his reason was affected, was another factor. At any rate, she rallied to the

Patriot cause with a fury that distinguishes her writing during the Revolution. She was no middle-of-the-roader; what she thought, she spoke or wrote. Her effect as a gadfly during the early years of the Revolution cannot be underestimated.

Describing her motives for writing her plays, she sensed "a period when America stood trembling for her invaded liberty"—a dramatic point in history requiring dramatic expression. Mercy Warren herself never saw a play on stage, but she had read both Shakespeare's and Molière's plays with pleasure and understanding. Perhaps instinctively, she expressed her emotional reaction to current events in play form even if it was meant only for reading.

Mercy Warren's first play, *The Adulateur; A Tragedy; As It Is Now Acted in Upper Servia*, appeared anonymously in two installments in the Massachusetts *Spy* (March and April, 1772). Attacking those who monopolized public offices such as Governor Hutchinson and Chief Justice Peter Oliver and praising the Patriots whom these officials angered, the play became immediately popular, so popular that some unknown person added two acts. Mrs. Warren acknowledged her unknown collaborator in a memorandum: "Before the author thought proper to present another scene to the public, it was taken up and interlarded with productions of an unknown hand. The plagiary swelled *The Adulateur* to a considerable pamphlet."[3] It was this pamphlet play, revised in five acts, which was published in 1773, still without her name. As a satiric attack it had a strong appeal for a people who easily identified the heroes and villains in the play although its stylized and exaggerated sentiment and verse do not give the modern reader the same pleasure.

The scene of *The Adulateur* is Servia; its form is blank verse. In Act I Brutus (James Otis) and Cassius (Sam Adams) discuss past and present patriotism and nationalism and urge their friends to action: "Let manly sense of injured freedom awake them." Meanwhile Rapatio (Hutchinson) and his group complain of their past treatment and plan to move against the Patriots. As Brutus and Cassius plot their cause in Act II, Rapatio declares war and attacks the citizens in "promiscuous slander," a reference to the Boston Massacre on March 5, 1770. Act III opens in "a spacious hall"; a ghost enters crying for revenge, and Brutus and Cassius declare that the revolution has begun. In another hall Rapatio argues with those senators who feel that the citizens are being abused and, later, blames the Patriot leaders. Act IV exposes a villainous Rapatio threatening economic revenge while showing a weak and repulsive character. In another scene Hazelrod (Oliver), speaking to the citizens, demands "arbitrary power." The final act of this loosely pieced together bit of propaganda strikes at the duplicity of the Tory leaders as Brutus weeps for his country.

A year later Mercy Warren, obviously pleased with her success, devised another attack in play form on Rapatio. This one, *The Defeat,* appeared anonymously in two installments of the Boston *Gazette* (May and June, 1773). Simpler in language and subject matter than *The Adulateur, The Defeat* presents a greedy and threatening Rapatio served by turncoats such as Proteus and a hired scribbler named Philalethes whom Mrs. Warren identified as Jonathan Sewall, the Tory activist for whom she felt only the greatest contempt. These men are opposed by Honestus, Cassius, Rusticus—Patriots all— who warn Rapatio that they will not be intimidated by his threats. The crisis occurs in the third act during a battle in which Rapatio, his abettors, and his fellow creatures are overwhelmingly defeated as freedom and happiness are restored to the people. Alone at the end of play and doomed, Rapatio laments his lost peace of mind which he sold for "flattering titles" and "sordid gold." With her heaviest satiric bursts reserved for Hutchinson, Mrs. Warren also defended those rights for which the Patriots would fight: right of assembly, freedom of the press, freedom from forced servitude, and the right to make just laws.

The Defeat, too, had a happy response, particularly so because it appeared at about the same time as some letters written by Hutchinson and Oliver which assured the British ministers that the belligerent colonialists were only a minor faction. Franklin had gotten possession of those incriminating letters, which Sam Adams then published after James Warren and his group had read them. The play and the letters further worsened the position of Hutchinson, who was removed from office the following year.

By this time the War of Belles Lettres in the drama was well under way with both Tory and Patriot plays, and Mrs. Warren's continuing career illustrates both the degree of her commitment to the Revolution and her contribution to its drama. With the recall of Hutchinson in 1774, General Gage took over the government of Boston; the colonial legislature, of which James Warren was a part, had moved its headquarters to Concord. During the winter prior to the momentous spring of 1775, Mercy Warren, always in touch with her husband by letter and occasionally riding with him on horseback as he went about his duties, wrote her third and most significant play. As usual her husband read her work and passed it on to John Adams in Philadelphia on January 15, 1775—"Inclosed are for your amusement two acts of a dramatic performance composed at my particular desire"—who rushed it into print.[4] It was immediately popular with Patriot readers, and John Adams, writing from Braintree on March 15, 1775, eagerly praised the author's ability in "classical Satyr, such as flows so naturally & easily from the pen of my excellent Friend." Although Mrs. Warren's name did not appear on the published work, *The Group* seems to have been the satiric play of which she was most proud. When years later, after she and Adams had had a serious falling out over different political views, she discovered that the authorship of *The Group* was being assigned to another, she asked Adams' help in identifying her work. His response by letter commended "Madam Mercy Warren, the historical, philosophical, poetical, and satirical consort of the then Colonel, since General James Warren of Plymouth, sister of the great but forgotten James Otis," and his note in the pamphlet copy at the Boston Anthenaem stated as follows: "August 17, 1814. The 'Group' to my certain knowledge was written by Mrs. Mercy Warren of Plymouth. So certifies John Adams."[5]

The sixteen characters in *The Group. A Farce, As Lately Acted, and to be Re-acted, to the Wonder of all Superior Intelligences, Nigh Headquarters, at Amboyne* represent the men who accepted appointments on the Massachusetts Council through a "royal writ of Mandamus" which usurped the rights of the electorate. For Mercy Warren and the Patriots of Massachusetts, these men were asserting their belief in the royal prerogative rather than in the Charter of Massachusetts and were worthy of particular contempt because as educated men they should have helped lead the colony toward freedom. Not all among the sixteen, however, were subjected to Mrs. Warren's scathing attack. In the play Sylla (General Gage) was treated with some sympathy as he struggled with his conscience as a man and with his duty as a soldier. Sir Sparrow Spendall (Sir William Pepperell) and Collateralis (Judge William Broune) were represented as relatively inoffensive, having inherited their wealth and managing to maintain some personal popularity among the people. Those men she treated as having some regrets for their positions on the Council. By this time, of course, Governor Hutchinson had departed for England; he is only talked about in the play (which includes other characters from *The Adulateur*). Those on whom Mrs. Warren's acid pen dripped vituperation and biting sarcasm were not too different from Rapatio: Hazelrod (Peter Oliver), Meagre (Foster Hutchinson, brother of the former governor), Hateall (Timothy Ruggles, a violent Tory), and Beau Trumps (Daniel Leonard, a Tory writer of some skill).[6] As a play *The Group* must be described as merely a dialogue, as all of Mercy Warren's political farces should be described. It lacks action, character portrayal, and a good conflict although it shows the author's excellent touch for satire. For that time, however—and all satiric propaganda must be judged in terms of the event satirized—it truly represented a view which attracted an enthusiastic reading audience. For later audiences some knowledge of the background is necessary, or the satire loses its effect.

The Group consists of two acts and a brief epilogue, all in blank verse. Although the play was probably never acted, it does not completely lack theatricality when, for example, the members of the Group are introduced as "attended by a swarm of court sycophants, hungry harpies, and unprincipled danglers, collected from the neighboring villages, hovering over the stage in the shape of locusts." In that atmosphere Hazelrod and Hateall revel in their cruelty in keeping the "dogs" down and boast of their villainy, Hazelrod having "sold my country for a splendid bribe" (I, i). Other members of the Group eventually confess that they have overcome conscious fears of godly retribution to become, as Beau Trumps explains, "the venal herd . . . mark'd with infamy till time blot out/ And in oblivion sink our hated names" (II, i). When immediate fears propel the Group to Sylla's camp to beg protection from the vengeance of the armed multitudes, Sylla has sympathy for the "injured nation" and hesitates to draw a "guilty sword" even as Hazelrod denounces "this ballancing of passions." Left alone, Meagre and Secretary Dupe bemoan the "unremitting vigilance" of the Congress, "the truths Nov. anglus [John Adams] tells," the "noble stand" of Brutus (James Otis), and decide that they must urge Sylla on "though injured justice stern and solemn frown." At their exit a curtain is drawn to reveal a Lady, who addresses the audience "in mournful accents" but with those references to nature which adorned Mrs. Warren's early verse. These are "painful scenes," the Lady explains, "Till British troops shall to Columbia yield,/ And freedom's sons are Masters of the field" (II, iii).

In May, 1775, British Generals Clinton, Howe, and Burgoyne arrived in Boston to begin an occupation which severely irritated the Patriots in New England. After the Battle of Bunker Hill on June 17, 1775, the siege by the Continental Army, together with a general lack of activity caused by severe weather, produced a restlessness among the British forces which, it is assumed, General Burgoyne attempted to remedy with a farce entitled *The Blockade of Boston*. At least, as the established playwright of *The Maid of the Oaks* (1774), he was capable of having written this skit which lampooned the efforts of the Patriots. Announced for performance in the *New England Chronicle*

(December 21, 1775), *The Blockade of Boston* was evidently presented also on January 6, 1776, in a performance which stimulated the creation of another political farce. No copy of *The Blockade of Boston* exists, but accounts of that night in January state that, at the moment a character burlesquing Washington entered the scene, a sergeant burst upon the stage to announce, "The Yankees are attacking our works on Bunker's Hill!"[7] The intrusion seemed at first to be a part of the play, but the immediate confusion among the officers present suggested another view. The resulting chaos inspired someone, possibly Mrs. Warren, whose violent antagonism to Burgoyne was well known, to write *The Blockheads; or, The Affrighted Officers*, a pamphlet play published in 1776.

Mercy Warren's authorship of this play has been seriously questioned, and despite both internal and external evidence which suggests that she could have been responsible, she remains an unlikely choice. While the social and political satire in the play is consistent with her usual attitude, the vindictive tone, though not out of character in her condemnation of Burgoyne, is absent in her other works. None of her propaganda plays, of course, carried her name, and she claimed only *The Group* late in her life. The argument that the language in *The Blockheads* is too crude and that the thought, too vulgar for Mrs. Warren is countered by her familiarity with all social levels in Barnstable and by the anonymity which she always chose. It is also noted that her publisher of *The Group* also printed *The Blockheads* and that several characters in the play, although with different names, appeared also in *The Group*. The differences from her other works that this play provides, however, are also noteworthy: the level of characters presented, female characters, the lack of subtlety throughout, an interest in plot, the use of prose rather than poetry, and an ending which included a popular flag-waving technique unused elsewhere by Mrs. Warren: "And let's conclude with huzza for America." Essentially, the authorship must remain something of a mystery.

The Blockheads, whoever wrote it, is a farce of three acts with a prologue and an epilogue. As in *The Group*, the characters in *The Blockheads*, at least the men, are keyed to real people.[8] While the British officers curse their poor food and their fate of being cooped up in Boston, their Loyalist friends find themselves in an equally wretched state. In contrast with the military, Simple and his wife, simple country folk, bicker over her social pretensions and his unhappy connection with the government. Their concern for food in these hard times brings forth some excremental humor, and the wife tells Simple bluntly that his lack of interest in her social aspirations may earn him the horns of a cuckold. Equally concerned with social position, their daughter plans to elope with Lord Dapper, a man who presumably "labors under the disgrace of Inability." When the British discover that the colonists have occupied Dorchester Heights, they condemn the Patriots as excelling "their very father Belzebub for fighting" and prepare to leave Boston. Simple, caught in the chaos, curses his fate: "to be yok'd to an old fool of a wife, and scampering after a herd of runaway cowards." The final soliloquy shows Mrs. Simple in Halifax pitifully asking that her injured country have a tear for her. The most interesting scenes in the play are those with Simple, where the dialogue is enhanced with good rural, farcical humor. As the social satire balances the political, the ridiculing of the British officers and their Loyalist friends in this play is underlined by a mocking emphasis on their disillusionment and dispair.

Another satire that may well have come from the pen of Mercy Warren is a short sketch entitled *The Motley Assembly: A Farce. Published for the Entertainment of the Curious* (1779). Although basically farcical in structure, there is something of the comedy of manners in this one-act play where the satire is aimed mainly at fashionable society, in particular at Americans who placed social standing above support of the Revolution. As is *The Blockheads*, it is in prose, with some rather stiff lines but also with some speeches that fore.hadow the wit in Royall Tyler's *The Contrast*. The play opens at the home of Mrs. Flourish, who will not let her daughter attend the legislative assembly for fear of social reprisals. Esquire Runt, a pretentious gallant and one of the managers of the assembly, speaks first:

> It is a very great mortification to the gentlemen, madam—your not permitting Miss Flourish to go to the Assembly.
>
> MRS. FLOURISH.   I mean it as such, Mr. Runt—if your sex are so weak and undiscerning, as to prefer the fading, short-lived, perishable trifle beauty, to the noble exalted, mental accomplishments, which only are of intrinsic value, Mr. Runt—it is fit they should be mortified.—O why has Heaven permitted our passive sex to be so long deceived and misled by the idle and groundless opinion of the superior wisdom of the male sex!—in animal strength I grant them their superiority—and I have found some capable of pleasing—but few—very few indeed capable of informing me.
>
> RUNT.   But, madam, you will be pleased to consider, that few ladies are so accomplished as you are allowed to be.
>
> MRS. FLOURISH.   Say no more, Mr. Runt—I am almost sick at the bare mention of the word—it is so horribly prostituted and misapplied upon almost all occasions.

Politics has forced itself upon society, and the assembly, once a simple diversion and entertainment for young ladies, now has a new significance. Will the British return? Perhaps it is best to be a "turncoat," as Esq. Runt urges, or the "versatile man," which Mrs. Flourish praises. The Taxalls also fear that attendance at the Assembly will affect their social prestige. Because the Flourishes and the Taxalls think rather more of scarlet uniforms than of blue ones, the American serviceman has a problem: shall he take "a little damn'd paracidical viper to his bosom because it is pretty?" Obviously not; honor and patriotism forbid it. Meanwhile "whigs and tories joined by fashion 'meet' in mixed assembly to their sires' disgrace." It is all very slight, distinguished only by the dramatist's vivid disdain for people who have nothing more substantial to direct their lives than the frivolous breezes of social fashion.

If *The Motley Assembly* was written by Mrs. Warren, it was the last of her satirical farces. Five years earlier her thoughts had turned to a different style of drama. In a letter dated January 19, 1774, to her close friend Abigail Adams, Mercy Warren wrote that "the solemn strains of the tragic Muse have been generally more to my taste than the Lighter Representations of the Drama. Yet I think that the Follies and Absurdities of Human Nature Exposed to Ridicule in the Masterly Manner it is done by Molière may often have a greater tendency to reform Mankind than some graver Lessons of Morality."[9] She was at this time, of course, deeply involved in writing plays that ridiculed particular activities of particular men and women. For historians of the drama, those efforts would certainly be classed as "lighter representations of the drama," and yet they were seriously written, not only to entertain, but to provoke thought. In fact, Mrs. Warren does not seem to have been a person with a great sense of humor. She had a good feeling for language, and she had a ready wit fired by strong opinions about life around her. She lacked the detached view of life that comedy demands, however, while personal sorrows and the solemn issues of the Revolution weighed on her. For reasons that are wholly her own, she claimed only one of her propaganda farces. Doubtless, she would have been surprised that they have lived so long, but that would not mean that she felt the issues and ideas involved insignificant. Those plays were written quickly and for a particular purpose. She wrote other plays and poems which she felt better represented her literary abilities.

In 1790 she published *Poems, Dramatic and Miscellaneous*, which included two long, dull tragedies: *The Ladies of Castile* and *The Sack of Rome*. As she had written her propaganda sketches for her husband and friends, she wrote these plays—each one taking about a year's time—for her son, Winslow, who was the U.S. consul in Lisbon. In blank verse *The Ladies of Castile*, the first of the two plays, showed a knowledge of the elements of drama not associated with her farces—plot, character, action, and conflict—but it does not raise her work above the conventional historical tragedy of the period. Taking as her thesis the last heroic struggle for liberty in Spain before the "complete establishment of despotism by the family of Ferdinand," she was able to indulge her interest in revolution and in patriots rising against a tyrant. Central in her play, as the title suggests, are women: the daughter of the tyrant is loved by a patriot; the tyrant's son loves the wife of one of the rebels; Maria, the major figure, wife and sister to patriots, defies the tyrant with a passion that suggests Mercy Warren's earlier convictions. But the revolution fails, and the play ends conventionally.

The Sack of Rome was no better, another historical play which she started as soon as she completed *The Ladies of Castile*. This was a period of personal sadness for Mrs. Warren, and her suffering seems reflected in the play. "Debilitated by the habits of every species of luxury," she wrote in the preface, "man has sunk to his lowest depravity and wants a lesson in morality, valor, and virtue." Traditional conflicts of love-versus-duty and honor-opposed-by-venality control a plot in which innocence suffers from the violence of those dominated by evil passions. If that was her lesson, it lacked her customary optimism, which at the time was being countered by periods of gloom. In the final act the invading Vandals sack Rome with the impartiality of degenerate arrogance. Although Mercy Warren had never seen a stage play, she had a strong desire to have *The Sack of Rome* produced and, hoping that he might arrange a performance, in 1787 sent a copy to John Adams in London. With considerable diplomacy, however, and some truth—"nothing American sells here"—Adams suggested that Mrs. Warren only publish her play and continue work on her history.

It was her *History of the Rise, Progress and Termination of the American Revolution, interspersed with Biographical and Moral Observations* which absorbed much of Mercy Warren's writing energies at this time. The first part was completed by 1791, and the entire work in three volumes was published in 1805. Soon afterwards there developed between Mercy Warren and John Adams a difference of opinion relating both to her strong opposition to Federalism and aristocracy and to comments which she made about him in her history. Neither person was restrained in letters which spelled out the injury and indignation each felt. Nor did her passion for freedom subside with age.

In a letter to Adams on August 4, 1814, when their views had become somewhat reconciled, she praised him for obtaining "an emancipation from the yoke of foreign slavery for this thoughtless, thankless race." The following October she died. Her life focused on the Revolution, and the little farces which she wrote in support of her opinions not only provide a substantial reflection of her talents as a satirist and political gadfly but serve as the best illustration of the way in which drama was used during the revolutionary period.

Long before Mercy Warren began to write, Whig and Tory points of view had been expressed in college dialogues. After her sketches began to appear, the Tories formed a more cohesive party unit and used the dramatic form as the predominant method for promulgating their opinions. One of their early efforts, *Debates at the Robin-Hood Society in the City of New York. On Monday night, 19th July 1774*, was published in New York, probably in 1774.[10] The nine "characters" listed might better be termed participants because the work is more a discussion than a play. The members of the Society, all impressed with their own importance, meet to oppose certain resolves or protests which the American colonists have drawn up against England. Mr. Silver Tongue, a powerful orator, presents the resolves: that the colonists should have "equality of rights," that they should be exempt from taxation without representation, that the opinions of the colonists should be represented at an assembly, and that the Boston Post Act subverts freedom. After a discussion the resolves are ordered published by John Holt, the Patriot editor of the *New York Journal,* and the play ends. Then, in a note, the anonymous author decries the fact that such people lead public affairs and assures the reader that the "wicked designs of the few" will be defeated. More subtle than other plays at this time—subtleties were never overwhelming in any of these plays or dialogues—it is the tone of the comments and the choice of words by the speakers that make the satire effective. The idea that the people have a right to rebel against a government is thoroughly ridiculed; the uneducated, common man is laughed at; his accents are mocked; even the elegant manner and language of Mr. Silver Tongue are objects of abuse. Generally, the play pictures the Patriot as an unbalanced part of society and finds the extent to which the Patriot carries the concept of liberty quite ridiculous.

It is reasonable to believe that the *Debates at the Robin-Hood Society* was a Tory reaction to the meeting of the First Continental Congress in Philadelphia during September and October, 1774. One of the acts of the Congress was to approve the so-called Suffolk Resolves, which, adopted by the Massachusetts Patriots on September 9, 1774, defied Parliament and declared their own rights and liberty seriously curtailed.

There is no question, however, that another Tory pamphlet, published that same year by the Tory printer, Rivington, was directed at the Congress. This was called *A Dialogue Between a Southern Delegate and His Spouse on His Return from the Grand Continental Congress.* The name on the title page is Mary V. V.; for literary purposes it is anonymous, but the point of view seems to be a woman's, and the work is "Inscribed To the Married Ladies of America." The sketch is exactly what the title describes—a brief dialogue, seven speeches by the husband and eight by the wife, in rhyming couplets of anapestic trimeter with irregularities. The wife's alarm begins the dialogue: "you'll repent of't," she says. And the same idea ends the piece: "Repent! or you are forever, forever undone." As she upbraids her husband for the foolhardy venture in which he is involved, he tries to calm her and explain that women do not belong in politics. But her chiding, her scorn, and her fear for his welfare do not abate as she sees stupidity in the approval of the Suffolk Resolves and utter absurdity in defying the "greatest power on earth." She ridicules the presumption of the delegates and, in some trepidation, warns her husband, "Make your Peace; Fear the King." The humor of the piece appears in the couple's bickering comments on women in politics, in the tirade that the husband must endure, and in the light touches of ridicule, while the propaganda value of the work rests in the seriousness of the observations underlined by the satiric tone. It is a clever plea, a warning to stop this foolishness before it is too late.

Another Tory tract in dialogue form may be remembered more for the length of its title than its value as drama: *The Americans Roused in A Cure for the Spleen; or, Amusement for a winter's evening. Being the substance of a conversation on the times, over a friendly tankard and pipe between Sharp, a country parson, Bumper, a country justice, Fillpot, an inn-keeper, Graveairs, a deacon, Trim, a barber, Brim, a Quaker, Puff, a late Representative. Taken in short-hand by Sir Roger de Coverly.* It appeared first in Boston in 1775 and was reprinted the same year by James Rivington in New York. Jonathan Sewall (1728–1796), a well-known Tory in Massachusetts, is given credit for writing this bit of propaganda, presumably just before he somewhat precipitously left for England in 1775. Known to favor Governor Hutchinson, he also welcomed General Gage in 1775. One consequence of his misguided enthusiasm was an attack on his house by a mob. Another can be found in Trumbull's description of him in *M'Fingal*:

Drew proclamations, works of toil,
In true sublime of scarecrow style
Wrote farces too, 'gainst sons of freedom,
All for your good, and none would read 'em.
[Canto II.]

The characters are the most interesting part of this conversation as they represent any village aristocracy which might gather in a tavern to consider the political situation. With the discussion completed, mainly through long, dull speeches, the Tory argument has been developed. Puff, the Patriot member of the Assembly, is a rather dense fellow who simply did not understand what was going on. The logical spokesman for the King and Parliament, the parson reflects the many New England preachers who still obstinately referred to the King as the "Lord's Annointed." The justice is also understandably friendly to England, whereas the barber talks on both sides to please his customers, and the landlord tries to stay neutral. In essence, none can imagine more liberty than they already enjoy, and their dialogue clearly but tediously satirizes the stupidity of the common man who is fooled by the Patriot leaders, the "wicked deceivers." Brim's benediction epitomizes their mood: "May the candle of the Lord within, lighten our paths; and may the spirit lead us in the way of truth; and preserve us from all sedition, privy conspiracy and rebellion." As propaganda, the dialogue preserved the usual tendencies of the pamphlet war while attempting to dramatize the happy conclusion that the Lord was on the side of the Tories.

Current events dictated both the timing and the subject matter of the War of Belles Lettres. As quickly as one political side published a tract or essay, the other side responded. The best of the propagandists was Thomas Paine (1737–1809), who arrived in America during the fall of 1774 with a letter of recommendation from Benjamin Franklin and who was at work editing the Pennsylvania *Journal* by February of the following year. Two dialogues are attributed to him. The first, published in the Pennsylvania *Journal* on January 4, 1775, is *A Dialogue Between General Wolfe and General Gage in a Wood Near Boston.* Wolfe had been a hero since his attack on Quebec in 1759, and Gage had been having problems with both Patriots and Tories since assuming the difficult task of replacing Governor Hutchinson in 1774. When the Parliament Act of Quebec in 1774 extended Quebec Province south to the Ohio River and west to the Mississippi River, the Patriots had more opportunities for complaints. Paine shrewdly resurrected the ghost of Wolfe to urge Gage to act strongly as a soldier and British citizen and to recognize what was hap-

pening. Wolfe then defends the Patriots' reactions to the Quebec Act and accuses the English of violating their own constitution and the "immutable laws
of nature" which every British citizen possesses. A Briton or an American,
Wolfe argues, ceases to be a British subject when he ceases to be governed
by rulers he has chosen or approved. Although the dialogue is slight, the
points are established with a fervor which was characteristic of Paine, who
wanted only to assure his readers that, indeed, the Quebec Act did violate
"the essence of liberty" and the British constitution.

A year later, after the battle at Lexington and the publication of *Common
Sense*, the *Pennsylvania Packet* (February 19, 1776) published another dialogue thought to be by Thomas Paine: *A Dialogue Between the Ghost of
General Montgomery, Just Arrived from the Elysian Fields, and an American
Delegate, in a Wood Near Philadelphia.*[11] In this work Paine made use of
another recognized romantic hero, one who had only recently been killed at
the head of troops attacking Quebec in the Patriot cause. As usual he employed no satire, just argument, and included some of the same ideas which
had just appeared in *Common Sense*. Essentially, the dialogue is a question-
and-answer script in which Montgomery uses his newly acquired supernatural
powers to persuade the delegate that "permanent liberty" can be achieved only
through independence from England. Calling the King a "Royal Criminal,"
he foresees the possibility of a "perfect and free form of government" in
America, where "human nature will *soon* receive the greatest military, civil,
and literary honors." There is, again, no character, no action, just powerful
argument. The concern for "literary honors," however, is intriguing. Whether
the author of *Common Sense* wrote this dialogue may remain disputable, but
it would seem that the unknown author knew Paine's essay extremely well
and could have been responsible for both works.

The most active year for pamphlet drama during the Revolution was 1776.
In addition to the dialogues just noted and *The Blockheads*, there were Patriot
plays by John Leacock and H. H. Brackenridge plus a scathing and anonymous
Tory attack called *The Battle of Brooklyn*. The most ambitious drama of this
period, however, and first American chronicle play is *The Fall of British Tyranny; or, American liberty triumphant. The First campaign. A tragi-comedy of
five acts. As lately planned at the Royal Theatrum Pandemonium at St. James's.
The principal place of action in America.* Internal evidence suggests that the
play was completed after the publication of *Common Sense* (January, 1776)
but before the news had reached Philadelphia of the evacuation of Boston
(March 17, 1776).[12] Soon after its publication in Philadelphia, editions of

the play appeared in Providence and Boston. For many years the identity of the author was uncertain, but it is now established that the play was created by John Leacock (1729–1802). A gold and silver smith during his early business life and a farmer later, Leacock was a prominent Philadelphian. As a member and perhaps one of the founders of a Patriot organization started in 1772 called the Society of the Sons of St. Tammany of Philadelphia, he was associated with important men in colonial politics. By 1785, with the publication of the first Philadelphia dictionary, he was listed as "John Leacock, Coronor for City and Country, & innkeeper." Although not a man of special literary talents, Leacock wrote poetry and at least one play that is an outstanding contribution to early American drama.

The scope of his play (from the causes of the Revolution in England to the end of General Montgomery's attack on Quebec on January 1, 1776) is matched by the complexity of its structure (five acts with twenty-six scenes). Presenting the accumulated actions and emotions which prompted the Patriots to rebel, the play was clearly written for one purpose: to bring people to the cause of American liberty. To accomplish his objectives Leacock uses several levels of actual or imagined society—the proud British aristocracy; the soldiers, citizens, and Negro slaves in America; and traditional shepherds. The language varies from forceful propaganda speeches to the vigorous exchanges of angry men, the conversation of common man, songs and poetry, and Negro dialect. There are the innocent victims on one hand and the villainous manipulators on the other. In sum, it is a sketchy view of all those years leading up to the Revolution as seen through events in the lives of a varied people.

Although the modern reader needs a knowledge of historical events and people to appreciate the satire and humor, the several editions of the play in 1776 suggest that Leacock's contemporaries, particularly those of his political persuasion, found the play fascinating. It is also quite possible that the play was produced. Although a public production in Philadelphia, in view of the city's civil regulations and the play's anti-British tone, might have been risky, the customary prologue and epilogue delivered by ficticious people—Peter Buckstail and Mr. Freeman—reveal the author's knowledge of the theatre. Paul Leicester Ford felt that *The Fall of British Tyranny* was performed more than once, but he had no real evidence.[13] Certainly, the play, in matter and structure, has nothing that would preclude production, and the absence of female characters would have made it more natural for college production at that time.

Leacock's alter ego, "Dick Rifle," dedicates *The Fall of Bishop Tyranny* to Lord Boston (General Gage) and Lord Kidnapper (the Earl of Dunmore), to their actors, pirates, and buccaneers, and to the Scots in America. His humorously satiric tone foreshadows the later scenes of the play that will treat the British: "I [the dedication reads in part] . . . dedicate the following Tragi-Comedy to your Patronage, and for your future entertainment; and as the most of you have already acted your particular parts of it, both comic and tragic, in reality at Lexington, Bunker's-hill, the Great-Ridge, etc. etc. etc. to the very great applause of yourselves, tho' not of the whole house, no doubt you will preserve the marks, or memory of it, as long as you live, as it is wrote in capital American characters and letters of blood on your posteriors." The first two acts present the cause of the Revolution. In Act I "at St. James's," the enemies—Lord Paramount (Lord Bute), Mocklaw (Lord Mansfield), Charley (Charles Jenkinson), the detested Scottish influences upon the King, along with Poltron (the Earl of Sandwich), Hypocrite (the Earl of Dartmouth), Catspaw (Lord North), Brazen (Wedderburn), and Judas (Thomas Hutchinson)—reveal through abstractions of their own political statements both their corruption and their complete disdain for the colonists. Act II shows America's friends in England. Lord Wisdom (the Earl of Chatham), Lord Religion (the Bishop of St. Asaph), Lord Justice (the Earl of Camden), Lord Patriot (John Wilkes), Bold Irishman (Edmund Burke), and the Colonel (Colonel Barre) tell of their opposition to their government's policies toward the colonists and predict a glorious future for America. In the manner of the position speeches in a debate, Leacock prepares the audience for subsequent action.

The action of the play then shifts to Boston for the reaction of the common man to the new British laws. Whig and Tory activities are debated; Lord Boston (Gage), reacts to the rout at Lexington. The tone of the play first changes abruptly as Dick and Roger, two shepherds, talk about the Lexington battle and celebrate with a song about St. Tammany. Again the mood changes, and a woman who lost the man she loved at Bunker Hill recalls that event in an emotional story. In Act IV the scene moves to a ship off Norfolk, Virginia, where Lord Kidnapper (Dunmore) tries to recruit Negroes to fight for the British. Here the language of the sailors provides some vigor to the dialogue, which is interspersed with snatches of song and dialect. Back in Boston the stupidity of and the lack of dignity and leadership among the British officers are dramatized in their "council of war after the battle at Bunker's Hill." Having thus presented colonial reactions and the continuing villainy of the British, the playwright provides a positive propaganda view. Captured by the British in his attempt to take Montreal, Colonel Ethan Allen reacts bravely and with dignity. At the Patriot headquarters in Cambridge, General Washington with Generals Lee and Putnam mourns the death of Montgomery as Putnam voices their determination: "I . . . swear by all the heroes of New-England, that this arm . . . shall wield this sword to the last in the support of liberty and my country, revenge the insult offer'd to the immortal Montgomery, and brutal treatment of the brave Allen" (V, v).

The popularity of Leacock's play is clear from its publication record. The drama would have been strong propaganda for a college stage publication, but such activity was not unknown in the colonies. Hugh Henry Brackenridge (1748–1816), for example, openly used his talent as a propagandist and dramatist to inspire his students at the Maryland Academy. Although best known as the author of *Modern Chivalry*, a novel generally satirizing society and politics, Brackenridge had careers as a judge, a legislator, and a chaplain. The ministry appealed to him particularly, and from 1776 to 1778 he was a chaplain in Washington's army. Certainly, a sense of mission and a belief in the power of persuasive oratory or writing are central to all of his work. Causes fascinated him, and, early in his academic career at the College of New Jersey, he had discovered a personal fulfillment through strong, emotional writing and a gift of satire.

In 1776 he wrote the first of two plays which were acted by his students at Maryland Academy. As Brackenridge explains in a note to his second play, he saw his plays strictly as school pieces, neither one finished as a drama and both certainly not ready for professional production. Writing in frequently powerful blank verse, he was always the teacher or preacher, definitely a man with a cause whose characters give orations on various subjects rather than participate in dialogue. Theatricality is completely overlooked; situations are reported, not dramatized. In fact, one must read *The Death of General Montgomery* very carefully not to miss the event of that death. Although Brackenridge once declared that he paid strict attention to the unities of time, place, and action and wrote according to the "prescribed rules of the Drama," he must not have looked over his plays before making that statement. He never forgot his message, however: "The subject is not love but valour. I meddle not with any of the effeminating passions, but consecrate my muse to the greatest themes of patriotic virtue, bravery and heroism."[14]

The Battle of Bunker's-Hill, A Dramatic piece of five acts, in heroic measures was published in Philadelphia in 1776 as written "by a gentleman of Maryland." Quickly composed, according to the preface, it was to instruct

Brackenridge's students as an "exercise in oratory." The prologue sets the tone of intense patriotism. First the American generals—Warren, Putnam, and Gardiner—and then the British generals—Gage, Howe, and Burgoyne—explain their objectives. All speeches are written in passable blank verse, but the acts are very brief. Act III, for example, takes only one printed page as Gardiner exhorts his men to be brave in battle, a contrast to the cowardice of Gage and the British soldiers described in Act II. Then in Act V, in ten brief scenes which skip back and forth between the armies, the battle of Bunker Hill is fought until the final American retreat, as both Howe and Burgoyne honor their enemies. But the "oration" is not yet over. There is an epilogue by a "gentleman of the army" ("who fights for freedom fights for the cause of Heaven") and three elegiac pieces: an ode on the glorious battle of Bunker Hill, a speech by General Washington, and a song in praise of the Patriot efforts that day. Rather than drama it might better be described as a patriotic display to encourage the colonialists in time of defeat.

Brackenridge's second play, *The Death of General Montgomery in storming the city of Quebec*, written and published in 1777 while Brackenridge was a chaplain in the army, also deals with a defeat. Essentially a eulogy rather than a tragedy—Brackenridge's term—it is an oratorical and poetic presentation of the imagined thoughts of the participants in a battle before, during, and after the event. Again it was propaganda, specifically planned to arouse and inspire Americans. Action and conflict are described rather than presented, while the drama involves only a brief moment encased in highly emotional poetry. But that was all that was necessary: a patriotic issue of sacrifice supported by the American leaders and the Ghost of Wolfe as well as by God and His Chaplain. It is its limited focus along with the propaganda power of the speeches which makes this work one of the best of the pamphlet plays of the Revolution.

The battle day dawns in Act III, "this auspicious morn" on which Montgomery recalls the hero, General Wolfe, feeling certain that Wolfe would oppose Britain's "unrighteous cause." In Act IV, after Benedict Arnold exhorts his men to "drive out these cut-throats homicides" Montgomery asks a prayer from the chaplain, and is persuaded to let the "gowns-man take a sword." "The cause is sacred," the chaplain argues, "and does sanctify,/ An action singular." Then a messenger appears. Their plans are known by the enemy; Montgomery now has difficulty urging his men on. He himself must advance first, his choice not to share their shame but death—"And God hath sent it. . . ." In the very next speech his aide-de-camp mourns "their deep

tragedy. Montgomery slain." It all happens very quickly, too quickly for co-
herent drama. A retreat is ordered, and the Ghost of Wolfe appears to inspire the troops "to win the contest." In Act V Arnold is wounded, and the
American forces are surrounded. When the British commander appears above
the wall with Montgomery's body, his "terms of peace" are accepted. With
good propaganda technique, Brackenridge has the British officer, Carleton, be-
rate the prisoners as "vile rebellious progeny of wrath" but not kill them.
The final speech of the play is spoken by an American, Captain Morgan,
who bitterly attacks this "deed of infamy" by the "earth-disgracing name of
Englishmen."

In this manner the Patriot cause was taken up by the pamphlet dramatists
in 1776, with plays by Warren, Leacock, and Brackenridge. Although there
were fewer Tory ventures in dramatic form during the War of Belles
Lettres, the Continental Army gave the Tories an excellent opportunity for
propaganda in the summer of 1776, and some anonymous Tory with a gift
for invective and satire took advantage of the occasion to write *The Battle of
Brooklyn. A farce of two acts. As it was performed on Long Island, on Tuesday the 27th day of August, 1776. By the representatives of the tyrants of
America assembled at Philadelphia.* Rivington immediately printed it in New
York, and the two editions which appeared the following year suggest its
popularity.

No one questions the idea that Washington was guilty of serious mis-
judgment as well as of a scandalously presumptive and casual attention to his
duties that August 27, 1776, when he was surprised by a British army that
disastrously defeated him and took control of Long Island. Men like John
Adams were furious at his negligence. During the Revolution Washington
was to make seemingly incredible errors, as the British did also, but the Battle
of Long Island was perhaps the worst. Along with his generals—Sullivan,
Sterling, and Putnam—his ineptness was excellent propaganda for the Tory
cause. The actual events of the situation did not require much exaggeration,
and historians have pointed out that some of the satirical observations made
in *The Battle of Brooklyn* are not far from the truth. The play, however, is
a scurrilous attack on Washington, his generals, and the Continental Army as
lechers, drunkards, horse thieves, counterfeiters, and cowards. Heavy-handed
ridicule and a sneering contempt mark the approach of the author, whose
sense of bawdy humor and low comedy give the play an occasional theatricality which most of the other dramatic pieces of the period lack. The attempts
at dramatized humor—Sterling's coming on stage half-dressed, for example—

are few, however, and the play generally follows the pattern of pamphlet drama by being light on action and heavy on description. Yet the dialogue shows conflicting emotions, and there is some attention to plot and characterization. This is a drama, in other words, not just a series of speeches. Yet, as usual, dramatic literature was of secondary concern; propaganda came first, and this episodic and libelous little farce was the best the Tories had to offer.

The first of the two acts presents the Rebel Chiefs before the battle. Sterling, caricatured as a dishonest, drunken fool, is suffering from the "gripes" after the previous night's drinking; two Rebel Colonels boast of the cattle and horses they have stolen. In a room at Brooklyn Ferry, two members of the "blushing trade," Lady Gates and Betty, discuss the generosity and aptitudes of Washington and Benjamin Harrison. "I almost puke at the recollection," says Betty. As a climax an apprehensive Washington curses his "ambition": "What have I sacrificed to thee?" The second act describes the rout in which "every man is now his own general." Washington and Putnam watch the disorder from Fort Green as the action follows historical fact rather closely. In the longest and last scene of the play, King and Noah, servants to Sterling and Sullivan, generally malign their masters, Congress, and the Patriot cause and decide to "renew our allegiance to the most admirable and virtuous Prince that ever swayed a scepter."

As the Revolution continued in its halting fashion, there was confusion and dissatisfaction on both sides, while the enthusiasm which directed the early action of both the Patriot leaders and the pamphleteers subsided. One little anonymous sketch published in 1777, *The Downfall of Justice; and, The Farmer Just Return'd from a Meeting on Thanksgiving Day*, comments bitterly but intelligently on local discomforts. Further described as "a comedy, lately acted in Connecticut," the play shows both anger and sensitivity in its clever satire. Sitting down to a good Thanksgiving dinner with his wife and daughter, the farmer offers a prayer for the food and for the poor and needy. Conversation turns to the high prices of firewood and food; the daughter ventures a laugh at the townsfolk who once scoffed at anything but the best and would now eat crusts with delight. Although the author's attitude suggests the effects of the war, the author is being ironic. Jack, the Negro servant of the family who talks in dialect, reveals the author's real beliefs. He is confused at the hypocrisy he sees. How can you laugh at townspeople who are hungry and still pray for the poor and needy? "Jack pitty poor folk," he says. Briefly but with good effect the author creates Jack as the only sympathetic character in the sketch and as the pivotal figure who directs the message and the satire of the play against those who profit from the war effort, particularly the profiteering Christian.

As the more violent war propaganda diminished, dramatists began to satirize the effects of the war on society. With *The Motley Assembly* in 1779, there also appeared *The Gubernatocial Collection*.[15] By contrasting the elegant balls held in Newport during the British occupation with a ball which forms a background for much of the play, the anonymous author of *The Gubernatocial Collection* satirizes Newport society after the departure of the British. Following his stated purpose "to give mankind a just idea of themselves," the dramatist provides a series of frequently unrelated scenes which capture particular qualities of people who represent a cross section of society. There is no plot, just one-dimensional, farcical sketches involving character types. A good part of the satire is directed toward war profiteers such as the husbands of Mrs. Cheatall and Mrs. Bankrupt, who got their wealth from the war just as Deacon Canteen made his money by making canteens for the British soldiers. But ridiculing a snobbish society is always basic to the author's approach whether or not war is mentioned. The newly rich General Cypher, the host at the ball, reached his position in society by kowtowing to the right people. Both Mr. Pomposity and Count Dipper Dapper, who have been abroad, find everyone at the ball who has not traveled "ignorant, illiterate fellows."

Although undoubtedly a Whig and concerned with social equality, the unknown dramatist was also strongly opposed to those who saw nothing good in America, those who not only held Tory views and profited by selling to the British but emulated the British in thought and action, copied their fashions, and praised their literature and culture while deploring anything American. Such an approach to society previewed the prejudices that stunted the growth of American drama, but it also stimulated some fine plays, from Royall Tyler's *The Contrast* through Mrs. Ritchie's *Fashion* to the dramas of Clyde Fitch.

Among the dramatists writing during the revolutionary period, there is one who does not properly belong in one political camp or the other. In fact, he did not take part in the pamphlet war, and his plays were not published until 1798, several years after his death.[16] The man is Robert Munford (1737?– 1783), remembered slightly as a prominent and influential landholder who served well in the Virginia House of Burgesses and in the House of Delegates prior to and during the Revolution but neglected and underrated as a dramatist. Although Munford did not consider himself a serious dramatist, his two plays, *The Candidates* and *The Patriots*, are the best written in America prior to the performance of Tyler's *The Contrast* in 1787. Both comedies read as well as many English plays of the period and contain some highly amusing scenes, while *The Patriots* presents ideas that are still meaningful to thoughtful readers. Munford's work also follows the dominant strain of satire that had directed American drama since Robert Hunter's *Androboros* in the early part of the century. His plays, therefore, fit into the drama of the War of Belles Lettres but with the distinct difference that he provided a balanced approach, that of a man of intelligence, sensitivity, and integrity expressing his views in the acceptable tradition of satiric comedy. His forte included an ability to imitate well, to which he added a rich imagination. More than other dramatists during the Revolution, he was concerned with the structure of his plays, the patterned development of plot and action, and the creation of interesting caricatures. If *The Disappointment* may be considered an opera-drama, Munford is America's earliest writer of comic drama.

The exact dates of his plays must remain a matter of conjecture. From all evidence, both internal and external, it can only be reasonably assumed that both were written during the decade of the 1770s. For *The Candidates* the earliest composition date is the winter of 1770–71, as indicated by the first line of the play, which mentions the death of Governor Botetourt (October 15, 1770). The setting of *The Patriots* is the year 1777, when the Scottish merchants were tried in the Mecklenburg Court House in April and the Virginia loyalty oath was a topic of discussion in May. The tone of this play suggests that it was completed by 1779.

Whatever the dates of his plays, Robert Munford had the necessary education, experience, and interest to do a surprisingly good job. Born into a wealthy family of social position and political prestige, he was educated in England (1750–1756) before studying law, marrying, and settling into the life of a planter in Virginia, where he was known to have a fair library and to have liked reading fiction and drama. Politics became a part of his life in 1765 when he was elected to the Virginia House of Burgesses. There he aligned himself with Patrick Henry and was an active supporter of the cause of liberty. As the Revolution approached, he was named head of the Mecklenburg County Militia and eventually commanded the militia of three counties, but his only active experience as a soldier was in the Battle of Guildford Court House. In 1779 he was elected to the House of Delegates. During the war years he had sufficient leisure to write *The Patriots*, but his major attendance at theatre performances was probably limited to the period 1770–1771. At that time David

Douglass and his American Company played in several Virginia towns before going into Maryland and then north for a final tour before theatre performances were prohibited by law. It has even been conjectured that Munford may have written *The Candidates* for possible production by Douglass' company.

The Candidates; or, the Humors of a Virginia Election is a brief and light satire on the manner in which elections are run and won. It was a popular topic, and Munford could have taken his ideas from numerous contemporary English models. In the fashion of such satiric comedy, he has some excellent scenes of farcical and racy humor which he intersperses with numerous references to local events and election practices. But, consistent with the motives of the good satirist, Munford was serious in his major plot sequence. He felt that voters and those running for public office should be responsible individuals, and the conclusion of the play shows his optimistic view.

As Munford points out, "an election brings out contrasting humors." Mr. Wou'dbe thoroughly dislikes the cajoling, fawning, and wheedling that seem to epitomize electioneering. Consequently, he bluntly refuses to support the candidacies of either Sir John Toddy or Strutabout. Among the voters to whom the candidates must appeal, Guzzle is a freeholder and lush who preserves a lizard in his rum bottle and who boasts that he understands the five "qualifications of the House of Burgesses"—eating, drinking, sleeping, fighting, and lying. At the candidates' barbeque Wou'dbe's attempt to give honest opinions on the candidates' promises contrasts with the racy humor of the voters and a hilarious scene featuring Guzzle, his wife, and Sir Toddy:

(*Enter* MRS. GUZZLE, *drunk.*)

MRS. GUZZLE.   Where's my drunken beast of a husband? (*Hickups.*) Oh John Guzzle. Oh John Guzzle.

GUZZLE.   What the devil do you want?

MRS. GUZZLE.   Why don't you go home, you drunken beast? Lord bless me, how the gingerbread has given me the hickup.

GUZZLE.   Why, Joan, you have made too—free with the—bottle—I believe.

MRS. GUZZLE.   I make free with the bottle—you drunken sot!—Well, well, the gingerbread has made me quite giddy.

GUZZLE.   Hold up, Joan, don't fall—(MRS. GUZZLE *falls.*) The devil, you will? Joan! Why woman, what's the matter? Are you drunk?

MRS. GUZZLE.   Drunk! You beast! No, quite sober, but very sick with eating gingerbread.

GUZZLE.   For shame, Joan, get—(*Offers to help her up, and falls upon her.*)

MRS. GUZZLE.   Oh Lord! John! You've almost killed me.

GUZZLE.   Not I—I'll get clear of you as fast as I can.

MRS. GUZZLE.   Oh John, I shall die, I shall die.

GUZZLE.   Very well, you'll die a pleasant death, then.

MRS. GULZZE.   Oh Lord! How sick! How sick!

GUZZLE.   Oh Joan Guzzle! Oh Joan Guz—zle. Lord bless me, how the gingerbread has given me the hickup.

MRS. GUZZLE.   Pray, my dear John, help me up.

GUZZLE.   Nay, my dear Joan, get sober first.

MRS. GUZZLE.   Pray, John, help me up.

GUZZLE.   Pray, Joan, go to sleep; and when I am as drunk as you, I'll come and take your place. Farewell, Joan. Huzza for Sir John Toddy!

[II, ii.]

Munford was clearly at his best in farce scenes with common characters. Unfortunately, the play loses some of its interest in the final act as the best candidates triumph all too easily.

The Patriots is a five-act comedy with a more conventional plot that mixes love and politics and reaches an acceptable denouement with the help of contrived discoveries and abrupt changes of character. Within these conventions, however, Munford shows marked talent in his handling, with different comic devices, of three sets of lovers on different social levels. The most original is the love affair of the cowardly Strut and Isabella, the "female politician," who not only knows her own mind and thinks in a combined romantic and pragmatic fashion but acts as aggressively as any dominating male. Although the characters are cleverly used both in the love episodes and in the propaganda scenes, Munford's attempt to relate the contrived love scenes to the more serious thesis of the play reveals his inexperience as a dramatist. Basically, he is concerned with false patriotism and the stupid persecution of minorities—serious considerations which Munford allows to intrude into his dialogue through occasional polemical statements that are a stuffy contrast to his more successful romantic and farcical scenes. As in *The Candidates* the ending of this play tends to be dull and contrived, but the humor and satire of earlier scenes provide a good antidote to Munford's deficiencies as a dramatist.

Munford's spokesmen in *The Patriots* are Meanwell and Trueman, "two gentlemen of fortune accused of Toryism." The three-pronged love plot involves Trueman, who is forbidden to see Mira by her father, Brazen; Isabella, the feminist who wants to marry a soldier but is advised by her father that she must marry Captain Flash, an egotistical superpatriot; and Pickle, Trueman's servant, who disguises himself as an officer in order to woo Melinda. Serious action begins with the plight of three Scotsmen whose offense before the people is in being Scotsmen and, therefore, enemies. (Hatred of Scotsmen in America, which reached serious proportions during the Revolution, was related to Lords Bute and Mansfield, whom the Patriots blamed for most of their problems.) After Meanwell and Trueman are exonerated when their accuser, Tackabout, is forced to reveal that he really is a Tory masquerading as a Patriot, awesome complications encumber the plot as Munford secures a happy ending for all three love adventures.

As the Revolution dragged on and the war among the propaganda pamphleteers seemed to become less spirited, a new note was sounded when the Americans signed a treaty of alliance with the French in 1778. Not all Patriots were happy with this agreement. France had been an enemy too recently, and it was also a Roman Catholic power. As the war came to an end, the American-French unity became an issue open to the satirist. One extant play which reveals the anti-French feeling is the anonymous *The Blockheads; or, Fortunate Contractor, An Opera in Two Acts as it was Performed at New York. The Music entirely new, Composed by several of the most eminent Masters in Europe.* Printed in 1782 in London, the opera could well have been a Tory play with the long title a common propaganda ploy rather than a description of production. Unfortunately, the supposed New York edition has never been found.

The work itself, a ballad opera, is an interesting mixture of allegorical characters and ordinary people both subjected to satiric treatment. With this fusion of the real and the symbolic, the author tries to disillusion Americans with their newly acquired French friends and to persuade them that England is their only hope. One plot revolves around Liberty's request that Americana help her save Freedom. With the assistance of Gaul, Americana goes to war with England, only to be betrayed by Gaul. Then realizing that Freedom is the child of England, she calls upon her "mother" to free her from Gallic chains. So runs the allegory. The other part of the opera is far more interesting while making the same point. In seven scenes with human characters, Old Shaver, a barber, figures prominently. He has three types of wigs (obviously a play on Whigs) which he places upon Blockheads. As his business thrives, he becomes wealthy and receives a title and a seat in Parliament, only to discover that he cannot maintain his commercial interests and follow his early ideals. In one scene a representative of America is blindfolded by a French physician, Deception, who then leads him wherever he wishes. In Congress, shown to be a divided and quarrelsome group, all members are put to sleep while "fiends" exchange their heads with French heads that do not suit their bodies. The series of sketches interspersed with songs provides some humorous satire before Americana ends the opera with the appropriate message by singing "Freedom, child of Albion's Isle."

Another brief opera-drama, or "Oratorical Entertainment," dealing with the relationship between France and America was Francis Hopkinson's *The Temple of Minerva* (1781).[17] This one stressed the happy cooperation between the two countries and was appropriately performed "by a Company of Gentlemen and Ladies" at the Philadelphia hotel of the Minister of France on October 11, 1781, as a part of the entertainment during a meeting between the minister and General Washington. As one of the signers of the Declaration of Independence as well as a poet and composer, Hopkinson knew the value of the proper political view at the correct moment. As the Genius of America and the Genius of France appear before the Temple of Minerva to learn the fate of America, they are regaled with predictions of a "future happy state" with France's friendship. There is no plot, of course, no character or action, just luxuriant praise of "Columbia's godlike son! Hail the glorious *Washington*," of the common soldier in America, and of the unity between the two countries.

The Temple of Minerva is clearly more opera than drama if, indeed, it could be said to contain any elements of the latter; however, it combines the propaganda approach to the drama that emerged during the revolutionary period with the college exercises of the 1760s. This form of eulogistic entertainment, employing dialogue and spectacle, continued for many years, always in celebration of a political, social, or moral issue relating to the new nation. One variation of the patriotic spectacle but without dialogue appeared on January 2, 1782, when Washington, still in Philadelphia, watched a performance of Beaumarchais' *Eugénie*. For the evening's entertainment Philip Freneau wrote a prologue in praise of Washington. The "illumination" which concluded the program outlined thirteen pillars which represented the states and which were adorned with the names of the military leaders of the Revolution.

With the war nearly over, colleges were again presenting dialogues and even plays. Students of Harvard College performed plays on national subjects by 1781, and students of Dartmouth College began to act out dialogues on different subjects possibly as early as 1774. Two of these, "A Dialogue Between an Englishman and an Indian" (1779) and "A Little Teatable Chitchat, ala-mode; or, an ancient discovery reduced to modern practice;—Being a Dialogue, and a Dish of Tea" (1781), were written by John Smith (1752–1809), a professor at Dartmouth. The first dialogue suggests the growth of Dartmouth from Moor's Indian Charity School in Lebanon, Connecticut, and makes particular reference to Eleazer Wheelock, who helped the school's transformation.

In it an intelligent and eloquent Indian responds to an Englishman's condemnation of Indians with a persuasive argument accusing the English of cruelty and unchristian actions. The second dialogue contains light satire on inflation, profiteering, self-serving assemblymen, and nonsensical tea-table chitchat.

College theatricals increased in number, and when Cornwallis' surrender on October 19, 1781, announced the climax of the "tragedy," as Lafayette described it, more people became interested in opening the theatres. John Henry was the first actor from the old American Company to return from Jamaica, but Philadelphia (which until 1789 did not repeal its law prohibiting theatre) was not ready for him and refused his request in July, 1782, to deliver his "Lectures on Heads." Baltimore, however, in January, 1782, opened a season in its new theatre, where Henry appeared before going to New York. There the British military actors were joined by a company managed by Dennis Ryan. Early in 1784 Lewis Hallam appeared in Philadelphia and, limited by the anti-theatre law, presented evenings of lectures and perhaps disguised plays in the Southwark until July, 1786. The next month the John Street Theatre in New York opened under the joint management of Hallam and Henry. Slowly and awkwardly an appreciation of dramatic activity was being nurtured in the new nation. And, with the ever-increasing theatre activity, American dramatists would find encouragement. Although it would still be nearly a century before American dramatists could achieve both personal fame and financial reward for their labors, the fascination of the theatre and the pleasure of seeing their art performed on the stage even for a single night was compelling. Soon America would have a few dramatists whose talents would be acknowledged and whose names would be recognized.

FIVE

Early Dramatists
of the New Republic

IN THE APRIL 18, 1787, issue of the New York *Daily Advertiser,* a theatre critic who signed himself "Candour" began his review of the previous night's play: "I was present last evening at the representation of *The Contrast,* and was very much entertained with it. It is certainly the production of a man of genius, and nothing can be more praiseworthy than the sentiments of the play throughout." The "man of genius," identified only as "a Citizen of the United States" in the announcements, was Royall Tyler; and his play was not only well received as the first native American comedy to be professionally produced, but it has impressed critics and historians ever since that first performance with the same sense of entertainment that "Candour" enjoyed. In his *History of the American Theatre,* William Dunlap commented on the production as the "commencement of the American drama united with the American theatre,"[1] and with this single play Tyler became recognized as a dramatist of some stature in America. During the period that followed the Treaty of Paris in 1783 and ended with Jefferson's election to the presidency in 1800, there were many plays written by amateur playwrights, actors, hacks, and members of the literati. From these years, however, four people might be selected for their significant or consistent contribution to the young and developing American drama. Tyler would be one; Dunlap, another; the other two are Susanna Rowson and John Daly Burk.

The political upheaval of the war was soon replaced with a social upheaval as the people—those same people who had demonstrably lacked a homogeneity and had prided themselves on their individuality while succeeding in a revolution only through the idealistic persistence of a few and the incredible errors in judgment on the part of others—tried to find a common bond. In fact, the years after 1783 were filled with a national disharmony which reached a crisis with the election of 1800, when the author of the Declaration of Independence faced the task of trying to put individual differences aside and to create national unity. To counterbalance the strain that accompanied the social and political factionalism, there had to be a comforting relaxation, and the theatre, as did the literature of the period, helped to provide the necessary change of pace. But the drama, because it demanded a more immediate reaction, more accurately and more readily reflected the attitudes of the people. Whereas satire had always been prominent in American drama, it now became for most of the dramatists a device to promote nationalism. Consciously or unconsciously, for idealistic or commercial motives, they began to write plays which reflected the constant and yet sometimes unsteady shaping of the new republic in America.

One of the major problems to be overcome in establishing a unified country was its size. It was soon discovered that the people could not afford to remain isolated in areas separated by great distances and linked only by miserable connecting roads. It took, for example, twenty-nine days for the news of the signing of the Declaration of Independence in Philadelphia to reach Charleston. In 1790, in the first census conducted in America, 4,000,000 people were counted. The largest city was Philadelphia, with a population of 42,000; the second was New York, with a population of 33,000. Only six cities had populations of over 8,000. The most interesting fact, however, is that those six cities constituted only three percent of the total population. America was clearly a country with isolation problems that would plague the rapid spread of theatre and, consequently, opportunities for the dramatist. If theatre companies undertook to travel between cities as little as possible and visited small towns not at all, it was because most roads were little more than tracks through the forests, and seasons for travel had to be carefully followed. Thus while the geography of America dictated its growth, the means for connecting the distant areas as well as the individualized rural and urban societies became a necessity for both the unification of the country and the development of theatre and drama.

During this period literature, which did not demand an immediate audience, remained as mainly an artistic outlet for instruction, either in politics or in morals. Fiction, poetry, and the essay did not flourish. Timothy Dwight stayed with tradition in *The Triumph of Infidelity* (1788), a satiric attack on the Roman Catholic church and on modern philosophy, and *Greenfield Hill* (1794), a defense of Calvinism. Neither attracted many readers. Joel Barlow, another of the Connecticut Wits, wrote *The Hasty Pudding* (1796), one of the most humorous and enjoyable poems of the period. Philip Freneau's postrevolutionary poems have a beauty and power which give him a much greater reputation as a poet of nature and humanity than as a poet of the revolutionary war. So much for poetry. As the last decade closed the eighteenth century, the writing of fiction in America was just beginning. William H. Brown's *The Power of Sympathy* (1789), an extravagant and carelessly written story which is extremely didactic and sensational, was typical of novels that would entertain America through much of the nineteenth century. Susanna Rowson's sentimental romances, particularly *Charlotte Temple* (1791), which lasted through 161 editions, also suggest the temper of the time. The same could be said of Hannah Foster's *The Coquette* (1797). Only Charles Brockden Brown broke the mold. Credited with being America's first major novelist, Brown wrote two novels, *Wieland* (1798) and *Armond* (1799), before the turn of the century.

With very few exceptions literature from genres other than drama was no more distinguished than were the plays written at the close of the eighteenth century, and some of the same reasons apply. Fiction writers at the time endured many of the same prejudices that harassed the dramatists. Poetry of a moral nature was acceptable; essays, tracts, and sermons were also approved reading. Fiction, on the other hand, suffered from religious prejudice in the North and a certain indifference in the South, where politics seemed to be taken more seriously. The novelist's response to such prejudices and indifference was to write domestic, sentimental, and morally instructive tales. Ever ready to copy a successful act, dramatists and theatre managers tried the same techniques. In Philadelphia, before the ban on theatre was lifted, the Old American Company disguised its productions as concerts or instructive lectures. Theatre managers reacted to prejudices by renaming their theatres opera houses or museums. Dramatists not only imitated themes used by novelists but adapted their stories for the theatre.

For the theatre of the period, however, it was necessary that the drama not only please and instruct in classical fashion but also somehow reflect American society and dramatize American ideals and American characters. In his farewell address on September 17, 1796, George Washington emphasized the new unity which the term *American* should symbolize. "The name of American," he said, "which belongs to you in your national capacity, must always exalt the just pride of patriotism more than any appellation derived from local discriminations." But what was an American? Those living in the new nation hardly knew, perhaps scarcely thought about it. Many simply rejected Washington's pleas and stuck to their "local discriminations." De Crèvecoeur, however, tried to provide an answer in the third of his letters from an American farmer, "What is an American?"

> *He* is an American who leaving behind him all his ancient prejudices and manners, receives new ones from the new mode of life he has embraced, the new government he obeys, and the new rank he holds. He becomes an American by being received in the broad lap of our great *Alma Mater*. Here individuals of all nations are melted into a new race of men, whose labors and posterity will one day cause great changes in the world. Americans are the western pilgrims, who are carrying along with them that great mass of arts, sciences, vigor, and industry which began long since in the east; they will finish the great circle.[2]

But de Crèvecoeur proved to be an idealist; people in America did not abandon their prejudices, manners, and customs. More important, however, they also remembered to carry along their arts. If they had not, the history of American drama and theatre might now be limited to the minstrel skit, the Wild West spectacle, and the Toby show.

In helping the American people identify with the new nation and understand their place in it, American drama and American theatre accepted important roles. More than other literary genres (and indeed with considerable strength throughout its history), the drama sought to foster that "just pride of patriotism" of which Washington spoke. Through ridicule and satire it encouraged people in the words of de Crèvecoeur to leave behind the manners and fashions of their former countries, particularly England and France. Taking obvious advantage of the immediate audience response which is peculiar to performed art, American dramatists chose material and themes to emphasize America. In this endeavor no playwright was more important than Royall Tyler, who explained "the contrast" as he saw it and created a typical Yankee character. Though not the first to be seen in American drama, Tyler's Yankee was the most fully developed to this point and one which despite personality refinements and changes in the future years, would be closely identified with the American character throughout history.

Royall Tyler (1757–1826) was that inspired person who could combine the joys of literary creation with a professional career. It must be noted, however, that he could not support himself with his writing, which included ten plays, at least fifty poems, a novel, and innumerable essays. As a lawyer, particularly as State's Attorney for Windham County, Vermont, he had some success, but his more lasting fame came with his twelve years' tenure as a justice of Vermont's Supreme Court, during which he presided over several celebrated cases. Even with this meritorious career, however, he had periods of serious poverty toward the end of his life.

The son of a staunch Boston Patriot, Royall was named William Clark until his father's death, when his mother legally gave him his father's name. Financially secure for a time and socially acceptable, he studied at Harvard, where he was considered an amusing conversationalist with a brilliant wit. After a brief stint in the Continental Army, in the Independent Company commanded by John Hancock, he studied law and wooed John Adams' daughter for more than two years before losing his romantic suit. Then, as his young and somewhat frivolous nature dictated, he went on to other ventures, which were described to Nabby Adams as disgraceful behavior. When Daniel Shay, who led the disenchanted and impoverished revolutionary war veterans in what came to be known as Shay's Rebellion, escaped into Vermont, Tyler was given the task of pursuing him. Although unsuccessful in his mission, he worked well with the governing authorities and was allotted another assignment, which took him to New York. There he also amused himself, as his previous activities in society suggested he might, and, five weeks after arriving in New York, he had written *The Contrast* and had seen it performed on April 16, 1787.

Tyler was remembered as a handsome man, his appearance no doubt providing him an advantage in his legal practice as well as in society. He was also fond of oratory and was a man of human compassion and understanding, qualities serving the dramatist and the lawyer equally well. In 1794 he married Mary Palmer, eighteen years his junior, under circumstances that still remain mysterious. Tyler then settled in Vermont, where he met Joseph Dennie, who became his collaborator in a large number of amusing and satiric essays, sketches, and verses which they signed as "Colon & Spondee." Light and topical commentary on society, literature, and politics, the joint creations continued until 1811.

During these years, despite a busy social life and active legal career, Tyler found opportunity to do considerable writing. Poetry interested him, and his best work was in the light, satiric vein that distinguished his plays and essays. From his first long poem, *The Origin of Evil*, published in 1793, until his last, *The Chestnut Tree*, written in 1824, he enjoyed the challenge of poetry but was never a poet of stature—and he knew it. His episodic novel, *The Algerine Captive*, which appeared in 1797, was occasioned by the Barbary Coast pirate activities. A brief work published in two thin volumes, it attempts to answer the demand expressed in the preface for realism, patriotism, and moral purpose. These qualities were conveyed through the experiences of a Dr. Updike

Underhill as he appears, first in America and then in Algeria, in some sixty oddly structured chapters of narrative. Tyler was clearly at his best, however, in short sketches and essays, which came easily from his pen. He seems to have been a person who had a natural talent for writing, one who took no interest in revision and had no pretense about his value as a writer. Yet he was a thoughtful man. He had something to say about fashion, literature, and politics and was seriously concerned with a native American literature and American ideas. Perhaps his essays collected in *The Yankey in London*, published anonymously in 1809 "by an American youth," best illustrate his work as a writer: a sprightly style, a reverence for America, and a varied subject matter. During his final years the cancer which took his life in 1826 prevented him from writing much for publication.

Tyler's reputation as a young man had been marked by a self-confessed "dissipation." That was one reason why John Adams was, at first, singularly unenthusiastic about Tyler as a possible son-in-law. Theatre in Boston, certainly considered a form of "dissipation," at this time was subject to particularly strong prejudices, and it is reasonably certain that Tyler had never seen a professionally produced play before going to New York in 1787. He had experienced amateur theatre, however, and his unfinished autobiographical work, "The Bay Boy," contains a section entitled "First Theatrical Presentation in Boston," which describes some difficulties in producing plays. Concerning his experiences with the drama and with the composition of his play *The Contrast*, however, it can be stated with certainty only that Tyler arrived in New York on March 12, 1787, that *The School for Scandal* was performed on March 21, and that the character Jonathan in *The Contrast* may have described that production in his commentary on "The School for Scandalization" in Act III.

Although *The Contrast* first appeared anonymously, reviews indicate that Tyler was recognized as the author. It is presumed that it was because he had written the part of Jonathan for Thomas Wignell that Tyler gave the copyright of the play to Wignell, who eventually arranged the first printing of the play in 1790. From that point on *The Contrast* became a part of American dramatic literature. In the theatre, however, it was successful only by the standards of the day. From 1787 through 1804 there is evidence of thirty-eight performances in New York, Baltimore, and Philadelphia by the Old American Company. Other companies produced the play in Alexandria, Georgetown, Fredericksburg, Norfolk, Boston, and Charleston, where songs were added, changes made, and the title revised to *The Contrast; or, the American Son of Liberty*. Between 1804 and a production in 1894 by the American Academy of Dramatic Art, changing tastes seem to have ruled out production. In 1912 and 1917 the play was again produced and by World War II occasionally appeared during college and university theatre seasons. In the fall of 1972, it opened in New York as a musical adapted by Anthony Stimac, with music by Don Pippin and lyrics by Steve Brown.

The Contrast lacks much of a plot and tends to be a talky play with little action, but it has many compensating strengths. Though imitative of the eighteenth-century British sentimental comedy, it is relieved by an originality in thought and in character presentation which distinguishes this play above all other comedies in eighteenth-century America. Structurally, it follows the traditional five-act pattern, while, in keeping with its thesis of "contrast," each act divides into two scenes which provide contrast in form as well as in content. Tyler was both well read and talented, and the play shows his familiarity with traditional dramatic techniques, idiosyncratic language, and literature of the period.

Basically, the play satisfied all the demands of the theatre audience of 1787. The prologue—"Exult each patriot heart!"—characterizations of Jonathan and Colonel Manly, the dialect, the issues, and the final line of the play—all emphasize the new nationalism. Although they may be caricatures, the characters' distinctive qualities delight the reader and viewer. Charlotte, for example, is a charming flirt, witty and full of life: "scandal," she notes, "is but amusing ourselves with the faults, foibles, follies, and reputations of our friends" (II, i). Colonel Manly, her brother, is a stiff and sentimental bore but a patriotic bore. Jonathan, in the tradition of the Yankee character begun almost a generation before *The Contrast*, provides good farcical humor which, with his rural eccentricities and "down east" dialect, makes him theatrically attractive, "a true blue son of Liberty," as he describes himself. Dimple is the typical fop, affecting the manners of the English and offending the American sense of manhood by not minding the main chance and by being careless with money and deceptive with women. As a strong moral was another *sine qua non* for American drama of the period, Tyler provided it generously in the actions of Manly, in the filial duty of Maria, and in the final scene of the play as Charlotte repents and Manly explains what probity, virtue, and honor can accomplish. Complementing the light wit of Charlotte is the farcical humor between Jonathan and Jessamy, Dimple's steward. Finally, there is the satire which American audiences had always enjoyed: satire on fashion, theatre, the English, and gossip. Additionally, to enliven the play there were songs, while superimposed on all elements was contrast—contrast between the people of England and those of

America, between affectation and straightforwardness, between city and country, between hypocrisy and sincerity, and between foreign fraud and native worth.

With all those characteristics assembled with a certain natural talent and an abundance of wit, it would have been surprising had *The Contrast* not appealed to Americans. Tyler in his youthful exuberance must have enjoyed ridiculing the stuffy romancing of Manly and Maria and the girlish gossip of Charlotte as well as the backcountry innocence of Jonathan contrasted with the hypocrisy of those tainted with English manners. Yet, with all the fun, a strain of honesty runs through the American characters. Tyler surely believed in them as he contrasted them with the affectations he despised. Although as a dramatist he was interested in provoking laughter, Tyler included nationalistic sentiments which he expected his audience to take seriously. One presumes that they did.

The play opens with Charlotte and Latitia gossiping wittily about men while showing compassion for Maria, who must give her hand to Dimple but without her heart. Poor Maria Van Rough, "her heart militating with her filial duty," is being forced by her father to "mind the main chance" and marry the man of *his* choice. Having thus presented two contrasting views of men and marriage, Tyler allows ever-chatty Charlotte and Latitia to open Act II with the topic of fashion while the staid opinions of Charlotte's brother, Colonel Manly, act as a foil to their light comments. When Jonathan and Jessamy, servants of Manly and Dimple, respectively, meet and the rural honesty of the one is contrasted with the sophisticated duplicity of the other, Tyler prepares for the contrasting views of love dramatized in the next act. First, Dimple, influenced by Chesterfield's comments on women and by his own increased debts, declares that he must break with Maria, marry Latitia because she has wealth, and have Charlotte as "a companion to my wife." Then Jonathan visits Jessamy and Jenny, tells of his experience in attending "the devil's drawing-room" (the theatre) unknowingly, and, with the hope of "Cherubim consequences," woos Jenny according to Jessamy's instructions. As a contrast to their hilarious scene, Dimple offers his views on courtship to Manly, who once explained to his sister that "the best evidence a gentleman could give a young lady of his respect and affection, was, to endeavor in a friendly manner to rectify her foibles" (II, i).

To this point in the play there have been delightful conversation and amusingly expressed contrasts with some farcical intrigue on the part of Jessamy. In Act IV Tyler provides a little more plot: Maria confesses to Charlotte that she has just seen the man whom she could love, and when Manly arrives it becomes clear that he is the man. But, above all, Manly is honorable, and, when Maria reveals her filial obligations, he unhesitatingly accepts the unhappiness which must be theirs: "it is your duty to obey your parent,—mine to obey my honor." Act V is introduced by a good satire on society as Jessamy teaches Jonathan to laugh in the proper manner and at the proper time. Scene ii provides a variation on the conventional eighteenth-century comic "screen" scene as people hide and listen in various attitudes. Finally, Manly unmasks Dimple as a conniving and unprincipled scoundrel; Latitia learns of his duplicity in love; and Van Rough discovers that he has not minded the main chance. Ruffled but untouched, Dimple takes his leave, dramatizing an ironic "contrast between a gentleman who has read Chesterfield and received the polish of Europe and an unpolished, untravelled American." It remains only that Charlotte admit the "littleness" of her tactics in attracting a man and that Maria and Manly receive the blessing of Van Rough and the "applause of the public."

Tyler went on to write other plays but never with the skill or appeal which *The Contrast* showed in sufficient quantity to give him an immediate reputation. A month after *The Contrast* appeared in New York, a comic opera in two acts by "the author of *The Contrast*" was announced at the John Street Theatre. *May Day in Town; or, New York in an Uproar* was performed on May 19, 1787, and not repeated. Neither play nor music is extant although it seems to have satirized New York society, with the principal character a "scold." The years passed. In 1795 Tyler's brother, Colonel John Steele Tyler, became stage manager of the Federal Street Theatre in Boston and asked Royall for plays. Presumably, *The Mock Doctor,* produced in Boston in February, 1796, was Tyler's adaptation of Molière's work. On May 6, 1796, *The Farm House; or, The Female Duellists* appeared on the Boston stage; no copy exists, but evidence suggests that it was another Tyler adaptation, this one of Kemble's *Farm House.* On October 30, 1797, *The Georgia Spec; or, Land on the Moon,* another afterpiece identified as Tyler's, appeared in Boston and then moved on to New York, where it was given at least three performances. Here Tyler was fairly successful in using satiric characters and language to ridicule the excesses of his day, in this instance, the Yazoo Purchase land speculation. Another play by Tyler that has been passed down only by title is the children's play, *Five Pumpkins.*

The only extant plays by Tyler, other than *The Contrast,* have been published in *America's Lost Plays.* The first of the four plays is *The Island of Barrataria,* a farce in four acts, based on the Barataria episode in *Don Quixote.*[3]

Buried beneath the complicated plotting and farcical techniques, which suggest Tyler's continued practice in writing plays, there is a message for the people of America. Carlos loves Julietta, daughter of the wealthy Alvarez, who has plans to wed her to the new governor, a "boorish" fellow named Sancho Panza. With wit and determination, however, Julietta gains her objective and carries the action of the play. The play's romantic device is Alvarez's ring, which Sancho accepts as a token of his pledge to marry Julietta after he divorces his wife. Then, in a long court scene in which Sancho administers justice to his people, Julietta, disguised as an old woman being abandoned by her husband, coaxes a proper judgment from Sancho, begs the ring as a token, and gives it to Carlos because Alvarez has sworn to give his daughter to the man who possesses the ring. All ends happily in the love plot, whereas Sancho, attempting to stop an invading army, is bound and trampled on only to be given credit for a victory. In his final speech he tells the audience that he knows he is unfit for office "but are there not some who govern it for years—bear abuse on abuse and have not wit enough to see that they are the Sanchos of the political play?" (III, ii). Like other Tyler works, the play is a satire, this time on the system of government, its concepts of justice, and its officials.

The other three Tyler plays are sacred dramas in blank verse. As his past habit had been to develop satire with carefully drawn morals, here he used his familiarity with the Bible to present similar moral attitudes. The first play of this group is *The Origin of the Feast of Purim; or, The Destinies of Haman & Mordecai*, a drama in three acts taken largely from the Book of Esther, dramatizing the conflict between Haman and Mordecai and the defeat of pride by righteousness. Although the final act builds upon the ironic change of fortune by which Haman is condemned, it ends on the positive note of the Purim celebration. In the next play, *Joseph and His Brethren*, in three acts, Tyler was able to accomplish the more difficult dramatization of Joseph's life with some success by building his climax around Joseph's revelation of his identity to his brothers. The play ends on a high note, dramatically and in terms of religious faith, as Jacob declares that his son is alive and that he will see him.

The last of the sacred plays, *The Judgement of Solomon*, dramatizes the well-known incident of two women claiming the same child. After introducing several people who question Solomon's wisdom, Tyler astutely shows the two women quarreling. It is, after all, a conflict for which a decision must be reached, and, as the women continue their arguments in court, Tyler underlines the basic confrontation with a background commentary between one who doubts and one who defends Solomon's wisdom. The play ends in the remembered fashion of glowing praise of Solomon's wisdom, largely in the phrasing of the King James Bible.

A lawyer would be interested in the question of justice, and Tyler's sacred dramas treat concepts of law, government, and justice as did *The Island of Barrataria*. With the exception of *The Island of Barrataria*, however, which deserves more critical attention than it has received, these late plays do not add much to Tyler's stature as a dramatist. They simply show his continuing interest in the drama and a consistent approach to ideas which were expressed in his literary and legal careers throughout his mature life. Playwriting was his avocation and a pleasant one; he earned his living as a lawyer and a justice.

As actors and actresses began to return to America after the Revolution and, joined by new recruits from England, began to play in the various theatres built by David Douglass, it became clear that theatre was to be a part of the new nation and that a playwright might even gain some slight fame and fortune. In truth it would be almost another hundred years before an American could sustain himself as an original playwright, but William Dunlap (1766–1839) is frequently called the first professional dramatist in America. Of course, he had to supplement that career with other jobs, some of which were related to the theatre. He managed the Park Theatre in New York, either alone or in collaboration with others, from 1798 until he went bankrupt in 1805, and he wrote biography and history, most notably his *History of the American Theatre*. Dunlap also brought a certain respectability to the American theatre. Considering its condition at the time, he deserves credit for a pioneering effort in an unproven field to which he brought a remarkable industry supported by talent and devotion. But it is his writing of at least sixty plays (twenty-nine of them either wholly or partly original with him) that makes him a significant figure in the history of the American drama. He made people aware of the American dramatist. It was his *Tell Truth and Shame the Devil* (translated from *Jérôme Pointu* by A. L. B. Robineau and performed at the John Street Theatre in New York on January 9, 1797), for example, which, as the first American play given an English production, was performed at Covent Garden, London, on May 18, 1799. At a time when little was being accomplished in American drama, Dunlap's work was a torrent of light. John Eliot, the so-called apostle to the American Indian in the seventeenth century, entitled one of his long essays "The Day Breaking if not the Sun Rising of the Gospel with the Indians of New England." Perhaps the attitude expressed in that title best describes Dunlap's work in early American drama. He appeared during a period when such a playwright as he was needed. Yet, in the larger view that time provides, his life appears as a succession of failures while his quantitative contribution to American drama is only occasionally distinguished by outstanding work.

The son of a prosperous storekeeper in New Jersey who had come to America as a British officer under General Wolfe and who remained a staunch Loyalist throughout the Revolution, William Dunlap would have seemed an unlikely person to become a patriotic American dramatist. Because he was an only child and because he was blinded in one eye in a childhood accident, Dunlap enjoyed a favored childhood. At his Perth Amboy home he had a friend in old Thomas Barlow, a man who passed his love for the classics on to the young boy. Later, in 1777, when the Dunlap family moved to New York, the youthful Dunlap was able to see the military plays produced by the British at the John Street Theatre. It is presumed that he started writing dramatic sketches about this time and was converted to the Patriot cause. Art also became something of a passion with him, and he combined it with patriotism by painting a portrait of Washington. After the war, thanks to an indulgent father, he went to London, where he studied painting under the guidance of Benjamin West. Contrary to his father's expectations, however, he did not spend enough hours at his easel. Instead, he idled his time away by attending the theatre and was called home in 1787. Back in New York he tried to make a career in art, but commissions were few. More to the point, the theatre still fascinated him, and, perhaps stimulated by Tyler's success with *The Contrast* (although he later condemned it in his *History* as "extremely deficient in plot, dialogue, or incident"), he wrote a play.

Dunlap took his first play, *The Modest Soldier; or, Love in New York* (1787), to the manager of the American Company, who praised it but kept postponing production. It was not long, however, before Dunlap learned an important fact: one must write a play with parts suitable for the important members of the company. In his next play, *The Father; or, American Shandyism* (1789), he provided a good part for the company manager, John Henry, and his work was soon "received with great applause" at the John Street Theatre. Years later a critic writing for the *American Quarterly Review* (June 1827) described *The Father of an Only Child*, the title Dunlap used for reprinting the play in 1806, as "one of the best plays we possess" for its "colloquial ease and sprightliness" and its "natural and interesting" incident. Critics since have not fully agreed, but, by following the sentiment of Laurence Sterne and by providing a complicated comic plot with disguises, devices, a good moral, an American soldier-hero, opportunity for much laughter, and a happy ending,

Dunlap wrote a play that acted well and appealed to audiences. He also showed the necessary theatrical *savoir-faire* by providing a prologue which praised the moral tendency of the stage.

The action of the play begins with the problems of Mrs. Racket, a ward of Colonel Duncan. Tired of an indifferent and dissolute husband, she tries to excite his jealousy by pretending an affection for Captain Ranter, a man with all the marks of a scoundrel. Meanwhile, her sister, Caroline, grieving for her fiance, Haller, whom she thinks is dead, is befriended by the Colonel. The device to connect the hero, the heroine, and the villain is a ring, given by the Colonel to his son, described by Caroline as belonging to Haller, and worn by Ranter. The action is stopped for comic scenes with Doctor Quiescent and various servants, and the necessary sentiment is provided by such scenes as that in which Haller, disguised as a blind soldier, talks with his father, who thinks his son is dead. The climax occurs when Haller reveals himself and identifies Ranter as his rascally servant who has stolen his ring. This revelation brings indescribable joy to his sweetheart and his father as Dunlap ties up his plot by reconciling the Rackets. In a revised version Dunlap made minor changes in this conventional play which are important in his developing career as they reveal his ability to adapt to the demands of both theatre management and audiences.[4]

That same year Dunlap wrote another play, *Darby's Return* (1789), a brief comic sketch for Thomas Wignell, who had acted the part of Jonathan in *The Contrast* and had asked Dunlap to write a play using the character of Darby from John O'Keeffe's *The Poor Soldier*. The result, as Dunlap explained in his *History*, was "an interlude, in which Darby, after various adventures in Europe and in the United States, returns to Ireland and recounts the sights he had seen" (vol. 2, pp. 160–61). Following an established pattern in American drama, *Darby's Return* was a satire but, different from other plays, a very gentle satire of the "gallant" soldier who returns to his village after the war. As Darby tells of his experiences, it is clear that the romantic concept of the soldier has no basis in actual military experience. Unfortunately, Dunlap's technique is narrative rather than dramatic and shows little of his later craftsmanship. In every sense the play is a trifle, but a delightful one with song and dance. One occasion which distinguished the sketch occurred when Washington was a member of the audience. When Darby was asked to describe the American president, Washington looked a little serious (according to Dunlap) and braced himself for the usual eulogy. After supplying numerous details concerning the president he thought he saw, however, Darby must finally admit that this person "was not the one." In this anticlimax Washington enjoyed a laugh with the audience.

During the next several years, Dunlap continued to write while adapting himself to New York society. He married in 1789, even worked in his father's business for a while, and hobnobbed with people of similar literary and artistic interests. The Friendly Club was one such group where he could exchange views although his adaptability within the theatre—his concern for giving people what they wanted in terms of melodrama, for example—suggests that he was a man who seldom expressed strong convictions. Instead, he was an accommodating man who could tolerate the activities of Lewis Hallam and John Hodgkinson. He could even put up with the extremely intolerant views of Timothy Dwight concerning the stage. A man of compromise and good sense, many would say; and a man who lacked these qualities could never have made Dunlap's contribution to American drama and theatre. It cannot be doubted that Dunlap believed that much drama and theatre was immoral; he particularly disliked the practice of setting aside a special section of the gallery for prostitutes. But he also believed that the drama could work "in Virtue's ways to fix the mind," as he stated in the prologue to *Leicester* (1794). As in all people his personal strengths could also be weaknesses, while his acceptable position in society and in the artistic and literary community enhanced his work in the drama.

The plays which he wrote during these early years indicate that Dunlap was exploring his own potential while trying to write something that would please audiences; his period of apprenticeship with actors and the theatre was not yet complete. Although he wrote *The Miser's Wedding* (1793) for Henry and Hodgkinson, the comedy somehow caused friction between the two actors and failed. *Shelty's Travels* (1794), written for Hodgkinson's benefit, was a brief sketch in which Dunlap tried to equal the popularity of *Darby's Return*. Shelty comes to New York, visits a theatre, comments on local sights, and makes one of the first references in American drama to American difficulties with the Algerian pirates.

On the same bill with *Shelty's Travels*, Dunlap offered *The Fatal Deception; or, the Progress of Guilt*, which was published in 1806 as *Leicester*. With unrelenting intensity, the major character of this play, Matilda, admittedly modeled on Clytemnestra, pursues a tragic climax in the manner of English heroic tragedy. A strong and sympathetic figure, Matilda had first been rejected by Leicester, whom she later indifferently married after being widowed by her first husband. Now in love with Henry Cecil, a weak man who poses as her brother, she sees the possibility of happiness until Leicester returns from wartime absence. From the crisis of his appearance, the action leads inevitably to tragedy as Matilda's determined plans for murder that will bring her freedom are frustrated by the ineffectual Henry and by Leicester's loyal followers. Written in average verse and boasting an exciting plot, this romantic tragedy suggests the type of heroic tragedy and melodrama toward which Dunlap would direct his talents either as playwright or as adaptor-translator.

Dunlap's next work for the stage was an opera, *The Archers; or, Mountaineers of Switzerland* (1796), which might better be called musical comedy. The setting is Altdorf, Switzerland where war with Austria is imminent. Dunlap creates a light tone with Conrad, who declares that he will enlist with the bowmen only if Cecily will marry him. After a duet with Conrad on the advantages of marriage, Cecily agrees, and the men converge to defend their native land. Among the governing officers, however, there is a concern for conciliation with the enemy, which William Tell opposes. Angered, the officials order Tell's execution, with the opportunity for freedom if he shoots the apple from his son's head. This he does, to the joy of his friends, but the Austrians are still approaching. There is a storm scene, a boat scene, and Tell's escape from the authorities before he leads his people into a successful battle. Conrad and Cecily provide comedy throughout, and the opera ends with their marriage. History is not important, but a strong hero is, and the songs must have helped make this good entertainment.

Dunlap then tried to capitalize on the popularity of Gothic melodramas with *Fontainville Abbey* (1795) and *The Mysterious Monk* (1796; published in 1803 as *Ribbemont; or, The Feudal Baron*). The first was based on Mrs. Ann Radcliffe's *Romance of the Forest*. In this play of storms and screams, sleepless hours, and supernatural activities, the heroine finally produces a scroll which proves that the marquis who owns the Abbey is really a murderer and that she is the daughter of his older brother and heir to the entire estate. Contrived but well received, the play was announced without Dunlap's name and became an early illustration of the automatic adverse criticism expected for plays with American authorship. In *The Mysterious Monk*, also in verse, Count Ribbemont, suspecting his wife's adultery with Narbonne, apparently murders them in a fit of revenge. The plot then unfolds a story in which the count learns that he was wrong to accuse his wife, contemplates taking his own life, and eventually experiences the proper remorse in a happy ending. The moral, false honor, became a subject of some controversy, while the play, even with the trappings of Gothic horror, was not very promising as an example of Dunlap's original work.

In June, 1796, Dunlap took a step which was a tribute more to his adventuresome spirit and innocent idealism than to his good sense as a businessman or a man of the theatre. He bought into the American Company by purchasing one-half of Hodgkinson's share. This meant that Hallam still retained his half-interest in the company while Dunlap and Hodgkinson owned a quarter each. According to the agreement Dunlap would act as manager, have authority over casting plays, and be able to produce plays that he wrote. These were distinct advantages for a dramatist, particularly so since some of the past prejudices against the theatre were beginning to be softened. (Two years earlier even puritan Boston had opened a theatre.) The immediate disadvantages lay primarily with the personnel with whom Dunlap had to work, and he was unequal to the task. It is doubtful, however, that anyone could have stepped into a situation embracing such jealousies as existed between Hallam and Hodgkinson and survived.

By the spring of 1797, Hallam had left the management; a year later Hodgkinson withdrew, and Dunlap took over the company in the new Park Theatre, which had opened in January, 1798. In his *History* Dunlap declared his inability to cope with the financial hazards of American theatre; he would rather have enjoyed, he wrote, "a theatre patronized by an enlightened government" (vol. 2, p. 38). Yet in December, 1798, Dunlap was able to rescue his theatre from financial chaos with an adaptation of Kotzebue's *The Stranger*, and as time passed his translations and adaptations of foreign plays kept him momentarily from bankruptcy. The seasons of 1800 and 1801 were his most successful. Then a number of things happened to cause his ruin: as Washington Irving started to review theatrical performances, his comments on the Park called attention to its inadequacies; Dunlap also lost some of his favored actors and actresses; and by February, 1804, the theatre was put up for auction. A year later, on February 22, 1805, as he recorded it in his *History*, "the theatre was finally closed, and the management of the man [Dunlap] who had sacrificed his health and property in the pursuit of that which eluded his grasp ceased" (vol. 2, p. 214). He did, however, leave the theatre well furnished materially and supplied with play manuscripts.

The Mysterious Monk had been Dunlap's first play as a theatre manager. His first play written for the new Park Theatre was *André*, which opened on March 30, 1798, and continued for three performances, a slight relief for the already financially troubled theatre. More than any other play by Dunlap, *André* has interested critics and historians, who frequently find it his best drama. Perhaps for the original performance, however, the theme was too subtle, and the dramatization, too close to the event portrayed. Major John André, the British messenger who conspired with Benedict Arnold, was captured by the Americans and hanged in 1780. Although André might be considered a major focus of the play, he has little overt action, and his conflict is concerned mainly with the manner in which he must die. The play revolves around the actions of those who would save him, each person applying pressure on the country as represented by Washington. André, who does not appear in the first act, is used almost as a device to help define a nationalistic thesis. The major conflict lies within a country which, as a newly established nation, feels that it must assert its rights yet at the same time nourish a fine sense of humanity toward André:

> One hapless hour [André confesses], thy feet are led astray;
> Thy happy deeds all blotted from remembrance;
> Cancel'd the record of thy former good.
> Is it not hard, my friend? Is't not unjust?
>
> [II, i.]

For man and country it becomes a matter of justice and mercy, a reconciliation of heavenly virtues which at that time in America's history could not be realized. André had been hanged, and Dunlap had to dramatize both sympathy for a young man who learns to "rise superior" and the sense of honor and justice which a new country must establish. At the final curtain Dunlap's reputation as a diplomatic moralist did not fail him. Through a spokesman he warns foreign countries of Columbia's determination yet declares that the past offenses must not undermine future relations.

Dunlap called his play "a tragedy, in five acts." Although it may be interpreted that André, an honorable man who took one false step, is the victim of a country's need to demand its rights, the play states clearly that it was not "fortune" but "misdeed" which got him into trouble. As the plot develops, André has very little struggle. Instead, Bland, a young American officer, dramatizes his own and his country's problem. Persuaded in the early scenes, before realizing that André is involved, that "all those who . . . seek to shake the Tree of Liberty" must fall, Bland is again persuaded by this argument at the final curtain. This is the positive, almost propagandistic view which *André* presents, but with a dignity absent in contemporary plays. Throughout, the speeches of M'Donald, an American general, reflect national and international views in contrast to the short-sighted isolationism of another character, and it is he who praises Washington and gives the final speech of the play.

The time of the action in *André* is 1780; the scene is an encampment where Bland discusses the war with his superior before learning that his friend, André, has been captured and sentenced to execution. Visiting André, Bland is incensed at the decision to hang him although André admits that he did doff his "martial garb, and put on curs'd disguise," an act which made him a spy. The scene changes to show his mother, Mrs. Bland, receiving a message which states that her husband, Colonel Bland, captured by the British, will die if André is hanged. Refused by Washington when he pleads for André's life, Bland "tears the cockage from his helmet," a gesture which Dunlap altered after it was hissed by the first night's audience. Mrs. Bland's pleading is also refused, and Colonel Bland writes a note to Washington to do "your duty." Bland is again frustrated and furious. Finally, Honora, André's fiancee, arrives from England. Denied a lover's petition, she goes insane. As the execution takes place, Bland apologizes for his insubordination and tries to understand.

In spite of the excessive romanticism, the sentiment, the obvious debts to English heroic tragedy and to Shakespeare, and the artificialities of the verse and the action, the play manifests a certain provocative power in the sensitivity of its argument. The characters are secondary; particularly weak are the women, who are simply pawns of the dramatist. As a rash youth in the early acts, Bland matures in the play as the country itself must mature. With a strong and unified approach, Dunlap provided fair exposition and a good change of pace from the frantic actions of Bland to the more philosophic atmosphere surrounding M'Donald and Washington. Of the serious plays written in America before James Nelson Barker's *Superstition* (1824), *André* must be considered the best.

It is a comment on the times and on Dunlap that he felt obliged to rewrite *André* as a patriotic spectacle entitled *The Glory of Columbia—Her Yeomanry*, which opened at the Park, appropriately, on July 4, 1803. The serious thesis of the original play was now replaced with scenic spectacle, song, and comic relief provided by America's soldiers and a spirited country girl as well as by a captured Irishman. The attempt to combine the story of André with the story of American soldiers fighting the British must seem a failure to all who read *André*, but it was a success on the stage for many years.[5] Patriotic plays, generally, were extremely popular about this time, and Dunlap contributed his share. *The Temple of Independence* (1799), was written for Washington's birthday. Odell quotes from the program to suggest the character of this spectacle: "At the sound of approaching War, the Scene draws and discovers through the Pillars of the Temple an American Encampment"; "at the call of the Genius of America, a Statue of Washington rises, which is afterwards crowned by a descending Aerial Figure, holding a Laurel Wreath."[6] *The Soldier of '76* (1801) and *The Retrospect; or, the American Revolution* (1802) were also patriotic pieces. Perhaps Dunlap's best-known effort in spectacle patriotism is *Yankee Chronology* (1812), which has been variously described as an anecdote, a sketch, and a monologue on stage. But mainly it is a song, "Yankee Chronology," in which Ben Bundle traces the Revolution from Lexington to Yorktown. Washington is praised in extravagant terms, and the battle between the *Constitution* and the *Guerrière* is described in a patriotic vision of victory in the War of 1812.

In 1798, less than a month after *André* was performed, Dunlap become sole manager of the Park Theatre. The fall season, planned for an opening in September or October, however, was delayed by an epidemic of yellow fever until December 3. Immediately, Dunlap began to lose money. Then on December 10 he produced *The Stranger*, his first adaptation of a play by August von Kotzebue, whose plays had been popularly received in England during the previous two years. *The Stranger* saved his season and inspired him to translate and adapt some thirty plays during the remainder of his writing career. Perhaps as many as sixteen of these came from the pen of Kotzebue; the exact number is difficult to ascertain because Dunlap was not careful in claiming or publishing all that he wrote. Although his version of *The Stranger* was never published, the play became well known as it was produced throughout most of the nineteenth century in America. On a count's estate, looked after by a young housekeeper who avoids society, there is a stranger, generous and honorable but sensitive and secretive. Then it is revealed that the housekeeper has left a good husband for a scoundrel and that the stranger hides from life to ease the pain of an unfaithful wife and to protect his children. When the two meet, it now having become obvious that they are indeed the husband and the wife, her honest repentance (and the timely appearance of their children) overwhelms his injured pride, and the curtain falls on a happy reunion. A heroic rescue, plenty of sentiment, plus the usual melodramatic devices and contrivances provided audiences with the emotional stimulation they wanted. Dunlap had been exceedingly wise in choosing *The Stranger*, and he was quick to exploit his talents as a translator.

Among his subsequent translations of Kotzebue's plays were *Lovers' Vows*

(1799), a story of seduction which eventually ends in marriage; *False Shame; or, The American Orphan in Germany* (1799), a tale of lost daughters and lovers and mistaken identity which includes a moral about the false shame which people hide; *The Virgin in the Sun* (1800), about a Virgin of the Sun in Peru who has married and is therefore condemned to be buried alive; *Pizarro in Peru; or, the Death of Rolla* (1800), a sequel to the previous play but better constructed with action involving Pizarro's attack on Peru and Rolla's sacrifice for love; and *Fraternal Discord* (1800), concerned with the manipulated separation of two feuding brothers and their final reconciliation. Kotzebue's plays saved Dunlap's financial life at various times but none as much as *Pizarro in Peru*, in which the romance of South America caught the imagination of American audiences.

Other German plays translated by Dunlap include Schiller's *Don Carlos* (1799) and J. H. D. Zschokke's *Abaellino, the Great Bandit* (1801). The latter was a romantic, blood-and-thunder melodrama in which a nobleman disguises himself as a bandit in order to overthrow the Republic in Venice. A contemptuous critic for the *Thespian Monitor* (December 9, 1809) faulted the translation as "tame" and "unintelligible" and the scene as too mysterious and lacking "sufficient connection." But it satisfied Dunlap's need at the time, and a reviewer of a later production, writing for the *Dramatic Censor* (January 1810), described the play as "one of those extraordinary productions which distinguish the present dramatic writers of Germany from those of all ages and all countries." Critics such as this one no doubt helped define Kotzebue as "the German Shakespeare." Contemporary audiences must have agreed, for Dunlap's *Abaellino* remained a favorite in America for years.

As a translator Dunlap had his greatest success with the plays of Kotzebue although, always searching for a novelty that would bring people to his theatre, he also looked toward France. There he found L. C. Caigniez's *Le Jugement de Solomon*, which he translated and adapted into a very popular play, *The Voice of Nature* (1803) and thus brought to New York the *mélodrame*, which made particular use of music and pantomime. As Guilbert de Pixérécourt had essentially established this form, Dunlap in 1804 adapted (making use of two earlier English versions) Pixérécourt's play, *The Wife of Two Husbands*, "a play in five acts, with Songs, Duets, and Choruses." As it turned out, this was Dunlap's last important work for the theatre he managed. It was very well received. Many years later he translated *Thirty Years; or, The Gambler's Fate* (1828) from the work by Prosper Goubaux and Victor Ducange. Typical of melodrama and of Dunlap, it provided a strong moral issue as it dramatized the life of a gambler who struggles with his passion. Victimized by a villain who tries to seduce his wife, he wanders for years. In the climax he rescues his son from a burning building, stabs the villain, and, a victim of his unhappy fate, takes his own life. All the trappings of melodrama were in this episodic work. From a distant point in time it seems hardly worthy of the earlier ambition of Dunlap, who was forced by the circumstances of his theatre management into the translations, which took much of his time and energy.

Of the original plays Dunlap wrote during and after his management years, only two deserve much comment. *The Natural Daughter* (1799) was unsuccessful on stage notwithstanding its strong moral sentiments concerning the man who marries a young wife and is reformed. Although *The Italian Father* (1799) owes its main plot device to Thomas Dekker's *The Honest Whore*, Dunlap considered it his best work. For those audiences of his day who enjoyed sentimental moralizing, he did, indeed, improve on his model. One interesting aspect of this production was Dunlap's insinuation, in order to relieve it of the burden of American authorship, that the play was one of Kotzebue's. It thus became yet another illustration of the growing prejudice that would seem anachronistic in a country concerned with its national importance. The bias persisted, however, becoming a very sensitive issue for American dramatists and the subject of numerous literary arguments.

Dunlap was less interested in his last play, *A Trip to Niagara; or, Travellers in America* (1828), which he described in his preface "as a kind of running accompaniment to the more important products of the Scene-painter." In this instance Dunlap was taking advantage of the panorama exhibitions which, having first reached New York in the late eighteenth century, became extremely popular entertainment during the 1830s. In Act II of *A Trip to Niagara*, the "Diorama, or Moving Scenery"—a stationary boat silhouette and a moving panarama—shows a steamboat passing up the Hudson River from the harbor through eighteen scenes to the "Catskill landing" and then on to "the little falls of the Mohawk" and the "Falls of Niagara" as the play action relates to the scenery.[7] Combining sentiment with a strong nationalism, Dunlap takes Mr. Wentworth, a stuffy Englishman who flaunts his arrogance, and his sister Amelia on a trip up the Hudson. Amelia is already persuaded of the quality and beauty of America, while her boy friend, John Bull, masquerades both as a Frenchman and as a Yankee to satirize the biased English traveler and to extol the virtues of America. At a time when stock characters were especially appreciated, Dunlap used the Irish, Negro, Yankee, and French to advantage in this episodic comedy. Earlier in the decade Dunlap had met and become a good friend of James Fenimore Cooper, who found it possible to help him financially during his last years. In this play Leatherstocking makes some of the more nationalistic statements and succeeds in changing Wentworth's ideas about America. There is not a great deal of plot, but sufficiently varied characters, humorous dialogue, and action combine with the spectacle to make entertaining comedy.

Although theatre historians have enjoyed Dunlap's acknowledged experiment with this new form of theatrical panorama, not all contemporary critics found it satisfying. One critic called it "the most satiating *namby pamby* production that ever disgusted our audience; words without ideas, scenes without conexion of probability; low jests; and mawkish sentiment clothed in the poorest language. . . . Such a play as this would stigmatize with contempt the name of any author, who had not given before, unquestionable evidences of dramatic talent and literary capacity."[8] Obviously, Dunlap's explanation in his preface did not deter the reviewer from what he considered his critical obligation.

After leaving his management of the Park Theatre in 1805, Dunlap tried off and on for the rest of his life to gain an income from his painting, but he was forced to rely on his writing and other jobs. In 1806 he returned to the Park as assistant to the management of Thomas A. Cooper, who dominated theatre in America for the next few years. In that position Dunlap's most noteworthy activity was to serve as companion to the great but alcoholic English actor, George Frederick Cooke. Cooke was a violent man, and, as a critic later declared, Dunlap "used every effort to check the intemperate habits of Cooke, but with little success."[9] When Cooke died Dunlap resigned his managing position and prepared the *Memoirs of the Life of George Frederick Cooke* (1813). Lord Byron is reputed to have found the biography almost unbelievable, first, that a man should have lived so long drunk and, second, that he should have found a sober biographer. Dunlap's next literary effort was *Life of Charles Brockden Brown* (1815), which was criticized for its shortcomings but which remained a major source of information on the novelist for more than a hundred years.

In 1832 Dunlap published his *History of the American Theatre*, an indispensable work for students of American drama and theatre once they realize its limitations. Dunlap's lapses of memory and personal biases frequently appear, but, as a dramatist writing about the theatre from his own experiences, he made many astute observations. "When we speak of the theatre in America," Dunlap wrote, "we mean the drama of the country. A theatre is used synonymously with a playhouse. But the theatre of a country may be its loftiest and most efficient literature, when its play-houses may be . . . the open marts of vice and portals of destruction" (vol. 2, p. 360). In an informal and anecdotal style, Dunlap explains his own relationship to the theatre and his contribution, with appropriate modesty, to the drama. Yet his opinions, however valuable, should not be mistaken for factual history. Nor did Dunlap actually claim to be an historian although his work provides a distinctive impression of the period treated. Two years after its publication, Dunlap, concerned with the other passion in his life, published a *History of the Rise and Progress of the Arts of Design in the United States* (1834). During the years following his theatre management and until his death, Dunlap gave more and more of his time to the writing of history—*History of New York, for Schools* (1837) and *History of the New Netherlands* (1836)—but, with the exception of his book on theatre, those works added little to his reputation.

Opinions on Dunlap have varied according to the mission which critics have felt that he was fulfilling. Odell referred to him as the "chief arbiter in the destinies of the New York stage" for a number of years and as manager of the prestigious Park Theatre. He was that. He also failed as a theatre manager while the most important part of his management was the production of his own plays. The observation of Oral Coad, Dunlap's biographer, that he established playwrighting as a respectable profession must be questioned because Dunlap's influence on later playwrights seems negligible if, indeed, it existed at all. Other people writing plays at the turn of the century—Tyler, Humphreys, and Barker—were certainly as socially respectable as Dunlap. Hornblow writes that Dunlap was a playwright of quantity, not quality, and a man of many trades, master of none. While insisting on some exceptions, many critics would agree with that view. And yet Dunlap deserves credit for his quantity and for his exuberance and idealism, which led him into situations where he could not cope although others under similar circumstances would later, and he made progress toward their success. If he was derivative in his playwriting, he at least imitated some of the appreciated dramatists of the time. By translating foreign dramas for American pleasure, he was in the foreground of a vast movement which for good or ill would come to fill a void and then stay to act as a deterrent to American creativity. With *André* he made a distinctive contribution to American drama; in his *History* he gathered his impressions for others to consider. Perhaps it is simply wisest to say that at this early time, as the theatre and drama in America struggled to get started, a person of ideals, one of talent and imagination who could write what an audience could appreciate in a society not yet thoroughly comfortable with the institution of theatre and one of courage and a capacity for hard work, was desperately needed as a substantial if not brilliant basis on which to build. Dunlap was that person.

Another dramatist who helped establish the basis from which American drama would develop was Susanna Haswell Rowson (1762–1824). A woman of considerable energy, she espoused strong moral principles and expressed her opinions on personal freedom and a woman's world with a vigor that seems to mark her determined march through life. Novelist, poet, dramatist, essayist, musician, editor, and teacher, she had the wit and intelligence to match her vigor. Lines from the epilogue which she wrote and spoke for her first play suggest her straightforward approach. In a clever twist the prompter (probably her husband) calls for "Mrs. Rowson," who comes breathlessly upon the stage to ask how people liked her play:

> "The creature has some sense," methinks you say;
> "She says that we should have supreme dominion,
> And in good truth, we're all of her opinion.
> Women were born for universal sway,
> Men to adore, be silent, and obey."

Whatever one's reaction to that particular sentiment, she did have "some sense."

Alert to life around her, Susanna Rowson aired her views on abolition, the Whiskey Rebellion, feminism, and English and American relations. National themes figure prominently in her plays, where women characters dominate or direct the action. She was an imaginative if sometimes too compassionate writer, and the courage and resourcefulness with which she endowed her heroines are representative of her own life. It was undoubtedly no small task for an actress and playwright to persuade the good people of Boston in 1797 that she was the proper person to provide moral and educational instruction for their daughters. But this she did, and she opened one of the best schools for "young ladies" of the time.

She had been concerned with the education of young women for some time and had published an essay on female education with letters of advice and moral tales in a volume entitled *Mentoria; or, The Young Lady's Friend* (1791). During her career as director of a school for young ladies, she published a spelling dictionary and put her drama experiences to work in the collection *Biblical Dialogues: Comprising Sacred History from the Creation to the Death of Our Savior* (1822). Writing in his personal memoirs, Joseph T. Buckingham, a contemporary critic and observer, remarks on her success as a teacher as well as her industry and intelligence: "Such were her accomplishments, her refined and moral principles, and her pious and charitable disposition, that her friends were numerous, and her pupils represented the most respectable families in the community."[10]

Born in England, Susanna Haswell Rowson was brought to America when she was five years old by her father, a British naval officer. The Revolution, however, forced them to leave America, and by 1778 she was back in England. In 1786 she published her first novel, *Victoria*, and that same year married William Rowson, a musician. Between that date and the summer of 1793, when she came to Philadelphia with fifty-five other men, women, and children as a part of Thomas Wignell's acting company, she wrote her most famous novel, *Charlotte Temple: A Tale of Truth* (1791) and gained some experience as an actress and singer in provincial theatre in England. The novel, which went through more than 160 editions in its long-lasting popularity, shows a courageous heroine who seems worthy of one's better sentiments as she is seduced by a British officer who deserts her in New York, where remorse and poverty bring about her death after the birth of her child. In America Rowson continued writing novels of a similar nature, one of which, *Sarah; or, The Exemplary Wife* (1804), revealed her own strengths and experiences in the description of a woman's acceptance into her home of her husband's illegitimate son. *Charlotte's Daughter; or, The Three Orphans* (1828), a final, posthumous sequel to her first success, became too humanitarian and pointed toward the work of E. D. E. N. Southworth and the domestic sentimentalists among Nathaniel Hawthorne's "damn'd mob of scribbling women."

In Wignell's company, which opened at the new Chestnut Theatre in Philadelphia on February 17, 1794, Mrs. Rowson played various secondary parts. Dunlap, who briefly described the company in his *History*, did not find the Rowsons of sufficient importance to mention. She was evidently an actress of only average ability but one who even then overshadowed her husband's activities in the theatre. For that first season William Rowson served as prompter while his wife played in the farces, did some singing, and acted such parts as Mrs. Fulmer in *The West Indian* and Lucy in *The Rivals*. She did not have parts in all the plays, and the Rowsons, staying only two seasons with Wignell, left after July 4, 1795. During the fall of 1795, the Rowsons worked at Rickett's Ampitheatre, where Susanna danced in the ballets for which John Durang was the master. The next year the Rowsons went to Boston, where they joined the company of the Federal Street Theatre for the season beginning September 15, 1796. At the end of the season, Susanna

Rowson retired from the theatre and opened her school at Boston, changing its locations over the years to Medford, Newton, and back to Boston. Writing occupied her as well as did the direction of the school until her death in 1824.

During her brief career in the American theatre, Susanna Rowson wrote at least four plays, perhaps more. John Bernard, actor and partner in the management of the Federal Street Theatre from 1806 through 1811, noted that for the 1810–1811 season "Mrs. Rowson, who had formerly been an actress, but was now superintending a seminary, favored us with another— 'Hearts of Oak'—a piece inferior to the other [W. C. White's *The Poor Lodger*], but which nevertheless displayed merits worthy of more praise than it received."[11] Among her other, more certain works, *The Female Patriot* was "altered from Massinger's *Bondsman*" for Mr. and Mrs. Rowson's benefit on June 19, 1795. *The Volunteers,* a comic opera which was performed twice in January, 1795, dramatized her enthusiastic reaction to the Whiskey Rebellion, which broke out in southwestern Pennsylvania during the early fall of 1794 as a result of the federal excise tax. Unfortunately, Mrs. Rowson's script for this musical play has been lost. The vocal score, composed by Alexander Reinagle, still exists, but it is difficult to know Mrs. Rowson's attitude from songs which are mainly about love and the joys of simple, frontier life. Her major concern, however, was for those "volunteers" whom Washington called to enforce the law. These militiamen, one of whom is called Trueman, sing of liberty and are finally welcomed home as heroes.

Susanna Rowson's last play, too, remains something of a mystery. Entitled *Americans in England*, it was written for her final performance at the Federal Street Theatre on April 19, 1797. It is presumed that she gave the rights of production to Hodgkinson, who renamed it *The Columbian Daughter; or, Americans in England* and used it for his benefit at the Mount Vernon (New York) Gardens Theatre on September 10, 1800. This playscript has also been lost, but it would seem to have praised America through a strong-minded woman, a daughter of Columbia according to Hodgkinson, the role Mrs. Rowson played in Boston. Such characters as Dick Rhymer, Jack and Arabella Acorn, Ezekiel Plainly, Folio, Snap, and Jemima (the heroine) perhaps suggest the farcical nature of this play which emphasizes English eccentricities and sturdy American qualities.

Susanna Rowson's first play, her best and the one for which she is remembered, is *Slaves in Algiers; or, A Struggle for Freedom. A Play interspersed with Songs* (1794). She prepared it, as she did *The Female Patriot* and *Americans in England*, for her benefit night. As did *The Volunteers* and the very popular pantomime dance of 1794 attributed to William Francis, a dancer, and to Rowson (with such songs as "America, Commerce, and Freedom"), it had music written by Reinagle. Beginning what would become customary with her, Mrs. Rowson acted one of the best roles for her benefit night of June 30, 1794. Repeated "with alteration" on December 22, 1794, it was also performed in Baltimore and may have appeared in New York although Odell records the title as *Slaves in Algiers; or, A Struggle for Liberty*.[12] For the first performance of the play in Philadelphia, the currency of her subject and the force of her opinions brought severe criticism from William Cobbett ("Peter Porcupine"). Cobbett, a strong defender of the aristocracy and the Federalist movement during his brief period in America, was as straightforward in his views as Mrs. Rowson was in the position she dramatized. Both had their supporters. It was a time when the United States, subjected to degrading abuse by the Mediterranean pirates yet unwilling to pay the tribute demanded by the Dey of Algiers, was beginning to think more seriously about its tiny navy. As Colonel David Humphreys, a dramatist and the minister to Portugal, attempted to negotiate the situation, Mrs. Rowson responded with a play which scourged tyranny and the lack of personal freedom. Cobbett found her attitudes completely distasteful and ridiculed the production for reasons which might have been more widely accepted had he reviewed the play as a theatre critic.

Slaves in Algiers was, at any rate, a hasty job of writing, completed in two months, as Mrs. Rowson admitted in her preface. But she had something to say. In addition to airing her views regarding personal liberty, she wanted to clarify a moral position, "to place the social virtues in the fairest point of view and hold up, to merited contempt and ridicule, their opposite vices." James Fennell, an actor who had come over from England with the Rowsons, was even more direct in the prologue, which he wrote and delivered, reprimanding the audience for not trying to free the captives held by the Algerians and praising Mrs. Rowson: "The reigning *virtues* she has dared to scan,/ And tho a woman, plead the Rights of Man." Her plea, as it were, has a contrived but moderately exciting plot about Americans, captured by the Dey of Algiers, making their melodramatic escape. In the opening scene Selina, daughter of the villain, Ben Hassan, sets the tone by explaining the love of liberty she learned from an American woman. Unfortunately, she never appears again although her confidante in the Dey's household, Fetnah, helps arrange the escape. Ben Hassan seems to be a friend of the Americans, but one of his songs reveals his true character: "I have cheated the Gentiles as Moses commanded" (I, ii). In fact, he turns out to be almost as much a comic as he is a villain. Rowson also manages very well to push patriotic and Christian sentiments into a melodramatic structure. The coy and witty Fetnah, clearly the most interesting character in the play, disguises herself as a boy to escape to the land of "peace and liberty" while Olivia, one of the Americans, is determined that the Dey's daughter, a converted Christian, take her place. When the escape does not succeed, Olivia further asserts her Christian martyr complex by declaring that she will remain and marry the Dey if her friends are released. But this sacrifice proves unnecessary as the playwright manages to free everyone: "No man should be a slave" (III, iv).

Aside from the contemporary issue, *Slaves in Algiers* has few distinctive qualities. Although its thesis would have been considered important, neither the characters nor the dialogue attract praise. There is considerable action, however, made more spectacular by foreign atmosphere. Unfortunately, other than this play there is little on which to judge Susanna Rowson as a playwright. Her versatility in the arts and literature, however, enhances her reputation, and her brief career as an actress and patriotic playwright who obviously was aware of the potential for drama in American society, provides an early glimpse of American women in the theatre.

John Daly Burk (1776?–1808), another major dramatist of the period, was a man of strength and purpose, an intelligent man with a compelling sense of humanity. Yet few of his contemporaries, judging him mainly on the basis of a single play, had kind words for him. Probably his belligerent and independent spirit did not encourage admirers. Inspired by truth as he understood it, he was destined neither to be fully appreciated for his work nor to live a calm and long life. Most critics remember him only for *Bunker-Hill*, an extraordinarily successful play on the stage (although frequently condemned), but mention the play mainly to apologize for the tastes of audiences. Dunlap called it "vile trash," but he produced it nevertheless, even with one of his own plays as an afterpiece. Most historians have simply discountenanced the play as a "patriotic effusion."

But Burk had more to offer than enthusiasm. While he lacked the wit and sense of humor that distinguished Tyler's appreciation of polite society and Dunlap's ability to compromise in both artistic and commercial worlds, and the talent of both in constructing a play, Burk had that understanding of human nature and the feeling for human inadequacies that a man of letters should possess. In his creation of Joan in *Female Patriotism; or, the Death of Joan d'Arc*, certainly one of the best American plays written in the eighteenth century, he showed his perceptive and inventive powers. With the spirit of the rebel and an original cast of mind, he contributed much to the early stages of American drama.

Born in Ireland, Burk attended Trinity College, Dublin, from which he was expelled for his republican and didactic views. A passion for freedom and a hatred of tyranny later forced him to leave the Ireland that he loved and subsequently wrote about in his *History of the Late War in Ireland* (1799) and in *An Historical Essay on the Character and Antiquity of Irish Songs*, which was printed in the Richmond *Enquirer* (May 1808). Enraged at seeing British soldiers take a man to be executed, he tried to rescue him, failed, and fled Ireland with the help of a Miss Daly (whose name he then added to his own in a typically gallant gesture) who gave him the clothes for his disguise as a woman while his dog held his pursuers at bay. Once in America he settled in Boston in 1796 and, by October of that year, began to edit a newspaper called the *Polar Star and Boston Daily Advertiser*, a brash and thoroughly anti-British publication which lasted only until February 2, 1797. It was this same month, however, that *Bunker-Hill* opened in Boston with considerable success. Burk then went on to New York, where he edited another newspaper, *Time-Piece*. This venture was cut short by his arrest for "publishing a libel contrary to the provisions of the sedition law of 1798," and he might have left America had he not been helped by Aaron Burr, to whom he had dedicated his second play, *Female Patriotism*, which was performed twice at the Park Theatre in April, 1798.

Soon after the turn of the century, Burk was in Petersburg, Virginia, where he married and continued his interest in literature. There also he developed an enthusiasm for the republicanism of Jefferson, that "energetic champion of the moral and physical production of his country." A theatre had been built in Petersburg in 1796, and Burk joined the Thespians, whom he directed in several plays and for whom in 1807 he wrote *Bethlem Gabor*, acting the leading part himself. During these years, while continuing to write poetry, he was also at work on a three-volume *History of Virginia*. Then there occurred the argument in a tavern where Burk, angry with the attitude the French people maintained toward the American republic, denounced them in his usual extravagant manner as a "pack of rascals." Unfortunately, there was a Frenchman present, a Monsieur Coquebert, who resented the slur on his nationality and demanded satisfaction with dueling pistols. On the first firing the pistols were ineffective. It was consistent with Burk's philosophy that there be a second attempt. The second shot went through the heart of the man whom A. H. Quinn called a "stormy petrel." It was April 10, 1808. At the time of Burk's death, he had already been all but forgotten in those places where earlier he had created some sensation. Writing his "Reminiscences of Newspapers," Joseph T. Buckingham noted that "about the year 1800, it was reported that he [Burk] was killed in a duel in one of the Southern States."[13]

Various historians have ascribed seven plays to Burk: *Bunker-Hill; or, the Death of General Warren* (1797); *Female Patriotism; or, The Death of Joan D'Arc* (1798); *Bethlem Gabor, Lord of Transylvania; or, the Man-Hating Palatine* (1807); *The Death of General Montgomery in Storming the City of Quebec; The Fortunes of Nigel; The Innkeeper of Abbeville*; and *Which Do You Like Best, the Poor Man or the Lord*? Only the first three are known to have been performed and have been published for the reading public; the authorship of the others has been questioned. (Dunlap is the source of the list, and his memory was often faulty. In the list he misspelled "Bethlem" as "Bethlehem" and divided the Joan of Arc play into two plays.) If Burk had written all the plays attributed to him, he would probably have been remembered differently by those writing in the nineteenth century. Virginians thought of him as a historian, whereas William W. Clapp, writing of the Boston stage, recalled him only as an editor. These were the two careers which enclosed his playwriting activity.

Bunker-Hill gave Burk his reputation—both good and bad. Opening at the Haymarket Theatre in Boston on February 17, 1797, the play boasted tremendous spectacle and concluded with a grand procession in honor of General Warren, with "American music only" played between the acts. That winter and spring it played a total of ten performances, and Burk made the unheard-of sum of $2,000 from his play. Audiences loved this grand "tragedy" of love and patriotism, which continued to be performed for many years, particularly on Evacuation Day, and was reprinted several times. Obviously, for a presentation of the Battle of Bunker Hill there must have been something constructed on stage which the soldiers could charge up. To prepare for the New York production, Burk wrote a long letter to Hodgkinson explaining in detail how they did it in Boston: the battle in Act V lasted twelve to fifteen minutes on a "hill" from which eighteen to twenty men could fire on the English, who would then roll back down, enveloped in smoke and flame as the noise of cannon and muskets resounded in the theatre.[14] With spectacular chaos plus pageantry and an overwhelming patriotic sentiment, it seems perfectly clear why emotional theatre-goers enjoyed the play, particularly at a time when America's image abroad was being challenged on many sides by the English, the French, and the Mediterranean pirates.

The odd part of the response to *Bunker-Hill* is the conscientious effort on the part of most early historians and critics to deplore it, particularly when the play was certainly no worse than many of the plays being produced at that time and even better than a substantial number. Although no one would contend that the play is great drama, the ardor with which some of the early condemnations seem to single out this play suggests a confluence of criticism for whatever reasons may be imagined. Dunlap's low opinion of it has been mentioned. Clapp concurred with the quick, adverse judgment of John Adams, who, considerably angered, felt that his friend General Warren had been maligned in the play. Clapp also quoted Buckingham: "The tragedy had not a particle of merit, except its brevity."[15] It is perhaps understandable that the manager of the rival Federal Street Theatre called it "the most execrable of the Grub Street kind," which, "to the utter disgrace of Boston theatricals, has brought them *full* houses."[16] Odell early refers to it as "Burk's rather discredited play" and then accepts it, as the managers of the time did, as a box-office success; Hornblow stated that it had "no literary or dramatic merit."[17] A critic for the *Thespian Mirror* (March 1, 1806), for example, writing in an article entitled "The American Stage," comments on *Bunker-Hill*: "The evening's performances consisted of trash—the representations with a few exceptions, beneath criticism." It is the tone of the condescension in the comment in the *Lady's Monitor* (November 28, 1801), in an article entitled "Our Drama," which arouses suspicion: "Mr. Burk brought forward his tragedy of *Bunker-Hill*; and it not only escaped *damnation*, but was received with much applause." The reviewer goes on to state, incorrectly, that "Mr. Dunlap revised the play before presenting it in New York—therefore, the success." When Odell quotes a favorable review from the *Gazette*, he assumes that it is a "manager-inspired burst."[18] And he is probably right. Yet these attitudes toward the play which Burk thought his "best offering" tempt speculation.

The prologue for the "tragedy of *Bunker-Hill*," as Burk describes it, plucks the proper emotional strings. There are references to the "patriot band" and "Columbia's Sons," a comparison of American and Roman heroes, and reference to America "secure on freedom's Ararat." Burk does not bother with character development, and his blank verse, no less the pompous than that of his playwriting contemporaries, is frequently as disjointed as his plot. The propagandistic speeches, however, and the anti-British–pro-American emotions aroused by the action and spectacle were sufficient stimulus for an audience. It is not a long play, and there is little time, or reason, to be bored even with Burk's contrived and ill-fated romance between the British officer Abercombie and Elvira, an American girl.

As the play opens a group of English soldiers "fly across the stage as if pursued," as the English leaders, Percy and Gage, damn the rout of their soldiers and wonder at the stubbornness of the colonists. Meanwhile, Elvira tries to persuade Abercombie that his argument for honor over love is wrong: "Let not the gorgeous pomp of laurell'd war/ Seduce thy mind from me" (I, i). Fusing the sentiments of romantic love and patriotism, Burk provides General Warren with a strong speech laden with propaganda—"Here in the face of heaven, I devote/ Myself, my services, my life to Freedom" (II, i)— as he takes command of the Patriot defense of Bunker Hill. After the audience endures the painful parting of Abercombie and Elvira, as the problems of their love echo the difficulties of the country, Warren and Prescot prepare for war with the rallying cry, "Liberty or Death." It is probably this scene, in which Burk made Warren act with strong determination for victory, that offended John Adams. Warren draws his sword and makes the following speech: "Now savage strife and fury fill my soul—/ And when my nature yields to self-compassion/ Let Boston's injuries rise before my view/ And steel my heart to pity" (IV, ii).

Theatre historians are correct in suggesting that Act V, the attack on Bunker Hill, provided the major appeal to audiences. As the English charge the hill three times and are three times driven back before Warren is mortally wounded, there were probably nights when almost anything could have happened on stage. The English, as well as the audience, view the slaughter after the Americans retreat, and Elvira finds Abercombie's body, faints, and is taken away only to be driven insane in the tradition of romantic heroines. Following the noble death of Warren—"O God protect this land—I faint—I die" (V, iii)— which Burk could have modeled on numerous popular plays, there is the grand funeral procession across the stage with all the proper emblems plus "two virgins" singing an original patriotic elegy to the tune of "Roslin Castle." The play does not read much better or much worse than many other plays and patriotic spectacles, but it could boast, in the event dramatized and in the timing of its creation, a popularity which managers could not afford to resist. Perhaps its repetition simply gave critics more opportunity to express their views.

Female Patriotism, published in 1798 as *The Death of Joan D'Arc*, a historic play in five acts, is—in its poetry, its structure, and the sensitive and original conception of the major character—far superior to Burk's first attempt. The play opens in a forest in France where the Dauphin, in despair over the latest English victory, hears about the Maid. Although firm in his belief that "in monarchies the King is paramount," when Pucella enters and explains her task, he gives her the leadership she wants. Soon Joan/Pucella challenges the British and arranges a meeting with Sir John Talbot, the greatest of the British officers. When anger overcomes him their meeting ends in a fight which is interrupted by Chastel, whose admiration for Joan has grown to a love which is returned. After helping the French win a victory (III), Joan explains that she is only a maid with no special call from "the skies." But she can inspire them. With this approach Burk creates a very human Joan of simply dignity.

Act IV opens with the procession to crown the Dauphin at Rheims. As *Bunker-Hill* reveals, Burk handled spectacles and processions expertly. Here Joan reveals her character and purpose in forceful, moving blank verse:

> T's not to crown the Dauphin Prince alone
> That hath impell'd my spirit to the wars,
> For that were petty circumstance indeed;
> But on the head of every man in France
> To place a crown and thus at once create
> A new and mighty order of nobility,
> To make all free and equal, *all men kings,*
> Subject to justice and the laws alone!
> For this great purpose have I come amongst you.
>   [IV, i.]

The major crisis occurs when the English finally outwit Joan, seize her, and sentence her to die as a witch for bringing "sorcery and war" to the world.

In the final act Joan is in prison, alone, abandoned, a very human figure caught in the world of men; her emotions direct her to anger, apprehension, and prayer, as she awaits her sentence: death at the stake. As Chastel pleads for Joan before the king and draws his sword in frustration, news is brought that Joan is dead. All are strangely affected and weep except for Chastel, who has a letter from Joan which bids him farewell and prophesies a good republic for France. More news: those who plotted Joan's death have been killed, and the revenge that Chastel demanded has begun: "The spirit of the lovely Joan of Arc . . . shrieks for vengeance" (V, ii).

Although Chastel assumes a major role, it is the character of Joan that dominates and distinguishes this play, a very human portrayal which displays more of the idiosyncrasies of Burk than it does of the qualities of the historical figure. She knows that she has power, and this knowledge is emphasized, perhaps in a way that shows more vanity than she should have. But her power is an inspiration for liberty, not a revelation of a divine mission. Act I introduces her and the task she conceives; Act II demonstrates her prowess in the fight with Talbot and her appeal to a veteran soldier; Act III tests her in battle but as an ordinary person: "I am no more of heaven than yourselves"; "I saw no sights but all of you did see" (III, iii). Act III also shows the plotting against her, which is carried out in Act IV. The final climax in Act V is consistent with the simple approach to life which marks Joan. There is no tragedy for Joan; it is a historical play (Burk took thirty lines from *Henry VI* for his first act and identifies them for the reader) with a thesis that would be expected of Burk and with the kind of action that shows a good sense of drama. In the final act, to which he adds a kind of agit-prop ending, he provides excellent sentiment as well as strong opinions. In his flamboyant style he uses Joan's character to hold the play together and, until her death, as a banner—female patriotism—to wave. Some have felt that the anti-French feeling in 1798 might have affected the play; Dunlap wrote that poor acting made it fail. Certainly, it deserved a better response than it got at the Park in April, 1798.

Nine years later Burk wrote another play which suggests a response to the violence in *Female Patriotism. Bethlem Gabor* is a revenge melodrama in which a character's sense of humanity dissuades the avenger, and the play ends happily. That Burk acted the title role suggests something about the man as well as his interest in theatre. Probably, he owed some debt to the major character in William Godwin's novel, *St. Leon* (1799), and to Charles Brockden Brown's novel, *Wieland* (1798), in which the villain's use of ventriloquism brings the hero to ruin. As the story of a man saved from madness by the words of another with the same problems, *Bethlem Gabor* includes the usual devices of Gothic melodrama, but the complications of the genre get out of control. Only the changes in Gabor as a man—as he fights the sense of humanity he must finally accept as true to himself—are interesting. In both theme and form, the play makes a statement about its author.

All of the dramatists discussed in this chapter—Tyler, Dunlap, Rowson, and Burk—had one thing in common: a sense of nationalism supported by a strong feeling for human nature. During the score of years that followed the Treaty of Paris, their plays were the best that Americans could offer, and with their work the drama of the nation called America rightly begins. And yet they were not alone.

SIX

Meeting the Demands
of a Growing Theatre, 1783-1800

IT IS relatively easy to pluck out of any given period of history the names of people who have made outstanding contributions to the drama. Winners become a part of the record books. But just as there are those innumerable details of everyday life which contribute to the creation of greater events, there are those lesser playwrights who help make a history of the drama: those who provide the prologues which introduce the main attraction, those who write the curtain raisers or afterpieces which fill out the evening, those who create the plays which keep the theatre open while a major production is being prepared or who try to catch the popularity of a current event and please both the theatre manager and the audience. A viable drama must meet the demands of the theatre, and even during such a brief period in early American history a variety of plays was written to meet that challenge.

With the Revolution over, the people began to look at their antitheatre laws, and, eventually, theatre managers cautiously remodeled the old theatres and opened new ones. In Pennsylvania, for example, the Dramatic Association was created "for the Purpose of obtaining the Entertainment of a Theatre in Philadelphia, under a liberal and properly regulated plan."[1] Frustrated by failure to reverse old laws in Boston, drama enthusiasts there decided to do things their own way and opened the "New Exhibition Room" in Broad Alley in August, 1792. Two years later Boston added the Federal Street Theatre and then, in 1796, the Haymarket Theatre. By this date there were theatres in Gloucester, Newport, Providence, Hartford, and Portland. Theatre activity in the South was also spreading, particularly in Charleston, where men like John Solee, Thomas Wade West, and Alexander Placide managed theatres which were served, according to Eola Willis in *The Charleston Stage in the Eigh-*

teenth Century, by at least a half-dozen plays written by Charlestonians during the 1794–95 theatre season. Ten years after the end of the Revolution, it was clear that America would have a theatre and would need dramatists.

The main character of America's early attempts to express itself in dramatic form rests upon the work of those dramatists. As might be expected, however, no strong, positive patterns in the drama distinguish the period. Because the theatre needed plays, it was natural that actors and actresses would help provide them. Because many people came to America from England, where theatre was popular, it was understandable that newly arrived Englishmen and even visitors from England would write and publish in America. And because the theatre was, and would remain for some time, the pleasure of relatively few people in America, where prejudice against it was still very strong, many playwrights wrote anonymously for moral, social, literary, or political reasons. Among the most successful poets and essayists, some wrote plays for the closet while others were obviously interested in theatre productions for their efforts. And then there were those more ordinary writers who enjoyed the theatre, had some talent for writing dialogue, and tried to meet the growing theatre's demand for plays.

As would be expected, the kinds of plays written reflect the diverse interests, objectives, and talents of the playwrights. Events, political and social, inspired a number of would-be playwrights, just as an interest in history and a strong patriotic feeling for the new country prompted others to write brief plays or spectacles with a little dialogue. Farce-comedy was the popular genre for the hack writer, while the more ambitious playwright would attempt melodrama or romantic tragedy in the manner of English and European writers. There were also adaptations and translations. What must be borne in mind, however, is that the history of American drama is limited to those plays which were published or were sufficiently discussed by contemporary reviewers that the plot and dramatic techniques are identifiable. Unfortunately, information is not always available from this early period when the theatre production seemed far more important than the play to the reviewers, who spent most of their time discussing morals or actors, scenery, and stage devices.

It must be remembered also that plays written by Americans occupied an exceedingly small part of the offerings in any theatre. Odell, in his *Annals of the New York Stage*, generally stops to comment when the play is by an American, and, except for the work of Dunlap, he was not able to do so for every season. It was the English or the European play, particularly the English play, which pleased Americans, just as it was the English actor newly arrived from England who attracted them to the theatre. Added to the broad prejudice against drama and theatre in America was a particular prejudice, even within the theatre management (which reflected the views of the audience), against American plays.

One traditional source for playwriting and play production in America was the college literary or social society. For example, the Honorable Fellowship Club of Yale (1767; later the Linonia Society) and another Yale organization, the Brothers of Unity, produced "dramatic exhibitions" and dialogues with such titles as *The Modern Mistathe* (1784) and *Upon the Disturbances in Massachusetts* (1787). Their single objective was their immediate pleasure, but one comedy written for the Linonia Society "by a Junior" in 1789 brought the ire of the president of Yale College.[2] After the Revolution two societies at Dartmouth College—Social Friends (1783) and the United Fraternity (1786)—competed with each other to perform the commencement exercises and occasionally produced original plays. Probably the best known of those early societies is the Hasty Pudding Club (1795) at Harvard. Although a number of years would pass before the debates which enlivened its meetings would be turned into exciting theatrical productions, Harvard students also wrote and performed plays during the Revolution.[3]

Among the first full-length plays to be written and produced for college production and the first to be published was *The Mercenary Match* (1784), a five-act tragedy in blank verse by Barnabas Bidwell (1763–1833). As does one of the characters in his play, Bidwell became a member of the state senate in Massachusetts (1805–1807) and then served as the state attorney general. He later embezzled $10,000 and fled to Canada, where he entered politics and remained for the rest of his life. The rather gallant villain of the play, Major Shapely, dramatizes a bit of irony for the author in his confession that he did it all "to satiate my desires." The scene of the play is Boston, where a Mrs. Jensen, having yielded to her father's demands for a "mercenary match," is deeply unhappy with her husband and ready to accept the advances of Shapely, an unsuccessful suitor from her past. Having sworn that he will ruin their marriage, Shapely insinuates his way into the confidence of both husband and wife and then maliciously creates such distrust and hate between them that Mrs. Jensen ironically gives her love and loyalty to the villain. When Shapely's and Mrs. Jensen's plans to murder Jensen are botched by their hired help, Shapely does the deed, with the result that Mrs. Jensen dies of shock and that he will be sent to the gallows and "everlasting woe."

In his *History of the American Theatre*, Dunlap called the play a "very pleasant and laugh-provoking tragedy" which he remembered as producing shouts of laughter when read aloud to a company of young men. One might hope that the author wrote the play for a comic effect. Shapely as a villain, for example, adding a few melodramatic gestures to his work as an intriguer, acts like a character in farce throughout. Only Mrs. Jensen as the restless wife deserves a sympathetic thought—and then only through the first three acts. As a farce-melodrama concerned with domestic problems, the play may have suggested a moral during the first four acts, but both characters and audience had trouble facing the catastrophe of the fifth act.

The French Revolution, an anonymously written play performed by the United Fraternity at Dartmouth in 1790 and published in New Bedford three years later, illustrates the political atmosphere in college as well as the long (seven acts), rambling type of verse drama that higher education seemed to inspire. Although the King, presented with a sympathy which the author felt obliged to justify in his published preface, feels that the "claims of the commons" have value, he is persuaded by his advisers to exile Necker, dissolve the assembly of the Third Estate, and send troops to disperse a gathering crowd. At this action, Lafayette, the political spokesman and advocate of liberty in the play, leads the people in revolt against the King, who finally signs a bill of rights: "So Gallia's Sovereign reassumes his glory" (VII). The revolt of the peasants also reunites the young lovers in the subplot. The time of the play encompasses many years—a breach of the Unities which was noted in the epilogue at a performance in Windsor, Vermont, in 1791—and its posture is primarily romantic with typed characters and strong nationalistic overtones evident in the frequent praise of freedom, in the contrast between the common man and the aristocracy, and in the comment on the French Revolution as an extension of the American Revolution.

Thomas Day must have been a rather serious-minded student to have written *The Suicide*, performed at the Yale University commencement on September 13, 1797, but he obviously believed in his play. He acted the role of the main character, a young man who attempts to take his own life after he has been disowned by his father but who is saved from disaster by an understanding friend. The subject matter of the play and the dramatized moral stance against suicide suggest a distinct gap between real and fictionalized life at this early period when suicide was a popular resolution in both romantic fiction and drama whether the hero or heroine was culpable or a victim of fate.

Another type of theatrical entertainment popular in America may best be described as a combination of pantomime, spectacle, masque, and pageant. It deserves some brief comment because dialogues were frequently part of the event and because the authorship, although seldom disclosed, was in most cases American. Considering the number of these pantomime-spectacle-pageant skits, there can be no question of their popularity, which shows something of the competition facing a prospective dramatist of the period. Even Dunlap contributed to the genre with *The Temple of Independence* for Washington's birthday in 1799. For an earlier celebration of Washington's birthday, John Parke had written *Virginia: A Pastoral Drama on the Birth-day of an Illustrious Personage and the Return of Peace, February 11, 1784.* It takes place on the bank of the Potomac, where shepherds and shepherdesses and hunters and huntresses sing, dance, and recite in honor of Daphnis' (Washington's) birthday. Finally, "a vast concourse of gentlemen" brings Daphnis on stage, where the Genius of Virginia summons the ghosts of past heroes (Warren, Pulaski, DeKalb, and so forth) to welcome him.

Most theatres provided such entertainments, and there were those such as Ricketts' Circus or Lailson's Circus where one could expect to see spectacles and pageants most of the time. For the ordinary theatre a seasonal event generally occasioned the piece, but a manager might simply celebrate something from the past. For example, in December, 1797, at Philadelphia's New Theatre, Thomas Morton's popular two-act play, *Columbus*, was performed "to conclude with a new additional scene written by a member of the Legislature of the United States." In the new scene, published the following year by its author, Alexander Martin, the Genius of America descends and describes to Columbus the future of America as it develops from the Spanish exploration through the English colonization to the Revolution. He then praises American leaders and warns against dissention. Three other productions in Philadelphia during May, 1798, suggest the scope and popularity of this type of entertainment: *St. Tammany's Festival in the Temple of Liberty,* "an occasional interlude consisting of Songs, Dances, and Spectacle"; *The Death of Major André, and Arnold's Treachery; or, West Point Preserved,* a grand pantomime in three acts "composed by a Citizen of Philadelphia"; and *The Sufferings of the Maddison Family; or, The Generous Indian,* "a Grand Historical Pantomime taken from the Memoirs of Mr. Maddison, an American painter." The next year Philadelphians enjoyed a "Song, Dialogue, and Dance" entitled *American True Blue; or, the Naval Processions* and *The Constellation; or, A Wreath for American Tars,* "with a Representation of the Chase and Action between the *Constellation* and *L'Insurgente* frigates."

On April 16, 1796, audiences in Charleston could have watched a spectacular fusion of pantomime, music, dancing, speeches, and odes entitled *The Apotheosis of Franklin; or, His Reception in the Elysian Fields* in which the Goddess of Fate proclaims Franklin's virtues and places a bust of Franklin in the Temple of Memory. Bowing to the interests of the French in Charleston, one manager produced in 1799 a "historical pantomime" called *The Man in the Iron Mask.* On January 25, 1795, Charlestonians watched a spectacle of local interest entitled *The Elopement; or, A Trip to the Charleston Races.*

Another spectacle, one presumably written by a Charlestonian during the Revolution as a musical and allegorical masque entitled *Americana and Elutheria: A New Tale of the Genii,* was produced by John Solee in Charleston in 1798 as *Americana; or, A New Tale of the Genii* and published in 1802 as an "Allegorial Mask in five acts." The scene of this spectacular bit of patriotic pageantry is the summit of the Allegheny Mountains, where Jelemnio, a friend of Americana, presents a masque for her entertainment. Having forsaken Britain, Elutheria, Genius of Liberty, comes to Americana's arms, where she will be defended against Typhon, Genius of Tyranny, and Fastidio, Genius of Pride, who reign hand in hand with Britain. In battles Americana uses a rod from which a "stream of electric fluid" is poured on the heads of Tyranny the Pride. Thoughts of war with Britain and the loss of Elutheria then plague Americana until she is joined by Galiana, Genius of France. In the climax Britain is defeated in battle and confesses to being deluded by Typhon and Fastidio, whose wings Americana then literally clips with shears presented by Elutheria. In great ceremony Americana and Galiana break Typhon's wand and place Elutheria's feet upon the necks of the two enemies. All hail America, "and Israel-like, they fling their chains away." Although the verse is rough and many of the speeches are impossibly long, the patriotic and moral atmosphere, along with the compassionate portrayal of Britain, evidently carries the piece. As usual, there was spectacle everywhere, but the modern mind must find that "stream of electric fluid" particularly intriguing.

For the New York stage, W. H. Prigmore, an actor, dancer, and singer, assembled in June, 1795, a "musical piece," *The Demolition of the Bastile; or, Liberty Triumphant,* complete "with a View of the Outside of the Bastile, Moat, and Drawbridge; the Inside of the Bastile, with the Cells, Gratings, Dungeons." It had been produced originally in 1793, the year New Yorkers could also have watched *The Siege of Gibraltar,* in which spectacle scenes presented "the shipping at anchor near the fort; an engagement at sea; Paul Jones taking the Seraphis; the fleet destroyed by bombs from the fort to be followed by Neptune and Arion; a shark swallowing a boat with men; the favorite scene of duck-hunting; the Gunner with his faithful dog." An earlier spectacle that came to New York, *The Convention; or, the Columbian Father*, "a Serious Pastoral in Two Acts," "by a Citizen of the United States," was produced on April 7, 1788. As were several other such entertainments, it was described by contemporary critics as a "scenic hodge-podge."

At this point in the history of the drama in America, actors and actresses performing on the American stage contributed measurably to the drama. Sometimes, as in the case of Prigmore, it was only a pantomime or an afterpiece; at other times, it was a full-length play. When the *Constitution* was launched in 1797, for example, John Hodgkinson prepared *The Launch; or, Huzza for the Constitution*, more a spectacle with songs and some dialogue than a play but popular enough for him to repeat it for his benefit the next spring. In June, 1796, an actor named Cleveland offered *Love Makes a Man*, a historical pantomime on the "Ever Memorable 4th of July 1776." A month previously, Madame Gardie, a dancer and the wife of a member of the orchestra at the John Street Theatre, had presented *The American Heroine*, a "Grand Historic and Military Pantomime." At the beginning of the 1798–99 season, an actor named Bates turned John O'Keefe's *The Positive Man* into *Preparation for a Cruise; or, The American Tars*, complete with Tom Grog as the true American sailor.

Such adaptations were very common, and it is probably impossible to know the full extent of the contribution to American drama made by American and itinerant English actors traveling among America's theatres during the late eighteenth and early nineteenth centuries. Even in New York, where information has been carefully recorded, far too many of the plays are known by title only, their authors and the plots they unfolded lost to posterity after the theatres darkened.

Fortunately, some of these plays were published. John Hodgkinson (1767–1805) came to America in 1792 and remained to achieve popular recognition for his acting as well as for his management of the John Street Theatre with Henry and Dunlap. In addition to writing his sketch *The Launch*, he had a hand in the Americanization of J. C. Cross's *The Purse* (1794), which was first produced in America in 1797 and repeated during later years as *The Purse; or, American Tars* and *The Purse; or, American Sailor's Return*. Hodgkinson's longest effort was *The Man of Fortitude; or, A Knight's Adventure*, produced first in 1797 and published ten years later. The story surrounding its creation must be told. Dunlap, it seems, had written a one-act play, *A Knight's Adventure*, which he gave to Hodgkinson to read. Evidently, the next thing he knew Hodgkinson had changed its title slightly and developed it into a three-act play which became quite popular with American audiences. Hodgkinson, who has not been remembered for his scruples, admitted the theft but pointed out that he changed everything, whereas Dunlap, with the tolerance that must have contributed to his failure in theatre management, did not feel that Hodgkinson had been guilty of conscious fault. It was, of course, an age when pirating was a constant if not always an acceptable theatre activity.

The Man of Fortitude combines the attributes of both Gothic and sentimental melodrama while managing pointed comments on justice and patriotism through the dialogue of a very Christian knight who speaks in stiff blank verse. The play has no real characterization or effective language, but Hodgkinson was a good actor who knew the value of excitement and expectation and the appeal of well-placed melodramatic devices on stage. After setting the knight and his humorous servant in a haunted castle—actually a bandits' hideout—where they are accosted by phantoms, bloody spectres, clanking chains, and blue lights, Hodgkinson twists his plot by having the captain of the bandits promise the knight freedom if he will woo for the captain a lady the bandits have captured. But the lady, Hortensia, turns out to be the knight's bride, stolen on their wedding night. The captain then shows his anger with all the thrills expected in a bandits' hideout until, for no reason at all, he suddenly turns sentimental. He wishes the knight and the lady happiness together and explains why he became a bandit. The knight, a man of fortitude, will take the captain's plea to the emperor, but it is Hortensia who speaks the epilogue (written by William Milns, a playwright and friend of Hodgkinson) as a woman of fortitude who got what she wanted.

The man who brought Hodgkinson to America, and then must have immediately regretted his act when Hodgkinson usurped his roles and made life generally difficult for him, was John Henry (1746–1794). Starting his acting career at Drury Lane, Henry went to Jamaica in 1762 and finally joined Douglass' American Company in Philadelphia in 1767 to become a leading man. During the Revolution he retreated with the other members of the company to Jamaica, where in 1783 he performed and published *A School for Soldiers; or, the Deserter*, an adaptation of Louis Sébastien Mercier's *Le Déserteur*. After the Revolution he became a partner with Hallam in America, where his play was produced in 1788. (Dunlap, borrowing from Henry's version as he wished, also adapted this play from the French.) Although Henry adapted his four-act play in Jamaica, he clearly had America in mind, for a manuscript note in the play states that the scene is laid in Philadelphia for performance in the United States of America. Short on characterization but long on scenes of soul-wringing and self-pity, all presented in stilted prose, the play offered a slight appeal through fast-paced action and the melodramatic thesis of honor, love, and forgiveness. The plot, in brief, follows Bellamy, a young man who became a soldier at his father's insistence, who deserts the army and hides in his sweetheart's house, where, unknowingly, his father, a major, is billeted. Discovered and arrested, Bellamy is presented in a court-martial before the unsuspecting Major who, under pressure from his commander, issues the severest penalty. With the regiment at the ready on the field of execution, the Major, who must give the signal, finally recognizes his son and throws himself in his arms. At this, the commander, who knows the relationship but had a grudge against the Major, relents and issues a pardon while everyone is overwhelmed by the goodness of everyone else.

Mainly, actors wrote melodramas and farces of a very ordinary or poor quality, but there were exceptions. One of the most interesting farces of the decade, for example, was written by J. Robinson, a comedian from the Old American Company who probably spent some time in Jamaica although the particulars of his life remain a mystery. As frequently happened, he wrote his play, *The Yorker's Stratagem; or, Banana's Wedding*, a farce in two acts, specifically for his benefit (which he shared with Ryan, another member of the company) on August 24, 1792. But it turned out to be so popular that he published it later that year. From the *Daily Advertiser* (May 14, 1797), a note suggests its popularity: "We are informed that the additional scene to be introduced in . . . the *Yorker's Stratagem* . . . is to consist of a Tragic-Comic interview between Banana and his forsaken *Prissy*." Robinson played Banana, a Jamaican native and a rather odd fellow but definitely comic in his actions and dialect. The plot is good farce: contrived action, disguises, intrigues, and a villain who gets what he deserves. The variety of the characters, one-dimensional as they are, helps set up the farcical situations, which are considerably enhanced by the humorous conversations in Yankee, Jamaican, French, and English dialects. Although Banana and his wedding are related to the main action of the Yorker's stratagem for gaining his girl, the play really breaks into two parts with most of the "stratagem" coming in the first act while Banana's wedding is the major action of the second. The structure of the play is not well conceived, but both halves are funny, and that was all that was necessary.

As do many farces, *The Yorker's Stratagem* has a complicated plot in which it is difficult to indicate all the comic action without getting bogged down with details. The main action of Act I follows a wealthy New Yorker who, disguised as a Yankee clown named Amant, arrives in a Jamaican town and finally finds his sweetheart, Sophia, who is kept by a cruel and greedy guardian, Fingercash. Much of the best humor, however, comes in Act II as the audience is introduced to Mrs. Banana, her son Banana, his Priscilla, and their love problems, comically expressed in Jamaican accents and metaphors:

MRS. BANANA. What is here fur do? You, Priscilla, you no hab de imperence of de dibel, to make such a noise in a my house?
PRISCILLA. I no hab right for come see my husband?
MRS. BANANA. Who do you husband?
PRISCILLA. Banana da my husband.
MRS. BANANA. Who tell you so?
PRISCILLA. Da, me tell myself so.
MRS. BANANA. Who, you, you?
PRISCILLA. Me, me, me, me, Priscilla.
MRS. BANANA. You mullatto Scafer, go tell de obasee for come turn dis imperence hussy out of doors.
PRISCILLA. Land a mighty in a tap, me poor one in a buckra country; you eber been hear de like of dat—me da imperence hussy—oh—who da you?
MRS. BANANA. Me da lady.
PRISCILLA. You da dible, look like a lady; tigh, dirty, so come dab me.
MRS. BANANA. Me hab plantation.
PRISCILLA. You, ye lookee like a mama; you mout like a bull-frog.

Poor Banana is dominated by his mother, who insists that he leave his Prissy and marry Louisa, the daughter of Fingercash. "Nibee mind," says Banana, "I will marry de fine lady for please my mumma, and go lib wid Prissy and poor little Quacka for please myself" (II, i). Meanwhile, Fingercash will allow Amant to marry Sophia only if Amant will dispose of an allegedly blackmailing clerk named Ledger, actually an old friend of Amant whom he thought dead. Only after Banana meets Louisa and blurts out his love for Prissy and their child are the plot lines tied together. Ledger, disguised as Banana, marries Louisa, whom he loves; Banana is happily returned to his mother (and, presumably, to Prissy); and Amant and Sophia see their future together. It should be noted, too, that at the end of Act I Louisa speaks the appropriate moral concerning greed and happiness as it relates to her father's love of money. Equally important, Robinson managed to include in his farce a number of the characterizations which would be popular in American farces for the next several decades. Although poorly structured *in toto*, the scenes with Banana make *The Yorker's Stratagem* one of the brightest American farces to appear on the New York stage.

In December, 1794, a Mr. and Mrs. Marriot appeared with the John Street

Theatre company in New York. Previously, Mr. Marriot had acted at the Theatre Royal in Edinburgh, but in New York both he and his wife played major roles during the 1794–95 season. By the end of 1796 they were in the company of the Haymarket Theatre in Boston, and the following February Marriot played General Gage in the first performance of Burk's *Bunker-Hill*. Rather little is known of their activity in America, but while they were here Mrs. Marriot wrote at least one play. Called *The Chimera; or, Effusions of Fancy* (1795), the farce she wrote for her benefit on May 22, 1795, and in which she acted the heroine, Matilda, was a failure. The *New York Magazine* called it "a farce certainly unequalled by anything except its own prologue." The plot reveals how Matilda pretends to be one kind of chimera in order to gain another kind, an ideal marriage, but, even as a play about a woman's wiles, it has very little, other than the woman's success, to recommend it.

On his 1793 trip to England, Thomas Wignell returned with a number of actors and actresses who would become popular in America. One of them was James Fennell, a talented actor, particularly as Othello, who had been popular in London for years. In America he led an odd life somewhat controlled by a mania he possessed for extracting salt from the ocean. Consequently, he invariably acted only long enough to gain money for his Jersey coast salt works and returned to the stage only when he needed more funds. And so his life swung back and forth. For his benefit at the New Theatre in Philadelphia on April 5, 1798, he wrote *The Advertisement; or, A New Way to Get Married*, but most of Fennell's playwriting took place after the turn of the century.

John Beete was a member of John Solee's company at the Church Street Theatre in Charleston. Beneath the title of *The Man of the Time; or, A Scarcity of Cash* (1797), which he declared was acted with "universal applause" in Charleston, he identified himself as a "comedian." Whatever his line of business, Beete revealed himself as a reasonably shrewd person. His ploy in the preface, for example, should have gotten him sympathy as he pleaded for support in his "maiden piece" from those "who wish to encourage native dramatic literature, so that our stage may not always exhibit foreign productions." This was an early time for advertising an interest in native drama. His two-act play is a satire on the greedy, speculating, "expedient" man of the times, the part Beete acted on stage. Besides being pro-American and advocating honor, the play is strongly anti-British. Beete finds real merit in the "threadbare coat" of the American and despises the "narrow souls" of the English. Although the play is strictly farce with characters determined by their names—Major Upright and Old Screwpenny—Beete's message gets in the way of his humor, and the farce loses some of its flavor. The omission of the Man of the Times from the final scenes also weakens the structure, which is otherwise quite carefully plotted through the love theme.

The villain of the play, Old Screwpenny, a Philadelphia speculator who takes "advantage of the weakness and folly" of men, sent his son, Charles, to England to teach him business chicanery, but while there Charles met Lydia, the daughter of Major Upright. Charles returns disgustingly honest, moral, and industrious. What is more, he now disagrees with his father's corrupt business practices. Old Screwpenny detests Major Upright, who will allow Charles to marry Lydia only if he bears "my name," and Charles can do nothing with his father, who rants about "Honor! the virtue of fools," brags of his manipulations in Congress, and eventually disinherits his son. But evil finally goes begging, and Charles repudiates the rumors of bankruptcy that might save his father's fortune. An interesting sidelight is supplied by two Irish indentured servants, James and Katy, who have come from Dublin to "Columbia's free land." When Charles accepts Major Upright's conditions to marrying his daughter, the Major also consents to the marriage of James and Katy and promises them a farm when their time has been served. Honesty, he says, is honor, as he castigates Screwpenny: "I am sure that the *Man of the Times* will be hated and despised, and virtue ever crowned with success" (II, iii). No one is allowed to be confused in this early condemnation of the practices of the American businessman.

William Charles White (1777–1818), the son of a merchant in Massachusetts, abandoned his father's counting room in 1796 to become an actor, making his debut at the Federal Street Theatre in Boston, where, in 1797 he played the lead in his own play *Orlando; or, Parental Persecution.* After four months of acting, however, he left the theatre, took up law, then appeared on the New York stage in 1801, with some chance of success according to Dunlap, but apparently returned to law, in which he earned a reputation as a country attorney and author. Eventually, he wrote at least two more plays.

Orlando, a gloomy and unrelieved as well as dull five-act tragedy in blank verse, was published with a romantic dedication to "the Fair Sex" and a prologue by Thomas Paine A. M. which asserted that "Tonight . . . our drama shines, by native genius grac'd." But the play suggests rather little dramatic genius. Because his son, Orlando, has dishonored him by marrying a girl, Cecilia, of "obscure birth," Dunfred is furious and plans revenge on both with the willing help of another son, Lysander, who later explains that " 'tis for gold that I have turn'd a villain" (IV, i). In an odd playwriting twist, White uses a servant to control or force the entire action of the play. It is the servant who tells Orlando's friend, Albert, of Dunfred's plan and who spurs Lysander to action by calling him a villain to his face. After the dense but honorable hero recognizes his danger too late, it is the servant who watches Orlando's "dissolution" in prison, announces Albert's death, takes away Cecilia's dagger so that she cannot kill her child, and gives the moral in the curtain line. Parents, he says, must remember children as blessings: "nor frown/ If virtuous love engage their tender hearts;/ 'Tis that which binds society, and gives/ A perfect finish to humanity." White evidently realized his dramaturgical weaknesses, however, and in the published version begged his readers to "consider it as the offspring of a pen, inexperienced in the field of literature: that it was composed in the short space of six weeks, during intervals from mercantile employment, and at those hours, generally dedicated to the drowsy god."

Persecution; or, the Hovel in the Rocks is an adaptation by John B. Williamson of George Lillo's *Fatal Curiosity*. Williamson was an English actor who managed the Federal Street Theatre in Boston during the 1796–97 season and produced his adaptation there on February 27, 1797. Eventually, he became the director of the Charleston Theatre and published his version there in 1800. It is interesting mainly as an illustration of an adaptation which changes a tragedy to a melodrama with a happy ending.

Generally, these early actors who wrote plays for themselves or others may be considered American because they came to America, no less than others, to stay and cast their lots with a theatre in a new land. One of the early actresses who brought excellent credits on her arrival in America in 1796 was Ann Brunton Merry. Having had a spectacular career, she is fully accepted as an American actress by historians. Yet it is difficult to consider her husband, Robert Merry (1755–1798), as an American dramatist even though he wrote at least one tragedy for his wife in America. The reason, however, clearly lies with the substance of his literary reputation prior to his coming to America and with his brief time here.

Born into the aristocracy, Merry established himself as a sentimental and rather superficial poet writing under the name "Della Crusca." In London he wrote a tragedy, *Lorenzo* (1791), and an opera, *The Magician No Conjurer* (1792); both failed on the stage. In America, where John Bernard found him a witty and truly "merry" fellow, one of Merry's first writing assignments was one-half of a special prologue for John Morton's *Columbus*, produced by Wignell's company. The following year Wignell went to some expense to produce Merry's tragedy, *The Abbey of St. Augustine*, on March 20, 1797, but it lasted only three performances perhaps because, as one critic suggested, monks and nuns were not so exciting as heroes and heroines. Later that month Merry retitled *Lorenzo* as *The Ransomed Slave* in an attempt to give his wife another good role, but this was also unsuccessful. On February 2, 1798, Merry's earlier adaptation from the French, *Fenelon; or, The Nuns of Cambray*, was brought out in Philadelphia and played a number of times. Then on December 24, 1798, a little more than two years after arriving in America, Merry had a stroke and died. John Bernard, who claimed a hand in rewriting *Fenelon*, said that Merry was working on another play when he died, but it is still difficult to see him as an American dramatist when he fits so securely into that "Della Crusca" mold that he fashioned for himself.

A man whose years in America are much more difficult, if not impossible, to trace is Thomas Pike Lathy (1771–?). A novelist born in England, Lathy wrote at least one play, *Reparation; or, The School for Libertines*, which was published in 1800 "as performed at the Boston Theatre, with great applause." As a tearful melodrama in prose with a happy ending, it is imitative of the English domestic drama. It is also typical of the numerous American plays written during the late eighteenth and early nineteenth centuries which are foreign in setting, characters, plot, and phrasing. There is nothing American about either *The Abbey of St. Augustine* or *Reparation* or, for that matter, *The Man of Fortitude* and *Orlando*. The classical tradition in American education influenced some writers in every aspect of their writing. Others, such as Merry and Lathy, brought their classical training with them. *Reparation* takes place in Switzerland, where the wealthy Lord Stanton is determined to help young Latouche win the girl he once was forced to leave because he was poor. Her father is equally determined that she marry Chapone, who poses as a rich Spaniard. Melodramatic action, songs, and local Swiss atmosphere enhance the play as the father relents, but the climax is provided by the sentimental subplot concerning a girl named Julietta, whom Stanton had once seduced and abandoned. For theatrical reasons their reunion takes place in front of a tomb, with Stanton praying before a candlelit altar as Julietta and her child in white robes enter from the tomb with music playing. The symbolism of the return from death seems a bit gruesome, but the author obviously thought it would provide an appealing climax of spectacle and atmosphere.

During the 1793–94 theatre season in New York, an Englishwoman came to town, as Dunlap explains with a slight acid flavor, "to instruct us in the history of the country, the value of liberty, and the duties of the patriot."[4] This was Anne Kemble Hatton, sister of John Kemble and Mrs. Siddons. Sensing the political power of the Sons of St. Tammany organization (established in praise of the chief of the Delaware Indians before the Revolution), she wrote an opera, *Tammany; or, The Indian Chief*, which was first produced under the auspices of the Tammany Society at the John Street Theatre on March 3, 1794. Because the Irish-Americans who supported the Society favored republicanism and the revolution in France, political antagonism marred the performance. The *Daily Advertiser* (March 6, 1794), however, described the opera as "subliminally beautiful, nervous and pathetic; its sentiment such as must be approved by every wise and virtuous person" and as the work of "a genius of the first order." Others objected; Dunlap called it a "tissue of bombast." But evidently the "republicans" supported the piece, and as this was a time when attitudes toward France were very strong, the opera served as a focal point for Republican-Federalist confrontation. For this reason rather than for its artistry, the opera was produced a number of times in New York, repeated in Philadelphia and Boston, and in 1795 reduced to two acts and called *America Discovered; or, Tammany the Indian Chief*. Mrs. Hatton became known as the "Poetess of the Tammany Society," but she wrote no more operas.

Tammany had a prologue written by Richard B. Davis and an epilogue which, according to a "Calm Observer" writing for the *Daily Advertiser* (March 7, 1794), were "brim full of the present popular notions of liberty; and of course went down with great eclat." The "Calm Observer," obviously a Federalist, also noted that the audience was composed of "poorer classes of mechanics and clerks, who would be much better employed on any other occasion than disturbing a theatre." The music seems to have been tolerable with various songs, which Mrs. Hatton eventually published, including solos, duets, choruses, and a full operatic finale. Unfortunately, the manuscript of the work was not published, and the plot is known only as it is revealed by reviewers and the songs. It seems to have had a rather simple story, however, revolving around the love of Tammany and Manana and the intrusion into the New World of the Spanish under Columbus. Tammany is lauded for an independent and noble spirit which proved too much for the Spaniards. In an attempt to separate the two lovers, Ferdinand, a Spaniard, carries away the lovely Manana, who is then rescued by Tammany. In the final act, filled with violence, the Spaniards set Tammany's cabin on fire and burn the lovers to death; but the atmosphere of this violence must have been different from what one might imagine because, as the "Calm Observer" explains, "Columbia, for this, was applauded also! merely for sooth, because he prophesied that favorable things should happen to US in the 18th century." Although *Tammany* is American opera rather than American drama, the merging of the two forms at this early time is critically defensible as many plays included music and songs and the separation of American opera and drama frequently becomes a moot point.

Mrs. Hatton also represents that English author who confuses the issue of the American dramatist. One more playwright will serve to illustrate the point: William Milns (1761–1801), a British citizen who came to New York, where he ran a school and wrote prologues and light farces for the Old American Company from the fall of 1796 through the spring of 1798. Odell refers to him as the "serviceable Milns," and Dunlap calls him a "friend" of Hodgkinson, a relationship which would seem to be accurate as he wrote everything for Hodgkinson. That he was a schoolmaster and a writer, interested in the art of writing, is also fact. As a member of the "St. Mary Hall in the University of Oxford," he published a composition text, *The Well-Bred Scholar, or Practical Essays on the Best Methods of improving the Taste, and assisting the exertions of Youth in their literary pursuits* (New York, 1797). His interest in the drama is shown in a few slight farces and in occasional prologues and addresses.

Among his farces, *The Comet; or, He Would Be a Philosopher*, which had been performed previously in London, proved most successful. A comedy in five acts with music by James Hewitt, it was first produced in New York on February 1, 1797, and its songs were published later that year. Dunlap notes that the comedy "was soon afterwards cut down to a farce, which it had been originally, when it was acted in London."[5] It was this play, *The Comet; or, He Would Be an Astronomer*, in two acts, which was published in 1817 in Baltimore as having been "performed with the greatest applause at the Philadelphia and Baltimore theatres." Before his early death Milns also wrote *A Flash in the Pan* (on which Dunlap comments, "It proved so.") and *Wives Pleased and Maids Happy*. Both were performed but, also, lost to history.

The only published play which Milns most certainly wrote in America was *All in a Bustle; or, the New House*, a comic interlude which he composed particularly for the opening of the Park Theatre on January 19, 1798. This hurriedly sketched "dramatic trifle," as he called it, written to answer "a local purpose," was repeated in the New York production and then taken by Hodgkinson to Boston the next fall to open the newly rebuilt Federal Street Theatre. There it was called *A First Night's Apology; or, All in a Bustle*. It is a very slight work as Milns recognized in his preface by suggesting that any formal attack on such a play which aimed only at raising a laugh "at the whimsical incongruities of a few local perplexities" would only identify "the very Quixotte of Critics."

The action of the sketch presumably takes place just before the theatre is to open and as the Manager, played by Hodgkinson, is plagued by a poet-playwright, Jingle, who wants to provide a few lines to open the theatre. "Damn his lines," says the Manager. "No," responds the Prompter, "let the audience do that." But Jingle, who speaks in phrases rather than in sentences, is persistent and finally tries to inflict his lines upon Mrs. Hodgkinson, who has been unable to find her dressing room. After commenting on the volubility of women, he tilts again with Hodgkinson as the author of *The Launch* and *Man of Fortitude* and refuses to leave his lines or his plays with him, as Hodgkinson had suggested, because they might be stolen. (It will be remembered that Hodgkinson simply took Dunlap's one-act sketch and made it into his own full-length play, but the fact that Milns could make this kind of reference suggests something about the atmosphere which the event must have created.) After the Manager is confronted with an actor and his wife who want jobs, the various members of the company complain about their dressing rooms. A shout reveals that Mrs. Johnson has "lost" herself. The scenery is in chaos; someone has walked over the new clouds with dirty feet; the rain is so dry that it rattles like snow; a dog steals someone's wig; finally the stage carpenters get into the act. Then the theatre doors are opened, and the Manager welcomes the audience. It is all a brief *tour de force*, but it does tell a number of things about the ways in which the late-eighteenth-century theatre operated.

While actors and actresses as well as visitors from England with varying ideas of permanency provided a substantial number of new plays which managers occasionally liked to bring out, there were also plays by American writers who showed an occasional interest in the theatre. Preserved by publication, those plays are representative of a greater productivity. At this early and strategic time in the creation of both a republic and a drama, all lines of contribution play a part, including the works of literary figures, amateur playwrights, hacks, and the would-be professional.

The subject matter which appealed to these late-eighteenth-century playwrights generally emphasized society, politics, patriotism, or, if the writer had a literary bent, some theme from classical tradition. At one extreme is the satiric farce such as *Sans Souci, alias Free and Easy; or, an Evening's Peep into a Polite Circle* (1785). A three-act farce of slight value either as literature or for stage production, it is sometimes attributed to Mercy Warren, but there is no hard evidence, and her authorship is most unlikely. As instruments for the author's satire, Young Forward and Little Pert compare Boston society with British "polite" society to the advantage of the former, while Mrs. Important and Mrs. Brilliance comment on fashions. Occasionally, there is wit such as that of the scene in which Forward and Pert become both the object and the means of satire as they plan to introduce plays on stage and then proceed to lectures on love and a "school of polite breeding." There are also two Negro servants who speak in dialect, but the work remains more a few scenes with satiric comments than a play.

A contrast in technique and subject matter, *The Fatal Effects of Seduction* (1789), a tragedy "by a friend of literature," shows the stuffy and too serious views of a pretentious writer at his moralistic worst. Writing in blank verse, the author attempts to dramatize the problem of Sophia Severus of Boston, the victim of "accursed seduction." Resisting all pleas, her dishonored father demands the seducer's name while ironically praising Lysander, the weakling Dimmesdale-type character whom Sophia will protect. "What not a single drop!" cries Lysander as he finds Sophia poisoned and tries to take his own life. Not until the epilogue, "spoken by an actor in female dress," is Lysander named and blamed as one who endangers female hearts. By attempting to make seduction in the abstract the villain, this work is more moral dissertation than drama, and, consistent with the practices of "Friends of Literature," the author evidently knew little about the theatre.

The morals of America were at least a pretended concern of a number of dramatists who could suggest national prejudices by finding a ready illustration of moral as well as social and political poverty in the British. *The Better Sort; or, The Girl of Spirit*, an anonymously written "operatical, comical farce" published in Boston in 1789, is a good example. After a prologue asserting that "a stage reforms the manners of a nation," the play, in ten scenes and an epilogue, satirizes moneygrubbing fathers and women who copy English fashion while showing how a "girl of spirit" wins the man she loves. Underlining the thesis is the British officer, Captain Flash, who is placed in constant argument with Yorick, a Yankee without an accent but clearly the voice of America. The plot is commonplace as Mira Lovemuch is being forced to abandon the man she loves, Harry Truelove, and to marry old Alonzo Hazard, whose money attracts her father. But Mira says "No!" and seems to mean it: "A virgin I'll live to E-ter-ni-ty" (iv). Politics enlivens the dialogue as Peter Lovemuch, Mira's father, declares, "I am a true Whig of '75 and a staunch Federalist of '89 and if you persevere to belittle my county, you'll anger me surely" (vi).

In a climactic nationalistic gesture, Flash, having endured Yorick's humorous dirge on the death of King George IV, drinks to the health of Mira and Harry and admits to being sufficiently instructed in the evening's conversation that, could he forget his king and country, he would settle in Boston. In his preface the author stated hopefully that his play would be a "very useful work," offered for the "amusement and edification of a credulous public." Better than did most playwrights at the time, the author used songs—"Had I a heart for falsehood framed," for example—to move the plot as well as to show local color. But the play is best appreciated as politically appropriate and topical satire, of interest more for some of the attitudes expressed than for theatre or literature.

Another play which mixed morals—the morals of business enterprise—with an American view is *The Wheel of Fortune* (1796–97), by St. George Tucker (1752–1827), a minor poet and lawyer who became a judge of the General Court of Virginia in 1788, and a professor of law at William and Mary in 1790.[6] Having before the Revolution visited relatives in New York and Philadelphia and been introduced to the theatre, Tucker became interested in native American drama. In the prologue to his play, he declared that the arts in America should "walk alone" without British influence and without the competition of imported plays—a fine early sentiment from the historical perspective but not a popular one at that time. The main plot deals with a miserly shipping merchant named Shee who tries to ruin an honest merchant in financial distress over a shipwreck by speculating on his cargo of flour. Underlying all action is a satire on Philadelphia merchants who speculate in money, goods, and land. As do many other ambitious amateur playwrights, Tucker wrote a complicated and unfinished play but one with some interesting characters. Shee's past activities in London, where he was known as Swindle, and his insistence on pro-British thought underline his villainy, while the references to the techniques of moneylending, the China trade, land speculation, and the intricacies of corrupt business transactions reveal something of the period. Wignell, with some comment about its inappropriateness at that time, refused to produce the play and Tucker, after some brief interest in the matter, went on to other things, returning to the drama briefly with *The Patriot Rous'd* and *The Patriot Cool'd* in 1812 and 1813, respectively.

Samuel Low (1765–18?) was an amateur poet and hopeful playwright who evidently made his living as a bank clerk in New York and as a Federalist officeholder. His play, *The Politician Outwitted*, written in 1788 and published in 1789 after being rejected by Hallam and Henry, shows a man of strong Federalist opinions who merged satire with comedy. As did some of the best satirists in English literature, he allowed himself a certain cynicism toward human nature. In "To a Spider" (from his poems published in 1800), he shows his distaste—"I like thee not, Arachne; thou art base"—by observing that "thou resemblist vicious *man* so much."

The Politician Outwitted is a long, five-act comedy combining some of the successful characters and patriotic attitudes from *The Contrast* with an ordinary comic love plot. Its *raison d'être*, however, was the new American Constitution, which had been finally ratified by the necessary number of states in June, 1788. Beginning with the opening scene, in which a character reads from a newspaper and comments on the events reported, there is a staunch defense of the Constitution and numerous references to local affairs in New York. The major plot revolves around Old Loveyet's admiration of Maria Aisy and his inability to see anything good in the Constitution. Although his name is a good clue to his comic abilities, his argument with Trueman, who favors the Constitution, shows the author's serious views. As a polemic, however, the play is wordy enough to be a little dull. "Your argument," Trueman tells Loveyet, "is heterodox, sophistical and most preposterously illogical" (II, ii). Finally, Old Loveyet is spurned by the flighty Maria and thus duped in both love and politics. To enliven the play Low adds a fop called Worthnaught, who uses French words, takes snuff, and flatters everyone, and Humphrey Cubb, a Jonathan-type clown who tells stories, misquotes proverbs, and doesn't know what the word *constitution* means. But they are not quite enough as the Federalist opinions get in the way of the comedy.

In the wake of the Revolution, all the major playwrights stressed nationalism while employing the devices and techniques of seventeenth- and eighteenth-century English comedy and heroic tragedy. Likewise, in the comedies and farces, pantomime-spectacles, and sketches by lesser playwrights, nationalistic gestures seemed mandatory. To the plays already noted, two more should be added. On April 17, 1797, *West Point Preserved* by William Brown was performed at the Haymarket Theatre in Boston, anticipating Dunlap's *André* by a year. Unfortunately, the playscript has not survived. *Columbia and Britannia*, "a dramatic piece," was published in New London in 1787, but its author is unknown, and it seems not to have been produced. The preface to the play identifies the dramatis personae: Fabius was Washington; Perjuris was Arnold. It is signed by "Philophron," who may have been a teacher because he wrote for the "improvement in Elocution, for a select number of students, at a public school." If he was a teacher, he was following the practice set by Brackenridge and those who wrote plays for the colleges.[7]

Commonplace in its nationalism, *Columbia and Britannia* was also typical of the spectacles which entertained the new country. The first of four acts opens in 1763 at the close of the French and Indian War when Columbia and Britannia enjoyed a child-parent relationship. Then, with a mixture of fact and myth, real and allegorical figures, poetry, song, and musical spectacle, the author chronicles the progress of Columbia. Threatened by Britannia's coercive measures to control the new land, Columbia declares war, with Washington her leader. Arnold's treachery is dramatized; Columbia asks Gallia for help; and Britannia begins to regret her role in suppressing liberty. There are harsh words for the British, but in the final act Columbia and Gallia are joined by Britannia in peaceful reconciliation: "unanimity and peace devine . . . in sweet'st contact bind."

A number of American writers tried to add plays to their contributions to the literature of the period. To help preserve those contributions, no matter how insignificant succeeding generations might regard them, Edmund Clarence Stedman and Ellen Mackay Hutchinson edited *A Library of American Literature* (1892), volume four of which, *Literature of the Republic, Part I, Constitutional Period, 1788–1820,* includes the work of one hundred writers, most of whom have been long forgotten. As would future American authors such as W. D. Howells or Henry James, perhaps these writers either felt a challenge to create for the theatre or accepted their success in one literary genre as an invitation to express themselves in another. The fact that they did have reputations in literature, however, reveals another response to the demands of the growing theatre in America. For the first dozen years of that "Constitutional Period," four of the writers listed by Stedman and Hutchinson tried at least once and with apparently little success to contribute to American dramatic literature: Elihu Hubbard Smith, Margaretta V. Faugeres, John Blair Linn, and William Munford.

Physician and man of letters, Elihu H. Smith (1771–1798) was during his brief life one of the brilliant young men of his age. Entering Yale College at the age of eleven, he graduated with the class of 1786 and then studied literature at Timothy Dwight's Greenfield Academy with the dream of being a poet. From 1788 through the winter of 1791 he studied medicine first with his father and later with Benjamin Rush. He then practiced medicine in Wethersfield, Connecticut, before moving in 1793 to New York, where he projected and edited the first American medical journal, *Medical Repository*, with two other doctors. In 1796 he was elected to the staff of one New York hospital. As a poet he is remembered as one of the "lesser" Hartford Wits, and his wider interests took him far beyond his medical career. In 1793, for example, he edited and published the first general anthology of American poetry, *American Poems, Selected and Original*, and, from the time he came to New York until his early death from yellow fever, he was an avid theatre-goer, a close friend of William Dunlap, and an active member of the Friendly Club. Considering all aspects of his dual career, however, there is no doubt that, for all of his intellectual brilliance and poetic skills, he was not destined to be a dramatist.

Smith's contribution to the American theatre, *Edwin and Angelina; or, The Banditti* (1797), an opera in three acts, illustrates one kind of play that theatre managers received from American writers and were forced to reject. There were exceptions, of course, but these were few. In this instance the interesting part is that Smith kept a diary which allows one to follow the mutual efforts and agonies of the dramatist and the theatre manager. Smith had written the script in 1791 and had added a scene in October, 1793, before the Old American Company accepted it for production the following June. Then came months of revision. Finally, by the fall of 1795, the music for the opera was ready, and Smith's diary shows that he followed the process of production very carefully. As time passed, he seemingly prepared himself not to be overjoyed if the play succeeded or greatly disappointed if it failed. Rehearsals did not go well, and he found the last one "most unpleasant." In terms of the way in which plays were usually produced at the time, however, it would appear that considerable effort was spent on the opera. But it failed, deservedly so. Looking back at its December 19, 1796, performance, Dunlap explained that it failed because it was "not sufficiently dramatic" in its structure.[8] In a letter to a friend on February 15, 1797, Smith explained that his opera "had not sufficient attraction for our laughter-loving citizens," and he then arranged to have his work published. Both Dunlap and Smith were right, but neither seemed willing to look at the work honestly.

The scene for this "serious" work in blank verse, as Smith described it, is a forest in Northern England where Sifred as head of the Banditti plans vengeance on Ethelbert, a tyrant who once imprisoned him and stole Emma, the girl he loved. In Act II Angelina, disguised as a pilgrim, meets Ethelbert, and there is much discussion of his regret of past actions and of her beauty, her virtue, and her desire for love. In a surprise attack Sifred and his men capture

Ethelbert, who admits his guilt and tells Sifred that Emma lives and loves him still. With this revelation the two men forgive and embrace. Act III has a divided plot that is difficult to reconcile. Because he was sworn to lead the Banditti, Sifred feels that he cannot leave them to be with Emma. Then Edwin enters the plot. Disguised as a hermit, he meets and recognizes Angelina but hides his discovery as she confesses her love for a youth whom she seemingly trifled with at some time. At a critical point Edwin reveals himself, and they embrace only to be discovered by Ethelbert, the object of Edwin's revenge until Angelina joins their hands in mutual forgiveness. The opera then ends as Sifred returns to Emma and vows to lead his men only in peaceful pursuits. Edwin also talks of peace and freedom as the chorus emphasizes this theme in its finale.

Obviously, the script posed difficulties, and it is probable that the music by Pelissier added very little. The involved plot is poorly structured, terribly disjointed, and burdened with unrelieved seriousness. In fact, it is difficult to determine the major characters or to know what the play is about. Neither Angelina nor Edwin is clearly drawn, and, whereas she appears first in Act II, he is not on stage until Act III, the final act. Emma, a major figure in the story, never appears. Sifred would seem to be the major character, whom Smith tries to portray as a wild, passionate, and distracted man, but his conflict is resolved early in the opera and by others. There is essentially no central conflict and very little action. Mainly, there is talk, long conversations in stiff, romantic language that is suited neither to the characters nor to the stage. Smith admitted taking some of the songs from Goldsmith's ballad "Edwin and Angelina," and the final act suggests that Smith was thinking of Washington and America in his concern for peace and freedom. But there was not enough substance or story to interest the theatre audiences. Nor would laughter have helped very much.

Less than a month after Smith's failure, on January 16, 1797, the John Street Theatre produced *Bourville Castle; or, the Gallic Orphan* by another brilliant young man, John Blair Linn. This was the second play by an American (in addition to two plays by himself) that Dunlap as comanager of the John Street Theatre had brought out this season, its appearance indicating an interest not shared by his colleagues. This play also had music, but by Benjamin Carr, and it survived a third performance, a benefit for the author. It was not published, however, and historians have done no more than to mention the play's title and to note that it was a serious drama in three acts. In his diary (February 28, 1796), Elihu H. Smith described it as "the composition of a young man" which was "eminently wanting in dramatic propriety," a comment which came after he read the play at Dunlap's suggestion. After the play's production, almost a year later, Smith called it a "serio-comico-musico-Drama" and noted that despite its three performances it was not well received except by Linn's friends, who "exerted themselves" in his behalf. Perhaps Smith's sense of competition flavored his bias, but he was at least consistent: he also described one of Dr. Linn's sermons as "miserable."

Others had quite different opinions of Linn's work, but none imagined the drama to be his forte. Deeply immersed in the classics, his writing showed little concern for the life around him. If his poetry provides a clue to his drama—and one might presume that it would—*Bourville Castle* was an unrelieved tragedy in blank verse with many classical references and an inclination toward that melancholy attitude frequently found in the romantic and the Gothic schools. A reviewer of Linn's poem "The Powers of Genius," in which he considers the nature, operation, origin, and progress of genius, complained, "When, oh when, shall the idolatry of learning be superseded by the worship of the truth!"[9] Perhaps Smith was not all wrong.

John Blair Linn (1777–1804), born in Pennsylvania, was a third-generation American with social and cultural credentials. According to Charles Brockden Brown, who married Linn's sister and who wrote a sketch of his "life and character," Linn enjoyed "the theatre [as] his chief passion" in college. After graduation he studied law under Alexander Hamilton but was evidently tired of that pursuit by 1796, the year that *Bourville Castle* was produced. Brown notes that Linn had written "many dramatic works" previously but that this was the first to be staged. By 1795, the year he graduated from college, he had also published *Miscellaneous Works, Prose and Political*, which included such works as an essay on Pelopidas and Epaminondas and "Melancholy. An Ode," in which one may find the following youthful lines: "On yonder barren isle in dreary cells,/ The dread enchantress, Melancholy, dwells." Almost immediately after the performance of his play, Linn decided to dedicate his "future to service in the church." No longer interested in the drama, he wrote during the remainder of his brief life sermons and the poetry for which he is remembered, if slightly, by historians of American literature.

Margaretta Bleecker Faugeres' *Belisarius* is another first-and-only play, also an unrelieved, five-act tragedy in verse. Probably never performed but published in 1795, *Belisarius* is a moral polemic with a protagonist not unlike the mythical all-American hero. Faugeres (1771–1801) was very romantic and idealistic if her poem "To the Moon" is any indication of her attitudes. In her play Belisarius (c.505–565), once a victorious general but now blind and banished by the emperor, Justinian, represents the power of love over hate. As public sympathy for the blind general builds, the emperor repents of his actions and the two men are reconciled. Belisarius, more pathetic than tragic, has the curtain line: "my men, when gathering wreaths of fame,/ Pause a few moments in their golden travel,/ and spend a casual thought on Belisarius." Although the play is a weak, beginning effort, the Gothic description of Roman prisons, the references to America, and the strong moral were obviously intended to satisfy the popular tastes of the day.

William Munford (1775–1825) was the son of Robert Munford, the Virginia politician and dramatist. William, in fact, was responsible for the publication of his father's plays and continued his father's interest in the drama and in writing in general. Perhaps his most significant work was a translation of Homer's *Iliad*, which he completed the year he died. Much as does that of Smith, Linn, and Faugeres, his drama shows both his classical education and his acceptance of the moral pressures of his day. And, as did those writers, he too created a play, *Almoran and Hamet*, more for the closet than for the theatre. Published with his *Poems* in 1798, the play was written, Munford stated, "to shew the evils of arbitrary power and to inculcate the proper sentiment of the passions and resignation to the Will of God."

Almoran and Hamet is a pseudoromantic tragedy in blank verse which employs both Western Gothic and Oriental characteristics in a classical framework following the unities of time (twenty-four hours), place (Persia in all acts), and action. The plot relates the efforts of Almoran, an evil tyrant, to rid Persia of his co-ruler and brother, Hamet, and seize the throne for himself. Most interesting, however, is the true cause of Almoran's unhappiness, which is also the source of his malevolence: through the help of a "Genius" he always gets his own way. Hamet, a man of goodness and values, is the complete opposite of his brother. Finally, Almoran asks his "Genius" for the death of Hamet and dies himself, for this is the one command which, his "Genius" said, "would be directed back on himself." The irony and the moral theoretically unite to good effect, but the problem, as with most of these plays by minor poets with a casual interest in the theatre, lies in the author's weak knowledge of dramatic structure and in his inability to develop a character through dialogue and action.

Although William Dunlap, through his close association with the theatre as a manager, is the single early example of the writer who might have legitimately called himself a professional dramatist for a certain period, there were others even before the turn of the century who aspired to that title. No one, of course, could earn a living writing plays at this time in America. Necessarily, then, those seriously interested in writing for the American theatre had other careers outside the theatre—that is, they were not actors or managers writing to supply their own needs. Nor were they basically literary people who might try the drama once and find it unsuited to their talents or interests. They might be inclined toward writing of some sort—journalism or belles lettres—but they were for the most part simply interested in writing for the theatre which they themselves enjoyed.

Peter Markoe (1752–1792) was such a person. Born on St. Croix, he was educated at Pembroke College in Oxford before being admitted to Lincoln's Inn. By 1775 he had taken up residence in Philadelphia and become a captain in the Light Horse, 3rd Battalion, of the Philadelphia City Militia, but he still took occasional trips back to St. Croix. After the Revolution he lived permanently in Philadelphia until his death. His writings show his classical training as well as his love of liberty and his dislike of government by aristocracy. He also seems to have had a good sense of humor and an ability to handle satire, which is best revealed in one of his prose works, *The Algerian Spy in Pennsylvania; or, Letters Written by a Native of Algiers on the Affairs of the United States of America from the Close of the Year 1783 to the Meeting of the Convention* (1787). This book contains letters from Mehemet as he comes to America, stopping first at Gibraltar, where his humorous satire centers on the Jewish merchants, then at Lisbon. Finally, he arrives in Philadelphia and lets his pen run wild on many aspects of society, including the three tyrannies—civil, ecclesiastical, and that of fashion. Throughout, however, he has great praise for Washington and the new society.

Neither of Markoe's two plays was acted. *The Patriot Chief* (1784), a five-act tragedy in blank verse, was evidently offered to Hallam, who refused it, whereas *The Reconciliation; or, the Triumph of Nature* (1790), was duly approved for production by the chief justice of Pennsylvania but subsequently withdrawn from the theatre manager after having been kept for four months without being produced. On reading *The Reconciliation* one can sympathize with the manager, but there is in *The Patriot Chief* occasional dramatic power as well as a strong thesis describing the dangers inherent in a government by the aristocracy. The opening scene of *The Patriot Chief* emphasizes that thesis as the villain, Otanes, complains that the people under King Dorus' rule in Sardia have too much control. Although Otanes' plans to murder the king are thwarted by his own son, Araspes, a member of the king's family is killed, and Araspes, confessing his foreknowledge, begs for justice. Years earlier Dorus had sent his son away because an oracle declared that Dorus' son, though guiltless, would be sent to death by a crowd. Now the crowd demands Araspes' death, but its temper is changed when ancient records reveal that Araspes is really Dorus' son. The basic irony of the father-son relationship carries much of the suspense of the play, but there is a great deal of emphasis on contrasts: war and peace, age and youth, and political horror and pastoral happiness. The play is as good as many produced at this time although the weakening of the villain's position in the final act and the overwhelming emphasis on the positive side of the contrasts show the dramatist's greater concern for message than for drama.

The Reconciliation is actually an opera in two acts, described as a version, with new songs, characters, and dialogue, as well as a "correction" of *Erastus* by the German writer Gessner. The plot is very simple. Wilson, as admirable as he is poor, has been renounced by his unreasonable father. Finally, Simon, Wilson's servant, decides to commit robbery. Why should he, with such a fine master, be poor while there are scoundrels who are rich? But the results are not what he expected, and his good master returns the money, along with "All I possess in undividing probity, and an unsullied conscience," to the victim, an old gentleman, who replies, "How enviable your situation!" Father—for the victim is Old Wilson—and son are thus united and reconciled. With his attitude toward life and his humorous actions, only Simon gives the play any distinction.

David Humphreys (1752–1818) does not fit neatly into any category. A diplomat and man of letters, he published one original play, *The Yankey in England* (1815), which is a small landmark in the progress of American drama. Prior to 1800 he adapted the French tragedy by Le Mierre, *La Veuve du Malabar; ou, L'Empire des Costumes*, as *The Widow of Malabar; or, The Tyranny of Custom*, a faithful rendering but not a slavish copy of his model. Although his letters reveal that he had other, original plays projected, none appeared, and he was best known in literary circles as a writer of prose and poetry. Having graduated from Yale in 1771, his association with John Trumbull and Timothy Dwight inspired him to poetry. Then the Revolution changed his plans, and he rose in the military ranks to be a colonel on Washington's staff. From 1784 to 1786 he worked in London and Paris (where he may have seen *La Veuve du Malabar*) with Jefferson, Adams, and Franklin in negotiating treaties of commerce. For the next two years, as a member of the Connecticut Assembly, he was recognized as one of the satirical Connecticut Wits, and, with Trumbull, Dwight, and Joel Barlow, contributed to *The Anarchiad*. In other poetry, some of which was extremely popular, Humphreys emphasized the beauties of America, which he served in several capacities, most particularly as minister plenipotentiary to Spain in 1796.

The Widow of Malabar, called a tragedy in five acts and written in blank verse of a very ordinary kind, was first produced at the Southwark Theatre in Philadelphia on May 7, 1790, and was performed in subsequent years in New York and Baltimore as well as in Philadelphia. Will the widow of the ambassador give herself to the funeral pyre? That is the question in Malabar as a young Brahmin argues the inhumanity of the law governing this practice with the high priest. The law also bothers the widow, who tells a friend about the young Frenchman she loved before her father forced her to marry the man who just died. When it is discovered that the Brahmin is the widow's brother and that her lover still lives, the plot is set. A French general in Malabar, aware of a widow about to cast herself on the funeral pyre, becomes incensed at "these abominable rites" and plans "to save the fair and abrogate your law" (III, v). As the widow prepares to do her duty, the Priest explains that "India calls/ For courage from a soul sublime, like yours" (IV, i). Then, in good melodramatic fashion, the general arrives at the pyre at the head of his troops. Recognizing him, the widow exclaims, "Oh! Montalban!—my deliverer!" and they are happily reunited. Unfortunately, the excitement of the last act is delayed by a tiresome argument on the issue between the Brahmin and the priest. There is, in fact, little action in the play, which is largely a discussion of the "abominable rite" presented from several points of view. Both the prologue and the epilogue, written with John Trumbull, contain some praise of America, and the epilogue, spoken by the widow, provides the single humorous line, a very understandable comment: "I liked a lover better than a grave."

Elihu Hubbard Smith observed in a letter to Samuel M. Hopkins (February 15, 1797) that Boston was becoming as "stage-mad" as it had once been "church-mad." Although it had been only since 1792 that Boston had provided any recognized theatre, by the time of Smith's letter both the Federal Street and the Haymarket theatres had opened, and dramatic entertainment seemed well under way. With popular encouragement some writers around Boston began to think about the theatre, not in a major way—that would come much later—but with a few offerings. One of these, Judith Sargent Murray (1751–1820) wrote two plays for the Boston theatre: *The Medium; or Happy Tea Party* was performed on March 2, 1795,[10] and *The Traveller Returned* was performed at least twice, once on March 9, 1796, and again "for the benefit of the poor widows and orphans of the town of Boston." For these performances Mrs. Murray was not identified as the author; in fact, her husband publicly denied her authorship of either play. In addition to avoiding the possible stigma attached to playwriting, Mrs. Murray may have chosen anonymity as a reaction to criticism, for between the fourth and fifth acts of the play, an "Apology for the Author," spoken by Mrs. S. Powell, implied that the author felt herself rudely handled by critics.

Mrs. Murray's reputation in American letters rests mainly on her work as an editor and on her essays, most of which were published in the *Gleaner*, Mrs. Murray's periodical, and signed as written by "Constantia." Primarily concerned with the rights of women, she published her first essay, "Encouraging a Degree of Self-Complacency, Especially in Female Bosoms" in 1784. Other essays included "Observations on Female Attitudes" and "The Equality of the Sexes." Influenced by the writings of Mary Wollstonecraft, she enthusiastically hailed "our young women forming a new era in female history" and assuming the equality "assigned them in the Order of Nature."

It was after her second marriage, to the Reverend John Murray, the founder of the Universalist denomination in America, that Mrs. Murray began to write in earnest, generally on moral, female, patriotic, and religious topics. After moving to Boston in 1793, she began to write prologues and epilogues for plays and to show a marked interest in the drama. Issue number 24 of the *Gleaner*, for example, contains "Panegyric on the Drama," in which she explained both her views and hopes: "From a chaste and discreetly regulated theatre many attendant advantages will indisputably result. Young persons will acquire a refinement of taste and manners; they will learn to think, speak, and act with propriety; a thirst for knowledge will be originated; and from attentions, at first, perhaps, constituting only the amusement of the hour, they will gradually proceed to more important inquiries."[11] Although idealistic in her observations, she was a sensible and intelligent person looking—she knew not how far—into the future. "From an infant stage," she wrote, "I look for improvement." Her own plays, unfortunately, add little to American drama. The imitative qualities of her work suggest that she was well educated, while her views reflect a strong character that seems to force contrived climaxes. This is particularly true of her first play. Her second play is better plotted but becomes a rather ordinary situation comedy. She published both plays—five-act comedies—in the *Gleaner* in 1798.

With publication, Mrs. Murray changed the title of *The Medium* to *Vir-*

tue Triumphant and provided an introduction by "Philo Americanus," who commented on the 1795 performance. The antagonist of the play is Maitland, a money-worshipping man who argues for self-balance, the "medium," and is angry with his son, Charles, who has forsaken the medium and who has declared his intention to marry Eliza Clairville. Although she has neither relatives nor wealth, Eliza is a strong and determined person, more heartless than Mrs. Murray might have intended and, indeed, the epitome of all snobbish virtues. She lets it be known that Maitland will never call her daughter-in-law without his "avowed desire." She will never, never marry "but on equal terms." As secondary characters, Mrs. Bloomsbury and Dorinda Scornwell, a fashionable lady who likes cards rather than conversation and a ballroom rather than a playhouse, enjoy a different view of marriage and are part of the author's satire on current fashion. After Maitland is persuaded to pay Eliza a "visit of acknowledgement" and is duly impressed, his objections quickly vanish, especially when the wealthy Colonel Melfort reveals that he is Eliza's uncle. "Virtue is still triumphant" says the Colonel for reasons that remain rather confused, and the curtain falls. Although the artifice of the climax weakens the play, the issue of the self-assertive woman is clearly stated and occurs very early in the history of America.

Taking America as her scene in *The Traveller Returned*, Mrs. Murray praised Washington and "the people of America" and introduced such characters as a Yankee named Obadiah, Irish servants, and a German landlord and his wife, all complete with accents. In a plot that is typical of the novels of the time, Rambleton returns to his home town after an absence of nineteen years and shares lodgings at an inn with young Major Camden. In another part of town, Mrs. Montague lectures her daughter, Harriet, on the seriousness of marriage and the necessity of controlling passion with reason. Many years back her worthy husband abandoned her and left her with their four-year-old son. As time and scenes pass, Mrs. Montague becomes suddenly aware that Major Camden, whom she wishes her daugher to marry, bears a resemblance to her husband. After the plot is interrupted by a drunk scene among the Irish servants and by a spectacular ballroom scene during which Mrs. Montague mysteriously receives a picture of herself, it is revealed that Rambleton is her husband and Major Camden, their son. It is a happy reunion, particularly for Harriet and Camden, both of whom had other partners in mind. The play ends with a dance. To lighten her inclination toward long, dull dialogue, Mrs. Murray used dialects, spectacle, and nationalistic scenes, but her plays are distinguished mainly by the issues she dramatized.

David Everett (1770–1813), another native of Massachusetts, enjoyed successful careers in law, oratory, and journalism, all of which are reflected in the two plays he wrote. For all his activity it is one of the ironies of fate that he is mainly remembered for what he must have considered an insignificant work of his youth: "Lines Spoken by a Boy of Seven Years," a poem he wrote for a student at New Ipswich, where he taught after graduation from Dartmouth College.[12] In later years he contributed to such periodicals as *Russell's Gazette* and the *Farmer's Museum* and wrote an essay of some distinction, "The Rights and Duties of Nations."

Everett's first play, *Slaves in Barbary*, a drama in two acts, appears not to have been performed professionally but was published in Caleb Bingham's *Columbian Orator* (1797). As does Everett's other writing, this play shows his interest in the affairs of America and his enthusiasm for personal freedom and liberty. Essentially, it is a propaganda piece with plenty of action on stage, stereotyped characters, stilted prose mixed with Irish and Negro dialects, and a contrived, oratorical ending. The major action of the play is a slave auction in Tunis which contrasts the views of Oran the slaver—"If there are lords, there must be slaves, and what must be is right" (II, i)—and those of Hamet, the humanitarian Bashaw of Tunis. At the slave market America seems to be represented by Kidnap, who has a Negro slave, Sharp, and when both are purchased by the same slave owner, Sharp is put in charge—a bold statement by Everett, who had very definite opinions. The last speech of the play also illustrates his sterling sentiments: "Let it be remembered, there is no luxury so exquisite as the exercise of humanity, and no part so honorable as his, who defends the Rights of Man." Ironically, this speech is given by Hamet, who, although a compassionate man, still traffics in human lives and seems a poor spokesman for the author's point of view. The humanitarian and pro-Negro sentiments plus the oratorical speeches give this play some distinction although, dramatically, it is typical of its day.

Everett's second play, *Daranzel; or, the Persian Patriot*, was performed at the Haymarket in Boston on April 16, 1798, and was revived for two performances at the Federal Street Theatre on January 29 and February 5, 1800. It was also published in 1800 with the comment that it was "improved" by a "literary friend" who is otherwise unidentified. In the prologue of this five-act historical tragedy in blank verse, there is reference to America and a concern that "dove-eyed peace succeed to war's alarm" with the inference to be drawn that Daranzel's struggle reflects the revolutionary struggle just completed in America. Dedicated to freedom in Persia as the champion of his people, Daranzel must contend with two villains, one dangerously straight-forward and the other cowardly. In contrast to many contemporary melodramas, women have a substantial role in the play in providing necessary exposition, establishing traditional themes (that is, refusing love until Persia is free, or honor before love), and reacting to reports of battle. Scenes in dark prisons, the capture of the castle, and the burning of the fleet enliven the plot, which is finally climaxed with a battle in which the strong villain—"Integrity, thou art the fool of fortune"—is killed while the cowardly one stabs himself ("Cursed fate!"). Daranzel, who is then united with his family, has the curtain line: "Now let this war of bleeding brothers cease." As had his other published play, this one has some moving speeches, obviously Everett's forte in the drama.

Ironically enough, rather little is known of one of the most productive playwrights writing for the American theatre during the last decade and a half of the eighteenth century. This was John Murdock (1748–1834), who published his first play, *The Triumphs of Love*, in the fashion of his time as "written by an American and a citizen of Philadelphia." He seems to have been a barber by profession; at least that occupation is indirectly reflected in his plays, which are filled with the topics of the day. Interested in the human nature that surrounded him, he was obviously a shrewd man with a good wit, a sense of humor, and a distinct talent for ridiculing society. Had he possessed friends in the right places or a wealthy patron, he would almost certainly have become America's first successful hack playwright.

There is no doubt that Murdock enjoyed the theatre and, by reason of his numerous nights there, felt that he knew something about it. Otherwise, his life is a mystery although he probably did not receive much formal education. In his preface to the publication of his third play, *The Beau Metamorphized*, he freely stated that "the author does not presume to rank himself among the learned; he is sensible of the disadvantage he labours under in point of education and situation in life." But he was a perceptive man who held well-considered opinions of theatre audiences as well as of local and national affairs. If not well read he at least knew what was happening in the limited world he saw every day, and he had the courage and determination to argue strongly when he felt that his plays were not being given a proper hearing. The play whose treatment he particularly resented was his first, *The Triumphs of Love; or, Happy Reconciliation*, which the manager of the New Theatre had produced on May 22, 1795, in a cut version but refused a second performance after it was published with a substantial subscription of seven hundred. As did innumerable playwrights who were to follow, Murdock complained that he had "been most shamefully treated by the managers of the New Theatre" and tried to take his grievances to the public.[13] And when this did not bring satisfaction, he reacted again in a manner that would become popular. The doors of the press, he subsequently maintained, were shut against him through the influence of the theatre managers. Finally, he simply published his three plays, of which only the first was performed. Perhaps he had a legitimate complaint. Although his topics were usually local and timely, his first two plays are still quite lively reading, whereas the third falls victim to what might have been a habit of verbosity. In background, education, and age, he seems to have been quite different from other identifiable playwrights of this period. Certainly, he wanted to write more plays and might well have done so with more sympathetic theatre managers. What he did write contributed well to the slight farce-comedy which was to be a staple in American drama for more than a hundred years.

In *The Triumphs of Love*, a comedy in four acts, Murdock shows his familiarity with contemporary drama as well as with the contemporary scene. And his view of both brings a humorous understanding of human nature that distinguishes the play. For his thesis he undertakes to comment on a traditional theme of heroic tragedy, love versus honor, in which honor must always be satisfied first. In a burlesque reference to Tyler's Colonel Manly in *The Contrast*, Murdock not only demotes his creation to Major Manly (although the name does become alliterative) but has him act in a way quite opposite to Tyler's character. In love with a certain girl, Major Manly debates the love-versus-honor topic with himself and finally discovers that "love has triumphed." Although Murdock's stern Quaker characters, with their clannishness and conservative views, reveal a serious interest in social problems, he pokes fun at the Society of Friends and their leader, George Fox, by calling his freewheeling hero George Friendly. Among the other characters George's servant, Sambo, is the best-conceived Negro in American drama of that period. Although a comic stereotype with the usual dialect, songs, and dances, Sambo is perceptive of his own situation as well as of others', and he is particularly clever in his imitation of the faults of his masters. Consistent with Quaker philosophy, George frees Sambo and treats him honestly as a human being.

Murdock also introduces a German watchman and an Irish servant, who enliven the dialogue, along with two American dandies, Trifle and Careless, whose actions ridicule the American tendency to imitate the foibles of English society. Throughout, Murdock is distinctly American and manages to include nationalistic comments on the Whiskey Rebellion, the problems in Algiers, and patriots in general. In a historical view his play contains the approach to native drama which Tyler initiated but adds more attitudes that are distinctively American.

With all of these interesting features, it is unfortunate that the plot of *The Triumphs of Love* is a contrived and rather formless mixture of some good incidents and characters terminating in a weak climax. Compensating virtues appear in the farce action, witty lines, and fast-moving dialogue. When Trifle tells George that he is in love, for example, George immediately surmises that the "damsel is black," knowing that Trifle is "fond of variety." George himself will not marry unless he can have a thousand wives, an idea that worries Jacob, his conservative father. George's foil is Major Manly, a stiff, formal, patriotic spectacle whose love for George's sister, Rachel, is thwarted by their father, who will allow her to marry no one but a Quaker. As a farcical interlude Murdock has George attempt an assignation with a seducible Mrs. Peevish only to be discovered by her suspicious husband, who dresses himself as a woman and hides in the closet. A bit of plot intrudes into the farce action when a man who is planning to leave the country asks George to look out for his sister, Clementine. Meanwhile, Rachel elopes with Manly as Murdock contrasts Manly's cloying patriotism with George and Trifle's light-hearted attitudes toward life, and climaxes Act III with a boisterous drinking scene. All problems are then solved before Act IV, in which a reformed George presents his wife, Clementine, and everyone asks forgiveness of Jacob who, having changed his views, joins with the others to declare that virtuous love has triumphed. Although the effect of the play is scattered, there is a pleasing vitality about it.

The Politicians; or, A State of Things (1798), Murdock's second play, is essentially a political argument in two acts. More fully than other plays of the period, it reflects the violent differences of opinion in America and the general uneasiness of a new nation. Washington's Neutrality Proclamation in 1793 had not stopped the English from selling weapons to the Indians or from attacking American merchantmen in the West Indies. Determined to avoid war and stay in the good graces of the English rather than the French, the Federalists sent John Jay to London, where he completed the Treaty of 1794, which by its concessions enraged the Jeffersonians. As a reaction, in 1796 the French refused to receive Charles C. Pinckney as a replacement for James Monroe as Minister to France. By 1797 the French were also seizing defenseless American merchantmen, and the new Adams administration was facing grave problems. By using farce characters Murdock was able to make telling comments on the political situation.

The play begins as Mrs. Turbulent argues abusively over the Treaty of 1794 with Mrs. Violent, who hates the French and "our devilish democracy." Partial, Hardy, and Crusty express their views with fanatic intolerance of each other as O'Callaghan Sarcastic chastizes Monsieur Aristocrat for his impudent and ungrateful opposition to the government. Reacting to much of this, the Negro servants, whom Murdock portrays with considerable skill, humorously argue their master's opinions. As Sambo explains, his master "damn French, damn English; he for his country." Sauney Biscuit's suggestion that they read the treaty impresses none of the group, whose discussion is climaxed with a dinner at Conciliate's house. There a disagreement on the subject they can toast erupts into a pitched battle, and the final speech, obviously the author's opinion, is quite without reference to the foregoing action and dialogue. It also suggests that the play was written before Washington left office in March, 1797: "I trust that people will know how to prize their singular happy situation among the nations of the earth, and join heart and hand in supporting the tired patriot who is at the head of their national affairs." Like Murdock's first, this play was published as "written by an American."

Murdock offered his third play, *The Beau Metamorphized; or, The Generous Maid*, an afterpiece in two acts, to the managers of the New Theatre in Philadelphia in 1800 only to have them reject it. As he had done previously, he built this play around a series of incidents rather than a structured story line. Most of the incidents, however, pertain to the efforts of a Mrs. Sprightly to change Vainly, "a young foreigner on his travels, carried away by national prejudices, but naturally of a good heart," to her "republican standard." Yet the process of his change is lost in the variety of entertaining episodes through which Murdock expresses his pro-American policies and his opinions on the American theatre. He also manages a comment or two for his critics. Bob Stubbles clearly refers to John Murdock, the barber, when he mentions a song written by a man "belonging to our town" named Tom Scribble, a cobbler. Says Stubble, "Swagger the lawyer, Dr. Sneer, and Parson Guttle run him down all they can; they say 'cobbler had better stick to his last'; they think, because he was not brought up in a high place of learning, he can't have any sense" (I, ii). The "Song of St. Tammany's Day" follows, a sprightly song in Murdock's pro-American style that should have brought him friends.

The American sentiments of *The Beau Metamorphized* are immediately apparent. Although Mrs. Sprightly is fond of Vainly, she is critical of his "prejudices in favor of his own nation; he won't admit that the Americans have any genius or any taste; he is continually ridiculing the American character" (I, i). Throughout the play Vainly is the target for Yankee comment. When he complains to his tailor that he makes clothes fit only for a mechanic to wear, the tailor responds: "Who has a better right to wear good and well-fitted clothes than mechanics? Are they not the most useful and industrious part of the people?" (II, i). Vainly's servant gets into trouble by saying that "the American government was something like our English one, but not so good" with the result that "a great big fisted fellow swore that if I made that comparison again, he would beat my English head flat as a flounder" (II, vi). When Vainly finally asks Miss Sprightly's forgiveness, she gives him her conditions: that he subscribe a gift for the poor, that he take "the pad from his neck cloth," and that he never ridicule the American character again. To this he readily consents and comments that love has "completely metamorphized [him] to your republican system" (II, vii). Although much of this farce is obvious flag-waving, it is done with spirit.

There is another aspect of *The Beau Metamorphized* (somewhat imitative of *The Contrast*) which deserves comment—the references to plays and theatre critics which occur in the first scene of Act I. Vainly has just seen a play which nearly "suffocated" him, and Sprightly replies, in words that practically repeat the current printed criticisms, that "it no doubt has its defects, as most dramatic pieces have, yet the audience were highly entertained with it; it went off with great éclat." When it turns out that the play was written by an American, Murdock's satiric barb catches a personal issue as Vainly sneeringly comments that "it is a mere farce for your [American] first classics to attempt a dramatic piece; your country affords no matter, no subject, no, nothing to lay the ground-work of a play upon" (I, i). This is early in the development of American literature for such a comment, which would, however, be repeated and far too easily believed for nearly a hundred years. Stubbles, the Yankee servant in the play, first saw Mr. Ricketts, whom he called "the devil on horseback," when he visited the well-known Ricketts Circus. Then he saw two plays—"one made me cry desperately, and the other made me laugh terribly"—and went on to describe them in humorous terms (I, ii).

Although frustrated by his failures with theatre managers, Murdock seems to have been a patriotic American, proud of writing. And for this time he wrote very well, creating comic dialogue that ranks with that of Tyler, Dunlap, and Munford. His major problem was an inability to structure a well-plotted play. Although his characters were usually stereotypes, he used them well in farce episodes. When one reads the innumerable plays by people with greater pretensions and fewer skills that were performed on the stage, it seems unfortunate that Murdock's particular talents were not encouraged.

That period between the end of the Revolution and the beginning of Jefferson's administration is generally discussed in terms of Tyler's *The Contrast* and the contributions of William Dunlap. This is an unfortunate oversimplification although the plays of those two dramatists are certainly distinctive. Vitally important in an assessment of the drama is the manner in which the managers of the newly developing theatres in America tried to satisfy their patrons. Mainly, of course, English actors controlled the theatre; English and European dramatists provided them with plays. It was not a time when Americans were encouraged to write for the theatre, and yet in some ways the demands made by a theatre which had to suit American audiences required new plays that only Americans could write. John Murdock, for example, felt very strongly on this point. The theatre is a mirror that reflects a society, and to reveal it the dramatist must be close at hand. Consequently, encouraged or not, quite a variety of Americans tried to satisfy the distinctly American audience and began to write, successfully or unsuccessfully, the kinds of plays that would be popular for years to come. A standard was not established, the playwrights mainly lacking the experience and talent to do so, but, in general, the early course of American drama was being decided during the period between 1783 and 1800.

SEVEN

"A Motley Spectacle":
Attempting to Focus the Drama
of a People, 1801-1814

MOVING INTO a new century, the people of the United States began to assert their independence and individuality. They had never enjoyed a feeling of complete unity, even during the Revolution, but under the leadership of General Washington there had been an understanding that an ability existed among the American people to form that "more perfect union." With the election of 1800 the disruptive force of the bitter factionalism that divided Federalists and Democrats filtered through politics into religion, social institutions, and the arts. Contradictory prejudices among the American people dominated the scene until the War of 1812. Presumably, the spirit of American democracy was revealed in every action—political, social, and artistic—but that "spirit" has always been difficult to define.

The theatre had been sufficiently established in the eighteenth century to penetrate the main settlements from Portland, in what would become the state of Maine, to Charleston in South Carolina, but theatres seldom have better drama than the audiences demand. Who, then, constituted the audiences for whom American dramatists must create? Without question, during nearly the first decade and a half of the nineteenth century, America held a diverse and, to the foreigner at least, an odd and uneasy population. According to Henry Adams, in his authoritative *History of the United States of America during the Administrations of Jefferson and Madison*, neither the character of the American people nor its government was substantially formed until 1815. Only then did Americans know where they were headed. Writing of "the Western World," that "long-wished-for sight," William Wordsworth saw only "a motley spectacle" in the new nation. It was not a kind view, but, in some respects, certainly through the eyes of an established European, it was not incorrect either. For the American dramatist, courageous enough to combat prejudice and disdain fame and honor, that "motley spectacle" was his to represent in the theatre.

In 1800 America had a population of 5,308,483; ten years later it had added nearly two million people. Of that earlier figure one-fifth were slaves, and fewer than 500,000 lived west of the Appalachian chain. Boston was a city of 24,800 in 1800 (32,000 in 1810). New York grew from 60,000 in 1800 to 96,400 in 1810 yet remained an unimpressive city, a seaport with attendant sanitation and security problems. Philadelphia in 1800 was a much more thriving city of 96,000 inhabitants with a good market, industry, and public spirit, but it was not destined to grow at New York's rate nor to reach that city's eventual importance as a social and theatre center. Virginia was the most populous and powerful of the states, while South Carolina had perhaps the greatest mercantile potential. With a population of only 18,000 in 1800, Charleston seemed to be the most promising of American cities. In 1810 it had a population of 24,700, but by 1820 it had added fewer than a hundred people.

Obviously, theatre activity is dependent on major population centers. During the 1800–1814 period theatre in America remained almost entirely east of the mountains, and managers were generally content simply to establish their activities in sites already penetrated. With theatre thus concentrated in the major towns and cities, travel between those cities was necessary as acting companies toured or individual starring actors played in the different theatres. But river travel was very poor; ocean travel, only a little better. On land one went by stagecoach—three days from Boston to New York on a triweekly schedule, two days between Philadelphia and New York with coaches leaving once a day. South of the Potomac one went mainly on horseback because there were no roads except between Charleston and Savannah. Early actors who published their memoirs did not fail to provide grim details of their travel experiences. As Timothy Dwight explained in his *Travels in New-England and New-York* (1823), however, "an inn is a very imperfect representative of the town in which it stands; and neither an inn-keeper, nor his servants, ought to be considered as standards of intelligence, character, or manners of the inhabitants at large" (vol. 4, p. 331). Dwight was trying to defend his country against the assaults on it by foreigners, and his protest, though not so dramatic as he meant it to be, had substance. Compared with the European, the American certainly had no literature, arts, sciences, nor history. Generally unable to express himself effectively, he was a sanguine, self-confident individual, intelligent, industrious, and inventive. His basic, simple conservatism, buttressed by severe prejudices in 1800, was forever at war with his idealism. Although his singular pride in his country revealed mainly the opportunity he saw for making money, it also showed his ignorance of much that was transpiring in the world around him. He was eager to work and ready for the power which he envisioned as a consequence of the ideal government he worked to establish. If his society was somber, it was because he had little time for social amenities, absorbed as he was in the pride of possession and accumulation which foreigners could little understand. From one point of view, the democratic concept, so poorly understood, lulled the citizenry into the cultural inertia which masks this early period in the nineteenth century.

People enjoyed entertainment, of course; at least, some did. There was some fashionable society in all three of the major distinguishable areas in the United States at this time. The social aristocracy of Tidewater Virginia, the Patroons of New York, and the socially elite of Boston were recognized, but these groups comprised only a small portion of the New World population, and the gap between rural and urban social levels in both Virginia and New England was great. In general, society was coarse and conservative. No Sunday travel was allowed in Massachusetts or Connecticut, and there was still a broad fear of the drama throughout New England. Yet, despite numerous admonitions to the contrary, some people persisted in attending the theatre. Dwight declared that for Americans in general "the principal amusements of the inhabitants are visiting, dancing, music, conversation, walking, riding, sailing, shooting at a mark, draughts, chess, and, unhappily, in some of the larger towns, cards and dramatic exhibitions" (vol. 4, p. 343). Balls and cotillions were more popular in the South, which was presumably less interested in money and more concerned with manners than was the North. For rural areas everywhere, there was horse racing and the rough-and-tumble fight as parallel entertainment with the card table, drawing room, or theatre of urban society.

Whatever their interest in entertainment as determined by social level, the greatest obstacle in the path of the American people was to be found "in the human mind." At least, this was the opinion of Henry Adams, who blamed, in part, conservative habits. People, for example, were hostile to banks although banks were necessary to their successful economy. They accepted roads as vital to a new democratic nation, but they were indifferent to paying for them. Although the education of that American "mind," particularly in New England, had been a strong concern during the colonial period, in 1800 Noah Webster declared that learning in America was possible only on a superficial level. Public libraries possessed fewer than 50,000 volumes, and one-third of these were theological. Colleges, too, were "disgracefully destitute" in their libraries and superficial in the education they provided. Even Harvard College, with four professors and four tutors in 1800, had progressed little in its past eighty years. Although there were several newspapers in America in 1800, advertising frequently took up half the space while the typical newspaper provided only a quarter-page essay on a literary or political subject. Everywhere there was a "condition of unnatural sluggishness," as Henry Adams described it.

As a possible response to this "sluggishness" the race for money on all social levels seemed a natural stimulant. And self-confident, money-conscious Americans, haunted by prejudices and fearful of the common mob, did not look kindly on literary people. Such a master of the world and its politics and society as J. Q. Adams had bluntly declared that one could not be both a man of business and a man of the arts. A businessman had honor in his country but not the man of letters and perhaps least of all the dramatist. For fear of damaging his dignity in the world of letters and sustaining possible injury to his reputation in his social and business activities, William Wirt, an important Southern attorney and political figure, had refused to have his play, *The Path of Pleasure*, either published or performed. Possible loss of honor was one thing; certain loss of money was another. There was little market for literature, and the mercenary spirit prevailing in America at this time clearly retarded progress in the arts. There was also, of course, no copyright protection for any author.

Although a surprising amount was being written and published during the years from 1801 through 1814, very little has proved to be of lasting value. The outstanding exceptions are *Edgar Huntley* (1801) by Charles Brockden Brown; Hugh Henry Brackenridge's *Modern Chivalry*, which appeared in installments throughout this period; and the early works of Washington Irving, who wrote for the *Salmagundi* in 1807 and published his delightful *History of New York* in 1809. Most of the eighty-seven volumes of native verse listed in Kettell's *Specimens of American Poetry* as published from 1800 through 1815 have been long forgotten. This literary activity is all the more surprising during a period when the reading public was a small part of the citizenry and when the financing of all publications either came out of the author's pocket or was raised by public subscription. The Boston *Monthly Anthology*, for example, reviewed some eighty-seven volumes in 1805 alone.[1] A great amount of printer's ink was seemingly spread to little purpose, but then, as later, most literary efforts became stepping-stones, minor and major, in the development of a literature.

A major influence upon these early literary efforts was the rampant political factionalism. Given the conservativism of many Americans, particularly the clergy and the educated citizenry, the election to the presidency of Thomas Jefferson, with his democratic and liberal ideas, was feared and denounced as a force of evil. A distrust of democracy affected all that they thought and did, and in some ways it served to place a barrier between an educated society and a democratic society. Fisher Ames bluntly stated that "a democracy cannot last."[2] The *Port Folio*, with its ultraconservative political theories, presented the view in 1803 that "a democracy is scarcely tolerable at any period of national history." As "democracy" became equated with "America," political movements such as the Essex Junto attempted to break away from "America," and a tendency arose among many educated people to avoid any feeling or thought that was "American." The result in literature was a basically dual approach that was as clearly observable in the drama as in other writing.

From one side it was fashionable and intellectually appropriate to imitate the English and to please the numerous Anglophile critics in America. Opponents argued the need to create a distinctly American literature. The moderate position between the two views, yet closer in practice to an imitation of Old World writers, was to create from a common knowledge of humanity while competing with the imaginative minds of other nations but avoiding the temperaments and peculiarities that distinguish a nation. Of these approaches, although few results were distinctive, the attempts to create an American literature were the most interesting and vital.

It should not be surprising that America's dramatists were more vocal than were other writers in urging an American literature. Concerned with the society that surrounded them and with the audiences that they must please, they sensed the advantages of social immediacy and, although clearly aware of the prejudices against native drama, undoubtedly saw nationalism as in their favor. James Nelson Barker, for example, advised writers to portray the manners and events of America where he imagined a "higher destiny" for the stage than it had yet attained.[3] George Watterston, in the preface to his unproduced play,

The Child of Feeling (1809), declared that the "peculiar duty" of the comic dramatists is "to confine themselves particularly to their own nations and to satirize such vices and foibles as are there most frequent and common."

CRITICISM OF THE DRAMA

One problem for all American writers at this time was to find a standard of criticism which they could follow. Years later James Russell Lowell was to declare that America first needed perceptive critics before it could have a literature. His astuteness in this observation is only emphasized by the early-nineteenth-century literature in America. Lowell himself, of course, was not without prejudices, and the acceptance of standards of criticism probably comes sometime after they have been effective. At this early time, however, there were some journals such as Joseph Dennie's *Port Folio*, established in 1801 and devoted to literature, and the *Anthology and Boston Reviewer*, established in 1805, which exerted critical standards and which might be compared to the English *Edinburgh Review* (1802) and the *Quarterly* (1809). (Not until the *Anthology* was revived in 1815 as the *North American Review* was there a continuous and substantial standard of criticism established.) Even the New York *Evening Post*, established in 1801, proposed "to cultivate a taste for sound literature" (November 16, 1801). Critics and writers alike, however, had learned part of their trade from Lord Kames' *Elements of Criticism* and Hugh Blair's *Lectures on Rhetoric*. Consequently, the influence of the English was strong, and a prevailing idea in America was to create "standards of taste common to all nations" or to express old things in new ways. Elihu Hubbard Smith, for example, contended that the belles lettres of all nations should unite mankind. American poetry, by that analogy, would be judged by the laws of English prosody, and one would speak of literature in America rather than of American literature.

This approach, however, did not satisfy everyone, particularly those who felt an obligation to express America's mission and to exult in its glory. Writers with nationalistic tendencies urged their colleagues "to leave European poets their Nightingales" (*Port Folio*, 1805) and emphasize, in the words of Noah Webster, the American "climate, plants, animals, arts, manufactures, manners, and policy." St. George Tucker of Virginia warned against European affectations and asked for a "manly species of writing." Americans were called on to reject what Royall Tyler described as the "ignis fatuus of the learned of Europe." Drama should not, as Barker explained, "lisp the language of Shakespeare." Rather it should be "plain-palated, homebred." In doing just that, however, American dramatists sometimes used American dialect and American idioms and thereby provoked adverse comment from such writers as Elihu H. Smith or a critic writing in the *Monthly Anthology* who was horrified to imagine that the notion of an "American tongue" or idiom would come from the "mouths of the illiterate." In their attempts to nationalize the English language, some produced what Joseph Dennie, the conservative Anglophile critic, described as "a vile alloy of provincial idioms and colloquial barbarisms." Even Irving poked fun at the unchaste American muse, calling it a "pawnbroker's widow." Somewhere between the excessive "fertility" of native oratory, as J. Q. Adams explained in his Harvard *Lectures on Rhetoric and Oratory* (1810), and an uncritical reliance on foreign models lay the best standards for American writing, but there was still the question as to who might create this literature—drama, poetry, fiction, or essay.[4]

It took a particular kind of individual to enter the field of American letters in 1800. Washington Irving, the only writer who published a work during the period 1801–1814 which would be critically acclaimed as well as widely accepted in modern times, was subsidized. Yet, there was a surprising number of Americans who began about this time to assess the literary resources of America as the slow process of cultural maturation got under way. As more products of the literary mind appeared, critics and readers found opportunity to comment. This was particularly true for the dramatist as newspapers and magazines, even books and pamphlets, paid increasing attention to the theatre. Although such comment was not generally the kind of criticism which Lowell described as necessary for the establishment of a literature, it was a criticism with which the dramatist had to contend if he wished to be produced by theatre managers whose careers depended on their ability to please audiences. For the person who would understand the drama of the early nineteenth century, an awareness of the purpose, quantity, and tenor of this criticism is basic.

A completely intolerant and adverse critical point of view, the clerical attitude toward the drama is a relentless and never-ending movement in the development of nineteenth-century dramatic criticism. Continuing the policy of their Puritan forefathers, the clergy, particularly in New England and the Middle-Atlantic states, maintained a constant attack upon the theatre. As a sinful act that could be easily observed in the cities, attendance at the theatre or an expressed interest in the drama was an easy and obvious target. John

Edwards' *Warning to Sinners; or, an address to all Play-actors, Play-hunters, Legislators, Governors, Magistrates, Clergy, Churchmen, Deists and the World at Large* (New York, 1812) is a good example of the kind of thought that went into such an attack. Playhouses become "the synagogues of Satan" and the "Devil's House"; "Devil's children . . . act the plays in those houses." What a shame, Edwards says, for a king or a president to waste "his precious time and money" at a play. With the weakness of absurd analogy, he compares the actor and the preacher while ridiculing the former by asking whether a sick person would "send for a play actor to comfort him." Bombast and excessive rhetoric, however, were the preacher's main weapons. "O! ye Legislators, Magistrates, &," Edwards expounds in his pious attempt to close the playhouses, "my conscience cannot be clear in the sight of God, until I have warned you to flee from the wrath to come." And for the perpetrators of this evil, "Repent, repent, ye managers of plays: beg of God to have mercy on your guilty souls."

Not all readers would take such attacks in silence. The writer of "The Drama" column in *Something* (1809), a short-lived magazine published in Boston, had pointed out "that the authors of its [the drama] institution in our mother country were ecclesiastics, that the preachers of the Gospel were the first and originally the only actors in the Drama, and that it was introduced to give a more impressive effect to the doctrines of morality and Christianity." Recognizing the fact that the drama does have a considerable "influence over the public mood," the writer went on to contend that "vicious and immoral" tendencies in the theatre would decline if the "aged and good laymen of our land" attended performances and that the presence of ladies in the pit would "refine" the rowdy character of the audiences.

When critics or reviewers of early-nineteenth-century American theatre made particular observations, they almost always commented on the actors or the staging of the play, or both. There are few comments that can be defended as dramatic criticism. Although staging was usually standard, there were some experiments which attracted notice. Writing about "The stage" in the *Ordeal* (May 6, 1809), for example, a critic told of the "various passions, ideas, etc. of the *dramatis personae* . . . conveyed to the spectators by means of a huge label, dangling from a pole, and brought on by some lubberly supernumerary." Following arguments put forth by the English such as in Jane Porter's *A Defence of the Profession of an Actor* (1800) critics other than the clergy frequently defended those who acted upon the stage and emphasized the techniques of their art: gestures, pronunciation, phrasing, seeming respect or disrespect for the audience—all received comment. And to understand the tenor of these comments it should be remembered that the critic or reviewer felt an obligation to oversee, instruct, or correct the performers. One actor was "interesting and impressive"; another delighted the house with "his gestures, his voice, his air, and above all, the speaking expression of his countenance." Or an actor "looked the part but his voice was hard and monotonous."[5] Actors were frequently chastised for weaknesses or sloppy work: "Mr. Mills' incorrectness this evening deprived us of the pleasure we might have received from Mr. Cooper's acting, as well as from his own."[6] Occasionally, an essay would supply background information on an actor—for example, "Biography: Mr. Caulfield" in the *Thespian Monitor* (December 9, 1809)— as well as advice concerning required improvement and attentiveness to duties. Essays in the *Thespian Mirror* include "Some Account of the Life of Mr. Fennel[1], the Celebrated Tragedian" (December 28, 1805) and *"The Wheel of Fortune*, and *The Romp"* (January 11, 1806), which compares the acting styles of Fennell and Cooper.

One fascinating text published in Boston in 1810 is *The Thespian Preceptor; or, A Full Display of The Scenic Art*, "including ample and easy instructions for treading the stage, using proper action, modulating the voice and expressing the several Dramatic Passions; illustrated by examples from our most approved ancient and modern dramatists; and calculated not only for the improvement of all lovers of the stage, actors and actresses, but likewise of public orators, readers, and visitors of theatre." Chapter one lists the essentials for becoming an actor—judgment, personality, voice, action, walk, plus an appropriate education as a classical scholar—defined tragic action as the expression of "imperious and incontrollable passions," and dictated such rules of acting as never to speak with profile or half a back to the audience. Then followed an enumeration of the characteristics of such parts as the Hero: "he cannot roar"; he cannot take short steps which indicate "meanness, trifling, indecision"; he cannot hold back his head, an action implying "inflated self-sufficiency and desire to extort slavish obedience." Chapter two explained some thirty "principal passions," of which the following provides the necessary illustration:

> *Fear*—violent and sudden, opens the eyes and mouth very wide, draws down the eye-brows, gives the countenance an air of wildness, draws back the elbows parallel with the sides, lifts up the open hand (his fingers together) to the height of the breast so that the palms face the dreadful object, as shields opposed against it. One foot is drawn back behind the other; so that

the body seems shrinking from danger, and putting itself in a posture for flight. The heart beats violently; the breath is fetched quick and short, and the whole body is thrown into a general tremor. Fear is also frequently displayed by a sudden start, and, in ladies, by a violent shriek, which produces fainting. The voice is weak and trembling [p. 35].

Such were the instructions which would aid both actor and audience.

Although the potential of the stage was a subject for considerable discussion, there was some agreement that performed plays had "an important influence on the morals, manners, and tastes of society."[7] It was up to the dramatist to focus that potential. A writer in the Philadelphia *Repository and Weekly Register* (April 11, 1801, p. 171), for example, declared that a well-conducted theatre had never existed because there were not enough good plays. He could admit that people needed that "intermission from duty," but he still found drama a "waste of time and money." The editor of the *Theatrical Censor* (December 9, 1805) found the stage a "direct School of Vice when it presents immoral scenes, when it utters base and corrupt sentiments, under the specious semblance of candour and truth." But he also believed in the art of his own theatrical criticism in holding "the mirror up to nature" and maintained that "under the proper management the stage becomes the School of Virtue, the School of Manners, the Great School of Society." Understandably, it was mainly as a "school of morals and innocent amusements" that the reviewers and critics for the several journals publishing theatre criticism saw the potential for American drama and theatre.

The obligations of the reviewer or critic were another issue discussed in the contemporary journals. The writer of "The Theatre" column in the *Thistle* (September 1, 1807) seemed to see himself as a superior authority and a safeguard for acting standards: "Should the actors be negligent in their parts; should they want a due understanding of the sense of their author; should they be careless in performance, and listless to applause; it is ten to one that they will be occasionally lashed in the *Thistle*. All theatrical criticism, however, will be tempered with candor and impartial discrimination." Although most critics obviously felt this same paternal duty to legislate from a position of authority, they expressed themselves differently. The critic for the *Theatrical Censor* (December 9, 1805) simply explained that he was neither the enemy of the drama nor the enemy of the public but the "voice of an enlightened audience."

Improvement or promotion of the drama and the theatrical performances, however, was always a primary concern. "We hope," wrote the critic for "The

Theatre" in the *Stranger* (January 29, 1814), "to induce the public, and particularly those who are qualified to form correct estimates, occasionally to notice with a view of improvement the management and performance in the theatre in this city [Albany]." Determined to avoid the indiscriminate praise that was common, the New York *Evening Post* was concerned with admonishing, correcting, and helping the actor. The *Thespian Mirror*, according to its prospectus of January 24, 1806, as devised by its youthful editor, John Howard Payne, was "to comprehend a collection of interesting documents relative to the stage and its performances; chiefly intended to promote the . . . American drama." Stephen Cullen Carpenter, drama critic for the Charleston *Courier* and publisher of the *Mirror of Taste and Dramatic Censor* during its brief life in 1810 and 1811, argued that the primary objective of dramatic criticism was to regulate the effects of the theatre on its audience, to interpose a discerning judgment on what otherwise might be a "transient, imperfect, and uselessly misleading pastime."[8] James Fennell, the actor who published *Something* in Boston from November 18, 1809 through May 12, 1810, and the *Whim* in Philadelphia between May 14 and July 16, 1814, contended in *Something* (January 10, 1810) that criticism should give "a more lively perception of the beauties and deformities of works of genius."

Although critics generally considered themselves watchdogs of public morals, guardians of the stage, and independent voices of the general public, it must not be assumed that all were both serious and honorable. Like people at all times, some, perhaps many, were for sale. One of these was John Williams (1757/1761–1818), an Englishman who emigrated to America probably in 1798, a year after his radicalism had gotten him into trouble and he had been prosecuted, fined, and judged a "common libeler" by Lord Kenyon. In America he wrote plays, edited a newspaper, and wrote for the *Dramatic Censor*, always using the pseudonym "Anthony Pasquin." Dunlap is very hard on him in his *History* as is John Bernard in his *Reminiscences*, calling Williams a paid puff, with money his only principle, who wrote what was "agreeable to price and order." It was said that "his ideas were as dirty as his clothes," which were evidently most disreputable. Williams died in poverty of typhus.

The best known theatre critic of this period was Washington Irving (1783–1859), who first contributed to the New York *Morning Chronicle* under the pseudonyms "Jonathan Oldstyle, Gent.," "Andrew Quoz," and "Jack Stylish." Of his nine "letters" published in this newspaper from November 15, 1802, until April 23, 1803, those numbered three through eight were playful but shrewd attacks on the struggling American theatre and drama. A few years later, with his elder brother, William, and James Kirk Paulding, Irving launched *Salmagundi; or, The Whim-Whams and Opinions of Lancelot Lang-staff, Esq. and Others*, which was published irregularly for a total of twenty issues from January 24, 1807 through January 25, 1808. This work, which Irving described as "juvenile" and hoped would "have gone down into oblivion," contains some of the liveliest and most astute comments on the drama and theatre of the period.

With wit and humor happily displayed, Irving managed to discuss all aspects of theatre: the audience, the staging and acting of plays, the drama performed, and even the critics. Concerning a performance of *Macbeth* (*Salmagundi*, January 24, 1807), for example, Irving observed through one of his alter egos, William Wizard, Esq., that Lady Macbeth "would have given greater effect to the night-scene, if, instead of holding the candle in her hand . . . she had stuck it in her nightcap." "From the Mill of Pindar Cockloft, Esq." (*Salmagundi*, April 4, 1807), Irving provides a long poem, parts of which no doubt describe some of the innumerable farces that lasted one night on the stage and never made it into print:

> And, last of all, behold the mimic stage,
> Its morals lend to polish off the age
> With flimsy farce, a comedy miscalled,
> Garnished with vulgar cant, and proverbs bald.
> With puns most puny, and a plenteous store
> Of smutty jokes, to catch a gallery roar.

Even more interesting are his observations on critics and their habits. After a review of a performance of *Othello* in the *Salmagundi* (March 20, 1807), he adds a telling note: "P. S. Just as this was going to press, I was informed that Othello had not been performed here the lord knows when; no matter, I am not the first that has criticized a play without seeing it." And in a letter to Jonathan Oldstyle, Andrew Quoz provides some impressions in which many still find solace: "The critics, my dear Jonathan, are the very pests of society; they rob the actor of his reputation—the public of their amusement; they open the eyes of their readers to a full perception of the faults of our performers, they reduce our feelings to a state of miserable refinement, and destroy entirely all the enjoyments in which our coarser sensations delighted."[9]

Whether the critics were worthy of Andrew's complaints is questionable. Perhaps they should have been. Following their stated objectives, however, critics generally said something about the plot and the acting and then praised, blamed, and questioned with an accuracy, astuteness, and honesty that is difficult to determine. Reviewing a play called *The Wanderer*, the critic for the *Thespian Mirror* (February 1, 1806) praised the author, "a young gentleman of this city," as one "who possesses talent which every lover of the drama should be proud to encourage." But the critic, John Howard Payne, was also the author of the play! A reviewer for the *Ordeal* (May 27, 1809) praised the love scene between Rolf and Pocahontas in James N. Barker's *The Indian Princess* as "superior to the composition of most of the modern European play compilers" but considered the play so "blended with the absurdities of melodrama" that he hesitated to recommend it. That this is the same writer for the *Ordeal* who had ridiculed the current vogue for German melodrama in two previous issues leads one to suspect a bias.

Faulting the productions came easy to the reviewers—for substantial reasons or, perhaps, out of habit. Arriving late at the theatre one night, the reviewer for the *Thespian Mirror* (January 11, 1806) wrote: "From what little we saw of it, however, we were not induced to regret not being earlier at the house." In the December 11, 1809, issue of *Something*, the critic expressed his entire response to the play in a single sentence: "And silence was in the galleries." Writing in the *Stranger* (February 26, 1814), a critic denounced a play called *Lake Erie; or, the Glorious Tenth of September* as containing only "barbarous rhymes, unconnected circumstances, partial dialogue from various sources and unfinished allegory tacked together in more confusion than Sybil's leaves, and forming in the whole a hotchpot which we imagine never has, and hope never will be again equalled." In a more authoritative manner, Joseph Dennie in the *Port Folio* (January 24, 1801) first framed a theory of farce and then presented his assessment of the play he viewed: "We do not expect from farce anything beyond the amusement of half an hour. The most extravagant eccentricity of character, and the most improbable situations are admissible in such a composition; provided the end of amusement be answered, without any violation of propriety. We conceive that the concluding scene of the piece under review is highly defective in this respect. . . . We hope that the ridiculous piece will be consigned in future to the oblivion which it deserves."

From their different personal viewpoints, the various reviewers or critics of drama and theatre tried to exert an influence on theatrical performance. Wanting to improve the drama in America, to guide the tastes of audiences, they assumed obligations which were in most ways no different from those directing modern critics, but they lacked the effective power of the modern critic. Whether they influenced the kind of plays being written would be impossible to determine. Criticism with an intent to instruct audiences, playwrights, actors, and theatre managers was just beginning in America, and if the playwrights listened, they still seemed to write the same types of plays: political and patriotic plays or celebrations for certain contemporary events, moral melodramas, plays in imitation of foreign models, and light farces and comedies. Every drama written during the period 1801–1814 is to be found under one or more of those headings, and there was remarkable activity among American playwrights considering the obstacles placed before them. Ironically enough, as explained very clearly in the *Ordeal* (May 27, 1809), the greatest of the obstacles was to be an American: "There exists in this country such a want of judgment, or rather determination, such an unconquerable prejudice against American plays, and even such a loathing to every allusion which is American in its nature, that an author is obliged to struggle in his fight to renown against an intolerable weight of prejudices and passions, which every moment threaten to sink him to the earth." Early American dramatists, however, seem to have had a remarkable determination, and if they did not reach the excellence or even acceptance that contemporary critics and later historians would have enjoyed, there was at least a good number of them trying, for whatever reasons, to write for an American theatre.

POLITICS AND NATIONALISM IN THE DRAMA

During the fourteen years separating the inauguration of Jefferson into the presidency of the United States and the Treaty of Ghent on December 24, 1814, there were about a dozen American playwrights who wrote and published more than one play. Another score published single plays, either after or in lieu of performance. Of this surprisingly large number only a few, however, could be considered serious playwrights. Among these, Dunlap and James Nelson Barker have been mentioned most frequently by historians. Although a man by the name of Charles Smith (1786–1808) figures prominently in Hill's *American Plays, Printed 1714–1830*, the seventeen titles listed are all translations of Kotzebue's plays, only three of which are presumed to be the actual work of Smith. The two most active playwrights of the time, each with five plays published, were Joseph Hutton and John Minshull. John D. Turnbull was doubtless equally active, but most of his plays have not survived. Whereas J. Horatio Nichols and John Blake White each produced three plays, their primary interests, as were those of most who wrote for the theatre, were elsewhere. Mordecai Noah's career as a playwright began during those early years, but his best work was to come later.

At this point in the development of American drama, the work of James Nelson Barker (1784–1858) is the most significant in suggesting the direction that American drama would take. More than that of any other playwright of the period, his work illustrates the varied focusing of themes, attitudes, and techniques to which others contributed in one way or another. *America* (1805) was essentially a patriotic effusion, whereas *The Embargo; or, What News?* (1808) dramatized a political issue. Generally, Barker avoided the excessive interest in upholding good moral conduct which infiltrated most American plays, but he did emphasize a conventional morality in both *Tears and Smiles* (1807) and *The Indian Princess* (1808). He also suffered the burden of his nationality, complained occasionally about it, and once consented to have his poetic melodrama, *Marmion* (1812), produced under the pretense that it was written by a popular English playwright, Thomas Morton. Mentioning the New York production on June 14, 1809, of *The Indian Princess*, Odell appended a sympathetic note: "It was to be many a long year before an American play would have a fair chance with an American audience in an American theatre. John Howard Payne was wise in going to London and remaining there for twenty years."[10] Perhaps because Barker never considered himself a professional dramatist, he was willing to stay in America and do the best he could in a theatre that was still largely English in its management and its actors. His best play, *Superstition*, would not appear until 1823, but his most active period in the theatre of Philadelphia, where he was quite closely associated with the management and with the actors for whom he wrote some of his plays, was prior to the War of 1812.

Barker came from a politically and socially influential family. His father, John Barker, had served in the Revolution and emerged a belligerent Patriot who capitalized on his sarcastic wit and his ability as an orator to become a fierce and popular politician and eventually mayor of Philadelphia. Some of his social, political, and patriotic views were passed on to his son who, having received an education befitting the family's social position, expressed them in plays, poems, and orations. In 1804 he began his first play, based on Cervantes and entitled *The Spanish Rover*, but never completed it.[11] *America*, a masque in one act "consisting of poetic dialogue, and sung by the genius of America, Science, Liberty, and attendant spirits, after the manner of the mask in the Tempest," was written in 1805 but was neither produced nor printed. Barker then attempted a tragedy, *Attila*, which was suggested to him by Gibbon, but, again, he never completed it although some years later he mentioned it as the play he would work on "should I ever be tempted to do anything more in the dramatic way."

Tears and Smiles, a comedy in five acts "written between the 1st of May and the 12th of June, 1806" was his next play. At a dinner party during which Charles Breck's *Fox Chase* was discussed, Barker (still, it must be remembered, a young man of twenty-two) was asked by William Warren, manager of Philadelphia's Chestnut Street Theatre, to write a play. Joseph Jefferson added the suggestion that it include a Yankee character. Inspired by both the invitation and his enjoyment of Tyler's *The Contrast*, Barker wrote the play which Warren opened at the Chestnut Street Theatre on March 4, 1807, to what the author described as a "complete success." In a typical stance Barker wrote a preface to the published play which reemphasized his strong support for native drama with native themes. He also showered contempt on a certain Anglophile, "my d———d good-natured friend," who found his play to be only a "collection of Columbianisms" and advised him to burn it. A "Columbianism," Barker went on to explain, is a "term of derision they apply to every delineation an American may attempt to make of American manners, customs, opinions, characters, or scenery." Fortunately, Barker had the good sense to reject that advice.

The setting for *Tears and Smiles* is Philadelphia, and the elapsed time of the play, in good neoclassical fashion, is twelve hours. It seems that in Europe, some eighteen years before the action of the play, a Frenchman had left two young children with a Mr. Campdon. Now, Campdon is terribly upset because one of the children, Clara, has run away, and the other, Sydney, has, before going off to do battle in Tripoli, seduced the affections of his daughter, Louisa. Faced with Sydney's return, Campdon is insisting that Louisa marry Fluttermore, a Europeanized fop whom she detests. There is also an "itinerant rake" named Jack Rangely who, with his servant Nathan Yank, is looking for the charming woman, the Widow Freegrace, whom he rescued in a runaway carriage. Alternating humor and mystery, Barker provides some lively scenes and fair suspense. Mingled with Rangely's search are the sprightly conversations of Yank, Fluttermore, and his Gallic friend, Galliard. To match the mysterious and unfortunate Madame Clermont, whom Louisa meets, Sydney returns with the equally mysterious Osbert. Finally, Fluttermore is revealed as Clara's lover and is persuaded to marry her; Rangely is accepted by the Widow if he promises to reform; Clara and Sydney discover that Osbert is their father, and Mrs. Clermont, their mother; and Louisa marries Sydney with the approval of Campdon.

The complicated plot of *Tears and Smiles* reveals all the structural inadequacies of a beginner's attempt to write comedy as the characters are shifted in and out of scenes to make discoveries and to be discovered. It is the wit and temper of the play, however, which lift it above the ordinary comedy of the time. An example is Fluttermore's encounter with his old college friend Rangely:

RAN. The grand tour?

FLUT. Yes; returned. Hey, monsieur? 'Gad, I beg pardon. This sudden *rencontre* with my friend—Give me leave—This is *monsieur Galliard,* from Paris. Monsieur, my friend, Jack Rangely, from—no matter. There; don't shake hands; that's antique. Talk English, Jack; Galliard prefers it; speaks it like a native.

GAL. Oh! lit, ver lit; *presque rien*; noting 'tall.

FLUT. No; believe me, he swears English with the best accent.

GAL. Oh! I'll be dam! You flatte me.

FLUT. Judge.

RAN. And what do you think, M. Galliard, of North America and its savages?

GAL. *Comment?* Sauvage! As I hope to be save, I have not seen—

RAN. I mean its inhabitants: for doubtless we must appear uncivilized to polished Europeans.

GAL. Your good pardon, sare; *c'est un bon pay*; ver good fine contrée; *tous les hommes,* all de peuple happy; all de vomen belle, beautiful! By gar, I am ravish'd!

RAN. You praise lavishly, M. Galliard.

FLUT. He does, indeed. For my part, I can't conceive what you possibly do in this corner of the globe. No opera; no masquerade, no *fete*, nor *conversazione*; a diabolical theatre; and not even a *promenade* where one might—(*Examining his figure.*) Then your women; such dowdies! No air; no manner. And your men: *O Ciel*! such beings!—Gad, Jack, you must go to Europe! You see what it can do.

[I, iv.]

Such dialogue, braced with French, Irish, and Yankee dialects, ridicules foreigners (the French rather than, as in *The Contrast*, the English), language, manners, gossips, and society in general.

Although the characters are stereotypes, they suggest something of Barker's potential as a playwright. Nathan Yank follows the Yankee tradition but with certain differences—still a servant but more of a country clown than is Tyler's Jonathan. With his European attitudes Fluttermore is the most successfully developed character although his impossible change in the final act detracts from that success. Sydney as the patriotic hero is dull and uninteresting, a stock hero;

Osbert has no individuality, Louisa shows only a little; while the Widow Free-grace is the best drawn among the women. It was an encouraging first play, particularly for its perceptive comments on the social manners of the time, and Barker did not wait long to try again. Between the writing and the pro-duction of his play, he had been off on another adventure to New York, where he may have caught some of the political excitement of the day which went into his next play.

Jefferson's Embargo Act of December 23, 1807, provided Barker with the necessary inspiration. Trying desperately to avoid war with England, Jefferson had signed the Non-Importation Act in 1806, but the English imprisonment of American seamen had continued, and the Chesapeake Affair of January 22, 1807, was interpreted as a direct insult by the British. The Embargo Act was Jefferson's answer, and for fourteen months American shipping was curtailed. As might be expected New England merchants suffered most under the act, which as an attempt at "peaceful coercion" proved a failure and was repealed in 1809. A rather ticklish affair, as Barker admitted, it only further divided Federalists and Democrats, but Barker, a staunch Democrat, defended the pol-icy which Jefferson stubbornly held throughout his presidency. A real dem-onstration of Barker's feelings appeared in *The Embargo; or, What News?* which he wrote for the benefit of Blissett, a comedian with the Chestnut Street company, which produced the play on March 16, 1808, as "a New Interlude written by a Gentleman of this City." Not all members of the audience agreed with Barker's dramatized opinions, but, as he explained in his letter to Dunlap, "the majority were of the right feeling, and bore me triumphantly through." The manuscript is lost, and the only information about the play is Barker's statement that he "liberally borrowed from Murphy's *Upholsterer*." It is pre-sumed that Blissett performed the comedy again in Baltimore, and it may have been performed by Bernard in Boston.

Meanwhile, Barker was reworking a play about Pocahontas which he had started sometime before and had taken up again only at the request of John Bray. An actor-composer, Bray provided music for Barker's songs in *The In-dian Princess; or, La Belle Sauvage* and used the three-act "operatic melo-drama" for his benefit on April 6, 1808. Although Barker took his theme and many incidents from John Smith's *General History of Virginia* (1624), he was not constrained by historical detail or chronology. Instead, he empha-sized romance and heightened his play theatrically by manipulating history and by creating an effective change of pace with scenes of humor, love, and action. Following a well-conceived patriotic opening scene in which Captain

Smith compares Virginia to a "stagnant Europe," the action shifts to the Indian camp where preparations are being made for Pocahontas' reluctant marriage to Miami, the brutal villain of the play. When Smith encounters the Indians, he is captured and then saved by Pocahontas in the traditional fashion. Rolfe's interest in Pocahontas then inspires the jealous Miami to declare war on the tribe of Powhatan, who defeats him with the help of the English. Eventually, this alliance of Powhatan and the English is destroyed by the machinations of Miami and the Indian priests, who plan a banquet for the English during which Smith and Rolfe will be killed. According to critics, a love scene at this time (III, ii) between Rolfe and Pocahontas, written in blank verse rather than in the prose of the rest of the play, was a high point of the production. The critic for the *Ordeal* (May 27, 1809) described it as "well wrought, replete with tenderness, and superior to the composition of most of the modern European play compilers." Finally, Pocahontas saves the English by leading the recently arrived Lord Delaware to their rescue, allowing Powhatan to be forgiven by the English as Rolfe and Pocahontas become engaged.

Whereas Robert Rogers had published *Ponteach* in 1766 and Mrs. Hatton had written her Indian opera, *Tammany*, in 1794, Barker's *The Indian Princess* was the first American play on an Indian theme to be performed.[12] Although Barker probably exaggerated when he stated that it played in "all the theatres of the United States," one good indication of its success is the fact that Dunlap chose it for his benefit on June 23, 1809. Critics also had good things to say about the play. Writing for the *Ordeal* (May 27, 1809), one critic enjoyed the "occasional touches of nature," the Indian character, and the tenderness in Pocahontas but objected to "the absurdities of the melodrama." A reviewer for the New York *Evening Post* (June 13, 1809) called it "one of the favorite modern productions . . . in point of dramatic composition, one of the most chaste and elegant plays ever written in the United States." From a modern view the Indian characters seem generally wooden, but Pocahontas offers a lively charm with her innocence, lack of pretense, and utter simplicity—a child of nature. The romantic flavor of the brave explorer as well as Barker's typical brand of patriotism obviously appealed to audiences. In structure the play is superior to almost all other plays of this period, but it still shows the problems of a young playwright, one who would, however, develop greater skills.

Barker's next play, an adaptation of Cherry's *Travellers; or, Music's Fascination*, advertised as "by a citizen of Philadelphia," was a patriotic spectacle, prepared at the request of the theatre manager. In its five acts scenes change from China to Turkey, to Italy, and, finally, to the "Quarter Deck of an American Frigate." Performed twice in December, 1808, and once the following January, it was then lost to both public and author. During these years Barker was also increasingly involved in politics, becoming active in a Philadelphia organization called "The Democratic Young Men" during the fall of 1808. More time passed. Then, early in 1812, some months before Barker enlisted his services in the War of 1812, he completed *Marmion; or, The Battle of Flodden Field*, "at the special request of [William] Wood," manager of the Philadelphia theatre. This, the most successful of Barker's plays, kept the stage for many years and was published in 1816 and again in 1826. Although the finesse of suggesting English authorship may have had some effect on its initial seven performances at the Park Theatre in New York in April, 1812, and on its Philadelphia performance the following January, the true authorship was then made public, and the play continued to please audiences. The fact that Walter Scott, Barker's primary source (along with Holinshed's *Chronicles*), was extremely popular in America may also have stimulated audience interest.

The times, too, were in some measure responsible for *Marmion*'s enthusiastic reception, and Barker knew exactly which emotions stirring in the collective American bosom he wished to touch. In his preface to the published play he asked his readers to note what must have been obvious to the theatre audiences: England's attitude toward Scotland in the sixteenth century was comparable to her treatment of contemporary America. The remainder of his preface is an impassioned plea for America's spiritual independence, in which he urged Americans "to acquire and maintain a steady, temperate, and consistent consciousness of our country's worth and value." These were tense times, and Barker was attempting to be an inspiration both for strong, patriotic feelings and for strong, sensible actions. In the spring of 1812, when many Americans were ready to go to war with England no matter how senseless it would have been, Congress was debating the issue. Indian problems, in which the British were said to have had a hand; maritime affairs as America maneuvered between England and France while being galled by Napoleon's sentiments; the issue of the western lands of America; the increased factionalism of Democrats and Federalists—all were coming into focus. And Barker's argument between Marmion and King James of Scotland (IV, iv) represented an accumulated resentment against England. During the first Philadelphia performance in January, 1813, King James' refusal to treat with England sparked a ten-minute patriotic demonstration. Congress had declared war against England on June 18, 1812.

During his years of playwriting, Barker had shown increasing improvement in the selection or the creation of his material as well as in his arrangement of it. In *Marmion* he chose a major dramatic encounter for each act. He then used Scott's lines and story or added his own ideas as he saw fit. By this time he had also learned that a successful play must have one outstanding character which would attract an actor, and Marmion appealed to such actors as T. A. Cooper, James Wallack, and John Duff. It is interesting to note that, as a mark of the times, perhaps an indication of an actor's preference, and as a foreshadowing of Barker's greatest play, *Superstition*, Marmion is a type of villain, one who is occasionally frightened and haunted by the probable consequences of his deeds. Other characters are more lightly sketched. DeWilton and King James are mainly noble; Constance, a woman of love and sacrifice; and Lady Heron, cold and calculating. Barker's major problem, as he admitted in his preface, was to focus on subject matter that was more epic than dramatic. Although the character of Marmion was his logical choice for emphasis, the play still suffers from loosely connected episodes which are, however, in themselves, carefully dramatized.

Appearing in the first scene of the play, after having presumably killed DeWilton and having had a love affair with Lady Heron, Marmion has designs on another woman, Clara. But he must first dispose of his current interest, Constance, whom he returns to the abbey from which he once abducted her. Later, in a scene well interlaced with pathos, Barker dramatizes the trial of the one woman who loved Marmion and her sentencing to the Vault of Penitence in the abbey. It was Act IV, however, which proved the most exciting for audiences in a country at war with England. Lady Heron, an English spy and lover of King James, urges the King to make war on England. When Marmion arrives a spectacular scene dramatizes his encounter with King James, who refuses in forceful tones to give up his sovereignty: "Do you not ask us here/ To throw our armour off, and cower at home,/ Patient, till England find a time to Treat?" (IV, iv). Disdainfully, the King goes on to refer to England: "The nation most selfish,/ Presuming, arrogant, of all this globe,/ Professes but to fight for other's rights,/ While she alone infringes every right." It is a powerful scene, and the play might well have ended there, but the melodrama was not over. The calculating female spy must be killed by the Scots; the lovers (Clara and DeWilton), united; and Marmion, forced to accept disaster during the Battle of Flodden Field.

The War of 1812 interrupted Barker's career as a dramatist. After combat duty as an artillery officer and service as a recruiting officer, Barker was discharged on June 15, 1815, as Assistant Adjutant General of the 4th Military District with the rank of major. He was now thirty-one years old, and his life had been spent in dilettantish pursuits as the son of a wealthy and social-minded family, with some attention to the drama and three years service in the military. He had little need to prove himself financially self-sufficient. He could, instead, indulge his fancies and give vent to that personality which seemed to show both the charm and belligerence of his father. Sometime in the spring of 1814, he had fought a duel with Major Wade Hampton in which he was shot through both thighs. Here was another illustration of that temperament which fiercely resented the treatment of American dramatists as well as the general attitudes some Americans had for English arts, letters, and fashions. At this point in his avocation as playwright, he was already being recognized to his advantage as an "American dramatist" when the phrase was generally subject to derision. The critic for the New York *Courier* noted that he should be "emphatically styled the *American* Dramatist" and went on to state that *Marmion* "produces emotions much more strong, an interest much more intense, and a moral effect much more salutary" than Scott's poem and "should be read by every man who is a lover of the drama, and who is disposed to foster American genius."[13]

As an identifiable American dramatist by 1812, Barker had written three reasonably acceptable plays and would write three more plays of which one would be the single outstanding American play written during the first quarter of the nineteenth century. His imagination, his natural talent for the drama, and his association with theatre people in Philadelphia were primary assets for Barker, but his social standing, financial independence, and personal temperament were also important. Such force of writing skill and personality, however, was very sparingly distributed among those contributing to the American drama prior to 1814.

Like Barker, James Philip Puglia was a citizen of Philadelphia and very much interested in the political system. His main career seems to have been that of a teacher of Spanish and Italian, but he wrote essays on politics, society, critics, and criticism and at least two plays. From what he wrote he would seem to have been a forthright man of strong opinions whose idealism did not always afford him the greatest personal protection. In an early book, *The Federal Politicians* (1795), he placed a strong emphasis on liberty and moderation. Using the pseudonym of James Quicksilver, he wrote *The Blue Shop*

(1796), "Impartial and Humorous observations on the life and adventures of Peter Porcupine, with the real motives which gave rise to his abuse of our distinguished patriotic character; together with a full and fair review of his late Scarecrow." Peter Porcupine was, as mentioned earlier, William Cobbett, and Puglia shrewdly applied his own patriotic and incisive wit.

Puglia obviously knew something about the theatre and probably belonged to a group of amateur actors for whom he wrote his two plays.[14] In both he used stage directions to good advantage and imagined his plot action in terms of the stage. He also created interesting characters, wrote fair dialogue, was clearly concerned with language, and plotted his stories reasonably well. Basically an essayist, however, he depended too much on monologues and asides (clever as they sometimes are) to explain his characters and action, and he appears quite unable to write an effective climax.

Puglia's first play, *The Embargo*, treats a subject that had interested Barker. It also supported Jefferson's act. The slight plot follows two sailors, one having signed aboard the *Maryland* for a voyage to Madeira, who contend for the love of the landlord's daughter, Nelly. The sailors feel that the "Dambargo" has spoiled everything from their chances at sea to their wooing of Nelly. While the sailors' language (with *damn*'s and *son of a bitch*'s) and fighting adds spice to the action, the dramatist's emphasis is clearly on the discussion between the *Maryland*'s captain and the merchant shipper, both of whom manage speeches defending the embargo. The play ends on the following lines:

> If ye are inclined to approve my CHOICE,
> Let American Genius th' EMBARGO defend,
> And thus with approbation's voice
> Expect that soon the Times will mend.

After this ending, the author noted on his manuscript that, if the play "goes on well," he would offer another comedy, *The Double Disappointment; or, A Touch At Modern Times.*

The eventual play, called *The Complete Disappointment*, has "MDCCCIX" on its title page and was dedicated to Simon Snyder, Governor of Pennsylvania, January 28, 1809, although it seems to have been written in 1808. As in *The Embargo*, the setting is Philadelphia, but its purpose was to entertain and to satirize society rather than to support a political view. The plot tells of a banker, Grabb, who is engaged to Lawyer Stark's daughter, Proserpine, but would rather marry Polly, the daughter of a rather unscrupulous broker named

Ferret. Unfortunately for Grabb, Polly loves Stark's son, William, a profligate who forges Grabb's name to a check and is arrested. Lawyer Stark, a garrulous person who uses at least three verbs in a series in every sentence and thinks only in lawyer's terms, is a good comic character, and Proserpine has a fine monologue before her mirror as she comments on her personal prospects and on society. Otherwise, it is a rather average farce-comedy with satire aimed generally at society and more particularly at bankers, brokers, speculators, corrupt police, lawyers, and the independent woman. Puglia draws no morals. As would have most other young dramatists at this time, he would have profited from more experience, which was not easily attained but, as did few of his equally amateur contemporaries who published their plays, he seems to have had a marked potential.

According to the opening line of J. H. Nichols' *Jefferson and Liberty; or, Celebration of the Fourth of March* (1801), "The hour approaches pregnant with destiny!" Indeed, it did. As a man of peace who did not wish to waste his energies, Jefferson ironically was plagued with problems along the Barbary Coast, intense political factionalism, the Federalist conspiracy in New England, and a constant harassment by the English and by that "Mephistopheles of Politics," Aaron Burr. To avoid war he purchased Louisiana in 1803, tried to maintain a neutrality in the difficulties that engulfed France and England, and signed the Non-Importation Act of 1806 and the Embargo Act of 1807. Nothing seemed to work, and he left office bitterly disappointed. Madison did little better during the early years of his presidency, and, whereas the war unified the independent Americans to some degree, it was also a degrading experience for many and a source of continuing anxiety for New England, which saw its affluence diminished by the expanding country. The year 1815 was one of self-recognition for America, but not until Madison had left office in 1817 did the Union become transformed into a modern state.

Much of the political activity of the period was noted in the theatres by any number of play characters who ventured a political or patriotic comment. For those who wanted purer strains of patriotism and nationalism on the stage, the theatre managers continued their policy of spectacle entertainment. "Written for the celebration of American Independence," William Dunlap's *The Glory of Columbia—Her Yeomanry* was first performed on July 4, 1803; joining John Daly Burk's *Bunker-Hill* as a popular patriotic spectacle. Another spectacle, *New York Volunteers; or, Who's Afraid?* (1812), placed Jupiter and Juno on thrones with Peace and the Genius of Columbia, "mixing allegory and myth in dire confusion," according to one critic. In Boston *The Pilgrims*

(1809) by an unnamed native author climaxed its brief, confused plot when the Goddess of Liberty appeared from a cloud, harangued the Pilgrims at length, and concluded by "telling them how great, powerful and wise their descendants were likely to be."

Of the purely political plays appearing during Jefferson's first term of office, most were written as closet drama. John Hodgkinson brought out *What News? or, How Goes the Election?* for his benefit early in 1801, but nothing is known of it. Nor is there any information on *Embargo; or, The Honest Countryman*, a farce by "a gentleman of Charleston" which appeared at the Charleston Theatre on April 27, 1808. One of the two plays which J. Horatio Nichols contributed to the reading public in 1801, *Jefferson and Liberty* (1801) was described as a "patriotic tragedy: a picture of the perfidy of corrupt administration in five acts." More appropriately styled propaganda than drama, this work in high-flown and ragged blank verse pieces together a number of episodes bolstered by scenes of farce humor, all of which make little sense. Act I introduces a triangle—the love of Horatio and Warner for Eliza, an indifferent coquette who feels "born to murder all who love me"—which eventually brings disaster to Horatio. Act II, scarcely a page in length, presents the Duke of Braintree (John Adams), an arrogant friend of the English who despises the "beastly, swinish multitude" and plans the murder of Robbins. In a more lengthy Act III, Peter Porcupine (William Cobbett, described in the dramatis personae as "Blackguard") intrigues with the minister from England. Other episodes show Alexander Hamilton caught trying to seduce a lady and subsequently tarred and feathered for his daring. Braintree swoons before Robbins' ghost as his crimes are recorded. Act V takes place in the Senate chamber as Jefferson presents his "Inaugural Speech." This is followed by a song denouncing Adams' "reign of madness and terror" and praising Columbia, where freedom will never expire "until ocean and land are dissolved on fire," and by an epilogue blessing the new administration "with Jefferson our head."

As propaganda *Jefferson and Liberty* extravagantly ridiculed the opposition but with little art or finesse and was much like *The Essex Junto; or, Quixotic Guardian*, which Nichols published the following year. In this allegorical play, however, there is a clear plot. The Duke of Braintree (Adams), having been given the guardianship of Virginia, the daughter of Old Patriot (Washington), sees the possibility of a crown and orders Creole (Hamilton) to kill Old Patriot. Instead, Creole kidnaps Virginia, who happens to be in love with Monticello (Jefferson), and tries to marry her; but she refuses him just as she has rejected the Earl of Indigo (Pinckney) and Braintree. Fighting among themselves, the disappointed suitors are disarmed by Monticello and his followers, and the Old Patriot climaxes the action by giving Virginia to Monticello. Although both of Nichols' plays oppose the Federalist tendencies toward a monarchial central power, the second play also attacks the conspiracy among the conservative "River Gods" of Connecticut and the Essex Junto of Massachusetts to break up the new country and offers the new Jefferson administration as the enlightened savior of the people. Both plays are also probably more interesting to political historians than to drama critics.

Another political satire published in 1802, *Federalism Triumphant in the Steady Habits of Connecticut Alone; or, The Turnpike Road to a Fortune* was written by Leonard Chester (1750–1803), a Yale graduate of 1769 whose family had emigrated to America in 1633 and settled in Connecticut. Published anonymously as "a comic opera or political farce" in six acts, it included a preface describing the work as "a slight amusement" created to suggest the ludicrous attitude of the state legislature. A reference in the preface to performances in Hartford and New Haven in 1801 is suspiciously part of the satire. Long and rambling, this work is essentially an argument composed of oratorical speeches and disjointed dialogue. It opens at the legislative session in New Haven on October 9, 1801, and what little plot exists revolves around a bill to be passed. Mainly, Chester shows a thorough knowledge of local and national events as he satirizes a broad range of politics and people: the influence and partiality of priests in political sermons, the stupidity and venality of lawmakers, those who want a monarchy rather than a government "dependent upon the fickle whims of popular elections," and corruption in general (one man was elected "on the express condition of sending endowments to Yale College"). Phrases in the title such as *Federalism Triumphant* and *Steady Habits* are part of the satire, while the idea of creating a turnpike from Hartford to New Haven satirizes the turnpike company which is controlled by the legislators for their own advantage and with the purpose of creating an aristocracy in Connecticut. With regard to individuals, Chester has particularly strong words for John Trumbull, who had satirized him as "Lag" in the *Anarchiad*. Chester berates Trumbull as McFingal, gives him long speeches (four pages in one instance), and burlesques him in the style of his own poem (*McFingal*): "Dispute and pray, fight and groan/ For public good, and mean your own." Essentially, the play is a violent and scurrilous attack upon the Federalists and their habits and dreams in Connecticut, fitting well into the tradition of dramatic satire practiced in colonial and revolutionary times.

Oriented more toward positive nationalism than toward bitter satire, Joseph Croswell (1786–1857) also presents a more salutary thesis in his five-act historical drama, *A New World Planted; or, The Adventures of the Forefathers of New England who landed in Plymouth, December 22, 1620* (1802). His is really an epic scene with an epic thesis: "What holy fires of zeal and piety,/ Inspir'd our great Forefathers to be Free?" (prologue). And in generally readable blank verse he tells of the English arrival at Plymouth, the welcome by Samoset, and the possible war with the Indians. Clearly epic in structure, too, the work has varied and dramatic scenes. The daughter of King Massasoit, for example, Pocahonte, is dressed in English clothes and has an English lover, while Massasoit occasionally adds an original touch by speaking in his Indian tongue: "Wame muckone nashpee, mesegheenk koh, wonnomittuoonk." The villains of the play, two white men named Lynford and Oldham, try to preach the Church of Rome, crush the Indian treaty, and cause rebellion. Eventually, they are captured by Captain Miles Standish with Massasoit's help, tried by the people in a rather interesting court scene that dramatizes the thesis of the play, and banished rather than put to death. From the large cast of characters, most of whom appear in history, William Brewster speaks the epilogue, emphasizing Washington and victory: "The splendor's of our unborn race, I see." Although Croswell provided some story and conflict, additional action and a little humor would have made his work more appealing. Perhaps he did satisfy himself, however. His purpose, he noted, was to write a eulogy to the age. Probably never produced, the play reads better than some which were.

In *Liberty in Louisiana* (1804), James Workman treated a contemporary issue and had his play produced successfully upon the stage. Workman (d.1832), Irish by birth, studied law in England and emigrated no later than 1799 to America, where he became a citizen of Charleston in 1804. Here his play was first produced on April 4. He then almost immediately left for New Orleans, where he became involved in civic and political affairs, served as judge of the county of Orleans, and was himself subjected to litigation through his involvement in the Burr Conspiracy although he evidently redeemed himself in the eyes of the citizenry of New Orleans. Among his writings *Political Essays* (1801) advocates those ideas which were to appear in his play: the oppression of Spanish rule, the idea that the United States should take possession of Louisiana, the stalwart character of the Irish.

With New Orleans as the setting for this farce-comedy, Workman's plot follows the attempt of a young Irishman, Phelim O'Flinn, to marry Laura, the rich ward of a lecherous old judge, Don Bertholdo, who is himself infatuated with the girl. Phelim's plans to impersonate Captain O'Brien, Laura's American suitor, are thwarted by Laura and Theresa, the housekeeper, who substitute Lucy, a girl Phelim left pregnant in Tennessee, for Laura in the marriage ceremony. The play ends as Lucy marries O'Brien, and the Americans raise their flag over New Orleans to establish "Liberty in Louisiana." All of the farce action, however, is peripheral to Workman's thesis, which is dramatized in the play through court cases brought before Don Bertholdo. Satirizing the Spanish despotic legal system through the corruption of this judge, Workman comments on the problems of heirs obtaining land they have inherited, on unjust imprisonments, and on bribery among officials. Workman's simple answer to the problems is to bring American rule to Louisiana. Although the play seems to have been widely read and successfully acted in New York and Philadelphia, among other places, its rambling character should have been a disadvantage. The love plot, though filled with colorful, realistic, and humorous material, is imitative of English farce, while the trial scenes are left to carry the burden of the satiric propaganda. The loosely connected episodes of those two major thrusts show the playwright's determination to try to please audiences with comic characters and farce action while, with his Irish eye for the dramatic situation, convincing them of his ideas through pointed satire.

James Workman is identified with a Southern school of playwrights that began to attract attention just after the turn of the century. Charleston, of course, had been an established theatre town for two generations of audiences, along with Williamsburg, Virginia. Playwriting, too, had been fairly encouraged from the efforts of those who created *Ye Bare and Ye Cubb* to the plays of John Beete, John Daly Burk, and a number of "gentlemen of the city." One of the first playwrights to be recognized in the Southern school was William Ioor (1780–1850), whose two comedies were performed at the Charleston Theatre. Ioor's forebears (the name is usually pronounced "Yōr") emigrated from Holland in 1714 and established themselves in South Carolina. Sometime before 1800 Ioor took a diploma in medicine from the University of Pennsylvania and became a registered physician in his home area of Dorchester, South Carolina, in 1805. In the interim he served in the general assembly from St. George, Dorchester, and may well have turned to the theatre as a natural platform for his political views. There is also evidence that he was engaged in farming, for both politics and farming provide the themes of his plays. Some time after his theatre ventures, Ioor moved to Savannah, Georgia, where he practiced medicine, and then returned late in life to the Greenville district of South Carolina where he died. A man of obviously vigorous opinions about both politics and drama, he dedicated his second play to the Republicans of South Carolina in general and, in particular, to those who saw the play in performance.

Independence; or, Which Do You Like Best, the Peer or the Farmer? (1805), a five-act comedy based on an English novel, Andrew MacDonald's *The Independent*, closely follows Jefferson's agrarian ideals while satirizing the rich, aristocratic society of England which Ioor accepted as having loose morals and a singular love of money. In the play Lord Fanfare is insulted because Farmer Charles Woodville is not only thoroughly unimpressed with the wealth and title he enjoys but refuses to sell his property to him. Fanfare's less-than-honorable nature is further revealed by his plans to seduce Woodville's sister, but his plans are cleverly foiled at a spectacular costume ball where Woodville is disguised as Dame Quickly and his sister as Pistol.

In other comic and melodramatic episodes of this loosely structured play, Fanfare plots against Woodville and is defeated by a comic, but honorable, figure, Sir Strutabout Talkbig. Later, he is frightened out of his wits in a haunted-castle scene in which Woodville and his friends pose as Lucifer and his devils. With the final ruination of Fanfare, everyone happily toasts "the honest farmer and Independence." In addition to its satire on English society, lawyers, legislation, and language, the comedy is an early expression in American literature of agrarianism and Jeffersonian Republicanism, which Ioor enthusiastically supported. As a play, however, it is slight on character and heavy on melodramatic devices, spectacles, and manipulated incidents. Although not a great deal is made of the farmer—in truth, a gentleman farmer—Woodville is a man of true Jeffersonian independence. It is this theme of independence as well as the fact that it is the first dramatic offering by a native of South Carolina which distinguishes the play in the developing American drama.

A firm believer in America and its independence, Ioor wrote *The Battle of Eutaw Springs*, according to a letter in the *City Gazette* (July 16, 1806), "to exalt the American character and, possibly, depress that of the British government." First performed in Charleston in January, 1807, and later, in Richmond and Philadelphia, the play employed the popular patriotic spectacles which mixed history and fiction, allegory and real people. After an opening chorus by Continental Soldiers, Generals Greene and Marion and their officers

cross swords and swear never to sheath them until independence has been won
or Congress releases them—an interesting alternative consideration. Next, the
enemy's positions at Eutaw Springs are being scouted; Greene is visited by the
Genius of Liberty, who tells him that America will succeed; patriotic speeches
are delivered before the historic battle; even Washington appears for a moment. Such seriousness requires relief, and it comes with a British soldier,
Queerfish, who provides good farce humor while escaping personal disaster
and supports the author's thesis by deciding to "become an AMERICAN
CITIZEN." To dramatize his politics Ioor contrasts the Tory plundering in
the South with a Whig family called Slyboots (a respected name in Charleston
at this time) who represent the admirable, patriotic Southerners. Structurally,
concern for Queerfish and the Slyboots overshadows Greene's actions, but the
climax is his as the British evacuate Charleston and Greene makes his triumphal entry in full parade with martial music.

For the reader, the long patriotic speeches in *The Battle of Eutaw Springs*
are dull, and the activities of the secondary characters, though welcome as
comic relief, throw the play out of balance and scatter the effect of some good
farce scenes, some moving patriotic spectacles, and, according to contemporary criticism in the *City Gazette* (January 14, 1807), "a faithful record" of
the battle. One interesting by-product of the work, suggesting the strength of
the play's political views, was the attitudes toward the drama, and toward
Ioor's play in particular, which appeared in current issues of the Federalist
and Republican newspapers in Charleston.

Britain was one source of irritation to the new nation, but, in as much as
the attacks on American shipping by the Barbary Coast pirates brought America its first military challenge beyond its borders, it is surprising that more
plays were not written on the subject. Susanna Rowson had offered one such
play before the turn of the century, but James Ellison's *The American Captive;
or, The Siege of Tripoli*, performed in the Boston Theatre in 1811, was the
only other important play on the subject before the War of 1812 gave the
military-minded playwright something else to think about. For the drama
historian the prologue to Ellison's play provides an unusual insight into the
delicate position of the dramatist of the time. Near the theatre in Boston, a
drunken sailor encounters a poet-critic who explains that his trade is "to
write—to puff—to ridicule—degrade." Inside the theatre the sailor again
meets the poet-critic and throws him out, explaining that the people are the
real critics of the play. Then *The American Captive*, in five acts, begins—the
usual complicated melodrama. Although it starts slowly with stiff and un-
wieldy language, the pace quickens as the Americans enter the scene. In

Tripoli trouble between the present Bashaw and the former Bashaw explodes when Anderson, an officer on a recently captured American ship, joins Immorina, the daughter of the former Bashaw, in her attempt to gain freedom and revenge for her father. As an American, Anderson is a man of honor and love; and in America all, including the blacks, are free. Songs and declarations support his attitude. It is, therefore, only proper that Anderson help Immorina through the horrors that melodrama invents, and in the final act an American frigate draws near, and the marines land to do battle. Anderson kills the villainous slave trader and delivers Immorina to her father: "Who fells the Tyrant—sets the Captive—Free!" Into that curtain line Ellison forced the thought of his play; the rest was fun and spectacle.

Although full-length plays about the War of 1812 were slow in coming, there was considerable activity upon the stages of America which reflected the progress of the war. Because America's most significant victories were fought at sea, many of the plays tested the ability of theatre managers and their crews to handle water on the stage. On the night of September 28, 1812, for example, the Chestnut Street Theatre in Philadelphia presented a "patriotic opera," *The Constitution; or, American Tars Triumphant*, complete with chase and battle. In Boston the following month, there was a spectacle called *The Constitution and Guerrière; or, A Tribute to the Brave*. James Fennell's *Hero of the Lake; or, The Victory of Commodore Perry* (1813) was a brief poem in iambic tetrameter rather than a play, but he often presented it on stage as a "patriotic salute." This would seem to be different from a dramatization of Samuel Woodworth's poem celebrating Perry's victory on Lake Erie, September 10, 1813, which appeared on the Boston stage as *Heroes of the Lake*. Other plays in Boston in December of that year included two patriotic sketches, *America, Commerce, and Freedom* and *The Genius of America*. The following April there were five performances of *The Battle of York; or, the Death of General Pike*. Generally, however, such spectacles illuminated the stage for only a night or two before disappearing forever. Newness and novelty were desirable features for American theatre at this time, and it is impossible to know fully the contribution of Americans to this fleeting wartime entertainment.

DRAMA: A UTILITARIAN WEAPON WITH A MELODRAMATIC TWIST

Nationalism was one concern of American dramatists which would only intensify as the country grew. Deeply imbedded in the American consciousness, also, was a concern for social and personal morality. By the first decade of the nineteenth century, the publication of sermons and patriotic orations might take up more than half the printer's time. With such inclinations toward oratory and propaganda, it is not surprising that Americans made considerable use of dialogues and plays as utilitarian weapons. Precedents had been clearly established in the early eighteenth century, and as time passed such techniques for instruction or persuasion became acceptable in church and academy.

One of the most extensive collections of published dialogues was Charles Stearns' *Dramatic Dialogues for the Use of Schools* (1798). A Unitarian minister preaching in Lincoln, Massachusetts, Stearns (1753–1826) also wrote religious poems. Another volume, published in 1800, was *Dialogues for Schools*, "selected, with alterations, from the works of various dramatic writers, to which is added an appendix, containing a selection of pieces for declamation," with titles such as "Money Makes the Mare Go," "Filial Confidence," "False Pride," and "The Dissipated Wife Reformed." Each piece conveyed a moral lesson with one character acting as the "sinner" who would be led by others to recognize his mistake or sin and to change his ways. Richard Salter Storrs (1787–1873) contributed *A Dialogue, exhibiting some of the principal and practical consequences of modern infidelity* (1806). More particularly related to religion, Edmund Botsford's *Sambo and Toney* (1808) is a dialogue in three parts in which Sambo, a hardworking, religious Negro, finally converts Toney, who helps things along by acting as a kind of vaudevillian straight man. By asking rather pointed questions, Toney allows Sambo to talk about religion for black people, about prayer, the "good life in Christ," and happiness for sinners. This particular dialogue in dialect became a favorite tool for Christian ministers and was included in an 1811 publication with the subtitle "A Dialogue; Between Two Africans in South Carolina, to which is added Biographical Sketches of Two West Indian Black Men." It also appeared in the Reverend William Meade's "Tracts & Dialogues" as appended to his edition of Bacon's sermons (1813). One of the Reverend Meade's original contributions to his collection was "A Dialogue Between Two Seamen after a Storm," in which Jack explains religion to Tom in terms of a sailor's experiences and warns him against drunkenness and adultery.

Traditionally in America the dramatist and the theatre manager frequently had to defend the stage as a platform for morality. Critics, too, took part in the argument and never seemed to tire of making an issue, either positively or negatively, of the morality in a play. Many, in fact, felt that it was the obligation of the dramatist to improve morals in society. While those who created dialogues for the explicit purpose of moral instruction used one element of the drama, they were not, obviously, writing for the professional stage, where prejudices still converged. Some who did write for the stage, however, readily accepted the critics' challenge. The anonymous author of *The Better Sort* (1789) was quite specific:

> For this the comic muse "first trod the stage,"
> And scourg'd the vice and folly of the age,
> Manners and sometimes principles she mended,
> And took her task up—where the preacher ended.
> [Prologue.]

In revising *The Father* William Dunlap increased the moralizing in direct response to his audience. The moral, as such, in almost all of the plays written at this time—romantic tragedies, sentimental comedies, even satires—was tremendously important in terms of the play's potential success with both a reading and a viewing public.

Expression of a concern for morals could be as vague as a reference to "sinning," but the dramatist generally chose a particular vice. One that bothered a number of people at this early time was dueling, particularly after the Hamilton-Burr duel on July 11, 1804, although dueling had long been practiced in America—and denounced. In a letter to Jeremiah Wadsworth, dated September 10, 1780, David Humphreys, statesman and dramatist, told of three duels in which two men were killed and three were wounded: "So you see what a passion we have for fighting—What a pity it was not gratified on a Common Enemy!"[15] *Favelle; or, The Fatal Duel* (1809) is a brief, one-act play of seven scenes by Charles L. Adams (1781–1851), who also wrote dramatic criticism. The scene is France, where Charles de Vineuil, who feels insulted by a comment Favelle makes, arranges a duel. Although Favelle tries to resist, the duel takes place, Charles is killed, and Favelle, in great agony over his deed, has to be prevented from taking his own life. At the climax he weeps over the body of Charles and for his own "hellish guilt" as a murderer and is haunted by a semblance of furies from which he tries to run before falling senseless to the ground. In ten pages it is not much of a drama, but it seems to have scrutinized some feelings of the day.

A more substantial play on the same subject is John Blake White's *Modern Honor* (1812), called a tragedy in five acts, which scourges dueling through the fierce machinations of the villain, Forsythe. As part of the author's protest, the action takes place in "any part of the *civilized world*." Relaxing in idyllic surroundings, Charles Devalmore anticipates a visit from Woodville, who is to marry Charles' sister, Maria. Posing as a mutual friend of both men, Forsythe seeks revenge on Woodville for being successful with Maria, who has rejected Forsythe. As a villain who believes that "in these rude days the only safeguard to a man of honor is the pistol" (II, i), Forsythe maneuvers Woodville into disgracing himself sufficiently with Maria to warrant a duel with Charles, whom Woodville unfortunately kills. In a second duel with Forsythe, whom he now suspects of villainy, Woodville is killed, leaving sorrow everywhere as the police pursue Forsythe. Act II and Act V contain long condemnations of dueling. *Modern Honor* is, in fact, the first full-length antidueling play written in America. Although the action is often deftly arranged, the dramatist is reduced to thrusting people on and off stage as his polemic demands. The blank verse is also quite artificial while the characters become vehicles for White's sincere outbursts against dueling.

Toward the end of the eighteenth century, when American fiction was beginning to reach an audience, it became popular to use "fallen" women to illustrate a moral point of view. Three-quarters of a century later, temperance speakers would place "horrible examples" on the stage to illustrate their ideas. Although the "horrible examples" of early fiction were far less real, their popularity cannot be questioned. Mrs. Rowson contributed *Charlotte Temple* (1790), which would eventually be dramatized; William Brown, *The Power of Sympathy* (1789); and Hannah Foster, *The Coquette* (1797). Sensing the popularity of that fiction, dramatists created domestic sentimental plays to illustrate better the potential of the stage as a platform for morality. A dramatization of *The Coquette* might have been expected, and, because Aaron Burr had been identified with the villain of the novel, it was not strange that such a strong anti-Federalist as J. Horatio Nichols, author of *Jefferson and Liberty* and *The Essex Junto*, would be the adaptor.

Nichols called his play *The New England Coquette* (1802) a "tragic drama in three acts" taken from the "history of the celebrated Eliza Wharton." Although it is difficult to make a tragic heroine of a girl who rejects a good man to give herself to a scoundrel who boasts of seduction and thanks God that he has no conscience, Nichols was only following the temper of the times when he tried. Friends try to save Eliza from the villain, but, when a message comes that Sanford wants Eliza back, her response is typical of Nichols' dialogue: "It is from Major Sanford; he who has undone me, robbed me of health and happiness, wishes an interview" (II, iv). Sanford finally discovers a conscience, however, and, tormented by his villainous actions (of which he has an abundance), he stabs himself when he learns that Eliza and her infant child are dead. The play ends as Eliza's friends stand before the monument of "our departed heroine": "Let charity draw a veil over her frailties, for great was her charity to others." The ambiguity here is tantalizing; in the play her charity extended only toward Sanford. In retrospect it all seems to prove that excessive sentiment is no better and no worse in drama than it is in fiction, but in this instance the novel was far more popular than the play.

Two other dramatists tried to use the popular contemporary sentimentalism in domestic situations to create didactic plays. One was George Watterston (1783–1854), a novelist and the first librarian of Congress, whose single play, *The Child of Feeling* (1809), was presumably composed at his leisure and at the request of his friends. A number of years later, in 1822, Watterston wrote a fictitious account of life in and about Washington, *The T . . . Family of Washington; or, A Winter in the Metropolis*. In his humorous commentary on society, politics, stagecoach and carriage travel, literary critics, and legislators, he suggests his attitude toward available entertainment by noting that the circus "is the only kind of exhibition they have at this place in the winter" and that "they have but one theatre here, and that is opened during a part of the summer months only by a company of strollers from Philadelphia who are scarcely encouraged to do even that."

The Child of Feeling, a comedy in five acts set in Philadelphia, is a long, wordy play in which the plot is moved by a succession of letters. Yet, despite the long and pointed speeches in which Watterston reveals his nationalistic feelings, the plot moves surprisingly well. George Montford, the "child" of too much feeling, cannot marry Julia because his father has been bankrupted by a villain who will send that worthy person to prison if Matilda, George's sister, will not marry him. To increase George's problems there is a simpering fop, Splash, who tries to discredit Julia in his eyes, and a lackey of the villain, Etymology, who constantly gushes word derivations. At a critical point in the plot, a mysterious, rich, and helpful man saves George's friend, Old Montford, and identifies himself as Julia's father. Of all humanity, Watterston explains, "the child of feeling is the most wretched." But he also compensates George for his agony by giving him Julia in marriage. Humor is provided throughout by Mr. and Mrs. Polemic, with whom Julia lives, she as the accomplice of Splash, he as a man totally absorbed with politics and Napoleon's activities. The play lacks good characters, but it has more than enough plot and were it considerably shortened would have compared well with other plays acted at this time.

After William Charles White had debuted as an actor in Boston and written *Orlando*, he abandoned the theatre to study law. But the theatre evidently still had a claim on him, and he wrote two more plays, both performed at the Federal Street Theatre in Boston with epilogues written by Robert Treat Paine, whom White extolled as "America's first bard." Both plays also made strong moral statements through the format of the melodrama, which was then gaining popularity throughout England and Western Europe. As did many of his contemporaries, White tended to write complicated plots with bloodless heroines who lacked noticeable ties to humanity. As a moralist employing a serious thesis, he also thought that he was writing tragedy.

Acknowledging a debt to McKenzie's novel, *The Man of the World*, White published *The Clergyman's Daughter* in 1810 after performances which, according to contemporary critics, had "many touching passages . . . which would be admired by any audience in the world."[16] The action of the play moves through a well-devised villain, Lord Sindal, who controls people for evil purposes yet puts on the face of a good man in society, even winning the confidence of the Reverend Annesley, his son Theodore, and his daughter Emeline. Sindal's objective is the seduction of Emeline, and his method is to take Theodore to London, introduce him to drinking and gambling, and finally fake his arrest so that Emeline will come to London. All of this takes place as planned, but by Act IV Sindal has tired of Emeline who, ruined and abandoned, loses her sanity and dies—but not before Theodore avenges his sister's treatment. Scenes in a London brothel and Theodore's declaration—"By heaven, I'll make cursed haunts of lust a scene of horrible desolation" (III, i)—suggest the kind of moral melodrama White envisioned, but all action is determined by the supremely evil qualities of the villain. The clergyman's daughter becomes simply the sentimental victim.

White's *The Poor Lodger* (1811) was also based on a novel, Fanny Burney's *Evelina*. Something of the confusion of the times that haunted dramatists appears in White's serious confession in his prologue that he didn't know whether to call his play a comedy or a tragedy. Finally, he settled on a "comedy in five acts" but noted his interest in alternating comic and serious scenes. For *The Clergyman's Daughter* James Fennell had written and delivered a prologue extolling the author as a native son. For this second play the prologue added a tentative quality to the nationalistic view: "Tonight, a town-bred bard, with fearful pride/ Awaits that fate, your voice must soon decide." Not all dramatists dared to confess authorship, but among the nationalistic-minded such bold pleas were becoming popular.

How White could have considered calling this play a tragedy stretches the imagination. The heroine, Harriet, has two suitors, the noble Lord Harley and the foppish Sir Harry Stormont. Dick Joblin, a humorous country bumpkin also has eyes for the poor heroine—alone in the world, her mother dead, and disowned by her father. At the Joblin's house there is a poor lodger who attracts little sympathy except from Harriet, whose tender care shows her to be an exemplary individual. And that is the situation around which love and mystery revolve. The good news in the last act of melodrama is sometimes even less understandable than it is bearable, and perhaps that is why White had the lodger reveal himself to the audience in Act III but make Harriet wait until Act IV to discover that he is her father. Then news comes that the man who stole his fortune has died and has willed it all back to him with the happy result that Harriet can marry Harley. One interesting aspect at the end of this play is Paine's five-page epilogue in poetic dialogue praising all of the characters in the play and concluding that love is wonderful, good fortune is nice, and "life is great fun." Both of White's plays suggest the popularity of adaptations and the audience enjoyment of sentimental stories. As a sometime-actor and playwright who wrote three professionally produced plays, he has some historical stature in a history of the drama but no distinctive qualities as a dramatist.

Nathaniel W. Eaton's *Alberto and Matilda; or, The Unfortunate Lovers* (1809) is a tearful melodrama in two acts. As the prologue modestly states, "a Shakespeare's fame is not projected here," and H. C. Delthorpe, in an epilogue, begs the audience's indulgence and apologizes for the first work of a young playwright, the "off-spring of Columbia's soil." If the irony on which the moral tale is based were not so serious, some of the lines would be humorous. As a melancholy hero rather than as a villain, Alberto confesses to the audience that he has been Matilda's seducer. With unexplainable foreknowledge and even less modesty, he foretells that "she little dreams that she will shortly be a mother." Then Matilda enters to say that her father is returning after two years' absence and wants her to marry a certain Charles Wilmot. Matilda has no mother; Alberto, no father. It must turn out, ironically, that the shipwreck seventeen years ago in which Matilda's father lost his son and wife was not fatal for either one. Much is left unexplained, but Alberto and Matilda's reluctantly recognize each other as brother and sister. As the husband and wife find happiness in reunion, their distraught children face a desperate situation, resolved as Matilda takes poison and Alberto kills himself with a dagger. Although the theme of incest was not new in the world of fiction, it was rare on the American stage and seldom was the moral lesson carried this far.

Sarah Pogson would seem to have written her "tragedy," *The Female En-*

thusiast (1807), as an exemplum of heroic and moral action, but it is little
more than a chaotic melodrama in erratic and highly romantic blank verse.
Charlotte Corday is the mad enthusiast who kills Marat because she sees him
as an enemy of freedom. Convicted by a court and in prison, Charlotte, who
is proud of her act, describes herself as a "victim of the times" before she is
taken away to the guillotine. But her reasoning is unclear. Much of the plot
deals with the actions of Charlotte's soldier brother who, somewhat removed
from his sister's difficulties, marries the girl he loves and at the final curtain
leaves for America "where quiet reigns." The play would seem to have a nationalistic thesis with Marat, who calls himself a "demigod," as the villain,
Charlotte as the instrument of progressive thought, and America as the utopia.
Although Pogson's enthusiasm for her heroine, whose ironic fight as a "victim" for the freedom of others can scarcely be doubted, her technique as a
dramatist was sadly lacking, and she remains one of the weakest among the
several women dramatists of the period.

THE FOREIGN INFLUENCE

Nationalistic literature was popular with some writers and readers, but
most educated people maintained a decided preference for the literature of
the "mother country." William Cullen Bryant was not yet writing, nor was
Irving particularly interested in his own country. Consequently, a good number of the plays written showed a strong influence from contemporary English
and European drama in form, thesis, and plot. Those who imitated or adopted
foreign material were most likely to be the classically educated Americans who
had some pretense toward life among the literati as well as in the theatre although the drama hack was perhaps just as apt to try to ride the popular wave
of foreign literature marked by the Gothic movement. A major difference between the two was that the classically educated amateur invariably wrote better
poetry but was deficient in character development, incapable of creating dialogue for more than two characters in a scene, and less familiar with the demands of good theatre. Some of those criticisms apply to most plays written
at the time—foreign or American—but if there was any aspect which might
save the play for its audience it was the Gothic spectacle that the writers
employed.

Charles Jared Ingersoll (1782–1862) achieved a reputation as a lawyer,
legislator, United States district attorney for Pennsylvania, and man of letters.
As an amateur dramatist he showed some facility with blank verse and his

classical inclination in two tragedies, *Julian, the Apostate* (1831) and the five-act tragedy in blank verse, *Edwy and Elgiva*, which was performed at Philadelphia's Chestnut Street Theatre in 1801. The critic for the *Port Folio* (April 18, 1801) noted that this "first born of a muse in her teens excited great expectations" and was "received in a most urban and candid manner." The story comes from English history and tells of the struggle for supremacy between the Church represented by Dunstan and the monarchy of King Edwy, whose marriage to Elgiva the Church considers incestuous, thus initiating the inevitable conflict between "allegiance" and "faith." The conditions laid down by the Church—divorce, penance by the King, disbanding of troops, confiscation of estates or death for the Queen—mean war. For a while Edwy seems to be winning the battle; then Dunstan escapes him, and his troops flee. On the battlefield Elgiva, distracted, finds Edwy wounded, and both die together. The spectacle of a tournament at the end of Act I and the sword play of battle in Act V provide some exciting changes of pace from the church-state argument, while the wit of the King's fool adds considerably to the overall effect of the play. The verse, too, although highly romantic, moves well with a dignity unexpected in such a youthful dramatist, who showed his deficiencies mainly in weak characters and a lack of motivated action. With more effort and experience, Ingersoll might have contributed something of value to American drama, but he chose other careers.

The most prolific of the Southern pioneer dramatists at the time—five plays, three of them performed—John Blake White (1781–1859) also revealed his classical training and, in most instances, his preference for European material. The exceptions are his *Modern Honor*, and a later play, *The Triumph of Liberty; or, Louisiana Preserved* (1819). As *Modern Honor* illustrates, White was a man of ideals and breadth of purpose. A lawyer and talented artist, he was a South Carolina legislator, a participant in the War of 1812, an active member of the Literary and Philosophical Society formed in Charleston in 1813, and a reformer strongly opposed to capital punishment as early as 1820.[17] As a young man he went to England to study art under Benjamin West. While there he enjoyed the theatre and became fascinated with the romantic and Gothic movements which would dominate the style in which he created several of his plays. Returning to America he soon discovered the impossibility of earning a living as a painter. From that point on, law, social reform, drama, and painting became his main interests in a life which the writer of his obituary termed "a synthesis of the cultural and intellectual forces of ante-bellum Charleston."

White's first play was *Foscari; or, The Venetian Exile*, a five-act tragedy in blank verse published in 1806, performed initially in Charleston and frequently repeated.[18] According to the *Thespian Mirror* (February 1, 1806), it was "received with a considerable degree of applause." A later reviewer in the *Ordeal* (March 4, 1809) forgot the young dramatist's plea in his prologue to "be not too severe—with gentle hand,/ Cherish this scion of your native land," and made the following observation: "Although the play of Foscari is somewhat better than American dramatick productions have generally proved, it is to the last degree common-place in the conduct of the plot, the language and the thought . . . . We do not recollect a single idea contained in the play which aspires to the praise of excellence." Perhaps the nationalistic plea was being overworked at this time—certainly most Americans who identified themselves used it—and reviewers reacted negatively while reinterpreting Samuel Johnson's definition of "patriotism." But this critic seems to have been reasonably accurate in his assessment of Blake's play.

Foscari, the son of the Doge of Venice, has been banished on the charge of murdering Count Donato, whose daughter, Almeria, he loves. The play opens with his return for more questioning by the Council which controls his future. The real murderer and villain of the plot is Count Erizzo, who not only plans to kill Foscari and seduce Almeria but, through his henchman, Policarpo, persuades the Council to continue Foscari's banishment. Although such unquestioning dominance of evil over innocence and truth was, and still is, standard in melodrama, the reviewer for the *Ordeal*, who seems to have been more demanding than were many critics and audiences, was dismayed. Further events in the play did not change his attitude. Foscari's escape from a would-be assassin precipitates a fight among the villains in which Erizzo is left for dead. Rescued by fishermen, he undergoes a drastic change of character and reveals his villainy to the Doge. But his repentance is too late. Foscari, dragged off in distress to the ship for banishment, dies of "the fatal moment" which "was too big with woe." Viewing the body drives Almeria mad—"Despair, despair, distraction and disgrace," she moans—and the curtain falls gradually to solemn music. Such plays as *Foscari*, with their exaggerated emotions and strong sentiments, reveal as much about actors' methods as they do the tastes of audiences, and dramatists probably do not deserve to stand alone, bared to the biases of a critic's pleasure.

White's Gothic melodrama, *The Mysteries of the Castle; or, The Victim of Revenge*, performed on December 26 and 29, 1806, and February 19, 1807, shows the usual emphasis on spectacle and a lack of interest in anything thought-provoking. Set in Castile, the play, written in prose, is long and complicated with innumerable characters, many of whom are brought on only to explain a twist in the plot or a Gothic device. As were most melodramas of this period, it is lively and confusing, and it includes a full array of Gothic features: a ruined castle, shrieks and moans, bloody daggers and bloody "drapery," a mysterious and beautiful lady, a Count de Mainfrois, who has been wronged, a strange hermit, a spectre, subterranean chambers, a villainous Count Leopoldo, a band of men seeking revenge, secrets, disguises, battles, chases, darkness, and a happy ending. All the dramatist had to do was place a couple of adventurous young men where they can solve the mystery, help the hermit (who is really the wronged count) find the beautiful lady, his wife, and get revenge upon the villain through the aid of the band of men and the timely arrival of an army toward the end of the fifth act. The trappings of melodrama were then distributed as the plot required. In a final irony the villainous count is buried alive in the ruined castle where he had kept the beautiful lady. Regardless of the description, the scenery for this piece was probably not too elaborate. Only a suggestion of horror was required to satisfy the strong taste for Gothic melodrama in America, a taste stimulated by Dunlap and maintained by William Ioor, Isaac Harby, J. D. Turnbull, and Mordecai Noah, among many others.

White's other plays include *The Triumph of Liberty; or, Louisiana Preserved*, published in 1819 but never performed, and *The Forgers*, published in five issues of the *Southern Literary Journal* in 1835. The first is a historical drama which uses the Battle of New Orleans as a major plot device while emphasizing a defense of Andrew Jackson's actions during the Seminole War of 1818. *The Forgers*, first entitled *Mordaunt; or, the Victim of Intemperance*, was one of the first temperance plays in America.[19] Similar in approach to *Modern Honor*, this play in blank verse condemns the evils of drinking, which White also attacked in *Intemperance* (1839), and gambling in the acts of a young man who is finally driven by an evil companion to forgery, attempted murder, and a horrible death in prison brought on by drinking poison. The attitude of the reformer is clearly shown in the author's comment on the manuscript: "Scene, in any City of the United States, where Brandy, Whisky, Wine, etc, etc, are freely drunk." White must be regarded as only a fairly talented regional and amateur playwright, but the acceptance of his early Gothic plays and his use of American subject matter in *Modern Honor*, *Triumph of Liberty*, and *The Forgers* allow him a position of some substance in early theatrical circles.

Isaac Harby (1788–1828) was another ambitious South Carolina dramatist. An intelligent, energetic, and confident man who openly admitted, "I am proud to own, I write for fame," he was a leader among Jews in America as president of the Hebrew Orphan Society and Founder of the Society of Reformed Israelites of Charleston. Harby was also a teacher, an editor of *Quiver* as well as of the *Investigator*, which he changed to the *Southern Patriot*, an esteemed and prolific drama critic, and the author of three plays. His first play, *Alexander Severus*, written when he was seventeen, was rejected by Alexander Placide, then manager of the Charleston Theatre, who later said that "dat Mons Harby vish to write like Shakespeare, and dat vas wrong, because Shakespeare vas old, but *he* vas young, and he made de people laugh, just after he make dem cry."[20] His other plays were *The Gordian Knot; or, Causes and Effects* (1807) and *Alberti* (1819). Whatever his intention, however, Harby found little fame with his plays. In fact, managers in Charleston and Philadelphia rejected *The Gordian Knot*, and he had to wait until 1810, the year he published it, before seeing it on stage. In a preface he described his difficulties and acknowledged that major parts of his first two acts came from the *Secreto Maligno* by an unknown Italian writer as revealed in Ireland's *Abbess*. Beyond this debt Harby went his own way. Rejecting the Gothic melodrama of his model and its attendant "monstrosities," he claimed to pursue "NATURE" as he saw it.

The scene of *The Gordian Knot* is Florence in the sixteenth century, and the plot is as complicated as the blank verse is forbidding. Following a worn pattern in drama, Harby has one major character, Ferdinand, swear vengeance upon another, Bertocci, for killing his father and brother. Adding a slight twist to this situation, Harby creates a mysterious priest who reveals that he gave Bertocci's infant son to a villain to be trained for the murder of his father. One of the best scenes is that in which Ferdinand incites Alphonso, his supposed son, to a frenzy of revenge toward Bertocci for some unexplained crime upon his mother. Bertocci's son, Marcello, precipitates little action but Marcello becomes the foil of the priest, who makes him swear an oath of secrecy which will be a "gordian knot" before finally revealing what will happen. Although the complication involving the sons suggests some imagination, the plot depends almost entirely on the manipulated secrecy—the "gordian knot"—and the resulting problems. So that the audience will not be completely lost, however, there is a repeated story that Bertocci will be threatened by one son and saved by another. Some sympathy for the theatre managers and audiences who held prejudices toward American drama is certainly not always misplaced, but there is also the tenable sentiment of a critic for the Charleston *Times* (May 11, 1810) who pleaded for "public favor" for this first youthful offering which, he felt, merited "protection."

While Harby was not successful with his two early plays, the achievements of William Ioor and John Blake White which influenced him to write for the stage in Charleston apparently also stimulated others to try their luck. One such writer was William Bullock Maxwell (1787–1814), a well-educated young man from a professional family in Savannah, Georgia, whose familiarity with theatre techniques suggests that he attended the theatre in Charleston although Placide regularly visited Georgia. Maxwell's single effort in drama was a Gothic melodrama in blank verse called *The Mysterious Father*. After Placide rejected the five-act play, Maxwell published it in 1807. Having been treated in a similar fashion by Placide, Harby reviewed the play with some favor in *Quiver*, reserving the latter part of his essay for an attack on Placide. Perhaps taking some material from Dunlap's *Ribbemont; or, The Feudal Baron* (1803), which had been presented in 1796 as *The Mysterious Monk*, and certainly showing knowledge of Shakespeare and the mysterious devices of Pixérécourt, Maxwell built his melodrama around the machinations of an evil monk named Antonio. One mystery surrounds Pirozzi, a nobleman who has disguised himself as a peasant. Another involves the influence of the evil monk on Count Veroni. The plot reaches its climax after Orsino, son of Count Veroni, kills Antonio in a bizarre Gothic scene at the tomb of his mother and is reunited with his sweetheart, Elvira, the daughter of Pirozzi. A derivative play, to say the least, with rather immature verse, and Placide seems to have shown good judgment in rejecting it.

John D. Turnbull was an actor who played in theatres in Boston, New York, and Charleston. During his brief career he either wrote or adapted a number of plays, many with foreign settings complete with elements of Gothic melodrama. With these he illustrated again the inescapable fact that before the War of 1812 actors wrote many of the better plays recognized as native efforts in American theatres. Among his plays are *Rudolph; or, The Robbers of Calabria* (1804); *Domestic Folly*, an "original burletto" (1805); *The Maid of Hungary* (1806); *Tars of Tripoli* (1806); *Victor; or, The Independents of Bohemia* (1806); *The Wood Daemon; or, The Clock Has Struck* (1808). Neither highly educated nor a poet, Turnbull mainly used the material that was close at hand for an actor and adapted the works of others. Although only two of his plays are extant, those suggest his talents well enough.

Rudolph closely follows its original—*La Forêt périlleuse; ou, les Brigands de la Calabre* (1797) by J. M. Loaisel-Tréogate—and, as an early adaptation of a French *mélodrame*, had considerable popularity on the stage. In three acts with "marches, combats, and choruses" and an interesting use of music throughout, *Rudolph* was an exciting, carefully devised melodrama. Searching for his betrothed in the Forest of Calabria, Albert and his humorous servant, Pablo, overhear a robber band planning an attack, conceal themselves in the robbers' cavern, and are locked in. There they find a girl, Rosalia, and together plot to destroy the leader of the band, Rudolph. Her attempt to poison his wine fails, however, and Albert is captured and sent off to be executed by Morgano, one of the bandits. When Albert is brought back on a bier, he unexpectedly rises, embraces Rosalia, shoots Rudolph, and explains how his life was saved by Morgano, who is really a colonel in the Sicilian army. The simplicity of the play added to its success, but it also had the necessary melodramatic ingredients of spectacle in the feast and drinking scene, action and thrills in the sword and pistol fights, and the Gothic charm of a cavern in the forest.

Although Turnbull's dependence on foreign scenes was a result of his models, he enhanced his materials with a talent for theatricality which has not been recognized. *The Wood Daemon*, described as "a grand, romantic cabalistic melodrama in three acts interspersed with processions, pageants, and pantomime," used a German legend and M. G. Lewis' *The Wood Daemon* as sources. The author also acknowledged unspecified suggestions by Robert T. Paine. This popular play had spectacle, Gothic thrills, some unusual devices for melodrama, and a story with good humor, sentiment, and a happy ending. It opens with the scene of a child chained to a post and about to be killed by the Wood Daemon, who feeds on human blood. But Auriol, a kind of nymph, explains that the child can be saved. Then the plot unfolds. Lady Una is about to marry Hardy Canute, the usurping Count of Holstein, who appears to be gentle but is in reality a fraud and monster who has made a covenant with the Wood Daemon whereby in exchange for wealth and position he provides him with a child each year. Thus far he has killed eight for the Wood Daemon. A crisis occurs when, at a pageant given for Hardy's amusement, Clotilda, Una's aunt, recognizes a young boy as Leolyn, the lawful count who was stolen from her safekeeping:

CLOTILDA.   'Tis as I feared!—The resemblance has struck him and we are ruined!
(*The bloody arrow stamped by nature on* LEOLYN'S *right hand meets* THE COUNT'S *eye—who starts from the bower, seizes* LEOLYN *by the arm, and points to the fatal mark.*)
COUNT.   Speak! Who art thou? That mark! What form is this which stands before me? Clotida, is this your child?
CLOTILDA.   Yes, my lord.—No—it is—
COUNT.   How! not know your own son? I'll know who he is! (*aside*) This is certainly the boy. No matter. (*To* LEOLYN.) Your pardon, my

pretty lad; give me the wreath—(LEOLYN *gives it and runs to* CLO-TILDA.) It is he, by my soul! the long lost son of Rusic! What's to be done?—Let the dance go on.

[I, ii.]

As a climax to the second act, the Wood Daemon appears and intones the single word, "Remember!" whereupon Count Hardy faints. Later, Leolyn is spirited away to a cavern where Una finds him chained to an altar and about to be sacrificed. Happily, Leolyn is able to slip a note to Una: "The clock shall strike, and you shall hear it—gain but a minute, and you are safe." Having been told by Auriol that she has the power to save Leolyn, Una gives him the magic wand with which he pushes forward the minute hand of the clock. The clock strikes. The Wood Daemon seizes and stabs Hardy as both fall into "sulphurous flames." The others are now free and happy, and Leolyn is recognized as the rightful count. Although the dialogue is weak, music and mystery enhance this play, which, with its delightful and well-paced story, must have provided an evening of fascinating entertainment. Both surviving plays by Turnbull show a fine awareness of the popular theatrical tastes of the day and the skill to satisfy them.

Mordecai Noah (1785–1851) was not seriously involved with drama until after the War of 1812. His interest in the theatre, however, started during his youth, and he recounts his early pleasures as well as his dramatic productions in a letter to William Dunlap, which appears in the *History*. His major career was in politics and journalism while his plays were, he admitted, "a kind of *amateur* performance." They were, however, as he progressed with his writing, an excellent brand of amateur drama. Growing up in Philadelphia, he had haunted the Chestnut Street Theatre in his youth, acted in an amateur "Thespian Company" in the Old American Theatre in Philadelphia, and helped cut and rework plays for performance by that group—all of which prepared him for his avocation as a playwright.

Barker's *Indian Princess* seems to have inspired him to write his first play, *The Fortress of Sorrento*, a melodrama. Although his work was never acted, Noah showed a shrewd interest in the drama by selling it to David Longworth's Dramatic Repository for publication in 1808 in exchange for a copy of every play that Longworth had printed. A "petit historical drama in two acts," taken in part from the French opera *Leonora*, *The Fortress of Sorrento* dramatizes the successful efforts of Leonora, disguised as a boy, Fidelio, to save her imprisoned husband from the cruelty of the governor of the fortress. It is a youthful work, artificial and slight, but the action moves well as touches of irony and sentiment are carefully introduced. Noah wrote that he "was almost ashamed to own it," but it was no worse than some being performed, and as a first attempt it suggested some promise.

Noah's next opportunity came in 1812 when in Charleston he was asked to write a play for the benefit of an actress. The result was *Paul and Alexis; or, The Orphans of the Rhine*; three years later it was acted at the Park in New York as *The Wandering Boys* and thereafter enjoyed considerable popularity. In 1814 the play was taken to London, where, somewhat altered, it was produced as *The Wandering Boys; or, The Castle of Olival*. One London critic anticipated the play as merely a melodrama "full of sound and show, and good for nothing, too dull . . . and too absurd to entertain the maturer frequenters of a theatre."[21] But he was mistaken, and the play was performed for eight nights—February 24, 26, 28 and March 1, 3, 5, 8, 12, 1814—at Covent Garden. Back in New York it was produced under its English title and finally published anonymously in 1821. Adapted from Pixérécourt's *Le Pélerin Blanc; ou, Les Orphelins du Hameau* (1801) rather than being a straight translation of the French work, Noah's play stresses plot more than the spectacle of the original and provides excellent sentiment and action with the young boys. Although there is little attempt at characterization, the dialogue moves easily, and the focus is sharp and clear, making this melodrama one of the best of the period.

The Wandering Boys opens as two boys enter the hamlet of Olival where years before a fire had destroyed a castle and, it is presumed, killed the wife and two boys of the owner, who was away on business. Suspense intensifies as the boys are recognized, first by the evil Roland and the baroness of the castle, who then plot their destruction, and second by a mysterious old count who masquerades as a castle porter. The high point and the crisis of the play occur at a dinner arranged by the baroness, who plans to poison the boys. But the count maneuvers their safety with heroic actions and eventually, after other suspenseful adventures, enters the scene richly dressed to embrace the boys as their father. There is something of the appeal of Kotzebue's *The Stranger* in this play, and it deserved its success. With these two plays written, Noah became United States consul at Tunis and in Morocco in 1813 and did not return to America for six years. It was after this date that he emphasized American themes and wrote some of his best plays.

WRITERS OF FARCE

The tendency of American dramatists to choose foreign themes and foreign situations continued to be strong and reached its highest point sometime during the second quarter of the nineteenth century, particularly among writers of poetic drama, who believed (and continued to believe far into the twentieth century) that poetic drama must deal either with the long ago and far away or with the legendary. On the other hand, those playwrights during the first decade of the nineteenth century who stressed patriotic or nationalistic themes and subject matter were in the vanguard of a trend in American drama that throughout the nineteenth century would continually place national events, historical characters, and problems upon the stage. The same would be true of the writers of moral melodrama, who would eventually attack intemperance, slavery, and the American business world. These were the major interests of early nineteenth century American playwrights—poetic drama imitative of foreign models, nationalistic plays, and moral dissertations.

What remains among the contributions of American playwrights are the innumerable farces and light comedies which at this time had little pretense other than to entertain and occasionally to ridicule. The number of those written during the period 1801–1814 can probably never be known. Most were never published; many were prepared quickly by actors who wanted a particular vehicle, a practice which would intensify once American actors gained a certain status and could demand plays. Essentially, however, those slight farces and comedies are a substantive part of theatre entertainment—either as curtain raisers, afterpieces, or a full evening's entertainment. Although their function in theatre would change as time passed, they provide a reasonable clue to the audience's enjoyment at the time. As some of the liveliest plays, without weighty substance or pretense, they suggest a norm of entertainment. They are the commercial hackwork of the period; yet some turned out to be more important than their creators could have imagined.

Love and Friendship; or, Yankee Notions was one of those. A three-act comedy, it was produced during the 1807–08 season at the Park, where the author, A. B. Lindsley, was a member of the company. He is quoted as saying that he wrote it when he was nineteen simply to pass the time. Later he revised it for publication in 1809, admitting that it was "designed for a farce but being considered too long has been printed as a comedy."[22] Doubtless he would have been surprised had he known that he was contributing to the development of the Yankee character in American drama. The scene of the play is Charleston, where Algernon Seldreer is in love with Augusta but is opposed by her father, who wants her to marry Dick Dashaway, a young profligate who "learned it all at college." Undaunted, Seldreer engages Jack Hardweather, a sailor, of course, and Jonathan, a Yankee complete with dialect, to help with his planned elopement. It is this Jonathan who is recognized as the first Yankee Pedlar in American drama and as the first Yankee to tell a story within a play—a characteristic which many Yankee actors a generation later would emphasize. To complicate Seldreer's plans, Catchpenny, a lawyer, falsifies a marriage contract between Seldreer and Mary Lightlove, who wants to marry Seldreer. When this ploy does not work for the villains, Jack and Jonathan, with his notions, go into action. The constable catches Catchpenny; Augusta catches Seldreer; and Jonathan and Jack discuss their future plans: "And say, amid this national commotion,/ We bid to live—each honest Yankee Notion."

It is all good farce with a fine drunk scene featuring Dashaway, Negro and Southern dialects, miscellaneous satire on education, lawyers, preachers, and national politics plus the Yankee character. Once a number of dramatists started to experiment with his character, Jonathan assumed more and more importance in plays. In Lindsley's play he sings "Yankee Doodle," dislikes being called "the notion man" or "brother blue skin," is a bit arrogant with Southerners, and maintains a strict moral view. He enjoys talking and likes to philosophize, but he is not a clown, just a good farce character who provides low humor and acts as an intriguer in the plot.

Jonathan Postfree; or, The Honest Yankee by Lazarus Beach was another farce which emphasized the Yankee character. A printer and publisher in New York, Beach wrote the play in 1806, never managed to get it produced, and finally published it in 1807. Songs that explain character and situation are important in this musical farce, which follows the problems of Maria Ledger. In love with Jemmy Seamore, who went away many years before, Maria is now being forced by a greedy and society-conscious mother to marry Fopling. Jonathan is the postman who reads all letters and has a word for everyone. In his opening scene he falls down, scattering himself and his letters, and then sings "Yankee Doodle." The plot is predictable as Seamore returns, a rich sea captain, rescues Maria from Fopling's attempt to kidnap her, and marries her; but Jonathan is not. Mainly a comic but without much dialect, he is not very bright although he is shrewd enough not to get involved with Fopling's abduction plans, and he even helps Seamore with the rescue. Such a great deal happens to Jonathan in the big city of New York, however, that he cannot wait to take the news back to Connecticut where he belongs.

Along the same line of farce-comedy, Everhard Hall wrote *Nolens Volens; or, The Biter Bit*, published in 1809. Hall, a lawyer in North Carolina, argued in the preface to his play that comedy could best improve the morals of the rising generation, but he also had to admit that his five-act play was a farce and his objective, amusement. John Daly Burk's Company of Thespians performed it in Petersburg, Virginia. As a satire on marriage, with occasional jabs at professional men and people with titles, it is a talky play and at best an amateur work. Intolerant of Farmer Downright, Sir Classic refuses to allow his son, Frederick, to marry Clara, the farmer's daughter. On the other hand, Downright has sworn to disinherit Clara if she marries a Classic. As the plot tumbles on, Frederick's indebtedness to Miss Markwell causes him problems, while Clara is wooed by two comics named Dennis O'Bodder and Le Trifle, a Frenchman. After Clara rejects both of them, Le Trifle and Miss Markwell are tricked into marrying each other. But not until it is revealed that Frederick is really Classic's nephew rather than his son can the lovers marry and Downright keep his word. The stock characters and situation provide the humor, but one of the more interesting aspects of the play is the prologue, which is delivered in part by a man in the audience.

The farceurs as well as their creations sometimes add a light touch to the history of American drama. John Williams (1757–1818), who reviewed plays under the pseudonym "Anthony Pasquin" and sold his comments to the highest bidder, also wrote several plays. *The Federal Oath; or, Americans Strike Home!* was performed in New York in June, 1798. In April, 1806, another Williams play, "A New Grand Local, Historical, Pantomimical, Melo-Drama" in three acts, *Manhattan Stage; or, Cupid in his Vagaries,* "by a gentleman of this city," was performed. With uncharacteristic fervor but probably good reasons, Dunlap reported in his *History* that the "gentleman" was a "wretched man" with a "wretched play."

Understandably, in terms of the management of American theatre, actors were responsible for most of the light comic farces. James Fennell (1766–1816) had written several plays before coming to America in 1793 and continued his contribution to dramatic literature in the country where he spent most of his adult life and achieved his greatest reputation on the stage. His *The Hero of the Lake*, which dealt with the War of 1812, has been mentioned; earlier, in 1804, he wrote and performed a farce, *The Advertised; or, A Way to Get Married*. Probably other plays that he wrote have been lost, but *The Wheel of Truth*, performed in New York in 1803, may well represent his talents, although one critic described it as a "silly farce," and it probably was. The plot idea was to put all suitors for a certain maid through the "wheel of truth," an action which would certainly have produced the kind of fun required in an afterpiece. Then John Hodgkinson conceived the idea of putting a critic through the "wheel" and having him come out a goose. As this was a time when the *Morning Chronicle* and the *Evening Post* were staunchly asserting their views on New York theatre, the resulting flurry of attack and defense provided some excitement.

It is likely that *Transformation; or, Love and Law*, a musical farce published in 1814, was also written by an actor, probably John Bray, who acted one of the major roles. Bray, it will be remembered, created the piano score for Barker's *Indian Princess*. In *Transformation* Mr. Makesafe wants his ward, Adelaide, to marry his nephew, Laglast. When he is called away on business, he leaves detailed instructions to allow only Malachi, a Jew, and Lady Pepperpod into his house. But Adelaide's lover, Camelion, disguises himself at different times as Malachi and as Lady Pepperpod and eventually wins the girl. As does *The Wheel of Truth*, *Transformation* exists only for love and a situation. In both, the opportunities for a romping farce would have appealed to actors.

John Bray (1782–1822) came to America in 1805 from England, where he had worked in theatres in York and Leeds, and made his debut in Philadelphia in December of that year. The critic for the *Theatrical Censor* (December 12, 1805) found him an actor "of much promise." A dozen years later, when Bray was acting in Boston, a writer for the Boston *Weekly Magazine* (December 6, 1817) described him as "an actor of merit in roles as a bumpkin, simpleton, etc." As a comedian Bray migrated from Philadelphia to New York and finally to Boston, where he suffered from a disease of "complicated disorders" according to W. W. Clapp in his *History of the Boston Stage*, and in 1822 returned to England, where he died. His free translation of an unidentified French comedy in one act was entitled *The Tooth-ache; or, Mistakes of a Morning*. Performed in New York on March 21, 1814, it excited laughter that was, according to Odell, "presumably inextinguishable for many nights of repetition."[23] The action takes place in the apartment of a prince where a chimney sweep who has entered surreptitiously disguises himself in the prince's clothes and, to hide his face from others, takes a handkerchief and feigns a toothache. Unrecognized, he is made privy to the extracurricular cavorting of the prince's wife. Finally, he is discovered by the real prince, who thanks him for unmasking the villains around him. The last line to the audience assures all that "smiles will cure our Tooth-ache." It doesn't amount to much—good farce action, a burlesque of the dentist's French, the usual mistaken identity—but it helps characterize American theatre and its audiences.

One of the most active American playwrights at this time was Joseph Hutton (1787–1828). With five published plays to his credit, he was also a respected actor in Philadelphia and with James Caldwell in New Orleans (1821–1823), where he was one of the principal actors in roles of tragic heavies and dignified old men. After his stint in New Orleans, Hutton left the acting profession to become a teacher in North Carolina, and there he escapes the drama historian. In "Dramatic Authors of America," *Dramatic Mirror* (September 11, 1841), James Rees described him as a better dramatist than actor and points out that his *Cuffee and Duffee*, a play now lost, was "highly applauded" for characters "most admirably drawn." Although his plays are minor contributions, they show versatility as they range through light comedy and musical farce to melodrama, and they reflect both foreign and native influences. Among the actor-playwrights of the period, Hutton was the most productive and seems to have had a potential in playwriting which for reasons unknown he did not pursue after his early activity.

Hutton's *School for Prodigals*, a comedy in five acts, was performed in Philadelphia in 1808 and published the following year. Essentially an English sentimental comedy, the play opens with a common situation: Lord Darnley is forcing Louise to marry his nephew, Edward, in spite of her love for his son, Henry, who has been estranged from his father for seven years. As plans for the wedding progress, the audience is introduced to Mordaunt, a beggar, who is really Henry returning to ask forgiveness of his father. That forgiveness and the proper identification, however, come only at the last moment when the banns are forbidden because Edward rushes in with the girl he has already married, leaving Louisa free to marry Henry. The uninspired plot and dull, romantic hero, however, are happily relieved by some good servant humor in Osbert and Fidget as the castle is readied for the wedding:

> FIDGET. Me master antient! and dare you presume to impeach me virtue and upright carriage? If I was not in such a hurry, I'd stay and give you a lecture—
>
> OSBERT. Good dame Fidget, rest easy a moment. I never impeached your virtue, marry for why? because I never knew you had any to impeach!
>
> FIDGET. Why you impudent, licentious old cork drawer, I shall inform his Lordship. Why did you not attend and hear our Lord rapping at the gate?
>
> OSBERT. That was impossible, dame Fidget.
>
> FIDGET. Impossible, when 'tis your duty to attend and be near the portal, and my ears were here saluted by it!
>
> OSBERT. Marry, dame, for two reasons. *Primo*, because it was not his Lordship that knocked; *secundo*, if it had been him, the infernal ding dong do bell of your clapper would drown the roar of Mount Vesuvius!
>
> [II. ii.]

Add to this a number of love songs—one concerned with the loves of Molly Mondoul—and the humorous dialogue of an Irishman named M'Gra and

Henry's uncle, a retired admiral. Although the subplots are far more attractive than the main plot is, the work displays a certain talent for a young playwright in handling a complicated story.

The Wounded Hussar; or, The Rightful Heir, a musical farce in two acts, was performed the next year, 1809, in Philadelphia. The plot is a repeat of the situation in Hutton's earlier play and is again distinguished only by the humorous dialogue and a clever servant whose curtain line—"What a concatenation of events!"—should sum up any audience's response to this slight whimsicality. Although Count Albourgh's daughter, Adeline, loves Bertolet, the son of a local witch named Buda, she is being forced by her father to marry Count Blenheim (who is in line to become Prince Pandolf) or suffer a "malediction." So Adeline dresses in men's clothing and flees, finding Bertolet, the wounded hussar, in the process. When they return to the castle, Bertolet discovers that he knows Blenheim and, in honor, restores Adeline to him only to be refused by the good count—all of which makes Adeline furious. Then Buda enters to announce that her son died in infancy and that Bertolet is really Prince Pandolf, identified by a mole on his arm. Now all are happy, and the father keeps his word to marry Adeline to a prince.

By the time he wrote *The Orphan of Prague*, a five-act melodrama published in 1810, Hutton had evidently discovered that there might be an advantage to being American and, in a prologue, begged some plaudits for "native genius." Although comedy seems to have been Hutton's forte more than was melodrama, he used servants well for his exposition and presented a less cluttered first act than did many of his contemporaries. His first two plays had shown that he used rather little imagination in his plot situations, and he did not alter his practice in *The Orphan of Prague* although he did begin to take more care with his characters. Because Leopold owes money to Baron Huberto, his daughter, Matilda, must marry the Baron even though she loves another and begs to be released from the obligation. The Baron's ugly humor suggests his guilt in the murder of his brother, Rudolpho, and of his wife and son some years previously in Prague. When a young stranger, Henry, appears, the Baron tries to have him killed. Acts IV and V present the plot complications that sometimes engulf playwrights, but the villain is finally dispatched, the chase brought to an end, and the gossip about substituted children proven true. As Huberto says with his dying breath, his servant can explain it all: "Long live Henry, Baron of Rosenheim." In true melodramatic style Hutton utilized confidants, disguises, and subterranean passages, but he was not adept at controlling either his characters or the element of time, which is always important in melodrama.

One would expect that *The Orphan of Prague* was produced, but evidence is lacking; *Venoni; or, The Maid of Savoy*, which appeared in Hutton's *Leisure Hours* (1812), was not. Written in two cantos of trochaic tetrameter quatrains with alternating rhyme and one canto of blank verse, the play is based on the highly romantic story of a Swiss patriot who helped a severely wounded French officer only to have the man seduce his only daughter and take her away. Hutton's scene is the bank of the Susquehannah River, where the hermit-patriot finds his daughter and her husband, forgives them, and sings "We may now the pleasures sing/ Which we knew in fair Savoy." The play's romantic and idealistic theme would seem to be one key to Hutton's character.

Fashionable Follies, presumably never performed although cast for production, was written in 1809 and published in 1815. As Hutton's best work, it clearly shows his progress as a playwright during the scant two years that he devoted to writing plays. It is also the most interesting of his plays because he embellishes a native theme with sentiments and characters that are peculiarly American. Somewhere in the background, too, there is the ghost of Tyler's *The Contrast*.

Ever since her father was somehow cheated of his fortune Maria Dorriville, the heroine of *Fashionable Follies*, has lived under the protection of Mr. Positive, a man who is never wrong, and now is in love with Edward Positive, the epitome of the virtuous, honest, honorable, sincere, unpretentious and patriotic American. The cad in her life is Charles Delancy, a young man with a French servant, a "meagre fop" who "takes snuff." Because it is fashionable to have a mistress, Charles tries to seduce Maria but is prevented by Maria's brother, whose determination to avenge his father has brought him to Delancy's house. Yankee characters and atmosphere are supplied by the Ploughboys, the incorruptible and conscientious farmers whom Maria visits. Finally, Dorriville, senior, appears, now a man of wealth gained from business in the East. Everything works out for the appropriate lovers, and Charles, a kind of American dandy, conscience-stricken at what he almost did, confesses his errors and concludes "that though Fashion may lead a man to the commission of many crimes, she can justify none." In this satiric comedy Hutton continued his interest in character portrayal and handled an intricate plot with some success. Never able to write a play that enjoyed great popularity, Hutton, nevertheless, deserves consideration both for the quality of his dialogue and for his skills in developing secondary plot action and farce characters.

A less productive and less skilled writer of farce-comedy than was Hutton, Charles Breck (1782–1822) has the distinction of writing *The Fox Chase*, the play which inspired Barker to compose his *Indian Princess*. Otherwise, he remains an elusive figure. In keeping with the habits and prejudices of the times, *The Fox Chase* was performed in Philadelphia in April, 1806, as "written by a gentleman of Philadelphia." Two years later it was published along with Breck's second, but unperformed play, *The Trust*. Both are identified as comedies but have the complications, mysteries, and devices of melodrama.

In Breck's first play the fox hunt is merely a device, being the scene of the action and having little to do with the plot except to provide a clue to the social level of the people. In his prologue Breck also stressed the patriotism and honesty presumably inherent in the rustic life which his play dramatizes. A young profligate, abandoned by his father, returns incognito to try to discover the man who ruined his father and to effect a reconciliation with his brother. In the process he manages to fall in love with the right girl. Though peripheral to the plot, there is one character, and only one, who presents a quality that is above the ordinary—a man who considers himself a botanist and plans such wild schemes as the introduction of wit into the human brain. His lengthy but clever discourses on his particularly odd philosophy of life, which is based on "equilibrium," the interaction of two impulses, generally enliven an otherwise average play.

With its overcomplicated plot and extremely artificial dialogue, *The Trust* is cut from the same cloth. Yet, again, one aspect adds a distinction—a couple of mendacious mendicants who try to parlay a letter they find into a few meals. The light moments they scatter throughout the play, however, are offset by Courland, father of Harry and, it seems, Louisa. Courland jails a righteous man for debt and proves himself unworthy of trust. Unfortunately, again Breck has created an interesting character or two but weighed them down with a cumbersome plot. Hebe, the object of Harry's affections, is a delightful girl. Mystery is provided by Old Ambert, who raves about his children, and by a letter, "a sacred trust held in charge for the only daughter of Mr. Mervin." All of the complicated relationships among the characters, however, would remain unexplained if it were not for Dorothy, who is introduced in the fifth act precisely to make that explanation. Ambert is really Mervin, Louisa's father; the villain is unmasked; and the appropriate lovers are free to marry. With this play Breck's career as a playwright apparently stopped.

Another elusive figure in the history of American drama, John Minshull wrote some of the best comedies and farces of this period, a number of them performed at the Grove Theatre in Bedlow Street. Unfortunately, he seems to have attracted the antagonism of the uptown New York theatre managers, perhaps because the competition of the Grove hurt Dunlap during his final year of management at the Park. Several actors from the Park also performed at the Grove at this time. For reasons unknown Dunlap did not list Minshull's plays although four of them were published. Odell referred to the "absurd Minshull" and "Minshull's assault" on playgoers in Bedlow Street. He also mentioned Minshull's participation in a "rather ungentlemanly chapter of our theatrical history," but he did not elaborate.[24] One presumes that the problem had something to do with Dunlap's failure and the advantage, foul or fair, which Minshull took of the situation. Whatever happened, Minshull was too active a playwright to be summarily dismissed from a history of the drama. It would be helpful to know more about him, but even his nationality is uncertain. Although he would seem to have been a resident of New York, the epilogue to *Merry Dames*, spoken by the author, states as follows: "I, a son of beef from the opposite shore." If this means that he was reluctant to accept his adopted country, his relationships with such nationalistic-minded people as Dunlap might have suffered. But an ambiguity still remains because Minshull's plays show a strong American patriotism. There is no doubt, however, that he was a man who observed life around him and possessed a marked talent for dramatizing his views in a clever and amusing fashion.

Minshull's three-act comedy, *Rural Felicity: With the Humour of Patrick, and Marriage of Shelty*, published in 1801, was founded on fact, according to his preface, and was intended to "harmonize the soul, and calculate a man for noble deeds." And perhaps it does that. There is certainly not much story in this musical portrayal of patriotism, love, and sentiment in a rural scene. Woodcutters and farmers get together to sing praises of their styles of living, their free country, and their government. Then an evening meal climaxes Act I and suggests the happiness of rural conviviality. Toasts are drunk: "May the wisdom of Washington be our base, and virtue our standard." Eventually, Jonathan appears along with a Cockney who sings a song about the "moose hunt" while Patrick and Shelty, celebrating their coming to America with songs and dances, prepare to marry village daughters. Essentially, the play glorifies the common bonds of people the world over in their various occupations and simple pleasures and has some of the same characteristics that would make *The Old Homestead* popular at the end of the century. Like that landmark in local-color drama, *Rural Felicity* boasts farm humor, word play, and a variety of characters, but it remains more sketch than play.

The Sprightly Widow, with the Frolics of Youth; or, A Speedy Way of Uniting the Sexes by Honorable Marriage, published in 1803, was, according to Minshull, "drawn from incidents that daily occur in human events." Evidently, the play was first written as *The Gig* and then revised as a five-act farce-comedy with the usual stated intent to praise virtue despite the fact that within the life being imitated there were no perfect human beings. It is certainly a slight yet sprightly play. Before it ends, a profligate young man named Britains Dash not only reforms his fashionable and pleasure seeking ways but learns to respect America. In this manner Minshull emphasizes both moral and patriotic sentiments. The title figure, the Widow Sprightly, is used mainly as an exemplum in her marriage to the ardent patriot and gentleman, Colonel Blunt. Working hard to reform Dash are his clerk, Teller, and Trusty, a man worthy of his name who turns out to be Dash's uncle and the guardian of Maria, Dash's eventual partner in marriage. Her late introduction in the story is a weakness, but plotting was rarely a strength of early American dramatists.

Minshull, instead, used his dramatic skill to create good conversation with just a touch of teasing improprieties. To this he adds intriguing wordplay, song and spectacle, and a variety of cleverly manipulated farce characters. The seducer of Dash's good intentions is Fanfarron, who appears in Act II "strutting and dressed like the knave of clubs with the addition of a pair of ear rings"; he reforms, of course, in the final scene. There is a well-devised spectacle scene in the public gardens as people wander around a waterfall and listen to an orchestra and a comic song about America, "the Columbian roast beef." Captain Trueman and Counsellor Gayly parade their interest in the Stockton girls, whose father makes the astute observation that "a good husband on viewing a beautiful woman is happy in the embraces of his own wife, provided her good sense directs her in pleasing his fancy." He also has an eye for the widow:

STOCKTON.   She is a charming woman—her shape—her air—her mode of address—her conversation captivating. A true academic figure—her lips inviting—her eyes sparkling like brilliants, and a chest, as white as hills covered with lillies to charm the eyes of the son of Mars, as reward for justifying his country's rights.

MRS. STOCKTON.   Sentimentally concluded, or I should have imagined you had been at the mill this morning.

STOCKTON.   For what, my dear?

MRS. STOCKTON.   To be ground young to be sure—Such rhapsody—from a father of a family—I protest I blush!

STOCKTON.   My dear, you know I was always fond of a fine sensible woman like Mrs. Sprightly.

MRS. STOCKTON.   Indeed—Does my size displease you? Is a woman of my figure and presence come to this?—It was but the other day I was counted an excellent piece on viewing the sumptuous gardens in France, in the presence of the Emperor—the Emperor—the Emperor.

STOCKTON. What of the Emperor?

MRS. STOCKTON. Joseph cast his majestic eye on me—Smacked his lips, as my lady Prominant did when she longed for the tail of the learned pig. It is an odd circumstance to relate, but facts are stubborn things—are they not, my dear?

STOCKTON. It is the inclination of your sex to be fond of stubborn things —There is no putting nature out of its place—My dear, was the Emperor content at smacking his lips?

MRS. STOCKTON. (*Setting his wig straight, glances at his forehead.*) That, my dear, is best known to myself.

[III, ii.]

In a clever fashion, as they play with fortune question-and-answer cards two by two, Trueman and Gayly make their marriage proposals to the girls, which are then approved by Mr. and Mrs. Stockton at another card table with the help of the same deck of fortune cards. All in all the play has good scenes and moves rapidly and colorfully, and in the epilogue Minshull manages a thrust at critics —"Better by far a Pit's critic to take"—as well as at his competition, whom he identifies as Dunlap Wignel.

Minshull's forte was his ability to sustain witty dialogue throughout a brief scene. Plotting gave him the kind of problems that appear in *The Merry Dames; or, The Humorist's Triumph Over the Poet in Petticoats, and the Gallant Exploits of the Knight of the Comb*, a three-act comedy published in 1805. In a long "prelude" he creates a comic story to prove that his play is founded on real life and explains that it is intended "to prove that vice and folly are not confined to Europe." That may be, just as his characters are as timeless and worldwide as farce itself. One part of his play deals with Mr. and Mrs. Lively, who decide to punish the lecherous old Dr. Catharticus, trick him into disguising himself in bonnet and petticoat, and send him "home like an old goat." Another part of the farcical action takes place in the shop of Comb the barber, who passes himself off as a Knight of the Comb to a ship's captain. Obviously, these two plot lines are only tenuously connected, but the Captain and Comb stage a good farcical fight. The first line of the play spoken by Comb suggests its bawdy quality: "I am just landed from Albany where the women keep close housed till they grow plump in the rear."

Imagery, metaphor, and one-line humor characterize *The Merry Dames* as well as *He Stoops to Conquer; or, The Virgin Wife Triumphant*, another Minshull farce in three acts, published in 1804. What distinguishes this from his previous plays is the coherence of its basic idea although the play as a whole is poorly developed. The setting is Rome, where Count Ludovico does not enjoy a husband's rights with his wife, Honoria. And, as he says, "to possess a fine park without the privilege of planting an acorn is against our national interest" (I, i). He is to be helped, however, by Sir John Patrick, who is himself assisted by a servant, Tickle Toby, a man who boasts of having seven women. Honoria, it seems, is too refined for shenanigans, but with her servant's help she will foil Sir Patrick's plot and, disguised as an Italian singer, receive her husband. It all ends happily, of course, in a scene of "rural felicity" as a matter of fact, but it is difficult to understand just why. Parts of this and other plays show clearly that Minshull had a good wit, if a bawdy one, and certain skills as a playwright which should allow him an important place among early writers of farce in America. Although most farce passes quickly across the stage, it was a substantial part of America's entertainment, and at this early time the plays of both Hutton and Minshull well represent this popular theatre.

From 1801 through 1814 America, politically and socially, was experiencing numerous problems for which it had no solution. There was as yet no direction on which the country at large had agreed. One finds the same situation in the drama, and just as there was considerable happening in the political and social worlds that provided help in determining direction, there was much activity among playwrights that suggested the direction of a dramatic literature. It was, however, a lean time for good drama. Dunlap was mainly involved in translation and adaptation; Payne had not started his playwriting career; Noah had just begun. The major playwright was James Nelson Barker, but his best work was still to come. Harby, Ioor, and John Blake White had written plays which suggested a Southern school of dramatists, but it turned out to be a meagre beginning which was not continued. Northerners Nichols and William C. White wrote a few plays of low quality and then stopped. Clearly, the hardest working playwrights—Turnbull, Hutton, and Minshull—produced farce. Other plays were the ventures of interested amateurs. Taken en masse, however, the number of plays and playwrights at this time represents both a considerable advance over the previous score of years and the multiplicity of interests and techniques that would be refined and developed by future playwrights.

EIGHT

Progress and Prejudice:
American Drama, 1815-1828

POLITICAL AND literary historians generally agree that the year 1815 suggests a new direction for America, one marked by changes in the attitudes of the American people. But in that area of creativity demanding cooperation between arts and letters, in theatre and drama, change and progress were less noticeable. The existing prejudices toward American fiction or poetry were multiplied and intensified two-fold when applied to the drama, while the control of theatre acting and management in America by Englishmen served only to underline the observation that the American stage, particularly in the major cities, was reserved for foreign plays and foreign actors. The most important play published in 1815, David Humphrey's *The Yankee in England*, had been performed early the previous year only by amateurs in Connecticut. In 1813 America's only actor of promise, John Howard Payne, had left for England to fail there as an actor but to become successful as a dramatist and adaptor-translator and remain abroad until 1832. A switch from the English invasion of America, it had clearly been a fortunate step for Payne to take; in America playwriting remained an avocation for interested amateurs or for actors. The one playwright during the 1815–1828 period who gained any lasting reputation, James Nelson Barker, did so, according to one contemporary critic, because he "devoted more of his leisure to the stage than any other American."[1]

For American drama 1815 was an important year only because the beginnings of new political and literary attitudes would be reflected to its eventual advantage. During the next dozen years a few American playwrights of more than casual talent would write for the theatre, the potential of the Yankee character in the drama would be refined, and three or four plays of some lasting merit would be written. The kinds of plays provided—farce-comedy, moral

221

melodrama, imitations of foreign poetic tragedy, plays emphasizing national-ism—were the same as those of the previous decade; and the problems were generally the same. The drama was still entertainment (it being clearly under-stood that this entertainment should be instructive if possible), and entertain-ment, though seemingly necessary to one's well-being, was only peripherally interesting to the pragmatic American. John Quincy Adams was a stern New Englander who enjoyed the drama and encouraged it; yet his views still sug-gest the limitations it held for him. In a letter (August 28, 1822) to Louisa Catherine Adams, he wrote as follows:

> You ask me why I frequent the theatre. First, because having paid for admis-sion for two persons by my two shares it is the only interest I get for my money, and the tickets cost me nothing. Secondly, because I have all my life had a very extravagant fondness for that species of entertainment, and always indulge myself with it, unless when motives of prudence, or propriety, or pride, or duty of some kind, real or imaginary, prescribe to me the self-denial of them. . . . But thirdly, my reason for going to the theatre now is that as yet I can do nothing else with the evening. . . . [Has seen Booth and Cooper but prefers] Jefferson to them all. The broader the farce, the more I enjoy it. But I expect that before it is over I shall be abused for it in the newspapers.[2]

Farce was preferred, and even the more sophisticated dramatic performances would be accepted mainly as entertainment; it was this attitude which would have to change before a drama that was both emotionally and intellectually stimulating could be created in America. Yet by 1828 entertainment in Amer-ica was developing some mature characteristics—as the country was, too. Public attitudes, dramatic criticism, a concern for an American literature, and a few plays provide the evidence of that development.

By 1815 the character of the American people and their government was being formed. After long activity the lines of struggle were beginning to con-verge, and Americans knew at least the directions they wished to go. With the presidency of Monroe the Union was transformed into a modern state. It was the "Era of Good Feeling" as America protected its manufactured goods with a tariff in 1816, chartered a Bank of the United States in 1816, began to de-velop its western lands (taking in six new states by 1821), and worked out treaties to establish its borders. Although the era ended in 1819 with the first of the economic panics which seemed to recur about every twenty years, by that time a certain national momentum had been established as the Federalist bias of Chief Justice of the Supreme Court John Marshall strengthened the federal government. One result of all of this activity, one most relevant to a developing theatre and drama, was the increased interest in roads, transportation, and expansion. The Cumberland Road linking Maryland and Illinois had been started in 1811; Monroe's administration began to use more federal money for roads, a national project which Adams supported during his term in office. River travel began in 1817 with steamboat connections between Cincinnati and New Orleans. That same year the Erie Canal was started, to be completed in 1825.

An expanding country was a challenge to theatre managers who saw the population west of the Appalachian Mountains grow from 1,080,000 in 1810 to 2,234,000 ten years later. The same expansion which would provide potential theatre audiences also created many problems for the new government and, as a by-product, material for native dramatists. As the American people jostled among themselves to set up that "more perfect union," they wanted no interference from Europe or from the new republics being established to the south— hence, the Monroe Doctrine. It was to be a government of the people and by the people, and the people insisted on their right to be heard. Although John Quincy Adams was a confirmed nationalist and worked for the people as he saw best, the cry of "Shall the people rule?" helped remove him from office and elect Andrew Jackson by a substantial majority in 1828. With a new constituency, Jackson brought something new to government, something of a political revolution to which all arts and letters responded as time passed.

The practical matters which engaged the minds of the American people during this period of change and progress had somehow to be infiltrated by a concern for the arts. And in view of the industrial advances being made in America—the work of John Stevens, Eli Whitney, Samuel Slater, and Francis Lowell—this was a monumental challenge, obviously heightened by the fervor of speculation which stimulated people in a variety of ways. People's heads were so filled with dreams of the main chance that they gave little thought to literature, which in 1815 was at a particularly low ebb, there being little incentive to write and a corresponding difficulty in getting things published. Some stimulating force was needed, and this appeared in 1815 in the creation of the *North American Review* (*NAR*), with the stated objectives of making Americans aware of their literary poverty and of encouraging a distinctly American literature. In its second volume, the *NAR* acknowledged the difficulties of the past in an essay entitled "Reflections on the Literary Delinquency of America" and then went on in the ensuing year to review just about everything of value that was published.

CRITICISM AND DEVELOPING
THEORIES

Following the theory that an effective criticism can stimulate and even guide good literature, critics and writers alike began to discuss America's literary needs and to urge an American quality. Added to the substantial criticism of the *NAR* were the views of Joseph Dennie in *Port Folio* (1801–1827) and the commentary in the *Analectic Magazine,* which until 1815 was edited by Washington Irving, and the *United States Literary Gazette.* Good criticism became more abundant when, in 1818, the *NAR* became a quarterly publication. Literary taste, however, comes slowly to a people and, as James Kirk Paulding somewhat facetiously noted in 1815, America had not yet arrived at "the manhood of a literary taste." What it did have was an unpolished vigor which seemed characteristic both of its few execursions into literature and of its people who were absorbed in creating a new nation. Many readers enjoyed this rough vitality; others did not. Then something happened which forced the conflict of literary tastes into the open. Sidney Smith, writing for the *Edinburgh Review* (January 1820), made a particularly disparaging observation that not only fired the tempers of American writers who already felt abused but also fluttered the patriotic dignity of some who might not otherwise have questioned a literary critic. "In the four quarters of the globe," Smith wrote, "who reads an American book? or goes to an American play? or looks at an American picture or statue?" It was all the more irritating to Americans because there was a touch of truth in Smith's assumptions. Purposely or not, however, Smith probably did a great service to American letters although he is not remembered with fondness.

The obvious conclusion that America's literature was wholly imported stimulated both argument and literary action. Was there an American literature? In 1820 this was a reasonable question even though the *NAR* had five years previously boldly declared its intention to encourage American writers, and George Pope Morris and Samuel Woodworth would soon state that their New York *Mirror and Ladies Literary Gazette* (1823–1842) was "literally and emphatically, AMERICAN." (It would be interesting to contemplate the influence upon literature in a masculine- and individual-oriented society which this plea to "ladies" assumed in the journals of the time.) At this early date a concern for America in stories and poems usually meant an inventory of scenery and objectively viewed peculiarities of people and materials. But perhaps this was not enough for a people solidly impressed by the romanticism of Walter

Scott, for, when the American Indian was urged upon them as a good subject, the Indian was either romanticized by Cooper or given a wild and intensely Gothic character by Robert Sands in his popular poem of 1820, *Yamoyden*. Still, there seemed to be a great deal in America that should attract writers, and John Neal dedicated *Rachel Dyer* (1828) to those ",abundant and hidden sources."

Would these materials, however, produce American literature or, more particularly, America drama? The erratic John Neal, whose experience in the theatre had not been pleasant, was bitterly adamant in his answer:

> *Comedies*—See Drama. No such thing in America. One Mr. White has written two or three; but we have never seen or read them. They are well spoken of—in America. *Drama*—Mr. Noah . . . has written some tolerable farces, and some intolerable entertainments. . . . The writers of America have no encouragement, whatever, to venture upon the drama. *Farces*—About a dozen or twenty sober, childish, or disagreeable "entertainments" have been produced, in the United States of America—by the natives—within the memory of man, we believe—under this title.[3]

Writing his *Notions of the Americans* (1828), Cooper found "no annals for the historian; no follies (beyond the most vulgar and commonplace) for the satirist; no manners for the dramatist." Cooper, of course, spent much of his time in France. Finding nothing else sufficiently native, some writers decided that a peculiar language or dialect would help establish an American literature. For *The Yankey in England* (1815) David Humphreys had included an extensive glossary of terms. The following year John Pickering published *A Vocabulary . . . Peculiar to the United States,* and in 1828 Noah Webster published his *American Dictionary of the English Language.* The argument concerning the existence of an American literature, however, was far from over.

In spite of a pervasive nationalism in American literature written from 1815 through the Civil War, it proved difficult to establish that "intellectual independence" for which Emerson so eloquently pleaded in the *American Scholar* (1837). English writers were not only truly superior to American writers; they were supported by the snobbery which appears among cosmopolitan and sophisticated people whose feelings of patriotism become moderated by taste and intelligence. Then, as time passed, the imitative, pseudo-sophisticates whose adherence to discipleship frequently destroys the godhead itself made more difficulties for an emerging literature in America. Compared with the writer of fiction or poetry, the dramatist, burdened with the strengthened prejudices of his potential audience and the difficulties of production and recompense, faced a more serious battle for recognition and eventual survival. As for American literature in general, Duyckinck's *Cyclopedia of American Literature* (1855) declared it still "thoroughly and essentially English." And for several more decades it was accepted by some critics only as a "condition of English literature."

Regardless of the continuing argument concerning the existence or quality of a literature in America, there was considerable activity among writers of poetry, fiction, and drama during the period 1815–1828. Among the best known are William Cullen Bryant, Washington Irving, James Kirk Paulding, and James Fenimore Cooper. Longfellow, Poe, and Hawthorne were also publishing their very early and immature works by 1828. Although the call for an American poetry and fiction was echoed by calls for an American drama, there was no magazine comparable to the *NAR* dedicated particularly to the welfare of the drama and to the encouragement of numerous dramatists whose efforts did not reach the quality of the best works of poetry and fiction. There was, however, an increasing attention paid to American drama in both literary journals and drama-theatre journals, and an excerpt from the *National Register* (July 27, 1816) suggests the tenor of that interest:

> It is to be regretted that the American drama is so little attended to. There is, perhaps, no country that affords so fine a field as this for the exercise of dramatic talent. The freedom of our political institutions, the variety and diversity of character which is to be found in the United States, and the unrestrained liberty of speech, which tends to develop all the peculiarities and eccentricities of our nature, must afford an unbounded field for the exertions of the dramatic muse. The prejudices, however, which rage for everything European, will have a tendency to retard the exertions of American genius; and while it reflects on the patriotism of our citizens, it contributes in no small degree to check the growth of our literature. . . . This slavish dependence upon foreign literary supplies must be destroyed, and the stage, now closed, must be entirely free to the dramatic productions of the American muse. We have been long enough a nation to produce dramatists, and I presume that no one will say there is a deficiency of genius. Let us strive then to overcome this melancholy apathy, and remove those numerous difficulties I have enumerated as retarding the progress of the American drama, and paralyzing the exertions of American genius.

Many of the journals of the period found an opportunity to review plays or comment on the drama: the *Albion* (1822–1830); the *American Monthly Magazine and Critical Review* (1817–1819); the *American Quarterly Review* (1827–1837); the Boston *Weekly Magazine* (1816–1819, 1824); the *Critic:*

A Weekly Review of Literature, Fine Arts, and The Drama (1828–1829), edited by William Leggett and merged with the New York *Mirror*; the *Minerva: A Literary, Entertaining, Scientific Journal* (1822–1824, 1825); the *Opera Glass* (1828); the *Theatrical Budget* (1823, 1828); the *Theatrical Register* (1824); the *Theatrical Censor and Musical Review* (1828). This is only a sample list of which some journals, as the titles suggest, dealt specifically with theatre. Added to these journals were a number of newspapers which also commented with some regularity on theatre production.

Throughout the period 1815–1828, writers and critics such as Samuel Woodworth, J. K. Paulding, G. P. Morris, William Leggett, William Coleman, and Robert Ewing supported American drama and encouraged good native dramatists. Among the several essays entitled "American Drama," the most significant appeared in the *American Quarterly Review*.[4] Basing his commentary on sixty American plays that he had in his possession, the writer decried the general decline in "the dignity and usefulness of the stage." The causes of this decline he enumerated as (1) the manager's tendency to cater to low public taste, (2) the alienation of the "fashionable" public through poor management of actors—that is, the star system—and (3) the lack of a national drama.

On the positive side the writer found a "present richness" in American drama, which he defended as "appealing directly to the national feelings; founded upon dramatic incidents—illustrating or satirizing domestic manners—and, above all, displaying a generous chivalry in the maintenance and vindication of those great and illustrious peculiarities of situation and character, by which we are distinguished from all other nations." With a scope of knowledge and understanding which no other critic to that time had offered, the writer then commented on the virtues and faults of a variety of American plays. Above all, however, he found much potential for an American drama which, he exclaimed, must be encouraged.

> The first requisite for producing a NATIONAL Drama is national encouragement. . . . The second, is a little more taste and liberality in the managers of our theatres; and the third, is the presence of competent performers, collected in companies of sufficient strength to give effectual support to a new piece, and sufficient talent to personate an original character, without resorting to some hacknied [*sic*] model, which has descended from generation to generation, and like all copies, lost something of the original in the hands of each succeeding imitator.

As an intelligent and even moderate analysis, this essay gave strong impetus to a gathering force which was championing American arts and letters, but it faced opposition and had a long way to travel for any lasting satisfaction, particularly in the drama.

Opposition to American drama came from a variety of sources, not only from the pseudosophisticated, but from intelligent and practical people. For all of those who wanted only American writing in American publications, there were others who argued that the superiority of English literature provided the necessary models for writers in America. It was a practical consideration and one which delayed the establishment of adequate copyright laws, which were being urged in America in the 1820s. Although tariffs during the Monroe and Adams administrations were a constant source of heated discussion, importing continued. "Dramatic entertainments" were also imported "from London as we do a great portion of our hardware and clothing from Birmingham, Sheffield, and Manchester."[5] The argument was one of analogy and therefore logically weak, but the people who held it also believed that American drama was really English drama. Consequently, they argued, America had a lawful claim on English literature as her own and, although a youthful nation, was still part of an old race and should wait upon its own maturing society to produce a distinguished literature.

Others who opposed too enthusiastic an appreciation of American contributions to literature did so from a position of intellectual moderation. They objected, as one critic described it, not only to putting out the moon (England) in order that the stars (America) might shine; they disliked the excessive false praise given to some American plays. Even William Leggett condemned the universal and extravagant acceptance of some plays which he called "nondescript polylogues." He faulted "the uncandid plaudits of friends, whose optics sometimes are unable to discern faults, though huge as high Olympus; and the partial approbation of critics, swayed from the upright rigor of truth by the influence of extrinsic circumstances."[6] Another critic deplored the popular tendency, particularly toward patriotic dramas, to "warmly and fondly cherish" even the least portion of dramatic merit shown by a citizen of the United States. "In that department of literature, as in others," he argued with unquestionable cogency, "we are not in the least disposed to encourage nonsense because it is native."[7] One can easily understand why the encouragement which American drama required also worked to its disadvantage both in its immediate critical reaction and in its long-term development. A nationalistic criticism had to be tempered with sensible literary standards, but objectivity was particularly difficult to sustain during a period of lively dreams and strong biases.

The critical advantage held by those who preferred English and European drama to American drama was the obvious superiority of the traditional foreign plays. With any honesty they could hardly have had the same preference for the contemporary English drama. Those critics, however, were aided in their position by the general control of the theatres by English managers and actors. Yet one must also confess that the majority of dramatic criticism, although greatly improved over that of a decade back, was only beginning to stimulate better drama. One basic reason for this situation, of course, was the obvious fact that there were very few American plays to review. In American theatres Shakespeare's plays were performed a great deal along with plays by Sheridan, Goldsmith, Otway, and Kotzebue. Otherwise, works by such minor and, at best, mediocre British playwrights as Frederick Reynolds, William Dimond, Andrew Cherry, or James Kenney took the place of possible American plays.

The position of American drama was further eroded by the critical approaches assumed by many who commented on the drama of this early date. The paid puffers, those "well trained house-dogs who/ shew their teeth to all but their master . . . the highest bidder,"[8] seriously diminished the value of contemporary dramatic criticism. If he were not a puffer, and perhaps if he were, the critic or reviewer (those who might deserve the title of critic were very few) spent most of his time commenting on the technical aspects of theatre—the spectacle effects, the conveniences or inconveniences of the house, the scenery, and the speech, dress, gestures, and deportment of the actor or actress. One of the "Croaker Papers," which were written by Joseph Rodman Drake and Fitz-Greene Halleck (both respected poets) and which entertained New Yorkers from the pages of the *Evening Post* for some weeks in 1819, satirized this type of technical criticism, as in "To E. Simpson, Esq.—On Witnessing the representation of the new tragedy of Brutus" (March 20, 1819).

Continuing that obligation to be guardians of public morals which had been established early in the century, reviewers tended to concentrate on qualities they found obscene or pernicious. They would also censure plays for having poor subject matter, unnatural sentiments, immoral characters, and indelicate or indecent language. Occasionally, an entire book such as T. Charlton Henry's *An Inquiry into the Consistency of Popular Amusements with A Profession of Christianity* (1825) would include a chapter entitled "The Stage" where those who supported the theatre were condemned for having "no taste for evangelical truth"; "attendance on the theatre is inconsistent with the duties and principles of Christianity" (chap. 2). From that point of view the theatre was continually attacked as a waste of time and money and as a place for smoking, drinking, and bad conduct in general. Yet while one critic would state that "from the stage men are directly prepared to go to *the brothel*,"[9] another would argue that the theatre should not be universally condemned for a few bad characteristics.[10] Occasionally, someone attempted a moderate point of view such as in George P. Morris' essay "Dramatic Mania" in the New York *Mirror*. While defending the drama, Morris agreed that it would be unwise to introduce the young to the theatre "before their minds were improved by education, their judgments ripened by reflection, and their principles established."[11] Whether defending or attacking the drama, critics most frequently used the moral and utilitarian approach.

Very little comment made in the many reviews could be interpreted as a literary evaluation of the play. Most writers dealt with the performance rather than with the play. Others were clearly too busy defending the drama to assess it intelligently. At odd intervals during these years, however, the few better critics looked at plays from an artistic point of view. The tired, old stereotyped characters and the unnatural language and cant phrases bothered them. There was some comment on lack of probability or realism, artificiality in plot and characterization, and deficiencies in structure. But no criticism was at all thorough.

In keeping with tradition a drama critic who was truly disturbed by what he saw would resort to satire. Back in 1803 the *Port Folio* had lampooned plotting difficulties by formulating a "striking and poetic plot" in which the author collected several "black-looking tragedies . . . interweaving and jumbling them together so that it will be impossible to develop or understand them."[12] In the preface to his play *Caridorf* (1827), Robert Montgomery Bird burlesqued poetic style in tragedy: "Make thou no stops, no commas, no colons, nor periods; but between sentences draw thou a long dash, for this is significant of passion." For the *Minerva*, "A Projector" devised a "Receipt to Make a Tragedy":

> About your subject you need not be very particular. Take a Romance . . . extract an improbable story, and compress it within the compass of twelve hours. Your heroine must be a great lady, tormented with the addresses of some powerful, warlike Lord, and in love with a black-eyed romantic young hero, who, at one time, had the good fortune to save his mistress from flame or flood. After a variety of distresses, soliloquies, and dialogues, let both resolve to escape.[13]

Actually, the critic and the dramatist in America had several similar problems. Mainly, the traditional stratification of society made writing for the theatre, or about it, an almost impossibly delicate task, particularly when the potential audience came from such a limited number of people. As dramatist or critic whom did one try to please? What constituted the audience? Was it the vulgar multitude of which Payne and Bird complained so bitterly or the enlightened few for whom they wished to write? For one critic, however, that was a begging question; it was simply a matter of understanding the logical place of the theatre in any new society:

> Its [the theatre's] origin and growth may be compared to the settlement of new lands. The first personage who penetrates the dramatical forest is the conjuror; who, to the utter astonishment of the natives, eats fire, swallows pins, transforms one substance into another. . . . After some time, this personage gives way to the strolling player, who enacts Hamlet the Dane in such a manner that deep tragedy is metamorphosed into broad farce. This may be regarded as the "Nick Bottom" period of dramatic progression. The mere strolling player yields, in turn, to the occasional visits of a regular theatrical company, which rescues the profession from ridicule and contempt, and gives to the pursuits of the actors a certain degree of respectability. The whole ends with an established theatre, the performances of which are fixed at particular seasons of every year, and upon which the inhabitants rely as a source of instruction and amusement.[14]

For that critic it all depended on which level in the progression of theatre any particular society seemed to rest. Other criticis, however, demurred. They argued that America need not have started at such a primitive level and that the final period already achieved in some cities should be producing a more sophisticated drama. But they did not fully understand the potential theatre audience in a new nation of rapidly changing population and shifting social structures.

When President Monroe took office, only the chief cities in the country had theatre companies, and these were uneven in talent and seldom satisfactory. The best actors played mainly in Boston, New York, Philadelphia, Baltimore, Charleston, or Washington, where theatre attendance might be a pleasant form of relaxation if one agreed with John Quincy Adams or a source of consternation if one sympathized with Mrs. Andrew Jackson. Newly arrived in Washington from Tennessee in December, 1824, she wrote to a friend: "The play-actors sent me a letter requesting my countenance to them. No. . . . Indeed, Mr. Jackson encourages me in my course."[15]

Perhaps the new sense of democracy illustrated by Jackson's appearance in Washington explains in part the changes that were being made in the theatre fare of the major cities in America during the 1820s. While melodramatic spectacles were sometimes condemned by theatre critics in the 1820s as harmful to a developing theatre, people seemed to require variety, excitement, and novelty. Legitimate drama continued, but New York theatre bowed to popular demands as Mary Hill played Richard III on horseback. In 1825 the Park Theatre first presented Italian opera; two years later the Bowery Theatre introduced French classical ballet; and the nearby Lafayette Theatre experimented with equestrian drama. By the end of the decade, still more changes occurred, and theatre competition increased. All three of the theatres just mentioned closed and converted their stages to dance floors to take advantage of the latest craze for masquerade balls.

This was clearly a difficult time for American theatre managers in large cities where they were increasingly dependent on the star system. Although it was a system they had created, it now tended to destroy theatre companies and bring agonies to the manager who must try to fill his theatre on off-nights when no star was available. Faced with such problems, the manager was reluctant to take a chance with an American play already floundering in prejudices, but it was a choice which the increasing nationalism sometimes made palatable.

Beyond the major cities was an expanding frontier for theatre. Even on the East Coast theatre seasons were irregular and companies were inferior in such places as Maine, Vermont, Rhode Island, Connecticut, New Jersey, and Delaware. In the Carolinas and in Georgia, theatre had a measure of popularity. But it was the West that seemed to attract theatre people during the period 1815–1828, people like John Bernard, Noble Luke Usher, Samuel Drake, Noah Ludlow, James Caldwell, and Sol Smith. People in Cincinnati, for example, witnessed stage plays in 1815, had two theatres by 1825, and by 1828 enjoyed a full season of drama. One early worrier about the encroaching theatre—perhaps the "National Panorama and American Museum of Wax Figures," which toured the West in 1815—expressed his views in the Chillicothe (Ohio) *Weekly Recorder* for January 15, 1815. Vincennes, Indiana, had a "Thespian Association" which staged plays in 1814; Detroit had amateur theatre by 1817, and one June 28, 1825, the Detroit *Gazette* reported competition among theatrical companies: "two traveling menageries and a great magician who ate fire and did a number of other odd things."[16] The next generation saw theatre spread throughout the Ohio and Mississippi river valleys—new opportunities for American dramatists and other critics.

PLAYS FROM THE TOWN CRYER:
NATIONALISM ON STAGE

In a situation bounded by the prejudices of theatre managers, dramatic reviewers, and a changing society, the American dramatist was not be envied. More definitely than poets or writers of fiction, however, the playwright helped establish the beginnings of an American literature as it was being defined in the first quarter of the century. Since before the Revolution, plays had revealed American manners and character, present and past glories, and national peculiarities. With the increasing stability which spread across the country after the Treaty of Ghent, the dramatists had placed more emphasis on the national past and the characteristics of the people. The American scene also became a recognizable part of the drama as Cooper's novels were dramatized and panoramas such as Dunlap's *Trip to Niagara* (1828) became popular. Mainly, however, dramatists seemed fascinated by the American people: the "fair" Americans, the immigrants, the Indians who were already there, and especially the Yankee.

Although by 1815 the Yankee had appeared numerous times upon the stage, he was not yet the great popular success that would attract actors and playwrights by the score in the 1830s and 1840s. He was, so to speak, having his character formed during the early decades of the century. In his *Retrospections of America, 1797–1811*, John Bernard explained that the Yankee, "who plays the 'title-role' in this part of the States," was the Yorkshireman of America with the Yorker's cunning, calculating, and persevering nature. A term denoting "character rather than locality," Yankee might also mean "Down-Easter." But he was, according to Bernard, "divisible into three species—the swapper, the jobber, and the pedler, all agreeing in one grand characteristic—love of prey—but varying in many striking peculiarities."[17]

It is probably impossible to know just how many playwrights tried to capitalize on Jonathan's popularity. *The Suffield Yankee; or, How to Sell Wooden Dishes*, written by a "gentleman of Albany" and performed at the Albany Theatre on March 30, 1814, suggests his early movement west. The glossary of terms accompanying Humphreys' *The Yankey in England* helped stabilize the character. Samuel Woodworth further delineated the character. It was Charles Mathews' 1822–23 tour of America, however, which stimulated the use of the Yankee as an acting vehicle. On his return to England the English actor created Jonathan W. Doubikins in a sketch entitled *Trip to America* and then collaborated with Richard B. Peake to write *Jonathan in England* (1824).

By 1828 James H. Hackett had started his career as a Yankee actor in America, an acting fad which did not end until the 1860s when the Yankee began to merge with the "local color" drama. During the period 1815–1828, however, the Yankee play and the Yankee character actor became a definite part of American drama and theatre.

Since his earlier excursion into the theatre before the turn of the century, Humphreys had relinquished his duties as a statesman but retained his title as a general and established a cloth and paper mill in a village in Connecticut which became known eventually as Humphreysville. Prefacing his published play with a letter to William Gifford, an Englishman who had read a version of *The Yankey in England* sometime very early in the century, Humphreys explained that he now called his play a "drama" in five acts rather than a "comedy," presumably to give it more substance in the eyes of his readers. In describing the characters in his play, he distinguished three classes of Americans according to their educational background. One character, Newman, belonged to the second class of well-schooled, useful, and respectable people, while Jonathan Doolittle, his Yankee character, had only the barest education, to which he added his own "judicious observations." Besides these qualities, Jonathan was "made up of contrarities—simplicity and conniving." At the end of his publication Humphreys added a rather extensive glossary of such terms as "Ax—ask," "Cute—acute, smart, sharp," "Kiver—cover," and "Nation— very extraordinary."

The setting for *The Yankey in England* is "a guest hotel in a seaport in England," and its plot is as complicated and badly structured as any Anglophile critic could have wished. Perhaps fortunately, it never came to the professional stage. Central to the main action are the Count and Countess St. Luc, the abductors of Maria. Mr. and Mrs. Newman are Americans working as servants to the Count. At the seaport are a general who has lost a daughter and an admiral who somehow lost a son and a wife. Soon Maria appears, disguised as a sailor, hoping to go to America and followed by her young lover, who is now masquerading as a French count. Only by dint of a fifth act filled with unparalleled discoveries (unparalleled except in another melodrama) can it be revealed that the woman who accompanies Maria is the admiral's wife; the disguised count, his son; and Maria, the general's daughter. Actually, the only way to straighten out such a plot is with a letter—which Newman kindly provides.

But all of this plot doesn't much matter. The importance of the play centers on Jonathan, who figures very little in the mysteries of the "drama."

Dressed as a sailor, eating a piece of bread, and sobbing as he complains of his great misfortune—all in good Yankee dialect—Jonathan appears before Newman at the beginning of Act I and, after a humorous dialogue, is given a position as footman to the Count St. Luc. Servitude does not appeal to this "free-born American," but that aspect of his situation is only one source of humor. In the course of the play, he tells where he was born, explaining what America means to him, and manages to sing "Yankee Doodle" twice. Jonathan is a proud and patriotic American, a moral man who meets Humphreys' description of the Yankee as "imaginative, prejudiced, docile, independent, obstinant, suspicious, ready to parry attacks with rustic and satiric retorts." Without him the play would have lost the interest which its title offers and probably disappeared into history without regret.

Another play which should be mentioned here is James Kirk Paulding's *The Bucktails*, which was written shortly after the War of 1812 but which was not produced or published until 1847. As a writer of fiction and as an essayist, Paulding was a strong spokesman for America and also a passable dramatist whose *Lion of the West* (1831) is a landmark play with its creation of the western backwoods character. As a social comedy, *The Bucktails* dramatizes the contrast between America as a land of freedom and equality and a tired and corrupt England. The plot follows the problems of an American heiress visiting in England, where she is courted by five disagreeable Englishmen who are primarily interested in her money, even to the point of attempting to kidnap her. But America is soon represented by two stalwart young men who win the hearts of the heiress and her companion while managing a considerable amount of pro-American propaganda. In this play, where both plot and characters have some clear development, Paulding provides a Yankee, Jonathan Peabody, who bears some resemblance to the Jonathans who came before him. There is also an Irishman, Paddy Whack, and together they bring a lot of humor to the play.

One of the best comic opera-dramas of the period featuring Yankee characters is *The Saw-Mill; or, A Yankee Trick* by Micah Hawkins (1777–1825). As a drama it has fair exposition, a well-structured plot, and clearly distinguished, if somewhat stereotyped, characters. Although the Yankee characters are really two old Princeton men disguised as Yankees and, therefore, corrupt models of the bonafide Yankee, the effect on the stage is the same. Nearly as interesting as the play is the dramatist, who seems to have been an extraordinary fellow. Raised on Long Island and at one time apprenticed to a coachman, he eventually became a grocer and, as an accomplished musician on piano, violin, and flute, kept a piano beneath his grocery counter and played a kind of running accompaniment to his customers' requests. Called a "Musician, Poet, and Grocer" by his contemporaries, he wrote patriotic and comic songs and probably more than one play. Only *The Saw-mill*, however, seems to have been published and produced.[18] Presumably based on a real incident which took place in 1824, this two-act opera-drama, in fair blank verse throughout, was performed at New York's Chatham Garden Theatre in November, 1824, and was repeated for four or five performances the following November at the Park Theatre. The New York *Mirror* found the scenery of the Park production beautiful, particularly the grand Canal and the Baron's house and barn at sunset.

The plot device for *The Saw-Mill* is a newspaper ad in which a rich Hollander, Baron Scaffderduval, asks for someone to build a sawmill on Oneida Creek. In order to marry the Baron's daughter, Elna, before she is forced to marry Count Phlegm, Richard Bloom disguises himself as a Yankee millwright, Ezeakiel Amos. With his servant, Jacob, and a friend, Herman, also dressed as a Yankee, he interviews the Baron and is hired with the promise of a parcel of land when the sawmill is finished. Most of the humor derives from the Yankee masquerade, but spectacular scenery and two love subplots undoubtedly added to the audience's enjoyment. Finally, Elna penetrates Richard's disguise. Then by conniving a bit on the placement of the sawmill and by taking advantage of the Baron's arrogant assumption of infallibility, against which he has pledged his own daughter, Richard manages to get the best of the Baron and win, not only the parcel of land where the sawmill is located, but Elna as well. As a whole, the comedy is fast-moving, with interesting and colorful characters, a number of witty and sentimental songs, and a nationalistic point of view which emphasizes scenery and people, in particular the Yankee as a shrewd and comic figure.

A play frequently mentioned as helping to establish the Yankee character in American drama, *The Forest Rose; or, American Farmers*, was written by Samuel Woodworth (1785–1842), one of the handful of playwrights who provides evidence by the late 1820s that the American dramatist was making himself known. Few could claim a better American heritage. Descended from one of the first settlers of Plymouth and the son of a soldier in the Revolution, Woodworth was born in Scituate, Massachusetts, and started his career by being apprenticed to a printer in Boston. By 1809 he was settled in New York, where for the remainder of his life he established himself as a poet, dramatist, and editor. From 1812 to 1814 he published a weekly newspaper called *The*

War; as a strong Swedenborgian he edited *The Halcyon Luminary and Theological Repository* (1812–1813); and with George P. Morris he established the New York *Mirror and Ladies Literary Gazette.* Throughout his life he wrote essays and popular poems such as the patriotic war song "The Hunters of Kentucky" and the poem for which posterity remembers him, "The Old Oaken Bucket." The latter he wrote in half an hour after a few drinks of a liquor that struck Woodworth as surpassed in taste only by the water from the old bucket that one got after a day's labor in the fields. Woodworth, who impressed some as having an almost childlike faith in man, also played several musical instruments and enjoyed the beauty of music as might be expected of a truly patriotic and idealistic poet. During his last years his creativity suffered from his eye troubles and what he termed "attacks of paralysis" which impaired his memory.

Woodworth wrote a number of plays, some of which are remembered only by name: *Blue Laws; or, Eighty Years Ago* (1833), a satiric farce; *The Cannibals; or, The Massacre Islands* (1833); *King's Bridge Cottage*, published in 1826 as by a "gentleman of N. York" and sometimes attributed to Woodworth; and *The Foundling of the Sea* (1833). This last work was concerned with the American Revolution, which also provided the inspiration for *The Widow's Son; or, Which Is the Traitor?* (1825). Woodworth's work was first heard on the stage on July 8 and 14, 1818, when his "Funeral Ode on the Obsequies of Montgomery" was spoken in the Pavilion Theatre in New York, and on July 10 of that year a young lady sang his song called "Freedom's Jubilee." In late December, 1820, and early January, 1821, Woodworth himself was involved with a Female Assistance Society, for which recitations were given at New York's Washington Hall, among them Woodworth's "The Tear of Gratitude." *The Deed of Gift*, his first play, opened in Boston in 1821 but was poorly received. With songs, a rural setting, and a strong sentiment for American liberty, this "comic opera" anticipated *The Forest Rose* but showed little dramatic skill. Perhaps some originality exists in the fact that the young hero was disinherited because he quit college to go on the stage; otherwise, it was the usual melodrama with the machinations of a villainous older brother defeated by the shrewd and determined sweetheart of the hero.

Woodworth's next play, *La Fayette; or, The Castle of Olmutz* (1824) anticipated the visit of the French hero to America. Taking his plot from the incident of Lafayette's imprisonment in Germany in 1792 and the attempt of a young German physician and an American to rescue him, Woodworth added a love match between the American and the daughter of the Austrian general who must keep Lafayette a prisoner. The ill-fated escape seems a disaster for all until a pardon from the emperor saves the American from execution and frees Lafayette. Throughout, Woodworth manages with numerous patriotic sentiments to appeal to the popular nationalistic prejudices. In the same year, 1824, Walter Lee wrote a play called *La Fayette; or, The Fortress of Olmutz*, which used the same historical incident as the basis for a romantic melodrama, but, whereas Woodworth's play appeared at the Park in New York, Lee's was evidently not performed.

The Widow's Son; or, Which Is the Traitor? had its source, as Woodworth explained in his introduction, in Margaret Darby, an eccentric woman who lost her husband at General Wolfe's defeat at Quebec and came to America from Ireland with her two sons. One son, William, was arrested for Royalist sympathies and later deserted the Patriot forces to give General Clinton the plans for Fort Montgomery. The resulting mental depression of the widow reduced her socially and economically until she was known as the "Witch of Blagge's Cove." Thereafter, and until Arnold's treason changed Washington's plans, "Crazy Peg" carried messages and got information for Washington while also posing as a spy for Clinton. It was excellent material for patriotic melodrama, but Woodworth weakened its potential by dividing his plot interests and by using Crazy Peg as a perpetual and mysterious *deus ex machina.*

One part of the plot revolves around an American officer, Champe, who fakes desertion, becomes an aid to General Arnold, and eventually arranges for the capture of a British transport before returning to his own side. Mainly, however, Woodworth emphasizes the widow and her two sons, particularly John Darby, who masquerades as a Dr. Stramonium. With a Negro servant, Scipio, they provide wit and humor and much of the action of the play. Lighthearted and indifferent to fighting in the army, Dr. Stramonium's character is the best that Woodworth created. Unrecognized by his brother, Captain Darby of the British forces, Dr. Stramonium is captured and gains admission to General Arnold's quarters, where the general is ill. At this point Woodworth tries to dramatize the idea in his subtitle, but loses it in the trappings of melodrama. When an American, Truman, thinks he has captured Arnold, it turns out to be Stramonium who is wearing the traitor's cloak. How do you identify a traitor? Had she been more seriously conceived, Crazy Peg might have helped with an answer, but she drifts in and out of scenes, singing songs, firing a pistol, saving one son from the British, another from the Patriots. In one song she tries to persuade her traitor son, Captain Darby, to change his views; in another she explains what is going on to Louisa, the girl loved by both Stramonium and Champe—and the only link between the two parts of the plot. By the end of the play, Champe has been successful, Stramonium will become a more serious man, while his brother, Captain Darby, remains safe with the British. While providing some interesting characterization along with fast-moving action, Woodworth unfortunately fails to dramatize successfully the one serious idea he ever put into a play.

A fusion of nationalism and sentiment inspired most of Woodworth's literary creativity, and *The Forest Rose*, his most important contribution to American drama, illustrates that combined approach. With music by John Davies, this pastoral opera-drama was first presented in New York on October 6, 1825, as an afterpiece to *The Lady of Lyons* and proved immensely popular throughout America for the next thirty-five years. It was also one of the several Yankee plays that held great appeal for the English. At London's Adelphi Theatre, for example, Josh Silsbee, an American Yankee actor, played ninety-nine performances as Jonathan Ploughboy in *The Forest Rose*. Although most of the Yankee actors at one time or another used this Jonathan as a vehicle, he is not one of the major characters in the primary love plot but rather a combination shopkeeper-farmer who shows some of the characteristics that would make up the Yankee of the future. Interested in girls but unable to woo them properly, sometimes easily duped but basically clever in a rural way, he has an offensive attitude toward Negroes and is essentially a simple person. Otherwise, Woodworth's rather conventional love plot, which is embellished by an English fop-villain, is supported by a farm-versus-city theme with strong pro-American overtones. As the good squire says, there is "no lot on earth more enviable than the AMERICAN FARMERS" (II, v). Woodworth tried to infuse some life into his rather stilted dialogue with a great many asides, a few soliloquies, numerous songs, and an occasional play upon words, but it is mainly Jonathan who brings some distinction to the play.

The opening scene of this brief, two-act musical play represents the idyllic qualities of rural life. The "overture expresses the various sounds which are heard at early drawn in the country commencing at the hour of silence when even the ticking of the village clock is supposed to be heard." Into this scene Woodworth introduces William and Harriet, the farmer's daughter, who coquettishly encourages Bellamy, an English fop. Jonathan woos Sally Forest, the deacon's daughter, who in a bit of rural humor blindfolds Jonathan and substitutes the Forest's Negro servant, Rose, to receive Jonathan's kiss. Blandford, another Englishman, and Lydia are the main characters in the love plot. Bellamy is the villain, who mistakes Lydia for Harriet in a blackhearted attempt at seduction and succeeds only in stealing her locket. This action and the lost locket create a misunderstanding between Lydia and Blandford, but Bellamy, still seduction bound, gets his just deserts when he is tricked in his abduction plans with a veiled girl who turns out to be the Forest Rose, the Negro girl. At the final curtain everyone is happy except Bellamy, who has the last word: "I will not fail to notice you when I publish my 'Three Months in America' "—a good parting thrust for Americans who had come to expect ill-treatment from their English visitors once they were safely home.

The Yankee was not the only character type in America that attracted play-wrights. The Irish, for example, came to America in great numbers after the War of 1812, and eventually the Irishman became a comic character on the stage almost equal in popularity to the Yankee. There was also the Indian, the Negro, and the Dutchman, or German. Hawkins' *The Saw-mill* had Dutch characters from Holland who spoke in dialect, and Carr's *Benevolent Lawyers* had a German moneylender. The stage "Dutchman," however, was really a German who would appear in the theatre most prominently about mid-century after the 1848 Revolution in Europe and subsequent German emigration to America. Before 1828 Negroes invariably had speaking parts only as servants. It took the efforts of Thomas Dartmouth Rice, an interest in minstrels, and the slavery issue prior to and during the Civil War to make the Negro a fea-tured character. And then there were those less identifiable characters who were simply Americans about whom one might write plays: farmers, soldiers, women, and the young and the old from any part of the country.

To assert an unmistakable national spirit, playwrights would frequently fasten their attentions onto one of the recognizable characters in America. They would then set their plays in a historical period and present scenes that were typically American—perhaps adapting a nationalistic novel that would serve the purpose. Their objective—and a major one for the 1815–1828 pe-riod—was to dramatize the American attitude, what they believed symbolic of the American spirit. Although they were generally not so successful in terms of literary accomplishment as were those who were writing poetry and fiction, the creators of American drama established some of the directions which would be followed in other literary genres.

By the 1820s the stage Irishman had already appeared in a number of American plays. *The Disappointment* by Forrest had a voluble Irishman named Truhoop whose servant, Terrence, also added to the comedy. Dunlap was an extensive user of the Irish character: *Darby's Return*, *The Glory of Columbia*, *Yankee Chronology*, *A Trip to Niagara*—all had definite, if conventional,

Irishmen. And one finds the Irish servant scattered through a number of early American plays. One of the earliest plays to make the Irishman the major character in a play and treat him as an immigrant is Charles S. Talbot's *Paddy's Trip to America; or, The Husband with Three Wives*, written and acted in either 1821 or 1822. Talbot, an Irish actor, came to America in 1820 and eventually published three plays. The hero of *Paddy's Trip to America*, a two-act farce, is Pat O'Flaherty, who came to America to make his fortune but first felt obliged to look up an old friend who had come to America much earlier. With these two characters Talbot shows the good and bad sides of the Irish—or of any people. Pat is the true and responsible person, the lover of life who must try to reform his boisterous and unprincipled friend who left a wife and children in Ireland, has wives in New York and Philadelphia, and is about to acquire another one. Some critics found this farce a tasteless burlesque, but Talbot protested that he showed only the fun-loving Irish immigrant.

One other play by Talbot, *Captain Morgan; or, The Conspiracy Unveiled*, published and acted in 1827, should be mentioned for its concern with a particular aspect of American history. Called a farce but really a melodrama, the play capitalized on the sensational activities of one Captain Morgan, a bricklayer in New York who, in 1826, was abducted and presumably killed when he threatened to publish the secrets of the Masonic Order. The eventual publication of his book touched the public indignation and helped found the Anti-Mason political party in 1829. Although Talbot's play is less exciting than the real episode, it shows, as does his Irish play, his inclination to take advantage of current events.

The Connecticut Emigrant (1822) "by a descendant of the Connecticut Pilgrims" provides another view of people in America. A dialogue in blank verse written mainly for the "Anniversary of the Connecticut Agricultural Societies, Cattle Shows, Fairs, and Exhibitions of Domestic Manufactures for 1822," it is also a strong bit of chauvinistic praise for the Nutmeg State. As people moved from England and Europe to America, so people moved from the eastern states to the unexplored West as new government land policies became enacted. This play dramatizes, or more accurately orates, the reasons why its hero decides to stay in the "charming land" of Connecticut. Not only a staunch supporter of his home state, the writer was probably influenced by the western land speculation which was mainly responsible for the panic of 1819.

Plays concerned with the movement westward were still a few years off at this time, but utopian living, a factor in the settlement of America, sounded its appeal throughout the nineteenth century. One such community, New Harmony in Indiana, stimulated "Peter Puffem" to write a short satiric farce, *Heaven on Earth; or, The New Lights of Harmony* (1825), an extravaganza in two acts. Fed up with life in Philadelphia, Gobbmouche falls prey to the seductive salestalk of Plausible, sells his property at a loss to Steadfast, and heads for Indiana along with a number of other dreamers. But "harmony" becomes a "bad joke" and Gobbmouche returns home, declaring that "if ever again I leave the old *drab coloured city* for a Heaven in the woods, may I be nailed to a chimney." Although not much of a play, it continues the pattern of comic satire in America.

Mary Clarke Carr is one of a number of women dramatists who provide a glimpse of Americans, particularly American women, during the early nineteenth century. Her view, however, is filtered through the eyes of a romantic idealist. Strength of mind, purity of heart, magnanimity of soul, and sweetness of temper replete with domestic virtues—this is the national female character as dramatized in Mrs. Carr's *The Fair Americans*, a melodrama in five acts, published in 1815 with indications on the script that Joseph Jefferson performed in it. Not much is known about Mrs. Carr. She wrote a short, patriotic play, *The Return From Camp*, which was not published but was enacted at Philadelphia's Chestnut Street Theatre in 1815. In the fall of 1814 she had begun to edit a woman's magazine, the *Intellectual Regale, or Ladies Tea Party*, which by the spring of 1815 she was also printing. Her two published plays— *The Fair Americans* and *The Benevolent Lawyers* (1823)—suggest an intelligent woman with that romantic strength of mind which she identified with the "national female character" plus a fusion of ardent patriotism and humanitarian impulses.

Carr's "fair Americans" are farmers, particularly farm girls, living on the banks of Lake Erie and going about their chores while the American military tries to recruit soldiers for a drive into Canada as the War of 1812 drags on. Although the farmers have difficulty seeing the wisdom of invading Canada, all belong to Captain Harley's Riflemen and are prepared to fight. News comes that York is taken; "the American eagle flies triumphant." Two of the farm girls are saved from Indians by two British officers who are then captured by the Americans. Throughout are patriotic speeches by both soldiers and women. With only a slight concern for character and with a scattered plot, there remains a certain charm to the play which is difficult to explain. It comes in the romantic fervor, the brightness of the girls in their innocent conversation, the comedy of an Irish couple, and the general humane quality of the play. In the final act, for example, there is no animosity toward the British; one of the officers is allowed to escape, and the other will marry the girl he rescued. Otherwise, the "fair Americans" enjoy a "sweet peace" and a united future. Of all elements of drama, theme—that is, nationalistic sentiment—is most important in *The Fair Americans*.

Mrs. Carr's second published play, *The Benevolent Lawyers; or, Villainy Detected*, dedicated to the "gentlemen of the bar," manages to satirize corrupt lawyers while upholding the profession. It also shows her continued interest in the variety of people who make up America. Among the characters are an Irish gentleman and a German moneylender, both of whom speak in dialect, and two Negro servants plus a hero, Trueman. As in her other play, Carr's thesis is eminently clear—"the depravity of a few of its members ought not to implicate the whole body," says the hero's legal clerk (I, i)—but in this play, too, her plotting is extremely weak. Charles Trueman believes that a lawyer can be a man who helps people, and he puts morals before money and the welfare of his clients before his fees. But there are other kinds of lawyers, those who charge 100 percent interest on money loaned, intrigue with their clients, foreclose without warning on notes, and try to force their attentions upon innocent females. In one scene, which attracted imitators, the abused heroine allows her disguised Negro maid to take her place in a meeting with the villain, picturesquely named Fairface. Interestingly enough, the maid, Kate, has some of the best lines in the play during this meeting and embrace. Finally, "the Science of Jurisprudence" is vindicated through the activities of Charles Trueman.

Another woman playwright, Maria Henrietta Pinckney (d. 1836), was equally concerned with presenting an American people. The daughter of a man of some importance—a leader during the Revolution, a minister to France, and later a Federalist candidate for the presidency—Miss Pinckney was known as a student of public affairs and as a very strong-minded person. In a volume entitled *Essays: Religious, Moral*, published in 1818 as written "by a lady," Pinckney included three plays, all intended for reading rather than for production.

The Young Carolinians; or, Americans in Algiers uses scenes of the Barbary Coast war as a background for some romance while contrasting them in about equal amounts with scenes of rural and upper-class life in South Carolina. En route to England the heroine, Ellinor, and her friend from the Carolina backwoods, Margaret, are captured by Algerian pirates and then rescued by Ellinor's fiance, already a prisoner of the Turks. Meanwhile, back in Charleston, certain class distinctions are revealed when Margaret's father, Homespun, visits Ellinor's sophisticated aunt. For the young people now in England, however, the answer to class differences is education, "not birth or fortune." Throughout, Pinckney emphasizes the ideal structure of democracy while requiring her Algerians to act more as romantic Christians than as Moslems. Another interesting aspect of this play and an ironic contrast to the democratizing of the classes is the defense of slavery provided by the Negro Cudjo, who also supplies some humor by using the Gullah dialect of Charleston.

Maria Pinckney's other two plays indicate her interest in a social morality as well as in democratic nationalism. In all that she wrote she had a definite purpose. *A Tyrant's Victims* is a tragedy concerned with Agathocles, the King of Syracuse, which according to the author is supposed to make one detest tyranny. In *The Orphans*, a five-act melodrama set in England, she dramatized social manners and morality through the actions of the rather fascinating Lady Flinty, the shrewish and grasping wife of Sir Spendall. Refusing to care for her orphaned younger sister, Lady Flinty reveals her bad temper, her ignorance, her malevolent heart, and her ability to "inflict," according to the author, "through criminal passiveness, evil upon others." Using the drama as a social weapon, Pinckney warns youth against the ways of such a person as Lady Flinty, a person who would, of course, be more easily found in England than in America.

As writers of fiction emphasized the American temperament as well as American history and scenery in their effort to create a national literature, the playwright, with his considerable experience in adapting foreign plays, found ready native material for the spectacular melodramas which parts of American society continued to demand in the theatre. No American writer had greater acceptance through the adaptor's skill on both American and English stages than did James Fenimore Cooper. His romantic idealism, so effectively presented through highly selective realistic touches of character, manners, and scenery, held great appeal for Americans whose dreams of the future and sense of past glories he depicted in an appealing world of wish-fulfillment.

A dramatization of Cooper's first successful novel, *The Spy*, appeared on the New York stage within a year, adapted by Charles Powell Clinch under the title of *The Spy: A Tale of the Neutral Ground* (1822). A businessman, government inspector, and later assistant collector of the United States Custom House in New York for more than forty years, Clinch (1797–1880) was a minor literary man by avocation and associated with such Knickerbocker writers as Bryant and Halleck. Although only *The Spy* is extant, he wrote four plays, all of which were produced on the New York stage: performed in addition to *The Spy* were *The Expelled Collegian* (1822); *The Avenger's Vow* (1824);[19] and *The First of May in New York* (1830).

The Spy follows Cooper's novel very closely, with the actions of Harvey Birch, the British spy and American counterspy, determining the plot and climax. One of the more theatrical scenes shows Birch escaping from prison disguised as a drunken, camp-following woman. The finale provided excellent patriotic melodrama as Clinch groups the characters around Birch's body while a sentimental eulogy is orated. But it was still largely Cooper's work on the stage. Clinch, depending on his audience's knowledge of the novel for his success, added only three original scenes. The disguises, the patriotic soliloquies, the songs, the humor of a Negro servant, a Doctor Sitgreaves, who is always eager to operate, a camp follower, and the difficult romance between an American officer and a girl whose brother is the British officer he has captured—all contributed to a lively evening in the theatre. The New York *Evening Post* (March 7, 1822) declared that the play possessed "uncommon merit": "The piece had every advantage of scenery, music, firing of small arms, and plenty of powder and smoke, enlivened with the blaze of a house a' fire, which was permitted guiltily to blaze on, undisturbed by any body near it." It was a popular play, and Clinch's version or other adaptations were performed for more than thirty years in the American theatre.

Several more of Cooper's novels were dramatized prior to 1828. An anonymous version of *The Pioneers* appeared in New York on April 21, 1823, as *The Pioneers; or, The Sources of the Susquehannah*, but dramatizations of *The Pilot* were more successful on stage. One anonymous adaptation came to New York in late October, 1824, and W. H. Wallack's *Paul Jones; or, The Pilot of the German Ocean* ran for seventeen weeks at the Chatham Theatre in 1827. Another version "adapted to the American stage by a gentleman of Philadelphia" played in 1827 in Baltimore, where it was considered attractive for its "scenic display" although it had "little merit as a literary production."[20] More interesting is Edward Fitzball's adaptation, which had a spectacular run of 200 nights at London's Adelphi Theatre in 1825. It is not generally realized that during the 1820s English theatre managers became increasingly aware of the drawing power of American peculiarities with the result that a number of hack dramatists in London made careers by adapting American plays and fiction for English audiences. Fitzball was one and William Bayle Bernard was another, and the popularity of their efforts covered more than a quarter of a century.

Another Cooper novel of the sea that became good spectacle theatre was *The Red Rover*. Adapted for production in 1828 by Samuel Henry Chapman, it also appeared on the stage in anonymous versions. Chapman (1799–1830) was recruited from England as an actor but is best known in America as the manager of the Walnut Street Theatre in Philadelphia where James Rees (*Dra-*

matic Authors of America) credits him with four plays—*The Red Rover, Dr. Foster, Gasperoni,* and *Mail Robbers*—of which only *The Red Rover* had marked success. In this play, exploiting the excitement of sea battles, Chapman followed the novel closely, using about a third of it, and added only two scenes of his own. In his adaptation he lost the idea of the pursuit of freedom which interested Cooper but created an average melodrama about the pirate Red Rover, who is really a sentimentalist at heart. After freeing the British agent sent to spy on him and after experiencing storms, battles, and romance at sea, Red Rover puts his crew and all passengers aboard the *Dart* with the sad words, "I shall soon be forgotten; Adieu." He then leaves his own ship, the *Dolphin*, which catches fire and blows up as the curtain falls. The use of fire and water fascinated theatre audiences at the time, but fire was perhaps the more memorable, a fact poignantly attested to by numerous theatre disasters.

For many writers interested in establishing a sense of nationalism in literature, the American Indians seemed ideal characters. They had been part of the lives of the early settlers in friendship and in disaster and had continued their dual role as the country developed. In either event Indians were a source of fascination. Early American dramatists had generally treated them as exceptional persons and most frequently romanticized them beyond recognition. The story of Pocahontas, perhaps because her achievements in both American and English society were remarkable, was particularly attractive to dramatists. But in real life, too, Indians entered the theatre, either as colorful witnesses to performances or as performers. For several nights during the fall of 1824, for example, six Indians danced a war dance between the play and the farce at the Chatham Theatre. Six chiefs from the Oneida tribe danced at the Lafayette Theatre during March, 1827. The following season, Odell notes, Indians were everywhere.[21] They even traveled to England. A notice in an English theatrical journal for January, 1819, stated that "the American Indian Warriors, who performed last season at the English Opera House, are now the attraction of the Dublin Theatre."[22] As material for American dramatists, however, Indians attracted only slight attention during the first quarter of the nineteenth century. Then, beginning with Edwin Forrest's performance in Augustus Stone's *Metamora* in 1829, Indian plays multiplied upon the stage for a generation until John Brougham burlesqued the noble savage with such effect as to help diminish the nobility of the image for decades of audiences to come.

After the War of 1812, a few years passed before any playwright used the Indian as a major focus; then in the early 1820s two plays emphasizing Indians were published, both dramatic curiosities yet in different ways and neither performed professionally. Nothing is known of Lewis Deffeback whose *Ooliata; or, The Indian Heroine* (1821) shows a familiarity with traditional melodramatic devices but little originality or talent in constructing a play. The main plot follows a love tria ₃le in which an old chief, Monomo, challenges the youthful Tullala as a rival for the love of Ooliata, the present chief's daughter. In action which abounds with love tokens, disguises, and incriminating letters, Tullala manages to thwart Monomo's plot on his life, but the news travels too slowly. Ooliata throws herself off a high cliff, and Tullala can only stab himself, leaving her unhappy father to moan their deaths. If this climax sounds familiar, there is a subplot in which a newly married American couple and their guide are captured by the Indians and saved by Ooliata in the traditional Pocahontas fashion.

The second play, *Logan; the Last of the Race of Shikellemus, Chief of the Cayuga Nation* (1823), was written by Joseph Doddridge (1796–1826), a clergyman, author, physician, and pioneer who was brought up on the frontier and knew the customs and speaking habits of the Indians. Seemingly uninterested in staging his play, he was concerned with historical accuracy. He had a purpose in his writing. "The tear of commiseration," he wrote in his preface, "is due to Logan." A man of peace who was friendly to the English, Logan, the Indian chief, was provoked by the murder of Indian women and children in 1774. The result was the War of the Earl of Dunmore, which ended with the peace of Camp Charlotte. In his fictionalized account Doddridge presents Logan as a strong and sympathetic character while the action of his play is seriously weakened by excessive argument, interrupted by war songs, and concluded only by a truce which leaves Logan alone yet with dignity ("Who is there to mourn for Logan? Not one."). Some of Logan's speeches, however, are romantically impressive and accurate in phrasing if one is to believe the author. There is no question of Doddridge's loyalties. He wrote more about Logan in his *Notes on the Settlement and Indian Wars of the Western Parts of Virginia and Pennsylvania from 1768–1783 Inclusive*. Despite weaknesses as a dramatist, Doddridge understood the Indians and manages to impart a certain fascination to his work.

Act I of the play opens as the British soldiers, having heard that the Indians are preparing for war, argue over the value of the Indians and finally vote to slaughter some who are living by the river. In their turn the chiefs assemble and plan revenge, but victory in battle is not easy; they must meet again to discuss war or peace. One argues that "the life of man is the life of War. The wolves cannot eat grass. Something must die before they can eat. The fox kills and eats the harmless birds." But another chief suggests caution: "Let us think a little before we strike. The panther before he springs on his prey, takes time to squat down, fix his claws, and mark his exact course with his eyes" (II, i). The chiefs finally agree to make peace with Lord Dunmore, and the play closes with Logan standing alone. As the last of his family, which was massacred, and as a chief who outlived the independence of his nation, Logan was, for Doddridge, a man of honor and stature.

Montgomery; or, The Falls of Montmorency, a three-act melodrama by Henry James William Finn, would not appear to be an Indian drama, but it was, and James Hackett, the actor, produced it as *The Indian Wife; or, The Falls of Montmorency*. Finn (1782–1840) first studied law in America and then left that career to travel to Europe, where he became an actor. When he returned to America in 1811, he achieved some reputation as a comic actor and a partner in the management of the Federal Street Theatre in Boston. With this experience he brought an exceptional theatricality to his Indian play, which opened in Boston in February, 1825, and, dedicated to Daniel Webster, was published the same year. More honest than most actor-managers, Finn disclaimed the usual pose of publication on the "advice of friends" and frankly hoped for a "profitable sale." He would write two more plays before his death aboard the steamboat *Lexington*, which burned in Long Island Sound, perhaps as spectacular an exit as an actor might wish.

Montgomery, which has little to do with the famous general, takes place on Canadian soil and dramatizes the attempt of L'Araignée to steal the halfbreed Indian wife, Altamah, of the French leader La Valle. After La Valle goes to Quebec to fight for Montgomery, whose death allows Finn an opportunity for patriotic sentiment, L'Araignée begins his skulduggery, which is eventually thwarted by the activities, both humorous and gallant, of two American soldiers, Welcome Sobersides and O'Shamrock. L'Araignée is that accomplished villain in melodrama whose ability to entertain nineteenth-century audiences is suggested by the final scene of the play. As L'Araignée flees down the river in a canoe with Altamah's child in his arms, Sobersides dangles over the water from the branch of a tree and snatches the child while the villain goes over the falls of Montmorency to a spectacular death. Although the Indian heroine is central to the action (and speaks in poetry), she is largely a passive figure. The play belongs to the comics and to the white men, whether pursued or pursuing.

Indians have limited roles in George Pope Morris' *Briar Cliff* (1826), and only one, Oonaliska, speaks, but the play shows how Indians were frequently used to help create popular theatrical successes.[23] Morris (1802–1864) was an essayist, poet, songwriter ("Woodman, Spare That Tree"), and influential editor, remembered especially for his founding, with Samuel Woodworth, of the New York *Mirror and Ladies Literary Gazette*, which he continued with Nathaniel Parker Willis as a weekly and finally as a daily paper. During his later years he lived at "Briarcliff," his country place across the Hudson River from West Point.

As were other plays at this time, *Briar Cliff* is a brief but spectacular melodrama, its strong nationalistic thesis supported by the Revolution. A listing of some of its sets and backdrops may suggest why it remained popular in theatres: View of the old North River; Crazy Bet's cave; View of the old Federal Hall in Wall Street, taken from the original view of 1783; sandy beach in Connecticut; Indians cross the Sound in canoes; characteristic dance by the Sons of the Forest; Parson Shepherd's house on fire; an original view of the Battery and Staten Island; the British ships at anchor in the Bay, taken from an original drawing made November 23, 1783; embarkation of the British troops.

The plot of *Briar Cliff*, which is based on Morris's novel *Whig and Tory*, follows the efforts of Mary Jensen, a Patriot in a Loyalist society, to rescue a wounded American officer, Leslie, from his English captors. One good episode shows Leslie, having escaped from Crazy Bet's cave, returning to his own camp disguised as a Methodist preacher and encountering the marauding cowboys who steal and burn without regard for Tory or Whig sentiments. The plot and Mary's problems are complicated by the jealousy of one British officer, Grant, and the anger of another, Waldron, who becomes suspicious of Mary's activities. Captured by Waldron and transported across Long Island Sound, Mary is first rescued by the Indians and later, by Grant, who, with his dying breath, puts her hand in Leslie's as the climactic tableau forms: "In the background appear American troops with Washington in the Center"—a *beau geste* with patriotic sentiment. Another popular thrust was shown by an English officer, Musgrave, who retreats among the defeated as he contemplates publishing his "Travels and Adventures in this horrid land." An Irish servant and a "learned" doctor also provide good change-of-pace humor in this popular melodrama, which was produced in four New York theatres: Bowery, Chatham, National, and Park. By 1826, however, Morris' more substantial contribution to American drama was as a critic.

George Washington Parke Custis' *The Indian Prophecy* excited some criticism because it linked Washington with the Indians and because the author's father was a stepson of the first President. Custis (1781–1857) identified himself as "a Southern Nabob, a man of acres (and good ones, too) and almost thrice a hundred slaves, and above all a writer."[24] With 8000 acres he was a man of means although he referred to slavery as "the appalling curse." Like several Southern gentlemen of his day, he enjoyed writing but published little. He wrote, in fact, at least eight plays, all but *The Indian Prophecy* after 1828; of that play he wrote that "I have even ventured on a little Drama, a slight work, but relating to a most intriguing event in the early life of General Washington. It was written for the 22nd Feb; but was too late for bringing out on that day."[25] Instead the play was produced at the Chestnut Street Theatre in Philadelphia on July 4, 1827. The "intriguing event" on which it was based was the declaration by an Indian chief in 1770 that years before, during Braddock's inglorious defeat, he and his braves had tried their best to kill the then Colonel Washington. When they repeatedly failed, even shooting the horse from beneath him, the chief decided that Washington was protected by the Great Spirit for some future duty and ordered his men to cease their attempts on his life.

Whether the play published in 1828 as "a national drama in two acts" was the same one produced on July 4, 1827, is open to debate. The published version opens with a long scene involving Woodford and his wife, who are then met by an old friend, Bishop, Washington's advance scout, and taken to see the General. At that meeting the Indians arrive, and Woodford instigates the joke of putting Washington's cloak on someone else and trying to fool the Indians. But the Indian chief recognizes the real Washington and delivers his prophecy: "He will become the Chief of Nations, and a people yet unborn, hail him as the Founder of a mighty Empire" (II, ii).

The acted version, however, was noticeably different. At any rate, at the Baltimore Theatre a week earlier than the Philadelphia performance, a reviewer described in a halting and peculiar, though interesting style, what he saw:

> Scenery mountains—some backwoodsmen with rifles—enter. Colonel Washington, accompanied by—we forget who—they discoursed of things and matters in general—talked about the scenery—prospects—Indians fighting. We had nearly forgot Bishop—who kept his place—behind his master—and like a trusty soldier, never spoke without touching his hat—Exeunt. Scene changes—a hunter's cot at the foot of the mountains—Mr. Darley—wife and child—enter Mr. Pearson and Mr. Forest—more talk—Mr. F. prophecies to the Col. about the mother country, etc.—pretty little Indian girl—just converted—exeunt—Indian girl, solus—soliloquy, the good, good missionaries —no applause—exit. End of 1st act.
>
> Act 2nd. The hunter, his wife, child, and the Indian girl, start for the camp

accompanied by Bishop—fall in with Indians—are captured in spite of Bishop's *coteau de chasse,* or whingger—only prevented from being scalped by Menawa—the fattest Indian we ever saw—who is on the way to make his prophecy—they conduct him to the camp, where in the meantime one of the Colonel's attendants is dressed up before the audience in his hat and cloak—Menawa comes in—with true Indian sagacity smells the rightful one out—is faint, won't drink rum, nor eat—strange things in an Indian—delivers his prophecy—dies. Col. in a stupor. Curtain falls.[26]

If nothing else, that summary suggests the changes that can be made between acted and published versions. The reviewer went on to question the theatre manager's discrimination in producing such a play and to "protest most solemnly against this dressing up a character to us so sacred as that of Washington." The afterpiece that evening, *The Fall of Algiers,* a new musical play in two acts (perhaps by John Howard Payne?), continued the nationalistic theme. With the growing force of nationalism in both literature and theatre during these years, the early interest in the Indian was only a prelude to what would come.

American history, particularly that concerned with war, also provided the dramatist with potentially spectacular material. Frequently, the results were simply staged spectacles, almost exhibits, in which the patriotic spirit was exercised through song, dance, pantomime, skit, or recitation. Two such presentations, for example, appeared in New York theatres during the late spring and early summer of 1815: on June 14 patriotic songs of Champlain and Plattsburg as sung by an actor in the character of a Negro sailor and for July 4 a "patriotic spectacle" entitled *4th of July; or, America, Commerce and Freedom.* Such events, of course, were in addition to the continuing popularity of Burk's *Bunker-Hill,* Dunlap's *Glory of Columbia,* and any Indian who might appear on stage. During the winter of 1822, as Clinch's adaptation of *The Spy* was becoming popular, M. M. Noah contributed a new "interlude," *Oh! Yes; or, the New Constitution,* as "written by a Gentleman of this City," and a full-length play for Washington's birthday celebration called *The Green Mountain Boys; or The Sons of Freedom,* "the first time of a Patriotic drama, written by a Gentleman of this City." In Boston, for the 1825 celebration of Washington's birthday, Henry J. Finn recited "The Triumphs of Liberty," a prize ode by one Ebenezer Bailey.

As an example of historical drama written between 1815 and 1828, C. E. Grice's *The Battle of New Orleans; or, Glory, Love, and Loyalty,* as did *The Fair Americans,* took its thesis from the War of 1812. Published in 1815, it was produced, along with Grice's much less successful *Battle of New York*, in New York's Park Theatre the following year. (Advertising indicates that Grice wrote at least three other plays—*Leonidas; or, The Grecian Father*; *Lorenzo, the Magnificent; or, The Merchant of Florence*; *Fraternal Feuds; or, The Lady of the Watch Tower*—whose titles suggest Grice's attempt to please theatre managers by imitating foreign models in style and scene.) Because the hero of *The Battle of New Orleans*, a "national and historical drama," was Andrew Jackson, this play also reappeared on the stage during his election year. The battle and most of the action of the play take place in Act V, but Jackson and his army tie together the various plot threads: the love of one soldier for the Colonel's daughter, the problems of the rejected son of another officer who returns from impressment at sea to join Jackson's army and who finds his wife and child, and the mysterious animosity between two of Jackson's officers which is resolved with an equally mysterious letter. The battle itself presents such scenes as that in which a girl saves not only her sweetheart but her country's flag: "Behold the banner, by a woman saved" (V, v). Although the dialogue is stiff and artificial, Jackson has strong propaganda speeches, and morality is linked to patriotism: "To venal acts let vassal nations yield,/ Duty and beauty are Columbia's shield" (V, v). In one sense, and for valid reasons, nothing more was required for the evening's entertainment.

As Jackson's national popularity grew, he became a more acceptable figure in drama. Surviving a close brush with the presidency in 1824, he was celebrated in *Old Hickory; or, A Day in New Orleans*, which Andrew Jackson Allen, a popular actor in America and namesake of the war hero, used as his benefit on February 11, 1825. Written by "two gentlemen of this city [New York]" (if all those "gentlemen of the city" were identifiable, American drama might claim some surprising dramatists), the play included a fighting Frenchman, three Kentucky sharpshooters, and a Negro soldier. In 1828 a play in one act, *The Cabal; or, A Peep into Jacksonism*, was published as written "by a Baltimorian." That same year James Frisby Brice published *Andrew Jackson*, an interlude in three acts, which treats the court-martial for mutiny of six militia men in Mobile, their conviction, and their death by shooting on the order of General Jackson. After an introductory argument between an Adams-man and a Jackson-man, the scene shifts to New Orleans, where a triumphal arch is erected to greet this "second Joan of Arc." As girls strew flowers in his path and as he is given a crown of laurel which he accepts but will not wear, soldiers and martial music make this less a play than a propaganda pageant of celebration.

Brice, obviously a loyal Jackson supporter, was apparently a lawyer in Annapolis who also held a top political office there in the 1780s. In addition to a romance, *Castle Crosier* (1827), and a monograph explaining the laws governing wills and codicils, he published two slight satirical farces. *Democedes,* presumably performed in Annapolis on August 18, 1827, is an odd sketch in three scenes which satirizes doctors. *Country Clown; or, Dandyism Improved* (1829), in one act, shows Arable arriving in town, meeting the local merchants, and being outfitted as a dandy ready for love. But he is foiled in his plans: "When I thought I had her beyond defalcation, she plays a devilish trick, and produces such a commotion in my umbilicals as to eviserate my cogitations." Brice's work might well have provided an interesting conclusion to an evening lodge meeting or social gathering.

Prior to the War of 1812, Mordecai M. Noah had written plays simply because he enjoyed the theatre. Essentially, his playwriting continued only as a demanding avocation to which he willingly apprenticed himself. After the War of 1812, during which he had served as U.S. Consul to Tunis, Noah returned to New York City to enter politics, work as a journalist, and dream of building a New Jerusalem, a haven of Judaism, on Grand Island in the Niagara River near Buffalo. He was also to write several plays, all emphasizing nationalism. The first one, *She Would Be a Soldier; or, The Plains of Chippewa* (1819), a "dramatic Gazatelle," was his most significant contribution to American drama. According to Noah it was written in three days for an English actress named Catherine Leesugg, but after first opening at the Park Theatre on June 21, 1819, it continued to be performed on the American stage for nearly forty years. It even attracted Edwin Forrest, who played the role of the Indian.

In his preface to the published play Noah explained his own role in the theatre. He was not, he admitted, a professional dramatist, nor did he want to be one. He was simply one of the spare handful at the time—Barker, Dunlap, Judah, Woodworth, Payne—who were contributing their unequal efforts toward the establishment of an American drama. As a man standing outside the professional theatre, Noah understood that encouragement for youthful attempts was necessary but, he wrote, "we must not expect . . . more . . . than may be sufficient to urge us on." And he gave the following sage advice: "We will succeed in time, as well as the English, because we have the same language, and equal intellect; but there must be system and discipline in writing plays— a knowledge of stage effect—of sound, cadences, fitness of time and place, interest of plot, spirit of delineation, nature, poetry, and a hundred *et ceteras* which are required, to constitute a good dramatic poet, who cannot, in this country, and while occupied with other pursuits, spring up overnight like as-paragus, or be watered and put in the sun, like a geranium in a flower pot." It is doubtful that Noah fully realized the length of time that acceptance would involve, but he was certainly aware that more plays must, and soon would, be written along the lines that he described.

She Would Be a Soldier did not meet Noah's demands. Instead, as most other plays of the time, it simply included as many surefire comic and melo-dramatic devices a three-act performance could bear. Although the play is thinly based on the Battle of Chippewa on July 5, 1814, it is more romance than his-tory. The plot unfolds the story of Christine, a young lady who, to avoid an unwanted marriage and to find Lenox, whom she loves, disguises herself as a man and enlists as a soldier, only to be discovered and condemned as a spy be-fore she is finally saved—in good melodramatic fashion—by Lenox, of course. There are songs, letters, miniature portraits; pastoral music, country parties, and rural dances; military splendor, fife-and-drum corps, parades, and a court-martial; a Frenchman who chases a chambermaid, an Englishman who is "fop-pish" and concerned with the "travels" that he will write, and a superior and intelligent Indian. There is also humor throughout—in dialects, situations, and dialogue—as well as satire on the English, patriotic sentiments for the Ameri-cans, a melodramatic recognition through a portrait, and a climax in which lovers and enemies are united. With such variety Noah assured his play some acceptance, but his only real accomplishment in the play is a heroine of singu-lar character and a certain imaginative persistence.

The Siege of Tripoli, Noah's next play, was first performed on May 15, 1820, at the Park Theatre. Here again Noah's nationalistic impulses, along with his personal experiences in the Mediterranean area, prompted him to write. The reviewer for the New York *Evening Post* (May 16, 1820) found it an interesting subject for American drama and praised the play as one that "awakened that national sentiment" and "elevated pride of character." On dif-ferent occasions the play was produced as *Yusef Caramalli; or, The Siege of Tripoli* and enjoyed some success. The romance of the Barbary Coast evidently still had an appeal, and other plays by Pinckney, Jonathan S. Smith (*The Siege of Algiers; or, The Downfall of Hadgi-Ali-Bashaw*, 1823) and Payne followed Noah's work.

For his next effort Noah took his material from the Revolution. *Marion; or, The Hero of Lake George* was written for the Park Theatre and performed there on Evacuation Day, November 25, 1821. He had, Noah confided in a letter to Dunlap, become "in a manner domiciliated in the green-room," but, he added, because he was daily involved in journalistic and political endeavors, he had "little time to devote to all that study and reflection so essential to the success of dramatic composition."[27] However, he was not without feeling for the dramas he wrote, and he dedicated *Marion* to the critic William Coleman, who, Noah complained, had abused his play in print without having seen it. The setting for the play is a village where Marion's estates have been confiscated by the British. Always on the brink of being captured, Marion is involved in one long melodramatic chase, which ends when General Gates' surrender on October 17, 1777, brings an American victory. There are no war scenes and few spectacles although a strong love plot features Marion and helps structure the chase. Noah's purpose, however, was to extol neither romance nor patriotic bravery but to remind everyone of the "soldiers of the Revolution and the struggle for freedom." Although it has some of the rural charm of *She Would Be a Soldier*, *Marion* lacks theatrical variety as well as a strong hero or heroine. The only other time that Noah dramatized the Revolution was in *The Siege of Yorktown*, which was performed in New York during Lafayette's visit in 1824.

Noah adapted *The Grecian Captive; or, The Fall of Athens* (1822) from *Mahomet II* (1820), a French *mélodrame* by Charrier and Joseph. He adapted the play for a friend in hopes of getting him a "good house" and even agreed that the hero could enter on an elephant—an act which brought a slurring comment from the reviewer of the New York *Evening Post*. For another public relations stunt of the evening, the play was printed in advance of performance, and each member of the audience was given a free copy as he entered the theatre. As to the play, Noah had this to say in his preface: "Let it take its chance with the rest of my little bantlings, which are vagabonding over the Union, playing in big and little theatres, adding a trifle to my reputation and nothing at all to my fortune." Although the play would seem to stress foreign scene and event, in sentiment and thought it is deeply American. The contemporary struggle for liberty in Greece was a source of great sympathy for Americans.

The captive from the play title is Zelia, the daughter of the Greek leader, Kiminski, and loved by the young Greek hero, Ypsilanti. The Turkish leader is Ali Pacha, who wants to win Zelia's love (and, in spite of his tyranny, he evokes a certain compassion for his feelings) while preventing the Greeks from retaking Athens. The plot follows the heroic actions of the Greek leaders and Zelia's planned sacrifice for her country until the Greeks, with the help of the American frigate the *United States*, are triumphant and Zelia can marry Ypsilanti. Generally strong on spectacle, Noah reached a new height in the final act of this play. Standing by the Acropolis Kiminski praises America and Washington while a procession of banners links Washington with Homer, Socrates, and Pericles. "Now," says Kiminski, "to merit freedom by the establishment of just laws—a free and upright government—a liberal, tolerant, and benevolent spirit to all." It is a typical play for Noah, who consistently emphasized the American point of view. It also shows, as he well knew, that his work marked only a very moderate beginning and a direction for more serious dramatists.

Another who helped with that moderate beginning, Samuel Benjamin Helbert Judah (c. 1799–1876), wrote at least four plays during his youthful and impetuous twenties and then disappeared from theatrical circles. Three of his plays were produced at the Park Theatre, where they had only average receptions. As did many of his contemporaries, Judah had considerable trouble plotting his action and providing adequate exposition. His usually extravagant and artificial dialogue contrasted his plays with the better work of both Woodworth and Noah, neither of whom approached the language facility of either Barker or Payne. Instead, Judah's forte was the brief spectacular scene, in which he rivaled his American and English contemporaries. Another outstanding characteristic of his writing is his concern for detailed stage directions and scene descriptions, as, for example, in an early scene from *The Mountain Torrent*:

> The Mountain Torrent; Marco's cottage perceptible to the right, at a distance, nearly shaded by trees and overhanging rocks; masses of crags are strewn around; to the right and left a hedge of wood, old and shattered, extending nearly halfway and supported by rocks; a fir tree felled and resting on each end of the bridge, and two crags projecting over the precipice make the crossing; a fall of water rushes over some rocks beneath the bridge, and joins a rapid stream which is also supplied from several smaller falls, from different parts of the rocks; the whole crowned on the summit by a thick forest; from the top of the first rock to the left is a winding footpath conducting to the bridge. The scene is nearly dark, and the glare of the lightning at intervals discovers the masses of rocks, and gleams on the waters, which are swollen and violently agitated by the wind; the storm becomes more terrible every moment. Marco is seen cautiously advancing down the footpath, making his way to the bridge.

The reader gets a clear view of the scene Judah imagined, and his placement of scenes clearly shows his interest in establishing dramatic effect. The well-written festival scene in *The Mountain Torrent*, for example, provides an ironic contrast with the sadness of the heroine, who is faced with sacrificing her love to satisfy her father's obligation. Although obviously capable of creating exciting scenes, Judah's usual fare was rather average melodrama that followed the common themes of the time, which he embellished with songs, choruses, and Gothic effects.

Some sketchy information about Judah's life, in addition to his writings other than drama from which conclusions may be drawn, is available. The romantic seems to have appealed to him, but he also seems to have had his idealism severely shaken early in life. Closely associated with society in New York, where he was educated along classical lines and admitted to the bar, Judah wrote three plays before publishing a dramatic poem in 1822, *Odofriede, the Outcast*. In blank verse with sources (several references to Milton's *Comus*) carefully annotated, he attempted to answer a serious question but succumbed to romantic mysticism. His hero, the Outcast, having sold himself for worldly pleasures and knowledge, becomes a fiend and is hateful to all mankind until events make him sensitive to human agonies and frustrated in his own lack of knowledge about death, which, he is told, must be experienced. Although this dramatic poem has interesting passages, the wandering and erratic movement suggests Judah's lack of concentration and psychological penetration. With the enthusiasm of youth, however, he sent copies to Thomas Jefferson and John Adams.[28]

In 1823 Judah published a vicious satire, *Gotham and the Gothamites*, in which he showed some powers of acute social awareness and attacked prominent New York citizens, one of whom was Robert Maywood, the actor who retired that year and to whom Judah had acknowledged a particular debt in the published version of *The Mountain Torrent*. At any rate, Judah seems to have shown a clearer sense of observation than of judgment; he was subsequently involved in a libel suit and spent some time in prison, from which he was eventually released for reasons of poor health. His frame of mind, however, evidently did not change. In 1827 he published *Buccaneers, A Romance of Our Own Country*, a play in which he further exploited his satiric attitude toward others. This time, however, he used a pseudonym, Terentius Phlogobombus. His next published effort in the drama was another romantic dramatic poem in four acts, *The Maid of Midian* (1833).

Judah's single produced play involving a nationalistic theme was *The Battle of Lexington*, performed in New York on July 4, 1822, and published the following year as *A Tale of Lexington*, "a national comedy, founded on the opening of the Revolution." The story of the clash between English soldiers and provincial farmers unfolds in a turgid manner as an English soldier, Ethlinde, woos Mey, the daughter of a farmer, Adam Bothel. Ethlinde soon discovers that Mey's young friend, Joscelyn, is his own son whose mother, Alianor, whom he abandoned, has gone mad. Alianor's actions provide the strong Gothic quality which was characteristic of Judah's work, while his attempt to present Ethlinde's struggle with his conscience before he accepts Alianor again as his wife shows the weakness of his psychological approach. Judah was much more at ease in melodramatic scenes, and Mey's escape from the English as she directs Joscelyn to retrieve the guns of the English guards through the words of the song "The Pilgrim Boy" is cleverly accomplished. There is also a certain amount of rough humor provided by two English soldiers, Haversack and Ambuscade, as well as some garrulous humor by a provincial farmer, Sheepshanks, who phrases every speech in Biblical terms or imagery. Overall, *The Battle of Lexington* depended largely on a few well-devised scenes for its appeal.

Judah's first play, *The Mountain Torrent*, a romantic melodrama in two acts, opened in New York in March, 1820, but had far better reviews four years later at Sadler's Wells in London, where critics praised its original plot, finely delineated characters, and pleasing incidents. It is, as a matter of fact, one of the earliest original American plays to find favor in the eyes of English reviewers. For Judah, however, it was but a trifle, the product of a few days' labor, he explained in a preface, and written solely to "amuse his mind" and please his friends. His major interest was not in the theatre, and he further declared that he would never become "a combatant for the drama," which he recognized as the victim of great prejudice when compared with English drama.

Although the plot of *The Mountain Torrent* is slight and all too familiar, the scenes and the incidents must have been spectacular on stage. To save himself from ruin, the Marchese D'Arenza persuades his daughter, Viola, that she must marry the treacherous Baron Trevasi rather than the orphan Alonzo, whom she loves. En route to the Marchese's castle for the marriage, the Baron is lost in a storm by a mountain torrent and waylaid by the servant of the Marchese, who has now decided to kill the Baron and save both himself and his daughter. When the Baron is rescued by Alonzo, whom he recognizes as the son of D'Almeida, a man presumably stabbed by the Marchese, he recklessly pushes his advantage until the full range of his villainy is discovered, and Alonzo and Viola can find happiness at the closing curtain. This "grand melodrama interspersed with songs" combines the traditions of romance and foreign intrigue, and the detailed descriptions of the scenery and actions suggest that it was undoubtedly a very attractive entertainment.

Judah chose a similar romantic setting, this time in Spain, for *The Rose of*

Arragon; or, The Vigil of St. Mark, a two-act melodrama performed in 1822 and published with a dedication to Edmund Simpson of the Park Theatre. A festival and a procession provide the spectacle for this slight and quickly written tale of Rosaline, a pretty girl who, after finally persuading her father to allow her to marry Aurelio, catches the eye of the evil Conde, who captures her and demands that she marry him. One original twist occurs when Conde is entertained by a masque presented by children dressed as the seasons. As might be expected, the "Ballad of the Rose of Arragon" is sung at a sentimental moment. Finally, Rosaline is rescued by Aurelio and his men, who are disguised as monks coming to the wedding after being delayed by their required vigil for St. Mark. None of Judah's plays provided anything more than the melodramatic entertainment of the period embellished and distinguished by the author's interest in setting and an occasional inventive scene. Had he tempered his libelous attacks and directed his satiric thrusts to acceptable comedy, his career might have been more significant.

By his own declaration, Judah's interest in American drama was casual and almost frivolous as he emphasized the foreign models that his classical education prompted and bowed only occasionally to national themes. Those two approaches guided the work of most playwrights, but the one who was most successful in following them was James Nelson Barker. With the possible exception of John Howard Payne, who did his best playwriting in England, Barker emerges as the most significant American dramatist of the first quarter of the nineteenth century. That his *Marmion* continued to be well received for a score of years suggests in part the popularity of Scott in America but more particularly Barker's skill as a dramatist. Other dramatizations of Scott's work such as *Mary of Scotland; or, The Heir of Avenel* (1821), adapted from Scott's *The Monastery* by "a Gentleman of this city" (New York), never approached Barker's success. Yet, unlike either Dunlap or Payne, Barker had no pretensions to being a professional man of the theatre.

After service in the armed forces during the War of 1812, Barker went into politics and was elected mayor of Philadelphia in 1819. Escape from his youthful avocation, however, did not prove easy. Once out of uniform he was again enthusiastically involved in the theatre, and the seriousness of his approach is revealed by the eleven articles on the drama which appeared under his name in the *Democratic Press* of Philadelphia from December 18, 1816, to February 19, 1817. About this time, too, he wrote a "melodramatic sketch in two acts," *The Armourer's Escape; or, Three Years at Nootka Sound*, which was first acted in Philadelphia on March 21, 1817. Never published, the play was written for John Jewitt, the armorer for the ship *Boston*, who acted on the stage his adventures in the Oregon outposts before the Northwest Boundary was settled. Indians are the principal characters in the play as the *Boston* is captured by the Nootka Indians, and the crew, destroyed, except for the "Armourer" and another American who are rescued by the Klaissat Indians and eventually saved by the arrival of an American brig. The playbill indicates customs, dances, and Indian ceremonies, which must have provided a fascinating spectacle.

Also in 1817 Barker published a sprightly comedy, *How to Try a Lover*, based on Pigault-Lebrun's novel *La Folie Espagnole* set in thirteenth-century Spain. For some reason the play was not immediately performed although it was cast and rehearsed. In his account published in Dunlap's *History*, Barker was unable to explain the withdrawal, particularly since "it was the only drama I have written, with which I was satisfied."[29] It was, however, eventually produced on March 26, 1836, at the Arch Street Theatre in Philadelphia under the title *The Court of Love*. Although the dramatist takes advantage of the usual conventions of secret letters, disguises, and stock characters, the play is skillfully derived and moves quickly through well-controlled intrigues. In search of amorous adventures, Carlos is lured into the castle grounds of Count Almeyda, the father of Eugenia, with whom Carlos has recently fallen in love. Unknown to the lovers, the two fathers have agreed that their children should marry, but the count first wants to test the young man. Carlos then meets many obstacles in his attempt to reach Eugenia and is finally arrested and tried before a Court of Love which the two fathers have devised and over which Eugenia will preside. But the fathers' intrigue is revealed to Eugenia, who, having a will and temperament of her own, almost spoils their plan by seeming to condemn Carlos. His punishment, however, is that he must marry Eugenia, and everyone is happy. The main characters are distinctly portrayed and enhanced by servants who reflect the dashing nobility and innocent purity of master and mistress in both manner and conviction. In both character and action there is a lightness in this comedy that is seldom found in early American drama.

Barker's crowning achievement, yet one which neither he nor his contemporaries fully realized, was *Superstition; or, The Fanatic Father*, first performed in Philadelphia on March 12, 1824, and published in 1826. The reviewer for the *American Quarterly* praised only the spirited dialogue of the play, while Rees saw it as "perhaps the best of Mr. Barker's productions."[30] The major theme of the play concerns New England intolerance activated by the superstitious mind. To this, Barker fused the incident of the Puritan refugee Goff leading the people against the Indians. Five years later Cooper employed the same story of the regicides of Charles I in *The Wept of Wish-ton-Wish*, and Hawthorne would use the tale of the Unknown in "The Gray Champion." Barker's work, however, is distinguished not only by its ideas but by the characterization of the villain, Ravensworth. There is, unfortunately, some stiffness in the dialogue and a weakness in plotting the climax which only the confusion of that moment makes believable, and the hero and the heroine are conventional representations from romantic tragedy. But Ravensworth controls the play, and if it is a tragedy, as Barker described it, the tragedy is Ravensworth's.

The fanaticism of the Reverend Ravensworth is immediately revealed in his hatred for Isabella and in his stern declaration that Mary, his daughter, must not see Isabella's son, Charles. A sense of mystery is introduced with Sir Reginald, who has come to America on an errand for the King and who is accompanied by his romantic nephew George, a libertine, whose wit and eloquence provide humor and a good change of pace. Charles increases the mystery when he meets the Unknown in the forest, recounts something of his past, and is strangely recognized. Barker then mixes melodrama and farce as Charles rescues Mary from the unwanted attention of George and is challenged to a duel, which adds some humor as George, wounded by a rapier, tries to compose a suitable epitaph while remonstrating with the stretcher-bearers for their inability to walk in step. Back at the village an Indian attack creates panic until the Unknown suddenly appears, organizes a successful resistance, and then disappears after mysteriously identifying Isabella: "Yes, 'tis she."

Act IV opens with a discussion of superstition in which Ravensworth defends his belief in sorcery to the great consternation of Walford, who expresses his fears:

> Oh, my friend,
> If reason in a mind like yours, so form'd
> So fortified by knowledge, can bow down
> Before the popular breath, what shall protect
> From the all with'ring blasts of superstition
> The unthinking crowd, in whom credulity,
> Is ever the first born of ignorance?

But Ravensworth is certain in his views and has determined that Isabella and Charles are the curse of the village. Meanwhile, Isabella explains some of the miseries of her own life to Charles but resists telling him the name of his father. She is interrupted in her story by a messenger who orders her and Charles to appear before the judge.

Inside the church, arranged as a Hall of Justice, Ravensworth ironically attacks Isabella as one "Who scorns religion, and its meek professors;/ And, to this hour—until compell'd, ne'er stood/ Within these holy walls" (V, ii). But the judge is not persuaded, and Ravensworth swiftly changes his plan and accuses Charles of the "contemplated rape and murder" of Mary. Heroically protecting the sensitivity of Mary, Charles refuses to plead his innocence (Ravensworth: [aside] "This is beyond my hopes.") and at the frenzied insistence of Ravensworth, who refuses to let Mary speak, is led off amid a raging storm and general confusion to be executed. Then the Unknown appears and claims Isabella as his daughter; Sir Reginald enters, too late, to identify Charles as the king's son; Mary goes insane and dies as the storm subsides; without Charles, "my only stay on earth," Isabella and the Unknown, one of the regicides, are left alone. The stage direction describes the final action: "Thro this scene, [Ravensworth] had shewn the signs of stern and settled despair, occasionally casting his eyes upon his daughter, or raising them to heaven, but withdrawing them again in utter hopelessness, now sinks groaning into the arms of Walford," having spoken the curtain line: "Dead! Dead!—"

Although the play occasionally falls into the weak patterns of romantic tragedy, there is an inevitability in its plotting, and the character of Ravensworth has no peers in the history of early American drama. He is a true villain-hero with intelligence, eloquence, beliefs, and passions. A clergyman who mistakes his own passions for the voice of God, he enjoys a powerful influence over his people and is able to mount a relentless revenge upon those who refuse to bow to his authority. From Ravensworth's first words Barker does a remarkable job in delineating the fanatical father who followed his god and destroyed his daughter, the two objects of his consuming love: "No, Walford, no: I have no charity/ For what you term the weakness of our nature./ The soul shoul rise above it" (I, i). His hatred of Isabella rises from his view of her as "a scoffer at things sacred/ At me; and my functions" (I, i); and he treats this personal slight with the vengeance of an Old Testament God. Because the Indians attack at the moment of Charles' return, he equates the two incidents and counsels "Prayer and sacrifice." Isabella's proud disdain for what she considers an unfeeling attitude then gives him reason to satisfy his jealousy with a victim for the sacrifice he counseled. Forcing the court's decision in a trial scene of great dramatic power, he shows fiendish glee at Charles' appointed destruction: "It is accomplish'd," he exclaims, "Guided by Heaven's vengeance" (V, ii). But he did not reckon with the very human love of his daughter. As does that of Hawthorne's Chillingworth in *The Scarlet Letter*, his revenge consumes all of his desires and life-giving energies. The actions of the final scene pass him by, and at the end he accepts an existence almost as life-denying as that of Mary.

This was Barker's final play. As poet, drama critic, and playwright, he had consistently emphasized a patriotic interest in the new nation; with *Superstition* he used America's past more successfully than did any dramatist of his period. Thereafter, government positions took most of his time and interest. His vigorous support of President Jackson earned him the appointment as Collector of the Port of Philadelphia in 1829, a position he held until 1838. It was during those years that he wrote and published the bulk of his poetry. Five years later Van Buren appointed him Comptroller of the Treasury. For the remainder of his life, politics and the changing administrations in Washington determined his career, most of which was spent in the treasury department. The drama tempted Barker's literary talents off and on for only twenty years of his mature life, but it was then that he left his mark on his country.

MORALITIES, MELODRAMAS, AND FARCES

Morality, as the dramatic criticism of the period 1815–1828 illustrates, was important as a force to be advertised as characteristic of the theatre. But as playwrights became more sophisticated and as the theatre became more professionally demanding, fewer original plays were written solely as vehicles for peddling morality. Perhaps the rising interest in the domestic sentimental novel answered part of the public demand for moral instruction while the adaptation of these novels to the stage satisfied the moralistic critics. Certainly the morality of such heroes as Cooper's Natty Bumppo could never be questioned on the page or on the stage. Susanna Rowson's moral lesson, *Charlotte Temple*, written in 1791 but popularly revived in numerous editions, was adapted to the stage at least three times. One version, *Charlotte Temple; or, The Victim of Treachery*, played in the spring of 1828 in Boston's Tremont Theatre, where it drew a very good house and was considered a successful first attempt for its author, G. W. Glascott.[31]

There were a few moral and religious illustrations dramatized for the public-at-large, but these probably were not performed. Rather typical is *Catherine Brown, the Converted Cherokee*, "a missionary drama founded on fact," published by "a lady" in 1819. Much more interesting is Erastus Brown's *The Trial of Cain* (1827), "by Rule of Court; in which a Predestinarian, a Universalian, and an Arminian argue as attorneys at the bar; the two former as the prisoner's counsel, the latter as attorney general." A rather strange but fascinating play, and quite different from the mass of religious drama, begins as follows:

> As I ascend the theatre of time,
> The mournful scene invites my soul to rhyme;
> The drama opens and the play's begun,
> Abel is kill'd by Adam's oldest son.

The charge of murder is denied by counsel, and witnesses such as Calvin, Foreknowledge, and Truth are called. But the verdict is that Cain acted freely: "We find him guilty of willful murder." Given this thesis and a more penetrating playwright, one less determined in his objective, the conflict could have been exciting drama, but this work remains strictly a tract.

Adaptations provided more conventional moral drama such as Perkins Howes' reworking of Catharine Maria Sedgwick's *A New England Tale* (1822), which he called *The New England Drama* and published, probably without performance, in 1825. This five-act moral, utilitarian play follows the difficulties of Jane Elton, about as good a person as one could possibly imagine: "Surely, the Kingdom is come in this dear child's heart" (II, ii). Left an orphan as the play begins, Jane is abused by Mrs. Wilson, with whom she is taken to live, is accused of stealing, and becomes involved with a lawyer who gambles, drinks, and "trifles with the obligations of religion" (V, i). Throughout, however, Jane is watched over by a good Quaker, Robert Lloyd, whom she eventually marries, and she becomes herself a Quaker, whereas Mrs. Wilson's children illustrate the degeneracy that visits the impure in heart. While trying to preach that the meek shall inherit the earth, this play, as did many others, only showed that domestic moralities can make tiresome dramas.

Whereas the American audience wanted the excitement and spectacle of melodrama or the wit and humor of farce, the American dramatists had not yet learned to use the melodrama extensively for utilitarian and moral issues. Their main utilitarian interest was patriotism; otherwise, they looked to farce. Some playwrights had translated the plays of Pixérécourt, but they had not completely understood the moral content of his plays—so clear to the French mother who was shocked when her son got into trouble after she had repeatedly sent him to watch Pixérécourt's plays. American playwrights would eventually demonstrate an awareness with temperance melodramas and slavery melodramas but not for a generation or two. Although the American Temperance Society was formed at Boston in 1826, it was some years before the great influx of Irish and Germans helped create a situation to which the theatre would respond. In the meantime Dunlap's translations of foreign melodramas such as *Abaellino, the Great Bandit* as well as the innumerable nationalistic melodramas already mentioned remained popular entertainment throughout the early part of the nineteenth century.

Surveying the number of farces which were either performed or published during any particular period in the history of American drama would be like sorting blades of grass according to size or shade of green—an endless task with little of consequence gained. The plays dealing with American character types were generally farces, and for the Yankee character alone there were hundreds of which only representative plays have lasted in manuscript or printed form. Following the tradition of the afterpiece in the early nineteenth century, new farces were in constant demand. At first, actors were largely responsible for those brief farces; later, the most popular actors established play contests to gain more and new material for an evening's work. Throughout this early period, however, it is clear that many slight farces were enjoyed or endured for a performance or two and then forgotten. Yet many others were published, and the *Checklist of American Imprints* includes an abundance of farce titles, some newly created by Americans and others reprinted from the popular English entertainment. Perhaps surprisingly, not all were written for theatres in the more populated eastern parts of America. Alphonso Wetmore, for example, wrote a farce in three acts, *The Pedlar* (1821), for the St. Louis Thespians. By the mid-1820s a number of cities and towns west of the Appalachian chain had theatres where comedies, melodramas, and farces were performed by professional or amateur groups. Entertainment was the key word in early American theatre, and farce was generally considered good entertainment which could be provided by amateurs or actors of lesser talents at a theatre which was not presently enjoying an engagement by one of the traveling "stars" of the period.

Most playwrights who contributed more than two or three plays wrote farces—Dunlap, Barker, Payne, Noah, Judah, and Woodworth, among others—and actors or managers still wrote plays, particularly the quickly composed farce, for their own needs. Henry J. W. Finn's *Woolen Nightcap; or, The Mysterious Flour Sack* (1828) is a nonsensical farce in which a king loses his nightcap, a scapegrace hides in a flour sack, and the "Nameless Assassin" comes out of the oven to confess the theft before hiding up the chimney. That is about all the nonsense there is to it; a note with the published play states that it was rejected by the theatre management. Sol Smith, another actor-manager, wrote a farce, *The Tailor in Distress; or, A Yankee Trick* (1823), which was performed in Cincinnati with a youthful Edwin Forrest acting a Negro character named Ruban. The Irish actor Charles S. Talbot wrote several farces. One, *Squire Hartley* (1827), has an English setting and is modeled after the eighteenth-century farce-comedy. In courting Emily Allcure despite her father's objections, Hartley is helped by his Irish servant, also in love, who dupes the girl's father through a disguise. Dialect and mannerisms are ridiculed along with Hartley's own stuffy reluctance to allow his sister to be courted by Captain Vernon. As might be expected, the farce ends with three weddings.

Beaux Without Belles; or, Ladies We Can Do Without You (1820), a musical farce by David Darling, was performed at the theatre in Fredericksburg, Virginia. A play of five scenes, it is perhaps indicative of amateur creativity of uncertain scope which was quickly produced and as quickly forgotten although it has some good lines and some passable farce action. It was a first play, according to the preface, "conceived, written, and delivered to the prompter in four days." The plot rests upon men disguised as women. Thinking that he has killed a man in a duel, Charles Safety is persuaded by his father to escape the authorities by assuming female disguise. Another character, Maxwell, for reasons of debt persuades his Irish servant, O'Diamond, to disguise himself as his niece until the real niece, a wealthy woman, arrives from India. To complete the situation the dramatist presents young Scapegrace, who must marry an heiress to reduce his debts. Scapegrace then becomes interested in Charles (as female) while Old Safety courts O'Diamond (as female). When the man in the duel recovers, Charles can again become a man, while O'Diamond, changing back into male clothes to escape his pursuer, allows Maxwell time to meet his niece and gain the money she represents to clear his debts. Obviously, these men do not need ladies to get along in life, and there are none in the play. The dialogue is weak, but the situation has opportunities for farcical fun.

Another farce from Virginia, *Nature and Philosophy*, was adapted from Auguste Duport's *Le Frère Philippe* (1818) "by a citizen of Richmond" and performed there in 1821. The "citizen" added one scene and freely translated and altered this tale of a young man who has been brought up in total ignorance of the opposite sex by a misogynist father. To complete his son's one-sided education, the father plans to have the ugly old governess in his brother's house be the first woman the son sets his eyes upon. But the brother has a daughter whom the boy sees first, and their meeting makes a considerable difference in what happens next. Although not an original American play, the adaptation has its merits.

A good number of the farces reflected some event or attitude of the times. *Things As They Will Be; or, All Barkers Are Not Biters* is a fair example. Published in 1819 "by Who D'ye Think?" (Vermileye Taylor), this farce in three short acts is dedicated to the "holders of Washington and Warren, and Exchange Bank bills." The year 1819 was a period of economic panic in America, and the play pokes fun at those who questioned the stability of the Washington and Warren Bank by having the heroine's fortune consist of stock in that bank and a beleaguered Quaker banker pay off his debts through the Washington and Warren. Contrived and sketchy, the play suggests the continuing interest of playwrights in a business-oriented America.

William Crafts' *The Sea-Serpent; or, The Gloucester Hoax*, a three-act "dramatic jeu d'esprit," is a broad satiric farce which first played in Charleston on May 12, 1819. Crafts (1787–1826), a South Carolinian, was a poet, essayist, and orator who graduated from Harvard College in 1805 and returned to Charleston to practice law and assert an ardent Federalism as a member of the state legislature. *The Sea-Serpent* was his only play, but he wrote theatrical criticism for the Charleston *Courier*, which he edited in 1821, and became something of a literary dictator of the period. Written in rhyming couplets of iambic pentameter, his play opens with a Gloucester fisherman describing a snake which breathed fire and which sufficiently interests the mayor and the justice of the town that they carry the news to Boston. At the Boston Museum the snake is discussed by such learned men as Linnaeus and Scepticus as Crafts flaunts his education rather ostentatiously. Back at Gloucester the little snake is kept in a glass container while $500 is offered for the giant sea serpent, which is finally caught: "(*Enter persons, bring a Horse-Mackerel or some fish, as much like the snake as can conveniently be procured.*)" Mainly, the play ridiculed a contemporary event in Massachusetts and serious attitudes toward sea monsters, but it might also have affected one of man's senses which has usually been abused only figuratively in the theatre.

Another Southerner who dealt in satiric farce was Lemuel Sawyer (1777–1852). A lawyer who served in the North Carolina assembly and who was also a member of the U.S. Congress, he explained his political and literary endeavors in his *Auto-biography of Lemuel Sawyer* (1844), privately printed in New York. Enjoying what he called his "Museum of Literary Curiosities," he wrote *The Biography of John Randolph* and two plays which were published but probably not performed. *Blackbeard*, called a comedy in four acts "founded in fact," appeared in 1824. Through a confusing and scattered plot, Sawyer satirizes the skulduggery of political elections, the manner in which wealth attracts women, the folly of people who believe in tall tales, and the usury rates in North Carolina. He cuts a broad path but not very cleverly. In concert with members of the Blackbeard Company, a political sharper and his accomplice hoodwink their victims into believing that money placed in a bag at the bottom of a river will be increased in amount through the devil's intervention. There is also a love plot and a rowdy scene or two as the dupes calculate their fortunes.

Sawyer was not above touching topics which might offend, and some critics found it difficult to accept the language in his second play, *The Wreck of Honor* (1824). Called a tragedy, presumably because deaths occur, this play in five acts with amateurish blank verse has two plot lines, both concerning love; yet the characters never cross plot lines. The play opens in Paris at the time of the Battle of Waterloo. In one plot Dumain, having sworn eternal friendship with St. Pierre, falls passionately in love with St. Pierre's equally passionate betrothed and is overcome with such a sense of dishonor that he welcomes death at the hands of the English. The other plot is more original as an American Captain Allen is taught French manners—the way to kiss, for example—by the Marshall and Madame Folard. But when Allen spurns Madame Folard's efforts at seduction as repulsive to American morals, he finds himself involved in a duel with the Marshall. Here Sawyer may have offended tastes by having the Marshall agree to withdraw his challenge if Allen will satisfy his wife. Seemingly deluged with women who want him to help them cuckold their husbands, Allen accepts but deceives the Marshall into going to the address where Allen himself was to meet Madame Folard. After Allen is killed in battle, the Folards, with faith in no one and malice toward all, plan to flee to America. Although Sawyer seems to have been a dilettante as a playwright, he had a sense of humor and an eye for the faults of society, particularly in France, where he found "the wreck of honor" everywhere.

POETRY IN THE THEATRE

That poetry was an acceptable medium for American drama was from the beginning the logical assumption for anyone with a background in England or Europe, where poetry was presumed to be the highest form of expression. Therefore, it was only logical, too, that early playwrights in America would model their efforts on Shakespeare or on the neoclassical dramatists of the eighteenth century. Not all new playwrights, of course, used poetry, but it would be a fair generalization to say that any American dramatist with ambitions to write a play on a serious theme or one with literary pretensions would create a play imitative of foreign models and written in verse.

Through the first quarter of the nineteenth century, poetic drama in America appeared with some frequency. Then, from 1829 until Boker's *Francesca da Rimini* appeared in 1855, it reached a blaze of popularity which was to be almost totally extinguished by the Rise of Realism. Never again has poetic drama been allowed to rise to such heights although there have been moments of achievement. The beginnings of the period of its popular acceptance came between the War of 1812 and the announcement in 1828 of Forrest's Prize Play Contest. Although Dunlap and Burk had written actable poetic drama before the war, it was afterwards, in the plays of Barker, Payne, and a number of lesser playwrights, that the power of poetic drama was first discernable. Payne, as an advocate of poetic drama, had complained that with the kind of audience that the American stage attracted and to whom the theatre managers appealed, a good poet became a poor dramatist. But the truth is that there were few good poets. Payne, certainly, would not be considered one of them. William Cullen Bryant, Richard H. Dana, and Fitz-Greene Halleck—among the best poets of the time—did not write for the stage. James G. Percival, John Neal, and James Wright Simmons—all minor poets—could not adapt their poetry successfully to the stage. Some of their attempts, however, along with the major efforts of Payne and Barker, helped establish poetic drama as one of America's major accomplishments in drama during the second quarter of the century.

Generally, a poetic drama in early nineteenth-century America would be a tragedy; it would be set in the historical past in a foreign land (exceptions would be the Indian plays or Barker's *Superstition*); with few exceptions its characters would reveal little psychological insight on the part of the dramatist and demonstrate only the virtuous hero, the beautiful and faithful or passionate and self-destructive heroine, and the evil and ambitious villain who frequently scoffed at democracy; the theme of the play would be freedom and patriotism, romantic love, marital infidelity, or parental tyranny and filial duty; the poetry in most of these plays would have very little to commend it as characters and their actions became lost in long rhetorical speeches, exaggerated poetic diction, and excessive imagery. This would be an acceptable generalization, but, as Oliver Wendell Holmes noted, no generalization is absolutely true—not even this one.

As a dramatic literature began to develop in America, certain geographical areas sustained an activity denied in others. The development of the theatre in the more populated areas, for example, encouraged playwriting in New York, Philadelphia, Boston and Charleston. For poetic drama, the South produced the earliest substantial activity. Robert Munford and St. George Tucker had written for the theatre in Charleston before the century got underway. John Blake White and Isaac Harby, both from Charleston, wrote poetic drama during the century's first decade and were joined by James Wright Simmons and E. C. Holland. Then, as the population and industrial and political centers shifted, the South lost its strong literary atmosphere for several decades.

From his several editing positions, Isaac Harby wrote a great deal and was considered one of the best critics of early drama in America. His essay "Defense of the Drama," for example, emphasized the wholesome quality of the mental excitement which good drama stimulates, the "spectacle of life" found in the theatre, and the drama as a "moral lever" to redeem youth while providing amusement as well as a sense of fashion and good taste.[32] In other essays he discussed T. A. Cooper's Othello and Coriolanus and Kean's Othello, Lear, and Sir Giles Overreach. Had he lived longer Harby might have contributed more substantially to dramatic literature. In 1822, however, he was working on the *City Gazette* and had established sufficient reputation that James Monroe attended the author's benefit for *Alberti*, a poetic drama.

The Gordian Knot (1807), Harby's earlier play, is far surpassed by *Alberti*, which was performed in the Charleston Theatre in 1819. Taking his plot from the political intrigues surrounding the Medici and the city states of Italy in the late fifteenth century, Harby created Alberti, a leader of the Florentine army, who seeks revenge upon his older brother, Ridolpho, for possessing and killing Alberti's wife many years earlier. Ippolito, the boy Alberti stole from Ridolpho in his early anger and raised as his own son, is to be the instrument of that revenge because Ippolito and Ridolpho's daughter, Antonia, have fallen in love. Some of the best poetry occurs in the lovers' scenes and during Alberti's forceful speeches to the Florentine senate. Both Alberti and Ippolito are warm, likable characters, and Harby's delaying tactics for revealing Alberti's secret (II) and his plan for revenge (III) provide good suspense and a crisis for the lovers. Although some critics thought that Antonia should have committed suicide upon learning that Ippolito was her brother (V, ii), Harby argued—with little evidence from the play, however—that her religion and morals would not allow this act. Instead, his plotting brought in the family priest, whose knowledge, explained in Act III, reveals that Ippolito actually is Alberti's son. The lovers—only first cousins—can marry, and all can end happily in this "revenge tragedy." Better than most of his contemporaries, Harby showed his skill in handling exposition and plot construction.

Edwin C. Holland (1794–1824) of South Carolina practiced law, edited the Charleston *Times*, and worked as a writer during a life ended abruptly by yellow fever. In 1814 he published *Odes, Naval Songs and Other Occasional Poems* and with Benjamin Elliott wrote a tract in 1822 refuting Northern criticisms of slavery in the South. Evidently, he also had a hand in writing the burlesque *Omnium Botherum* with William Crafts and Henry J. Farmer. His only published play, however, a melodrama in four acts which he described as a dramatic essay and entitled *The Corsair*, was produced in Charleston in 1818 with music supplied by Charles Gilfert. Using Lord Byron's poem as his inspiration, Holland tells about Conrad, the Corsair, who leaves his beloved Medora for a pirating adventure and who is captured by the Turks. When the beautiful Gulmore helps him escape and joins the band of pirates, their love grows until he decides to return and to take his farewell of Medora: "Silent and dark I go, and go alone" (IV, ii). With its spectacular use of pirate signals, a hero held in chains in a dungeon, beautiful women, and the Byronic touch, the work has a certain romantic charm but is generally more essay than drama.

James Wright Simmons (1790–1858) was a minor poet from South Carolina who studied at Harvard and traveled at home and abroad in the typical fashion of a Southern aristocrat. In New York he worked for the *Mirror* and the *Courier*; later he became a coeditor of the *Southern Literary Gazette* with William Gilmore Simms, who expressed ambiguous views concerning Simmons' contributions to literature. Among Simmons' published plays are *Manfredi* (1821), a tragedy in five acts; *Valdemar; or, The Castle of the Cliff* (1822), a dramatization of Scott's *The Bride of Lammermoor*; and *Julian* (1823), a dramatic fragment. Two other plays, *The Master of Ravenswood* and *De Montalt; or, The Abbey of St. Clair*, were performed at the Charleston Theatre on April 12, 1824, and February 2, 1843, respectively, but never appeared in print. *Manfredi* is typical of the kind of melodrama which Simmons wrote. Taking his plot from Byron's *Manfred*, Simmons dramatized Manfredi's determined actions to save the beautiful Francesca from a forced marriage to Osma, a shadowy villain whose name brings shudders to the young girl. Visions, wild dreams, insane raving, disguises, melancholy, and mysteries characterize this play in rather artless blank verse which ends as Francesca dies, and Manfredi, laughing hysterically after having killed Osma, fatally stabs himself. There is no evidence that the play was ever performed.

Toward the end of the first quarter of the nineteenth century in America, New England had not yet reached the distinction in literature which Longfellow, Emerson, and Hawthorne would soon bring to it, but its educational system and cosmopolitan atmosphere in certain population centers fostered a great deal of literary effort, particularly in poetry. In dramatic literature, however, there had been little activity although William Charles White, David Everett, and Elihu H. Smith had attempted poetic drama around the turn of the century. New England would never be distinguished in contributing to the popular poetic drama prior to the Civil War, but a number of poets and writers were tempted by the spectacle of the stage. Representative of those literary men during the pre-1828 period are John Neal, James Abraham Hillhouse, and James Gates Percival, each with a reputation as a poet which none managed to transfer to the theatre.

John Neal (1793–1876) is the most exciting of the three, though not for his dramas—he wrote only one, and that was not produced. He is remembered mainly as an editor, a minor poet, a critic of some substance writing both in America and in England, and the author of five novels, including *Logan* (1822) and *Brother Jonathan* (1825). He was also admitted to the bar in 1820. A substantial part of his contemporary reputation came from the erratic, arrogant, and frequently condemning opinions in his essays.

Neal wrote his single play, *Otho*, a strong Gothic melodrama, for the actor Thomas Abthorpe Cooper, who rejected it, according to Neal, for being too melodramatic and for requiring too many changes of costume. According to his letters to the Reverend John Pierpont, Neal finished writing the play in London in November, 1818, and sent it to Cooper, who returned it because he could not read the handwriting. Even after revisions over the next two years Cooper remained unimpressed with the "great tragedy," as Neal described it: "As a poem . . . I have gone far beyond it. As a drama I have never conceived anything to be bad with it."[33] Finally, Neal published *Otho* in 1819 with a preface in which he acknowledged his debt to Byron's *Corsair*. Eventually, in 1828, he republished the play in the *Yankee*, a magazine he edited.[34] His most detailed comments on the work, however, appear in his letter of June 29, 1819, to Pierpont: "The plot is my own—new and forceful—and the only objection is whether one gets confounded as to who is who—whether the Devil has anything to do with Otho or not."[35] Clearly, the play meant a lot to Neal, who revealed some of his own frustrations in this character study of a gifted, Byronic hero whose tragedy is his birth and an empty future.

The plot of *Otho* begins with a battle pitting Irman against Otho the

Bastard, who allows himself to be captured—in despair and undetermined whether to live or die. In prison he is visited by Ala, Irman's betrothed, who is attracted by Otho's virility and mystery. When Ala finally consents to marry Irman, she is abducted at the altar by a mysterious stranger, Lord Ola, who is, in reality, Otho, Irman's lost brother. Not realizing his identity, Irman's father avenges his death by killing Otho—his son. It is a strange play but one with a passion and an incoherence which were as characteristic of Neal as the occasional brilliance of his verse.

James Gates Percival (1795–1856) was another erratic individual, whose career spanned law, medicine, chemistry, geology, and the brief editorship of a poetry magazine. Throughout his life he wrote a considerable amount of poetry, which his critics found excessive and diffuse with a sweetness that became monotonous. The same comments may apply to his single drama, *Zamor*, written in blank verse and published with his poems in 1821 but written during his earlier years at Yale College. *Zamor* dramatizes a portion of the life of a determined and unprincipled villain who cannot forget that Abdallah, the King of Granada, once did him an injury. As the play opens Granada is involved in battle with the Spaniards, and the King, whose ironic trust of Zamor stimulates the action, asks that he be forgiven for his earlier action. But Zamor lives only for revenge: "How terrible is vengeance in the bosom of a Moor," he soliloquizes as he plots Abdallah's death (II, i). Finally, Zamor, who is defined only by evil qualities, is killed by the reigning Prince of Granada: "And let us know, ruin and death await/ The ambitious wretch, who darest o'erturn the state" (V, ii). Perhaps Percival intended a nationalistic thesis; if so, it is lost among the image-laden verses which attempt to substitute a flow of words for thought.

Although James Abraham Hillhouse (1789–1841) has been only briefly mentioned by historians of American literature, for a time he was rated high among New York writers, his work praised by Bryant, Irving, and Nathaniel Parker Willis. A major part of this work was poetic drama, which he was always anxious to have performed, but it is a comment on his plays that most of his contemporaries assumed that he was writing for a reading audience. Yet Bryant considered his modern tragedies "well worthy of notice," and even the prejudiced English critics found *Percy's Masque* "admirable" throughout. In the history of American drama, however, he best represents those of the respected literati who generally wrote carefully plotted plays in fluent blank verse while lacking a familiarity with the particular requirements of the drama which might have allowed their plays an opportunity in the theatre.

Hillhouse attained his literary reputation in New York, but his years and interests at Yale (class of 1808) determined his career. There he had debated the topic "Are theatres beneficial?"—and lost—and had delivered a lecture entitled "A Defense of Theatre." Unfortunately, he had also been influenced by Timothy Dwight, who deeply admired Shakespeare but condemned theatre in general and the melodramas of Kotzebue and his peers, which he considered "movable brothels," in particular. Immediately following graduation Hillhouse wrote a five-act Gothic drama, *The Castle on the Danube*, in which a knight after an absence of several years returns home to find his father and his betrothed in the power of an evil cousin whom he must destroy to regain the estate and deserve the girl. A fair youthful start, Hillhouse followed it in 1809 with another romantic tragedy, *The Convent*. The next year he wrote *Geneviere of Brabant*, a five-act tragedy in blank verse concerned with a crusader's jealousy of his innocent wife. None of these was produced, but Hillhouse was hopeful and offered his next play, *The Spanish Lady* (1810), a three-act prose drama, to a theatre manager in Boston who read it and gave it "unqualified approbation" only to revise his hasty opinion and decide that the work was better for the closet than for the stage. In 1811 Hillhouse completed a draft of *The House of Belvidere*, which he revised for publication in 1837 as *Demetria*.

Obviously entranced by the theatre, Hillhouse was, unfortunately, poorly prepared to write for it as it existed in early-nineteenth-century America. He was also poorly advised. As his energies became more involved with his plays, he began to send his work to his Yale mentor, John Trumbull, for his comments, but Trumbull's opinion that *Percy's Masque*, which Hillhouse wrote in 1817, was "superior in its plot and execution to any new tragic drama exhibited in England in the last half-century"[36] only revealed his ignorance of good dramaturgy. With the enthusiasm which marked his adventures with theatre, Hillhouse went to England in November, 1818, and presumably tried to get the play performed. Perhaps there he received better advice, probably from Washington Irving, who read his play. At any rate he published his play in England in 1819 and again the following year in America, where Bryant reviewed it favorably in the *NAR* (October 1820).

The incidents surrounding *Percy's Masque*—as do those surrounding Neal's *Otho*—illustrate the chasm separating the literary figures in early America from those who wrote successfully but generally without distinction for the contemporary theatre. As did many of his peers, Neal assumed that his success as a poet and writer of fiction warranted success in the theatre. A certain jealousy and arrogance began to form between active playwrights in America and the much more successful writers of poetry and fiction. Two distinct groups were created, and animosities developed as the efforts of one were demeaned as inferior literature, while the works of the other lacked the qualities necessary for success in the theatre.

There was the traditional dramatic literature which certain writers enjoyed and tried to imitate, and there was the growing American theatre developed by entrepreneurs who, with their prejudices against American dramatic composition, would occasionally accept plays which they thought would satisfy their customers. The two sets of interested people seemed to exist on different levels —intellectual and perhaps also moral—in terms of their attitudes and beliefs. Among the successful creators of American literature there were several who wanted to write for the theatre but lacked the necessary skills; on the other hand, most of the men and women writing plays were not acceptable in the best literary circles. Who ever heard of John Minshull? or John Turnbull? Some writers such as Robert M. Bird would bridge the gap successfully at different intervals in their lives; Washington Irving would hide his contribution; Longfellow and Cooper would try unsuccessfully to write for the stage; many would complain of the problems from both sides. But it would be a long time before the two groups would work together and approve of each other.

All of Hillhouse's four published poetic dramas well illustrate the strengths and weaknesses of the poet's attempt to write for the contemporary theatre. *Percy's Masque*, a five-act drama in blank verse, deals with Percy's plan to regain his lost heritage, Northumberland. Although the final act has some good melodramatic scenes, too much is told or argued, and too little, dramatized. The ending is inconclusive; the characters are colorless, even Percy; and the dialogue is romantic and exaggerated. The irony in Hillhouse's dedication of *The Judgment, A Vision* (1821) to John Trumbull, who should bear some responsibility for Hillhouse's dramatic style, passed without notice.

Hillhouse worked on *Hadad*, a dramatic poem in five acts, for about four years before publishing it in 1825. Taking his scene from the Book of Tobit, he tried to dramatize the conflict he saw in Hadad, an infidel held hostage in Jerusalem, whose actions ("like an evil angel") reflect the conflicting spirits which inhabit his body. One of Hillhouse's best characters, Hadad focuses a plot which makes substantial and interesting use of religion and the supernatural. Unfortunately, the dependence on the supernatural reduces the intellectual content of the play, one element in Hillhouse's dramas which critics almost invariably respected.

Demetria, a domestic tragedy in five acts, appeared in 1837, completely revised from its earlier version. The story is one of love and jealousy in which Cosmo, happy in his adoration of Demetria, is seduced into a disastrous marriage with her sister, Olivia. Although the verse has occasional strength and beauty, there is little in the play that would be attractive on the stage. The exception lies in one potentially fascinating character, Jacqueline, Olivia's Iago-like servant who manipulates the course of events for her own evil purposes:

> Freed from the abject lot imposed upon me,
> By faithless, purjured man—enriched—
>   revenged—
> I'll shrive, do penance—peradventure deck
> Some shrine, and feed the holy candlesticks,
> Till virgin wax hath cancelled virgin shame.
>   [III, ii.]

A Satanic force, Jacqueline controls all action and characters; Demetria does not even feature in the play until Act IV. But Hillhouse's work lacked theatricality; it was too ponderous for the stage. Ambitious and even persistent for a time, he failed because he did not have the right teachers for his objectives. He could create finished and tasteful dramatic poems which boasted picturesque descriptions and controlled imagery, but he could not write good plays for the stage—although they are frequently more interesting to read than some of the violent Gothic melodramas which appeared in American theatres.

Other practicing poets wrote poetic dramas for the stage with little more knowledge of its requirements than had Hillhouse. Some were performed and forgotten; others were published with the same results. *Alfred the Great* was published in New York in 1822 as written by "a young gentleman of this city" (perhaps Julian Magnus) without a previous production. With the usual help of disguises, witches, and an abundance of action, sometimes without much clear purpose, the dramatist somehow combined romance, nationalism, and Christian morality as Alfred saves his queen and his kingdom from the invading Danes. James Lawson, a New York editor and poet, wrote *Giordano; or, The Florentine Conspiracy* for the Park Theatre, where it was performed on November 13, 1828. William Leggett, reviewing the play for the *Critic*, praised its language and poetic embellishments but thought the circumstances of the plot too complicated.[37] Perhaps they were, but no more so than in many other plots. The play deals with the unsuccessful attempt of the ambitious Florentine general, Giordano, to kill a young hero who has found favor with the Duke. Reuben M. Potter was another minor poet who chose a foreign land for his play. *Phelles, King of Tyre; or, The Downfall of Tyranny* first played at the Park Theatre on June 13, 1825, and eventually, deservedly or not, brought a typically condescending observation on "the infant phenomenon—the American drama" by Odell, whose views have helped create the bias reflected in modern criticism of American drama.[38]

Another play which attempted to capitalize on the popularity of foreign history and romance and which caused some commotion during its early performances in Philadelphia was the tragedy *The Usurper* by Dr. James McHenry (1785–1845). An Irishman who came to America in 1817, McHenry contributed historical novels—*The Wilderness; or, Braddock's Times* (1823) and *The Betrothed of Wyoming* (1830)—and a play to the literature of his adopted country. He also founded the *American Monthly Magazine* in 1824 as competition for the *NAR*. Setting his play in Ireland at the time of the Druids, he described the cruelties of Cartha, who conspires with a wicked Druid to murder his brother and seize the Irish crown. In the slaughter Mahon, a nephew of the tyrant, escapes, grows to manhood, and returns to the palace of his father. His future is then decided by his mother, a Druidical priestess, who gives him her blessings before killing the usurping Cartha in a fight during which she is fatally wounded. First performed at Philadelphia's Chestnut Street Theatre, on December 26, 1827, *The Usurper* showed itself to be a slow-moving play with considerably less attention paid to the subtleties of drama than to spectacular action. Trying vainly to give the play the proper tone, James Nelson Barker wrote a prologue which noted that "Our poet's pencil paints the moral scene,/ Teaching what ought to be by what has been." But McHenry, to whom narrative history came easier than did dramatic dialogue, was unsuccessful in his determination to show his audience the disaster which comes to tyrannical ambition. When the manager, Wemyss, refused an author's benefit, the coterie audience rebelled, but the author's only recourse was to publish his play and attack the manager in his preface—which he did.

Another event in the history of this play perhaps helps to explain why more writers did not attempt to create for the American stage. Two years after its initial performances, *The Usurper* appeared at the Arch Street Theatre, where the audience greeted it with uproarious laughter, stimulated, according to a reviewer, by both the "merits of the play and the exertions of the performers."

> The tragedy of *The Usurper* affords a striking instance of the success of an author whose course is decidedly original. Formerly, the writer of a play was expected to bring to the task some knowledge of nature and some power of language—some little capacity for forming a plot, and a slender acquaintance

with stage effect. But it was reserved for the author of *The Usurper* to show the fallacy of the belief that these were indispensable requisites, for he has produced a play in which there is not the least evidence of his being possessed of any one of these qualifications, and which yet is capable of affording the highest entertainment to an intelligent audience. He has relied altogether upon his comic powers; and has so mingled the serious with the burlesque as to excite the admiration of the gods.[39]

Poor McHenry deserved this treatment no more than did many of his contemporaries—who frequently were not spared the critics' fun, either. To appreciate the observations of this particular critic, however, one must fully understand, not only the kind of dramas being written, but the kind of production that any play could receive and the varied objectives that reviewers might have.

Among those contemporaries of McHenry who would have brooked no condescending reviews even if deserved was Frances Wright (1795–1852), reformer, freethinker, playwright, and *femme extraordinaire*. Her single play, *Altorf*, which was produced at the Park Theatre in New York on February 19, 1819, attracted less attention than did the other activities of her life, but it merited the praise it received. The critic for the *Evening Post* (February 22, 1819) summarized its deserving character: "The plot is neither dark nor intricate, nor is there any difficulty in following its details; the language is clear and elegant, the characters natural and interesting, the morality pure, the probabilities and rules of drama all observed." It is a play of strength and passion in which the nobility of woman dominates, qualities expected in the work of Mrs. Wright.

Born in Scotland, orphaned in infancy, and raised by a grandfather in England, Frances Wright showed her early independence by running away to Scotland with her sister when she was eighteen. In 1818 she came to America, where she wrote *Altorf*, and then returned to England in 1820 to write *Views of Society and Manners in America* (1821). After meeting in Paris Lafayette, with whom she possessed the "most intimate private and political confidence,"[40] she accompanied him on his American tour in 1824 and remained to work for the emancipation of Negro slaves on an experimental farm in Tennessee and to become involved with Robert Owen's utopian society at New Harmony, Indiana, particularly with the Educational Society and the *Harmony Gazette*. It was in New Harmony that she met and married William Phiquepal D'Arusmont, whom she later divorced. A tall (five-feet-ten-inches) woman with handsome, masculine features, she was, according to one contemporary, "the most intelligent female defender of liberty in the present age."[41] Certainly, she knew and expressed her mind. She attacked religion, the influence of the church in politics, education based on authority, and marriage based on legal rather than moral obligations. Most acceptable to Americans was her certain belief in this country as the land of liberty, an idea which she put into practice with her flamboyant freethinking.

Indicative of her faith in America was her statement in the preface to her printed play that this country would one day revive the "sinking honor of the drama." America, where she found the art of government brought to perfection, should also "in its maturer age . . . foster and advance every other art, and be at once the land of liberty and of genius." Hers was the kind of romantic and overwhelming faith which all young countries need. In *Altorf* her own belief in freedom was transferred to the Swiss struggle for independence; she hoped that the audience would "associate with a magic spell/ The name of WASHINGTON with that of TELL." Here she dramatized the inner struggle of Eberard de Altorf, former Austrian and now captain in the Independent Swiss Army. Married to Giovanna, Altorf is suddenly faced with the conflict of love versus duty as he meets again the Rosina of his youthful passion, the daughter of the Count of Rossberg, who is trying to force Altorf to help bring the Swiss under the Austrian flag. Recognizing that he does not love Giovanna, Altorf finally leaves with Rosina for the Rossberg castle, where, hunted as an outlaw, he is overcome by his own sense of dishonor and kills himself. His despair has also affected Rosina, who regrets her part in the tragedy and takes her life. Giovanna, given the clearest characterization in the play, is the understanding and loving wife who has vainly bid her husband to "guard thy honor" and, at the climax, feels both a sympathy toward and an envy of Rosina, for whom her husband has sacrificed himself:

> Thou might'st have known ere this Giovanna's peace
> Was one with thine. I would not seem to boast,
> Yet as I have an urgent prayer to put,
> I will recount my claims—not on thy love,
> But on thy gratitude and thy respect.
> Be patient, Eberard, and answer me.
> Say, have I not in summer of my youth,
> When that the heart is warm, and temper smiling,
> Resign'd myself unto a husband's service
> Who never gave me for my pains a smile?
>
> [IV, ii.]

And at the curtain she speaks the author's thoughts:

> Art gone? Both gone? Poor maid, I envy thee.
> In life thou wert belov'd, in death—united;
> And ye shall have one grave, poor, hapless lovers;
> And one sad, only mourner there to weep you.

As romantic and idealistic as its creator, the play shows less the struggle of man than the force of woman, but it has a movement, a strength of verse, and a sense of humanity which place it well above the average level of poetic drama at this time.

The American dramatist with the strongest reputation during the first quarter of the nineteenth century did not write his best plays in America. He was John Howard Payne (1791–1852), the youthful prodigy who showed his talent for the drama as actor, critic, and playwright long before he reached his maturity. The son of a schoolteacher whose work took him to Boston in 1796, Payne was early involved in school plays and found the English boy actor, Master William Betty, a model for his endeavors. In Boston Payne met Samuel Woodworth and helped edit the *Fly*, a magazine "for the improvement of youth of both sexes." By 1805 Payne was sent to New York to work in a countinghouse, where his activities did little to absorb those energies he soon exercised by attending the theatre and by publishing the *Thespian Mirror*, (December 28, 1805–March 22, 1806) which was "to promote the interests of the American drama." This journal was the kind of ambitious undertaking which attracted the attention of William Coleman, editor of the *Evening Post*, and brought Payne some notoriety among the socialites and literati of New York. Even at this early day, Payne was asking the question which remained unresolved during his lifetime: "Why is native genius allowed to waste itself in obscurity when editions of foreign publications are multiplied in our city?"[42]

Payne's first play, *Julia; or, The Wanderer*, a comedy in five acts, was performed at the Park Theatre on February 7, 1806. The plot follows the distressing problems of an orphan, Julia. Rescued from a villainous uncle and the unwanted attentions of a young profligate by the usual brand of hero, Julia finds a good home with a man who turns out to be her father, and she eventually marries the hero. The play includes farcical tricks played upon the uncle, some satire on the practices of polite society, and enough cynical and questionable language to condemn it for certain audiences: "An obliging girl is worth all the wives in heaven"; "What signifies the loss of one girl? The country's full of them"

(III, iii). Following the usual practice, the play appeared as "written by Eugenius, a gentleman of New York," a "gentleman" who would not celebrate his fifteenth birthday until the following June. Reviewers quickly condemned and defended the play, but its questionable delicacy offended too many people, and this quite remarkable work from such a young person was withdrawn by its rather embittered author.

By the following June, Payne was en route to Union College, where he was something of a misfit both academically and socially. Perhaps to compensate for his inadequacies, he did some acting and edited another paper, the *Pastime*, which for its twenty-one issues emphasized, not theatre, but "the cause of polite literature." With his father's bankruptcy in the fall of 1808, he left college and soon debuted in the part of Young Norval in Home's *Douglas* at the Park Theatre on February 24, 1809. Dunlap recorded Payne's success, stimulated no doubt by the novelty of a new and youthful actor in America. That winter and spring Payne acted successfully in New York and in Boston. During the 1809–1810 season he appeared in Baltimore, Philadelphia, Richmond, Charleston, Norfolk, Petersburg, and Washington. He acted many roles during these early years, including Romeo, Rolla in *Pizarro*, Hastings in *Jane Shore*, Edgar in *King Lear*, and Hamlet. Although well received in Baltimore particularly, he was disappointed with his inability to find acting assignments in New York. Perhaps unconsciously, but certainly with a shrewd purpose, he then started a trend among American actors that has never stopped. On January 17, 1813, with the financial help of some friends, he sailed for greener theatrical fields in England. But he was to be disappointed there, too. Not until June 4, 1813, did he have an opportunity to appear on the London stage—as Young Norval in *Douglas* at the Drury Lane. Although the response was satisfying, his engagement was not a long one, and he was soon forced to try to establish himself by acting in the provinces—Liverpool, Manchester, Leeds, Birmingham. During the summer of 1814, he toured Ireland. By the next spring he crossed the channel to Paris, where he met Talma, the foremost French actor of that time, and then almost immediately and quite casually slipped into another career.

Earlier, in 1809, Payne had published a version of Kotzebue's *Das Kind der Liebe*, which he had adapted from two English translations by Inchbald (1798) and Benjamin Thompson (1800). Dunlap's version was more popular in America than was Payne's but it is the method which Payne used to create his play that is important. An analysis of the various English versions of Kotzebue's play extant at that time indicates the remarkable ability Payne pos-

sessed to select those distinctive characteristics of a story which he then emphasized with a high sense of theatrical effect. Six years later, having translated
the current Paris hit, *La Pie Voleuse* by Louis Charles Caigniez and Jean Marie
Théodore Baudouin, as *The Maid and the Magpie*, he approached the manager
of Drury Lane only to discover that he had just accepted another translation.
He did, however, make an agreement with the Drury Lane management which
offered to pay him to translate the latest Paris successes for its stage.

  The Maid and the Magpie dramatizes the story of a young servant girl,
Annette, who innocently chooses a hollow tree in which to hide a piece of
silverware given to her by her father, a deserting soldier. Wrongly accused of
theft by her mistress, she cannot tell the truth for fear of condemning her father. But she is eventually saved by a peasant who retrieves the piece of silverware from the cache of a thieving magpie. The happy ending not only frees
Annette from suspicion but allows her father a pardon. It was a simple and
familiar story, but the play was sufficiently popular to have three versions playing in London by the time Payne's translation came to New York in the spring
of 1816. Clearly, Payne had found his place in the world of theatre and drama,
and it took him only a week to prepare his second translation, a version of
Frédéric du Petit-Méré's *Le Vol; ou, La Famille D'Anglade*, which he called
Accusation. Opening at Drury Lane on February 1, 1816, and at the Park in
New York City on May 10, 1816, this moralistic three-act melodrama of robbery, blackmail, and accusations finally ends in revealed innocence and triumphant virtue. It seemed a good beginning, and Payne soon learned the value of
publication for his plays and the opportunity a preface offered for enlarging
upon a thesis or discussing problems such as play piracy or the difficulties of
translation.

  At that point, Payne's business relationship with the Drury Lane management broke down. It was a matter of money, and he could not get proper consideration or even fair terms from either Drury Lane or Covent Garden. Three
manuscripts—*The Rival Heroes, Charles XII*, and *Peter the Great*—which he
sent to the Drury Lane management were misplaced by O. W. Ward, Secretary
to the Committee of the Drury Lane Theatre. Payne also complained (September 14, 1818) to Stephen Kemble, the newly appointed director of the theatre, that he was denied free admission both before and behind the curtain, "an
established privilege of every person who has produced a play at any house."[43]
The results of his rather vehement protest against this "restraint upon my right"
are unknown, but, when he finished *The Tragedy of Brutus; or, The Fall of*

Tarquin for Edmund Kean, he offered it to Drury Lane, where it opened December 3, 1818, an immediate success—success, that is, for Kean and for Drury Lane but additional agony for Payne.

In spite of billing as the "American Roscius," Payne's acting career had floundered with only 106 performances during his first five years in England while his quarrels with managers added to his anxieties. Then, because he had used seven sources for *Brutus*—sources he readily admitted—Payne was accused of plagiarism, a ridiculous cry at a time when pirating was openly practiced.[44] Added to the unpleasantness of the charge, which was eventually cleared up, was the indignity of receiving monetary recompense equal to that of writing an afterpiece for a play that enriched Kean by fifty pounds a week, saved the theatre from an embarrassing season, and became a favorite vehicle for major actors on either side of the Atlantic.

Payne took his two main themes from history and myth: Brutus' use of Sextus Tarquin's rape of Lucrece to expel the Tarquins and Brutus' dramatic condemnation of his own son, Titus. The scene of the play is Rome, where Sextus has seized the throne by murdering the father and the brother of Lucius Junius, who now lives with the victors and feigns the "fool." Upset by a prophecy that "the race of Tarquin shall be kings, till a fool drives them hence, and sets Rome free!" (I, iii), Tullia, Sextus' queen, suspects Lucius Junius and names him Brutus. One night Sextus, having heard Collatinus boast of Lucretia's faithfulness as a wife, rapes her and describes his feat to Brutus, who then dramatically casts off his mask of idiocy and uses Sextus' action and Lucretia's suicide to rally the Romans in battle. At this turning point of the tragedy, Brutus provides a memorable curse for dramatic literature:

> The furies curse you, then! Lash you with
>   snakes!
> When forth you walk, may the red flaming sun
> Strike you with livid plagues!
> Vipers, that die not slowly, gnaw your heart!
> May earth be to you but one wilderness!
> May you hate yourself,
> For death pray hourly, yet be in tortures
> Millions of years expiring!
>
> [III, i.]

He then swears revenge in that language of emotion which made this play a popular vehicle for actors:

To the death I swear
My burning vengeance shall I pursue these
    Tarquins!
Ne'er shall my limbs know rest till they are
    swept
From off the earth, which groans beneath their
    infamy!

                                        [III, ii.]

At the climax Tullia dies, Sextus Tarquin is stoned to death, and Titus, having fallen in love with Sextus' daughter and been controlled by those who conspired against Brutus, must be condemned. After making that judgment, Brutus cries "Justice is satisfied, and Rome is free!" and falls senseless, a final victim.

Better than any other play Payne wrote by himself, *Brutus* shows his method of composition, his power as a dramatist, his genius, not for creating the original drama, but for recognizing dramatic material and extracting moments of theatrical power. From his five major sources for *Brutus*—Nathaniel Lee's *Lucius Junius Brutus, Father of His Country* (1681); Voltaire's *Brutus* (1730); a translation of Voltaire's work by William Duncombe (1734); Hugh Downman's *Lucius Junius Brutus; or, The Expulsion of the Tarquins, an Historical Play* (1779); and Richard Cumberland's *The Sybil; or, The Elder Brutus, A Tragedy* (1813)—Payne constructed a play that not only provided an excellent role for a leading actor but emphasized a strong moral basis for the popular themes of liberty and freedom. The conflict is well set up, with a drastic change of events in Act III leading to the dramatic ending that links the two plot threads, which in themselves provide a good change of pace. In language the play is irregular. Payne lifted many lines from his models, but his blank verse shows the occasional power and dignity that attracted the nineteenth-century actor.

Over all *Brutus* was a tremendous stage success, playing first in America on March 15, 1819, and holding the stage for more than seventy years. A critic writing for the Petersburg *Intelligence* probably suggests the feelings of many Americans after hearing of Payne's success and reading his play:

The circumstance of a young American, destitute of patronage, and without literary celebrity, having produced a *successful tragedy* on the British boards —taking too, as the ground-work of his Drama, the identical foundation attempted to be built upon by several of their own writers in vain; we confess sharpened our appetite, and created in our mind high expectations. . . . We read it with deep attention, and upon concluding it, we knew not whether we felt most of admiration for the performance, or of gratitude towards its author. Mr. Payne has not only reared a monument to his own fame, but has conferred honor upon the land of his nativity.[45]

The editor of *New York Drama* collected *Brutus* in the first volume (1876), commenting that *"Brutus* is still a favorite performance in the hands of an adequate personator, and has found able representatives in this country in the persons of Forrest, Hamlin, Edwin Booth and others, and is still played to the satisfaction of admiring audiences."

Payne's apparent success, however, also attracted his creditors, for whom he had no satisfaction. After a disastrous season as manager of Sadler's Wells Theatre, he found himself in debtor's prison, where under a black seal inscribed "Octavius," he received a package containing two French plays. From one of them, Victor Ducange's *Thérèse; ou, l'Orpheline de Genève*, he adapted in three days a potboiler called *Thérèse, the Orphan of Geneva*, which opened at Drury Lane on February 2, 1821, and brought enough money to free him from prison. The plot of *Therese*, a typical melodrama, shows how the orphaned heroine is abused by society and accused of forgery and murder by a villain who also saves her through an unintentional confession as papers which establish her birth and inheritance are discovered.[46] Payne's next play, *Adeline, the Victim of Seduction* (1822), adapted from Pixérécourt, is a pathetic and sentimental melodrama about a "victim" who drowns herself during a festival despite the pleas of the villain's wife and her own blind father.[47]

These were years of tremendous activity for Payne, who did not rest in 1822 with *Adeline* but also adapted Scribe and Dupin's *Michel et Christine* as *Love in Humble Life*, in which a rather tolerant soldier returns home and encourages the marriage of his former girl friend to another before going back to his company, and Frédéric and Boirie's *Le Maréchal de Luxembourg* as *Peter Smink; or, The Armistice*, in which the hero in disguise prevents his capture by signing an armistice. From two acts of a play by Boirie, Carmouche, and Poujol, *Les Deux Forcats; ou, La Meuniere du Puy-de-Dôme*, Payne adapted *The Galley Slaves; or, The Mill of St. Aldervon.* He also cut and transposed enough of Hyacinthe and Alfred's *Ali-Pasha* as *Ali-Pacha; or, The Signet Ring* to make a drama better than the original. As usual, audiences in America were made aware of Payne's work with productions at the Park Theatre in New York not long after London openings. But, also as usual, such performances brought no money for Payne, who complained about the situation in his preface to *Thérèse*, which was taken down in shorthand from the theatre pit and thus stolen by other theatre managers in London.

One of Payne's most popular plays was *Clari; or, The Maid of Milan* (1823), which he adapted from a French ballet-pantomime in three acts, *Clari; ou, la Promesse de Mariage*. The plot is sweet and moral, although slight, but the sentiment of one song, set to music by Henry Bishop, carried the play through many performances in England and America. That song was "Home, Sweet Home." The play tells about Clari, the daughter of an Italian farmer. Clari is flattered by the Duke Varaldi's promise of marriage and is whisked away to all the magnificence of the court, where she remains both happy and virtuous until a chance entertainment provided for her amusement tells her own story. When the father in the sketch curses his undutiful daughter, Clari stops the performance, sees both her foolishness and her danger—deviating from his source, Payne insisted that Clari keep her virtue—and steals away to her home. As she approaches her village, she hears the haunting song ("Mid pleasures and palaces though we may roam,/ Be it ever so humble, there's no place like home."), and it remains only for the Duke to come after her, confess his villainy, and ask for Clari's hand in marriage.

Payne's next major work was his best comedy, *Charles the Second; or, The Merry Monarch*, which played first at Covent Garden on May 27, 1824, and at the Park Theatre in New York on October 25, 1824. Consistent with his past methods of composition, the play is a free adaptation of Alexander Duval's *La Jeunesse de Henri V* (1806), which in turn was based on *Charles II, roi d'Angleterre, en un certain lieu* (1789) by Sébastien Mercier. In order to win the hand of Lady Clara, Rochester must disgust the King with the "nocturnal rambles" which they both enjoy and "bring him back to reason." Mulling over his task, Rochester decides to visit a young barmaid, Mary, whom his page and protégé, Edward, is wooing in the guise of a music master named Georgini and, at the same time, to give King Charles "his first lesson in morals." Disguised as common seamen, Rochester and the King arrive at the tavern of Captain Copp, Mary's uncle and rowdy old tar. There Charles, exhibiting the "merry" nature that has brought him a reputation, begins to take liberties with Mary:

CHARLES.   (*To* MARY.) And so you are fond of music, my pretty lass?
MARY.   Oh, I love it of all things.
CHARLES.   A pretty hand to beat time with. (*Taking her hand.*)
MARY.   Sir—(*Withdrawing it.*)
CHARLES.   And as pretty a little mouth to warble a love-song. I warrant, there come none but sweet notes from these lips. (*Offers to kiss her.*)
MARY.   (*Resisting.*) Sir, give over—let me go, sir.—Mr. Georgini—help, help!

(EDWARD *bursts from* ROCHESTER, *who is laughing. At this moment, enter* COPP.)

COPP. Avast there, messmate! What the devil, yard arm and yard arm with my niece!

(CHARLES *desists, a little confused.* EDWARD *approaches* MARY.)

MARY. (*Flurried.*) I am glad you are come, Uncle. This rude stranger—

COPP. (*Taking her arm under his.*) Thunder and lightning—what! insult Captain Copp's niece in his own house! Fire and furies!

CHARLES. (*Pretending to be a little gay.*) I insult your niece, messmate? Since when has an honest tar's kissing a pretty girl been considered an insult? As to the young woman, if she takes offence at a piece of sailor civility, why, I ask pardon, that's all.

COPP. (*Softened.*) Oh, as to a piece of civility, d'ye see, that alters the case; but guns and blunderbusses! If anyone should dare—

[II, ii.]

The evening then passes in pleasant enjoyment until Rochester sneaks away, leaving the King with a tab he has no money to pay.

Suspect and locked in a room when he offers a diamond-studded watch to Copp, the King finally bribes his way to freedom about two steps ahead of a blast from a double-barreled shotgun. The next morning Copp and Mary appear at the palace to return a watch which obviously belongs to the King and are shocked to recognize both the King and Rochester, who, after further conversation, turns out to be the brother of Mary's mother and, therefore, her uncle. But they can all keep secrets, and the play ends happily; Rochester will become a "rational" and submissive husband to Clara; Mary will marry Edward; and Charles swears that he will henceforth abjure nightly frolics.

London critics were quick to point out that *Charles the Second* was not true comedy but rather farce or low comedy. The critics also had some understandable difficulties in recognizing it as Payne's work and for some time accepted Thomas Dibdin as the author. A year later, when the King of England, George IV, attended a performance, the *Chronicle* referred to the author as Dibdin, who encouraged the misconception by stating publicly that Payne had stolen the play from him—a play by Dibdin was called *Waggeries in Wapping*—and had altered it only slightly. In his preface to the 1824 publication, Payne argued that the translation of a foreign play by any individual did not allow that person complete ownership and stated that he had written his play during the fall of 1823 in Paris. He further explained that "my manuscript has been revised by a literary friend to whom I am indebted for invaluable touches."

The "friend," it turned out, was Washington Irving, and the degree of his complicity in *Charles the Second* has never been satisfactorily resolved.[48] For reasons that can only be surmised, Irving insisted that his name not be "implicated" in this or in other collaborations with Payne, and the particulars of his contribution remain conjecture. There is little doubt, however, that much of the wit and humor in the dialogue may be attributed to Irving. The creation of Captain Copp presents more of a problem. Payne claims him in his introduction to the 1825 *French's Acting Edition*, whereas Irving's biographers insist that Copp was Irving's invention. From the correspondence between Payne and Irving, it is clear that Irving contributed substantially to the play, and Copp, whoever may have been responsible for him, was a major part of its success, particularly with the song which he was never allowed to finish.

> In the time of the Rump,
> As old Admiral Trump,
> With his broom swept the chops of the channel:
> And his crew of Tenbreeches,
> Those Dutch sons of ——
>
>   [II, ii.]

Whatever his part in the creation—dialogue, character, or plot—Irving evidently was serious in his efforts. After watching the second performance of *Charles the Second* at Covent Garden, he wrote to his nephew that "it succeeds very well, though the critics attack the language. . . . I shall assist Payne in pruning the piece today, and I have no doubt it will have a good run."[49]

It did have a good run and was revived for many years in both England and America. In America Joseph Jefferson received excellent reviews for his low-comedy acting in the part of Copp. All the major characters in the play, however, are individualized, and in later years Fanny Kemble had considerable success in the part of the charming Mary Copp. Audiences and critics enjoyed the "smartness of dialogue," the "choice of situation and incidents," and the delineation of character. Captain Copp has a suggestion of humanity— a sentimental heart, an honest mind, the language and temper of a sailor, and a sense of humor—which distinguishes him in Payne's work. By combining a literary quality with those characteristics which make a stageworthy play, *Charles the Second* was distinctive on the American stage at this time. With more than one good part and with excellent farce action, it is weakened, however, mainly by its ending, which is more moral than probable and simply ties events together in the manner of situation comedy or of farce. The characters determine their futures, and, in both the society dramatized and the language used, there is a suggestion of social comedy. It was soon published in England in two versions—in 1824 in three acts and in 1825 in two acts combining Acts I and II of the previous version plus other changes—and was published also in America.

Irving and Payne worked together on six plays, only two of which were performed—*Charles the Second* and *Richelieu*.[50] Even after Irving decided in January, 1824, that he could not allow any more time for playwriting, the two Americans remained close friends in England. It would appear that Irving's efforts in the drama were well known at the time. In fact, Payne not only dedicated *Richelieu* to Irving when it was published but openly thanked him for his aid in writing the play. Irving, however, never admitted his collaboration. For *Richelieu*, which opened at Covent Garden on February 11, 1826, Payne had again used a Duval play as his source, *La Jeunesse du Duc de Richelieu; ou, le Lovelace Français*. Unfortunately, Payne's work had the particular fate of being opposed by the French minister at the Court of St. James, who was a descendant of Richelieu. Later, acted under the title *The French Libertine*, the play became very controversial among English critics, who found it, at different times, "distasteful," "extremely tiresome, vulgar, stupid, commonplace," or "the most successful of dramatic productions of its kind which we have seen for many years, and its merits are of a high order."[51] In America it was produced both as *Richelieu* and under the title *Remorse*. Meanwhile, Payne had written *The Fall of Algiers* (1825); a number of farces including *'Twas I; or, The Truth a Lie* (1825), which one critic described as "rendered laughable by the performers, but in itself is light as air";[52] and several other plays.

In July, 1832, after an absence of nearly twenty years, Payne returned to America and was treated to benefit performances of his plays and to testimonials in New York and Boston. In New York he was greeted as "Our distinguished countryman—John Howard Payne. The family of literature welcomes him to the home whose praises he has so sweetly sung." Happy at this reception, he responded, in part: "My feelings for the literature of the drama, and my sense of its importance to the community, must be inferred from my past attention to it, and will, I trust, be obvious from my future efforts to desire a place among those of my countrymen who have shown, and some very recently, the power of achieving great things for our fame to come in this most difficult pursuit."[53] But Payne's future in America did not come up to his expectations. Although his plays were being performed both in England and in America, the lack of adequate copyright laws denied him proper financial reward, and the monetatry problems which had haunted his earlier years continued after his return to America. His attempt to establish a journal failed; he seemed to feel that people were out to "crush" him; he complained that no one recognized him or that, at one time, Cooper's benefit conflicted with his; trivial things upset him. At a benefit in New Orleans in 1835 he unburdened himself of his bitter feelings—yet understandably so—toward copyright laws and those theatre managers who expended no efforts for American plays while they maintained their theatres by paying prompters to smuggle over the latest English novelties with which they pushed American plays off the stage. After that date, Payne's life was no longer associated with the drama. For a while he traveled among the Cherokee Indians and tried to help them in their relationships with the United States government and to gather material for literary work. In 1842 President Tyler appointed Payne as consul at Tunis. Recalled in 1845 and reappointed in 1851, he died in Tunis in 1852.

In many ways Payne epitomized the plight of the dramatist in America during the formative years of the new nation. Although his particular genius was not in creating the original play, he had considerable skills in recognizing, selecting, and combining the works of others into successful stage productions. He obviously had also a great deal of energy. His attempt to combine acting and playwriting, however, was not so satisfactory an undertaking as that of Dunlap, who combined management with playwriting; yet even Dunlap went bankrupt and was always hardpressed financially. Prior to 1828 these two were America's most prolific professional dramatists—in fact, America's only playwrights who did not have primary careers elsewhere. Not a shrewd businessman, Payne was easily victimized by English managers although his plays were produced, and he did make a reputation as a dramatist with more than sixty plays to his credit. The American theatregoer recognized his work as a major contribution to American drama. "Jacques" (Robert Ewing), reviewing plays for the *United States Gazette* during the Philadelphia season of 1825–26, commented on three productions of *Charles the Second*, two of *The Maid and the Magpie*, one of *Brutus*, one of Dunlap's *Abaelino*, and three of Barker's *Marmion*.

Although Payne proved that he could reach some popularity as an American dramatist, he also proved that the American dramatist would have to do without financial recognition. It is ironic that an American could go to England and be recognized only to return to America and be ruined by that preference for English creativity which directed American taste. Before Payne returned to America, however, the situation for American dramatists was slowly changing. Their artistry was becoming recognized, their efforts were even sought, and their tormentors would no longer be English managers but American actors.

NINE

Wanted: American Dramatists

By 1828 there was strong feeling among critics of the drama that an American drama should be encouraged, but not all were sure of its future. One critic even declared that "American genius, it appears, is excluded forever, by insuferable barriers, from tragic excellence; and Melpomene seems determined, that it shall never enter her temple, with what she considers its worthless offerings. The tragic muse disowns her votaries in America, and even denies them the poor favour of following her triumphal car."[1] Other critics could look into the past and note plays by Dunlap, Barker, and Payne that deserved recognition while remembering passages from other dramas that held some merit. Undoubtedly, it was as much an emotional reaction as an artistic or intellectual assessment that influenced critics. Certainly, pride was involved— pride in a growing country which saw power in a nationalistic approach, and pride among those interested in dramatic literature who saw both American poetry and fiction awarded a recognition denied the drama. The frustrations and irritations that would prompt Ralph Waldo Emerson to make his plea in "The American Scholar" in 1837 were clearly felt in the 1820s. But the drama, because it was produced in the theatre and therefore subject to special prejudices in the very heart of that Puritan land where some of the best literature would be created, attracted less attention than did other literature. Nationalism, on the other hand, is seldom determined by taste. The theatre had long been a means for patriotic declamation and spectacle, and, if not for art, certainly for nationalistic pride the drama deserved encouragement.

Artistry was also considered by those who saw beyond the relatively barren past of American drama and envisioned a potential that a few select plays had suggested. "Whatever talent there may be among us, it has to be encouraged"

291

was the somewhat desperate plea of the author of the long essay, "American Drama," published in June, 1827, in the *American Quarterly Review*, which had just been established by Robert Walsh, a Baltimore lawyer. "The first requisite for producing a National Drama is national encouragement," the author continued, as he outlined the steps to success. "We do not mean pensions and premiums—but liberal praise and rewards to success—and a liberal allowance for failure. . . . The second is a little more taste or liberality in the managers of our theatres; and the third is the presence of competent performers, collected in companies of sufficient strength to give effectual support to a new piece, and sufficient talent to personate an original character, without resorting to some hackneyed model, which has descended from generation to generation, and like all copies, lost something of the original in the hands of each succeeding imitator." There was nothing new in these requests, except perhaps the right to fail, which, unfortunately, had been exercised all too frequently in the past. English managers had been the butt of criticism for years; so had the concern for competent performers, but the timing of this comment was important. Changes were being made in the formulation of acting companies, and those changes would affect the writing of plays.

In the 1820s New York was assuming a new position of importance in America. It was, according to Vernon Lewis Parrington, the literary historian, becoming the "chief repository of the new capitalism," and the effect of its economic vigor was felt in the world of theatre. These were the "Palmy Days," according to Odell, seasons during which theatre was at its most competitive and interesting. Several new theatres appeared. The rebuilt Park Theatre (destroyed by fire in 1820) opened in 1821; Chatham Gardens, a summer tent theatre, added light drama in 1823 and in 1824 moved into a permanent building where until 1827 it was a serious contender for the Park's fashionable audiences; the Lafayette Theatre, large enough for equestrian and dramatic performances, was built in 1825; the beautiful New York Theatre opened in 1826 but failed to attract audiences and eventually acquired the name of the Bowery Theatre, subsequently going through more changes of name, management, and entertainment policy than any other American theatre. There was also William Niblo's museum theatre, the Sans Souci, which opened in 1828, and the Mount Pitt Circus, which opened in 1826. All were in addition to the several theatres already actively producing plays in New York. This expansion of theatre, of course, was not limited to New York. These were years of growing theatrical activity not only along the East Coast but also west of the

Appalachian Chain and throughout the Mississippi Valley. Even Salem, Massachusetts, erected a "temple of dramatic art" in 1827.

Growth in theatre was necessary to meet the needs of the rapidly increasing population, particularly in urban centers. But the big change was in the practices of theatre management. No longer could managers employ the old stock system of rotating a set number of plays around a permanent resident company. Instead, the star system, which English actors like Cooke, Cooper, and Kean brought to America, was becoming popular with the result that stock actors played to near empty houses as audiences waited for the celebrity. Along with that problem, managers encountered another. Toward the end of the 1820s, when the spirit of Jacksonian democracy had created a lasting impact on American society, the tastes of theatre audiences began to change. Audiences craved excitement, something new. Even the Park, that bulwark of traditional theatre, resorted to more spectacular entertainment and, in 1826, was chastised for its poor taste by the New York *Mirror*. On a summer night in the 1820s, for example, New Yorkers could watch melodrama, equestrian drama, circuses, fireworks, balloon ascents, Shakespeare, and concerts or perhaps attend a theatre which had been converted to a ballroom for a special occasion. Theatre managers, hard put to stay solvent in an increasingly competitive world, looked for answers: if stars attracted audiences, one response was to provide more stars; and novelty for audiences meant more plays as well as different performers. Both answers meant encouragement for American actors and dramatists.

The first American actor who was given billing equal to such English contemporaries as Edmund Kean and William Macready was Edwin Forrest. Fighting the same English prejudices that haunted American dramatists, Forrest wisely chose to gain experience in provincial theatres from Albany to New Orleans. Achieving success with some speed, he represented an ideal of manhood which Americans applauded, and, when he first played in Boston in February, 1827, his potential was recognized. "The young gentleman is commencing a proud career, and with continued study and perseverance, must eventually become one of the first actors of the stage," wrote one prophetic critic.[2] And Forrest rose to heights equalled by no other theatrical performer before the Civil War. As he gathered a following first in America and then in England, his star went from horizon to zenith with a dazzling speed.

Although Forrest was first of all a spectacular actor, he is important for another reason in the history of American drama. On November 22, 1828,

Forrest placed an advertisement in the *Critic*, a journal just started by William Leggett:

> To the author of the best tragedy in five acts, of which the hero or principal character shall be an aboriginal of this country, the sum of five hundred dollars, and half of the proceeds of the third representation, with my own gratuitous services on that occasion. The award to be made by a committee of literary and theatrical gentlemen.

It was a new concept which not only recognized the American dramatist but would also reward him. The linking of the literary and the theatrical worlds was also a shrewd move.

American dramatists were now actually wanted, and Forrest deserves considerable credit for an idea which stimulated a new interest in American drama. What he did with the results of his contests and what others did with the plays they got in this fashion—the contest idea was repeated many times by Forrest and others—deserves considerably less than enthusiastic praise. Of the fourteen plays which Forrest's advertisement elicited, he chose John Augustus Stone's *Metamora*. During the next quarter of a century, hardly a season passed in which Forrest did not act the title role, and he made quite literally thousands and thousands of dollars from this one play; in despondence and poverty Stone committed suicide. Robert Montgomery Bird, another winner of a Forrest Contest, finally stopped writing plays when he discovered that he could not make a living while Forrest was growing tremendously wealthy producing his plays. Forrest's idea for a playwriting contest had been exceedingly shrewd for his own advancement, but it should be noted that his treatment of dramatists who wrote for him was consistent with the times and in no way illegal in spite of seeming unfair. It was a time when speculation was a watchword in America, and Forrest speculated. Although dramatists in America had been slowly improving their lot since 1815, as the increased number of plays and playwrights indicates, by a single act Forrest stoked the fires of their potential artistry. He had the remarkable wit, or good fortune, also to strike a responsive nationalistic chord. Without question, he encouraged American dramatists to emerge from their obscured and generally undistinguished past, but he had no intention of rewarding them unduly.

A second American actor who reached star billing at this time was James H. Hackett, who first appeared on the New York stage in 1826. His debut, however, did not impress audiences, and, as did Payne, he took himself and his aspirations to England. There his performance of a Yankee character suggests some influence from the eminent English comedian Charles Mathews, whose story relative to America is worth telling for the eventual impact it had upon the American dramatist. During his 1822–23 tour of America, Mathews was particularly impressed by the people—the Yankee and the Negro, their manners and dialects—and their "national peculiarities." On returning to England he expressed his impressions in an entertainment called *A Trip to America*, one part of which was a "monopolylogue" called *All's Well at Nachitoches* in which he played all of the following parts: Colonel Hiram Peglar, a Kentucky shoemaker; Agamemnon, a poor, runaway Negro; Jonathan W. Doubikins, a real Yankee; Monsieur Capote, a French emigrant tailor; and Mr. O'Sullivan, an Irish improver of his fortunes. From that display of "national peculiarities," the character of Jonathan inspired Richard B. Peake to write a farce, *Jonathan in England* (1824). With typical enthusiasm Mathews not only helped Peake with phrasing but acted the title role with considerable success. At first, in an unusual display of English sympathy, English critics saw the character of Doubikins as an affront to Americans, and Mathews was attacked in the press. One critic, however, found *Jonathan* no more a "libel on American character" than "Leatherlip Grassfeeder is an unjust and liberal caricature of a city alderman."[3] Most accepted the blunderings and pleasantries, although farfetched, as simply humorous and entertaining. Mathews was quick to respond that his creation was never intended as a "national portrait."

Using Mathews' work as a model, Hackett achieved some slight recognition in the London theatres in 1827 as a Yankee storyteller. That summer he returned to the United States. Impressed by Mathews' success, Hackett adapted George Coleman's *Who Wants a Guinea?* (1805), a comedy about a Yorkshireman named Solomon Grundy, into a sketch he called *John Bull at Home; or, Jonathan in England*, in which he changed the major character to Yankee Solomon Swap. Evidence suggests that he made the adaptation himself, cutting the action considerably, eliminating some characters, editing Solomon's lines to provide the right dialect, and adding the appropriate Yankee phrases. This work was published in 1828 and first played at the Park Theatre in New York on December 3, 1828. Whether Hackett's play is more or less a hodgepodge than Coleman's is a moot point. Any audience enjoyment had to come, not from the scattered story about a family home where young Fanny seeks a job, but from the assorted individuals assembled there, particularly Solomon Swap. All Swap does is to "run about and talk," one of the other characters says; "he's all legs and mouth, like a Dutch oven upon a trivet. He knocks the furniture about as he does his English, and makes as much havoc in a house as in a language" (II, i). But audiences enjoyed him, and that was all that was necessary.

With that play Hackett started his career as a Yankee impersonator, and the play itself lasted through many Yankee actors. Hackett also introduced other Yankee plays and soon resorted to the technique which had brought Forrest such success:

> Premium—Mr. Hackett, of New York, has offered a premium of $250 for the best comedy in three acts, in which the principal character shall be an original of this country.[4]

Here again, American dramatists were encouraged, indeed, needed. But by 1830 the play contest was already becoming suspect, and a critic, quoting Hackett's notice, explained some of the problems:

> We doubt whether there will be many competitors for this premium, as no pledge whatsoever is given that men of even common capacity will be judges, or that the premium, when earned, will be paid. The practice of offering rewards in this loose and irresponsible manner is the height of absurdity, and it ought to be discountenanced by the whole fraternity of authors and publishers. The names of the judges should be made known— the author has a right to know the character of the tribunal before which his production is to appear; and as the promise of pay is the main inducement, he should be perfectly satisfied that everything will be fair and honest. . . . If this system of offering literary prizes were properly conducted, much benefit would result to the character of our country, and something solid to the pockets of our authors.[5]

Thus corruption appears before encouragement gets fairly started, but the progress of the dramatist is suggested by the rights the critic felt could be asserted. Most important, however, both an awareness of and a need for American dramatists had become established, and that was the epochal note first sounded in 1828.

The contests also drew attention to the increasing number of plays being written. Although John A. Stone's career seemed to start with *Metamora* in 1829, he had been writing plays for several years. Stone (1800–1834), a native of Concord, Massachusetts, combined acting and playwriting careers. As did many other hopeful actors, he debuted at a Boston theatre in Home's *Douglas* but in the role of Old Norval. Presumably by personal inclination and because of physical appearance, Stone played eccentric comics and old men. Although he never reached star level, he was a favorite with New York audiences from 1822 through 1831, after which he acted in Philadelphia theatres. During his brief career he wrote at least ten plays. Prior to 1828, however, he had written only two plays—*Restoration; or, The Diamond Cross*, which played at New York's Chatham Garden Theatre in November, 1824, and *Tancred; or, The Siege of Antioch*, which was printed in 1827 but never acted although published with the play is a letter by Joseph Jefferson, who praised its "elegant" language and found it "perfectly dramatic." The time of this second play is 1097 during the First Crusade as the Christians besiege Antioch under the leadership of Alexius, Emperor of Greece. Almost victimized by Alexius' jealousy before his involvement in the invasion, Tancred is a character of some potential in an otherwise disjointed story. A suspenseful spy scene also shows Stone's ability to create humor. His depth of thought is revealed in a Yorick-like scene involving a skull which he carefully interlaced with a philosophy of human nature. Yet in spite of a sensitivity that was not common in much of American drama, *Tancred* is not a successful play. Whereas parts of the play suggest the skills of a man who could create *Metamora* two years later, prior to the announcement of the play contest in the fall of 1828, Stone was simply one of a number of actor-playwrights in America.

In 1828 Robert Montgomery Bird, the man who would become the outstanding American dramatist of the early 1830s, was just completing his playwriting apprenticeship. Bird (1806–1854) was truly one of the remarkable men of his generation. His varied interests and equally responsive talents carried his active mind through medicine, science, music, art, history, politics, pedagogy, and the creation of criticism, poetry, fiction, and drama. Had he ever decided to concentrate his efforts, he might have made his mark in any of these fields, but he even planned the staggered and disjointed activity that his mind pursued. He determined early, for example, that in his literary career he would begin as a poet and dramatist, turn next to novels, and finally write history late in his life. For the drama he projected at least fifty-five plays, but he cut this part of his literary career short when he became disenchanted with the demands placed upon dramatists by theatre managers and actors. He was particularly unhappy in his dealings with Edwin Forrest, for whom he wrote four prize plays which enriched the actor considerably but brought very little to the author. In his *Secret Records* Bird explained his feelings: "What a fool I was to think of writing plays! To be sure, they are much wanted. But then novels are much easier sorts of things and immortalize one's pocket much sooner."[6] Had there been adequate copyright laws in America at that time, his contribution to American drama—distinguished as it is but limited to a few plays—might have been far greater.

During 1827 and 1828 Bird was actively involved in writing plays, both comedy and tragedy. At least two of these deserve some comment despite an aura of closet drama that attaches to them. Bird was a scholarly individual; he read widely from classical literature, but he was also very much a product of and a part of the more recent romantic tradition. Taking his degree in medicine in 1827, he practiced only a very brief time before becoming seriously involved in the literary career in which he had been dabbling during his medical education. At this point in history, Romanticism exercised a strong influence upon American literature. A convenient term to describe some changes in literature, Romanticism meant many things: the untamed and emotional attitude toward nature that distinguished Wordsworth's poetry; the idealism and imagination that would spark the writings of Emerson and of Thoreau; the interest in the Gothic that inspired Hawthorne and Poe; a sense of freedom; and a realistic attitude toward physical scenery that marked the historical romances of Cooper, Kennedy, Paulding, and Simms. Although Bird belongs among those novelists, he was a major force in bringing Romanticism to American drama. While his early works only suggest his eventual contribution to the drama, his combined interest in classical poetry and contemporary Romanticism produced vigorous and flamboyant plot and dialogue that would appeal to an actor such as Edwin Forrest. Bird also had strong opinions about dramatic composition which he was beginning to express in the quite voluminous notes and records that he kept during the early years. He wanted to write for the stage, wanted to demonstrate that superior "gift of poetry and a knack for dramatic effect" which distinguished the stage dramatist from the person who wrote only for the closet. Essentially, his career as a dramatist did not begin until he wrote *Pelopidas* for Forrest in 1830. By the time he stopped writing plays four years later, he had provided Forrest with three more plays which give remarkable evidence of his distinctive skill in understanding the essential dramatic situation, creating well-developed heroes, and writing the kind of rhetorical and exclamatory poetic speeches that fitted Forrest's robust style of acting.

Bird was not careful in dating his early playwriting efforts. *Bachelor's Hall; or, All in A Hobble* and *The Masque of the Devils; or, The Canterbury Clock*, two slight, unfinished comedies, seem to be his first attempts. *News of the Night*, an ambitious farce set in Philadelphia, concerns two young ladies, their lovers, and their guardian uncle, who encourages their elopements in order that he may keep half of their inheritance. Much of the farce humor and action derives from Bird's skillful use of a large box as a kind of moving trap for various characters. Bird set *'Twas All for the Best* in England, and this comedy is as imitative of Congreve as *News of the Night* was of Ben Jonson. Complicated in plot and improbable throughout, *'Twas All for the Best* follows the activity of Sir Noel Nozlebody, who does everything wrong but for the best reasons. Bird's notes indicate that he had the Chestnut Street Theatre in mind as he wrote, but evidently nothing came of the plan.

The City Looking Glass (dated July, 1828, but, as the other two plays, neither acted nor published during Bird's lifetime) shows the continuing progress that Bird was making as a dramatist and a particular success in writing social comedy that has long gone unrecognized. It is easy to see its derivative nature, but the play also shows fresh and original touches in form, character, and point of view. In the prologue Bird explains the "looking glass" metaphor:

> We've only made a "mirror for the time";
> Where ye may look, and see such knaves and asses
> As, we hope, can't be seen in your own glasses,
> Playing before ye certain tricks and capers,
> Such as you look for daily in the papers.

The plot revolves around the attempt of a rakish villain, Ravin, who explains his philosophy to his brother in the first scene:

> I have introduced you to a circle, where, to be as genteel as the rest, it is only necessary for you to dress well, to drink deeply, to be knowing with the ball and pasteboard, and to swear abominably. Follow them in their frolics, invite them to the tavern, let them be often drunk at your expense, and they will suffer themselves to be gulled out of sheer gratitude. You will find Bolt, the lawyer, an excellent introduction to all the rakes and profligates in town: therefore be tender of his purse. Keep up the Doctor; the character is respectable, and will be an excuse for want of manners.

Ravin's plan is to arrange two marriages for himself, whereby he will gain an immense fortune. To carry out his plan, he must deceive, lie, destroy by false accusation, manipulate people, and contrive self-serving situations—all reflected in the city's looking glass. But his plans explode into a near-grotesque chaos in Act V which only careful revelations can clarify. Finally, Ravin is identified as the very rogue whom by his base insinuations he had accused the hero of being, and the girls involved marry men of honor and social acceptance.

Although the comedy is basically Restoration in temper, it includes the characters and the devices of melodrama such as well-timed rescues and farcical actions. Bird also demonstrated considerable ability to handle a complicated plot in a variety of frequently well-structured scenes. Cleverly combining sophisticated and bawdy wit with a touch of sentiment, he produced an anti-sentimental view to which he fused a realistic lowlife in Philadelphia as a background for his social situation. Nathan Nobody, a comic servant, wants to be paid in part with theatre tickets—to "learn wisdom." Topical interest appears in an argument over politics and slavery between a Southern gentleman and a Philadelphian capitalistic aristocrat. Those and other scenes ridicule aspects of society and show that Bird was much aware of the use of language as support for the comic mood and of the necessity of entertainment as superior to moral preachment. His skill in characterization was equally encouraging. His villain-protagonist, for example, has a dramatic quality lacking in the more conventional heroes whom the girls will marry as he controls the movement throughout the third act in terms of social mood as well as of melodramatic plotting. Perhaps in keeping with the spirit of the time, Bird also introduced a patriotic theme and provided a Yankee sailor, Taffrail. *The City Looking Glass* is surely not a faultless play, but it shows the work of an intelligent and thoughtful playwright who was learning his craft.

Bird planned to write several tragedies in 1827 and 1828, but only three fragments and two completed plays exist. Of the fragments, *The Fanatick* is set in Germany and based on Charles Brockden Brown's *Wieland*; a second fragment, *The Three Dukes; or, The Lady of Catalonia*, deals with love in Spain as one man finds his beloved too cool while another complains that his is too passionate; *Giannone* takes place in Naples and describes a plan for bloody revenge within the family of a usurping duke. In the essay "Dramatic Authors of America," James Rees remembers "perusing the manuscripts of two [plays by Bird] which gave promise" of the distinction that might have awaited him as a dramatist.[7] Those were entitled *The Cowled Lover* and *Caridorf*.

Dated June, 1827, *The Cowled Lover* is largely melodrama with a plot imitative of Shakespeare's *Romeo and Juliet*. The hero, in love with the daughter of a bitter enemy, gains entrance to the castle where the heroine feigns madness to forestall marriage to her father's choice. There the hero is discovered by a servant and meets death with his beloved at the hands of her father. Unfortunately, situation rather than character controls the plot, in which Gothic elements are strong and characters declaim broadly about freedom and liberty. *Caridorf*, written in August, 1828, is a Gothic melodrama which traces the destruction through jealousy of the violent, gloomy hero. His major faults of jealousy and anger are well established in Act I, and few changes occur as one degrading act follows another until Caridorf, by falsely accusing the blameless heroine of infidelity, brings disaster to both of them at the final curtain. Characterization is again weak although in both plays Bird tried to emphasize and build his plot around the peculiar characteristics of a major figure. Few would see Bird's very considerable potential in these two apprenticeship plays, which, in contrast to *The City Looking Glass*, are more typical of the average American efforts during the first quarter of the century.

Another American who would contribute to early American drama under the aegis of Forrest was Richard Penn Smith (1799–1854). In 1828 he, too, was just getting started. A Philadelphian, Smith was a grandson of William Smith, Provost of the College of Philadelphia, whose enthusiasm for drama and theatre was revealed in his pressure on the Pennsylvania Assembly and his support of Thomas Godfrey. Richard Penn Smith was, for a brief time, the owner and editor of the *Aurora*, but he made his living mainly as a lawyer. From 1825 through 1836, however, he managed to write some twenty plays, the best being *Caius Marius*, another Forrest Prize Play. His two earliest plays, *The Pelican* and *The Divorce*, both dated 1825, exist only in manuscript. The first, a one-act farce, was not performed; and the second, an attempt at romantic comedy, was rewritten as *The Deformed; or, Woman's Trial* and performed in 1830. Smith's first play to be acted upon the stage was called *Quite Correct*, a comedy of sentiment and romance concerned with an innkeeper who insists on being "quite correct" in all that he does—even while his establishment provides a meeting place for two lovers and a separated couple. Based on a story by Theodore Hook called "Doubts and Fears," which was adapted from a French comedy, *L'Hôtel garni; ou, La Leçon singulière* by Désaugiers and Gentil, *Quite Correct* opened in Philadelphia on May 27, 1828. This was the beginning for Smith, a dramatist with recognizable talent as a craftsman who, as did Dunlap, adapted many foreign works. The following year Smith wrote six plays, five of which were performed.

With the literary promise that was appearing in America by the late 1820s and with the political changes which exercised some influence upon that promise, the future for the American dramatist seemed markedly hopeful by the time Forrest advertised for plays. Stone, Bird, and Smith all wrote plays that achieved particular popularity through Forrest's acting, but they also represented a broader interest in playwriting that was emerging with the literary renaissance in certain areas of America. Philadelphia seemed an especially fertile spot for playwrights. Barker and Noah were joined by McHenry, Bird, Smith, David Paul Brown, and Robert T. Conrad. Stone, as had Woodworth, had started in New England, where Longfellow, New England's most celebrated poet of the nineteenth century, would attempt to write poetic dramas. Other New England dramatists such as Epes Sargent and Nathaniel Parker Willis migrated to New York, which attracted a number of dramatists and tempted native sons and daughters to write for its developing theatre. By 1828 Charleston was losing its prestige as a drama and theatre center, but, with Sawyer from North Carolina, N. H. Bannister from Baltimore, James M. Kennicott from New Orleans, and Caroline Lee Hentz from Kentucky, a diminished tradition was being carried on.

And there was other evidence to show a growing interest in American drama and theatre: more published plays, for example, and more collections of plays. There were also odd little plays such as Josiah P. Smith's *Who Ever Saw the Like!* "A tragi-comedy, or rather a comico-tragedy; portraying the last elections of Knox County, with references to the neighbouring counties," printed in Knoxville at the "Enquirer Office" in 1827; *The Cabal; or, A Peep into Jacksonism* (1828), "A play in one act, By a Baltimorian"; and *Sophia; or, The Bandit of the Forest*, "a play in three acts, By a gentleman of this City," printed in New York in 1828. Publications from "Elton's theatrical, play, print, and song store" include *Theatrical Commicalities, Whimsicalities, Oddities and Drolleries* (1828), a collection of songs and monologues which actors used to build their individual popularity, pieces such as "The Yankee Militia Muster," "Jonathan's Visit to a Wedding," "Major Longbow's Appetite," "Adventures of Major Longbow," a comic song entitled "Wery Pekooliar; or, The Lisping Lover," and two monologues, "L. A. W.—Law" and "The Assembly Hall," by the English comedian George Holland, who enjoyed more than fifty popular years on the American stage. *Acting American Theatre*, "containing the most popular plays, as they are performed at the Philadelphia Theatre; carefully corrected and published from the prompt books," appeared in 1826–27. Publishers such as David Longworth in New York had published innumerable plays during the first quarter of the century, but with greater activity among American playwrights plus the population and theatre growth, both the number of individuals publishing plays and the variety of published materials relating to drama and theatre increased.

Both Forrest and Hackett helped make 1828 a distinctive year in the development of American drama and theatre with the contest announcement and with the production of *Jonathan in England* in New York. Two other events in that year brought the American drama closer to the American theatre, where the preference for English plays and English performers was a growing irritant among audiences who took their nationalism seriously. One of these events was the performance on May 26, 1828, at the South Pearl Street Theatre in Albany, of the first-known dramatization of Washington Irving's story "Rip Van Winkle." Irving's creation had first appeared in *The Sketch Book* in 1819. The Albany adaptation by some unknown person was entitled *Rip Van Winkle; or, The Spirits of the Catskill Mountains*. Thomas Flynn starred as Rip while his wife played Rip's daughter, Lowenna; and this brief sketch evidently initiated the love affair between Knickerbocker, the village schoolmaster, and Alice Van Winkle which later versions by John Kerr and Charles Burke emphasized. One reviewer of the Albany production printed the prologue, written by "one of the citizens of that sedate city":

> If scenes of yore, endear'd by classic-tales,
> The comic muse with smiles of rapture hails;
> If when we view those days of Auld Lang Syne,
> Their charms, with home, that magic name combine;
> May we not hope, kind friends, indulgence here?
> Say, (for I speak to yonder fat mynheer,)
> Say, shall our burgomasters smile to night?
> Shall they from woe-worn care divert one wrinkle,
> To crown our hero, far-famed *Rip Van Winkle*?
> Shall Knickerbocker's sons, that gen'rous race,
> Whose feelings always beem upon their face,
> Excuse the efforts which the muse affords,
> And greet each buskin'd hero on these boards?
>
> Shades of the Dutch! How seldom rhyme had shown
> Your ruddy beauties, and your charms full blown!
> How long neglected have your merits lain?
> But Irving's genius bids them rise again.
>
> To you, Albanians, grateful as we are,
> We offer trembling our bill of fare.
> Yours was the soil of Dutchmen. Here they trod,
> When leaving glory's waves, fair freedom's sod.
> 'Twas here a Stuyvesant and Chrystyoner reigned,
> And kept their honor and their name unstained.
> *Oranje Boven*, be their motto, too,
> And be their sons like them, to freedom true,
> Let then our gen'rous friends one smile bestow,
> Friends perched *aloft*, and you my friends *below*:
> Save us, we ask you, from the critics' jaw—
> We know your answer, 'tis a cheering *yaw*![8]

Other dramatic versions of the story appeared over the years—Kerr's in 1829, Burke's in 1850, Thomas Lacy's somewhat later—culminating in the Dion Boucicault–Joseph Jefferson version of 1865, in which Joseph Jefferson III, born in 1829, starred for forty years. But it all began in 1828.

A second event in 1828 involved a young man named Thomas Dartmouth Rice. After some acting in New York, Rice went west in the fall of 1828 and joined Ludlow and Smith's theatre in Louisville, Kentucky, as a kind of general handyman and novice actor. Later that year he transferred to Samuel Drake's company in the same city. It was during a performance of Solon Richardson's *The Rifle*, in which Rice played a cornfield Negro, that he first "jumped Jim Crow." The date could have been late in 1828 or early the following year; the exact time is unknown. But Rice was the man, the place was Louisville, and the repercussions of his act were tremendous. Walking around his hotel Rice wandered into the livery stable of a man named Crow whose Negro helper, calling himself Jim Crow, was currying a horse.[9] The Negro was rather unhappy looking and crippled with rheumatism, but he nonetheless sang a song as he worked. At the end of each verse, he gave a little jump and, as he landed, set his "heel a'rickin." Rice was fascinated. He paid the Negro to teach him the song, and he quickly learned to mimic the voice, the shuffling gait and mannerisms, and the little jump at the catchy refrain:

> Turn about and wheel about,
>   An do jis so;
> And ebery time I wheel about,
>   I jump Jim Crow.

Rice added verses to the song and took his act back East, where his success eventually made him a part of American folklore with the usual embellishments to accounts which make accuracy very difficult. His act encouraged theatrical extravaganzas that become known as Ethiopian Opera; Jim Crow as a character stimulated the creation of other Negro characters in American drama; in 1843 American minstrelsy began with the Virginia Minstrels; and Rice, the itinerant actor of 1828, was eventually given the title of Father of American Minstrels.

One of the seemingly encouraging aspects of the developing American drama at the end of the first quarter of the nineteenth century was its closer tie to the actors in America, who were by this time more apt to be American by birth and attitude. Unfortunately, the advantage turned sour when these actors began to exert a degree of prejudicial control over plays and playwrights which tended to discourage original dramatists. This was another confrontation which would slow the development of an American drama. Yet both the greater acceptance of the American actor and the increased efforts of American writers to make their readers aware of an American literature—both coming with the era of Jacksonian democracy—momentarily helped the American dramatist. In 1828 relief for the dramatist—relief from the double prejudice of being an American writer and of writing for a theatre regarded by many as Satan's den and largely controlled by men unsympathetic to American creativity either for financial or artistic reasons—seemed to be more than a flickering dream.

During the first 230 years of the white man's recorded interest in theatre while in America, the American dramatist accomplished relatively little in terms of the amount of drama produced. But he did mark up a few decided achievements which still rank high when compared with all artistic accomplishments in America to 1828. Playwriting during the colonial period was a sketchy and tenuous affair. Although the New World was America, it was an English colony rather than an independent nation, and the drama—what little there was—would, at first at any rate, be an extension of English drama. What individual character it might claim would be a tendency toward satire, which might again be considered an imitation of eighteenth-century English writers. Clearly, the kind of people who came to America during the colonial period determined the arts of the country. Hence the prejudices of New England and Pennsylvania exerted an influence for a long, long time, while the more liberal Southern colonies permitted a freer expression in both arts and letters. War is a period of social and political upheaval, and the drama and theatre of the Revolution, while individualized by certain issues and people, might belong to any period of comparable stress. For the drama historian the significant aspect of the conflict in America is the importance which drama and theatre assumed during the struggle, an importance not achieved in America until World War II and the subsequent conflicts in Asia.

It took nearly fifty years for the new nation, the United States of America, to show an interest in its own literature. Irving would be called the "American Goldsmith" and have to be persuaded by an Englishman to write about America. Cooper would be the "American Scott," and both Cooper and Irving would spend a great deal of their time abroad. Then Longfellow clearly helped set a new direction when he chose an original and somewhat daring topic for his graduation address to the Bowdoin Class of 1825 and spoke on "Our Native Writers." Throughout these fifty years the drama was subject to such social and literary questioning that the more serious, and perhaps pretentious, writers withheld their names when they wrote plays. Consequently, America could boast few dramatists worthy of the title, few plays that should be remembered other than as steps marking the progress and direction of a slowly developing art. Yet there were a surprising number of people who aspired to write for the theatre. A few were serious students of the drama; others were simply imitators; some were strong-minded women who wrote some of the most interesting plays; many were hacks writing for the nonce.

Dramatists from this early period who created plays comparable to the achievements of their colleagues in other literary genres are Royall Tyler, William Dunlap, James Nelson Barker, and John Howard Payne with Washington Irving. Yet only Payne might be considered a professional playwright, and he, as were other literary figures of the nineteenth century, was aided by a government appointment late in his life. As a Hawthorne or a Poe might attest, one could not make a living in literature. The best plays from these dramatists—those plays that reveal both theatrical effectiveness and a literary quality—are *The Contrast*, *André*, *Superstition*, and *Charles the Second*. Yet with the exception of *The Contrast*, none would compare with the best works of Bryant, Irving, or Cooper. Perhaps that goes without saying. It is difficult to compare a play written to be produced on the stage and subject to the creativity of the actor on a particular evening with a novel to be enjoyed in private forever. All four of these plays, however, still read well although, with the exception of *Charles the Second*, none held the stage for long. Barker's *Marmion*, Dunlap's *Leicester*, and Payne's *Brutus* all had better reception in the contemporary theatre.

The best plays of Tyler, Dunlap, Barker, and Payne are significant contributions to drama in America, outstanding for their time and worth the careful appraisal of the literary historian. They reveal the skills of the competent, and sometimes inspired dramatist as well as the imagination and insight of the man of letters. Although one misses a consistency of excellence and a sensitivity to language that would make first-rate drama, those qualities would be long in coming to drama in America. Americans would have to be satisfied with a few simply good plays and to delay excellence for future generations which would make greater demands upon their dramatists. But the lack of superior qualities does not constitute a great condemnation either of American drama of this period or of the playwrights mentioned. In the history of drama in the English language there is a noticeable hiatus between the plays of Sheridan and those of Shaw, with few dramatists worthy of note writing during the first half of the nineteenth century. Among those Englishmen who were producing theatre fare for the London audiences at this early time, there were none whose works might not be mentioned in the same breath with Hutton, Minshull, Turnbull, Noah, Woodworth, or several others. They were equally good and equally weak, and they provided the entertainment on which theatres must exist until the exceptional dramatist appears.

During the early development of American drama, just about all forms of drama were written or attempted. The only distinctive accomplishments, however, were in comedy or, more accurately, farce-comedy. *The Contrast*, of course, provided a fine beginning. Dunlap's *The Father; or, American Shandyism* is also fair comedy although diluted with a moral instruction that most American dramatists accepted as necessary while the best avoided it. Barker's *Tears and Smiles* and *How to Try a Lover*, Bird's *The City Looking Glass*, and the Payne-Irving *Charles the Second* demonstrate the comedy that would distinguish the drama of the period. Many of the lesser farce-comedies also continued to emphasize satire, that single distinctive feature of colonial drama.

Although American playwrights wrote both farce and melodrama, they so mingled the forms that few good examples of either—with the exception of some adaptations by Dunlap and Payne—appeared. Part of the reason lay with the dramatists' lack of experience and a weak knowledge of the requirements of those particular forms of drama, which were only vaguely understood. It must also be remembered, however, that, for all but one or possibly two of these playwrights, the drama was only an avocation, an interest of spasmodic intensity which generally lasted for only a brief time. Some dramatists tried to write tragedy, but here again the weaknesses of the dramatist—lack of psychological insight, poor use of language, inability to develop characters, and misunderstanding of the structure of tragedy—made acceptable tragedy all but impossible. Only Barker, with *Superstition*, provided an outstanding exception. As time passed less interest would be shown in tragedy as American playwrights discovered a strength in creating melodrama, which would give their work worldwide significance.

Caught up in the fervor and excitement of the new nation, most American playwrights felt only an obligation to entertain with an underlying current of moral instruction. If they did have something to say, it was generally to be patriotic or to love freedom. Nationalism was ever the dominant force in American drama, appearing even in dramas with foreign settings such as Wright's *Altorf*, and plays on historical subjects or ones emphasizing the Yankee character were among the most popular of the period. Even those few plays such as *André* or *Superstition* which do have thought-provoking themes present their ideas against a nationalistic backdrop. Mainly, however, through 1828 the American dramatist, having endured the worst of the Puritan strictures and gotten around them, was interested in entertaining the audiences. Intellectual stimulation would have to wait; American playwrights needed encouragement even to exist. There were everywhere sufficient prejudices and objections that it was not to their advantage to create additional conflicts or to make themselves controversial. Some did, of course, and their plays are frequently more interesting to the social historian than to the drama critic. By 1828 the necessary encouragement was appearing—from some critics, from the play contests, from the new atmosphere of nationalism. Although there were still obstacles in all directions, changes in the democratic society and in the theatre generally benefited the American dramatist. It would be a slow process—years, decades—but the future for the American dramatist was looking brighter.

NOTES

1. Introduction

1. See a pioneering essay on Indian treaties as "theatre-in-life" by A. Drummond and Richard Moody, *Quarterly Journal of Speech* 39 (1953):15–22. Laurence C. Wroth ("The Indian Treaty as Literature," *Yale Review* [Summer 1928]) supports a view of the Indian treaty as dramatic literature.

2. "The Destruction of Schenectady," *New York Historical Society Collections for 1869*, pp. 165–72, reprinted in Richard M. Dorson, *America Begins: Early American Writing* (Bloomington: Indiana University Press, 1971), pp. 314–20.

2. Colonial Attitudes and the Beginnings of Drama in America

1. Quoted by Robert E. McNicall, "The Caloosa Village *Tequesta*: A Miami of the Sixteenth Century," *Tequesta* 1 (March 1941):11–20.

2. See *Massachusetts Historical Society Proceedings* 49 (December 1915):99–106.

3. For publications against games and plays (1699) and the establishment of Watch and Ward societies (1699) see the *Ancient Charter, Colony, and Province Laws of Massachusetts Bay* (Boston: Thomas Watt for the Commonwealth, 1814), chap. 63, pp. 334–38, and chap. 65; for the 1712 Act Against Intemperance, Immorality, and Profaneness, and For Reformation of Manners, which became the prototype for all censorship laws in the United States, see ibid., chap. 105, pp. 395–99.

4. Joseph Tisdale, *Speech . . . Against the Bill then before the House of Representatives for preventing Stage Plays, and Other Theatrical Entertainments* (Boston, 1767).

5. Reprinted in Arthur Hornblow, *A History of the Theatre in America from its Beginnings to the Present Time*, vol. 1 (Philadelphia: J.B. Lippincott, 1919), p. 102.

6. For example, David Douglass' "grateful thanks" in the *South Carolina Gazette and Country Journal* (August 24, 1773).

3. Experiments with the Drama in Colonial America

1. *Historical Magazine* 9 (April 1865):118.

2. See [Anthony Aston], *The Fool's Opera, or The Taste of the Age. Written by Mat Madley. And Performed by His Company in Oxford. to which is Prefix'd, A Sketch of the Author's Life, Written by Himself* (London, 1731), pp. 20–21.

3. Frank Pierce Hill, *American Plays Printed 1714–1830: A Bibliographical Record* (Stanford, Calif.: Stanford University Press, 1934).

4. Printed in the *Virginia Gazette*, nos. 37–39 (1737).

5. "Printed at Moropolis since 1ˢᵗ August, 1714." The unique copy remains in the collection of the Huntington Library, San Marino, California.

6. For a more detailed discussion of Hunter's political problems and adversaries in the situation which prompted the writing of *Androboros*, see Lawrence H. Leder, "Robert Hunter's *Androboros*," *Bulletin of the New York Public Library* 68 (March 1964):153–60.

7. Quoted in Lawrence H. Leder, "Cadwallader Colden's Letters on Smith's History," *New York Historical Society Collections for 1868,* p. 202. Colden's comments suggest that people either saw the play performed or read it.

8. Smith provided considerable support for the theatre in his *American Magazine*, where he praised the profession of acting and even dreamed of a theatre established by law.

9. Originally written by Thompson in 1740 and revised by Mallet in 1751. Smith commented on his production in the *Pennsylvania Gazette* (January 20, 27, February 3, 10, 1757), saying that "the Youth having from Time to Time delivered proper Speeches and Acted Parts of our best dramatic Pieces, before large Audiences with general Applause" chose the *Masque of Alfred*.

10. *The Paxton Boys. A Farce. Translated from the original French, by a native of Donegall* (Philadelphia, 1764). Anthony Armbuster printed and sold this play whose popularity is suggested by second and third editions printed the same year.

11. The identity of the author of this play is not beyond question although Thomas Forrest is generally accepted as the author. John Leacock, the author of *The Fall of British Tyranny*, has been considered a possible author; Andrew Barton, whose name appears on the title page, has proved difficult to identify as a playwright.

12. See W. B. Cairns, "American Drama of the 18th Century," *Dial* 59 (July 15, 1915):60–62.

13. *Pennsylvania Gazette* (February 17, 1773).

4. Drama and the "War of Belles Lettres"

1. See the extensive pamphlet bibliography in Thomas R. Adams, ed., "American Independence: The Growth of an Idea," *Publications of the Colonial Society of Massachusetts* 43 (1956):17–202.

2. Quoted in Katherine Anthony, *First Lady of the Revolution: The Life of Mercy Otis Warren* (New York: Doubleday, 1958), p. 120.

3. Quoted in Alice Brown, *Mercy Warren* (New York: Charles Scribner's Sons, 1896), p. 178. Memorandum in the Massachusetts Historical Society.

4. Quoted in Brown, p. 164. Two scenes of the play were published in the *Boston Gazette* (January 23, 1775). John Adams mentions in a letter (May 21, 1775) from Philadelphia that "one half the Group is printed here, from a copy printed in Jamaica." Its first complete form as a pamphlet was published in Boston on April 3, 1775; later editions appeared in Philadelphia and New York.

5. Quoted in Anthony, pp. 243–44.

6. Arthur Hobson Quinn (*A History of the American Drama from the Beginning to the Civil War* [New York: Appleton-Century-Crofts, 1943, p. 40]) assembled a key to the characters in the play, which originally appeared without such an interpretation because one was obviously not needed at that time:

Lord Chief Justice Hazelrod	Peter Oliver
Judge Meagre	Foster Hutchinson
Brigadier Hateall	Timothy Ruggles
Hum Humburg, Esq.	John Irving, Jr.
Sir Sparrow Spendall	William Pepperell
Hector Mushroom	Colonel John Murray
Beau Trumps	Daniel Leonard
Dick, the Publican	Richard Lechmere
Simple Sapling, Esq.	Nathaniel Ray Thomas
Monsieur de Francois	James Boutineau
Crusty Crowbar, Esq.	Josiah Edson
Dupe, Secretary of State	Thomas Flucker
Scriblerius Fribble	Harrison Gray
Commodore Batteau	Joshua Loring
Collateralis, a new-made judge	William Browne
Sylla	General Gage

7. George O. Seilhamer, *History of the American Theatre* (Philadelphia: Globe Printing House, 1889), vol. 2, p. 20.

8. The dramatis personae were identified in the printed play as follows:

Captain Bashaw	Admiral Graves
Puff	General William Howe
Lord Dapper	Lord Percy
Shallow	Grant
Dupe	General Clinton
Meagre	Harrison Gray
Surly	Timothy Ruggles
Brigadier Paunch	William Brattle
Bonny	John Murray
Simple	Josiah Edson

9. Quoted in Brown, p. 237.

10. *Debates* is in the *Hayaud Pamphlets*, vol. 44, Library of Congress.

11. In June, 1776, it was published as a pamphlet in Philadelphia.

12. Moses Coit Tyler, *Literary History of the American Revolution* (New York: G. P. Putnam's Sons, 1897), vol. 2, p. 198 (note).

13. *Some Notes Towards an Essay on the Beginnings of American Literature, 1606–1789* (n.p., 1893), pp. 20–21.

14. From "The AUTHOR to the PUBLIC" printed with *The Death of General Montgomery, in Storming the City of Quebec* (Norwich, Conn.: Trumbull, 1777).

15. *A Farce. As acted at C——t H——l. Which points out a variety of characters that have arisen in the political uproar, since the confusion of distructions.*

Together with other scenes for the amusement of the curious (Newport, R.I., 1779).

16. Robert Munford, *A Collection of Plays and Poems, by the late Colonel Robert Munford, of Mecklenburg, in the State of Virginia* (Petersburg, Va., 1798).

17. The libretto was published in the *Freeman's Journal* (December 19, 1781).

5. Early Dramatists of the New Republic

1. William Dunlap, *History of the American Theatre* (New York: J. and J. Harper, 1832), vol. 1, p. 136.

2. Hector St. Jean de Crèvecoeur, *Letters from an American Farmer* (New York: E. P. Dutton, 1912), p. 43–44.

3. See, in particular, chapters 45, 47, 51, and 53 of Part 2.

4. The play was printed in New York in September, 1789, and reprinted in the *Massachusetts Review* (October and November 1789).

5. Some of the scenic action was described in a program as follows: "During the Finale, A Transparency descends, and an Eagle is seen suspending a Crown of Laurel over the Head of General Washington with this motto, 'Immortality to Washington.'" Reprinted in George C. D. Odell, *Annals of the New York Stage* (New York: Columbia University Press, 1927), vol. 2, p. 182.

6. Ibid., p. 51.

7. For information on panoramas and dioramas in America see "Moving (Dioramic) Experiences," *All the Year Round* 17 (March 23, 1867):304–7; and the bibliography of Richard C. Wickman, *An Evaluation of the Employment of Panoramic Scenery in the Nineteenth-Century Theatre*, Ph.D. diss., Ohio State University, 1961.

The terms *diorama* and *panorama* require comment. As a theatrical form the panorama was invented in 1787 by Robert Barker of Scotland and was a large, stationary, circular painting requiring for exhibition a special building and special lighting effects. The first panorama, opening in London in 1794, exhibited a painting sixteen feet high and fifty feet in diameter. The diorama was invented by the Frenchman L. J. M. Daguerre in 1822 and is a painting, viewed from one point, which achieves a transparent effect through a regulation of the color and intensity of the light shining on it. As time passed, the term *panorama* encompassed the dioramic effect, and the two terms were used interchangeably.

8. *Irish Shield and Monthly Hilenan: A Historic, Literary, and Dramatic Journal* 1 (January 1829):30–31.

9. "A Reminiscence of George Frederick Cooke," *Spirit of the Times* 18 (July 15, 1848):245.

10. Quoted in William W. Clapp, Jr., *A Record of the Boston Stage* (Boston: James Munroe, 1853), p. 42.

11. John Bernard, *Retrospection of America, 1797–1811*, ed. Mrs. Bayle

Bernard (New York: Harpers, 1887), p. 365. This play may have been an adaptation of J. T. Allingham's *Hearts of Oak*, which played at the Park in New York in 1804, or its mention may reflect a misunderstanding by Bernard.

12. Odell, vol. 2, p. 411.

13. Quoted in Clapp, p. 54.

14. Burk's letter is reproduced in Dunlap, vol. 1, pp. 313–15.

15. Quoted in Clapp, p. 53.

16. Quoted in Dunlap, vol. 1, pp. 312–13.

17. Odell, vol. 2, p. 60; Arthur Hornblow, *A History of the Theatre in America* (J. B. Lippincott, 1919) vol. 1, p. 240.

18. Odell, vol. 1, p. 460.

6. Meeting the Demands of a Growing Theatre, 1783–1800

1. See the minutes of the Pennsylvania General Assembly (February 16, 1789).

2. See Ota Thomas, "Student Dramatic Activities at Yale College during the Eighteenth Century," *Theatre Annual* (1944):47–59.

3. In his *Nouveau Voyage dans L'Amerique Septemtrionale, En L'Année 1781* (Philadelphia, 1782), p. 25, L'Abbé Claude C. Robin writes: "ils sont jouer à leurs Elèves des Tragédies; le sujet en est toujours national: tel que l'incendie de Charles-Town, la prise de Burgoyne, la trahison d'Arnold." Robin also noted that the plays enjoyed "plus d'effet" than did English or French plays.

4. William Dunlap, *History of the American Theatre* (New York: J. and J. Harper, 1832), vol. 1, p. 213.

5. Dunlap, vol. 1, p. 305.

6. The only manuscript copy of this play is owned by Colonial Williamsburg, Virginia.

7. Oscar Wegelin, *Early American Plays, 1714–1830* (New York: The Dunlap Society, 1900), p. 18. Wegelin suggests that the author may have been Nathaniel Niles because the first two stanzas of his poem, *The American Hero,* appear in the play.

8. Dunlap, vol. 1, p. 302.

9. *Monthly Anthology* 2 (1805):531.

10. M. B. Peladeau ("Royall Tyler's Other Plays," *New England Quarterly* 40 [March 1967]:48–60) is mistaken in his argument that Tyler wrote this play, as were the contemporary critics such as "Candour" who implied that Tyler was the author. Using the pseudonym "Philo Americanus," Mrs. Murray claims the play in an introduction to the published version: "The author of *The Medium* . . . now entitles her play *Virtue Triumphant.*"

11. Judith S. Murray [Constantia], *The Gleaner, A Miscellaneous Production, in Three Volumes,* vol. 1 (Boston: I. Thomas and E. T. Andrews, 1798), p. 230.

12. Published in Caleb Bingham, *Columbian Orator* (Boston, 1810), pp. 57–58. Memorable lines are as follows:

You'd scarce expect one my age
To speak in public on the stage;
And if I chance to fall below
Demosthenes or Cicero,
Don't view me with a critic's eye,
But pass my imperfections by.
Large streams from little fountains flow,
Tall oaks from little acorns grow;

13. The *Philadelphia Gazette* (February 24, 1796) carried Murdock's "A Fair Recital of Facts." Subsequent responses were published in this newspaper and in others along with Murdock's rebuttal and insistence that managers "trample upon native productions."

7. "A Motley Spectacle": Attempting to Focus the Drama of a People, 1801–1814

1. Forty-five of these were pamphlet sermons or Fourth-of-July orations. Fred L. Pattee, *The First Century of American Literature, 1770–1870* (New York: D. Appleton-Century, 1935), p. 180.

2. Fisher Ames, "The Dangers of American Liberty" (1805), *Works of Fisher Ames* (Boston: Little, Brown, 1854), vol. 2, p. 382.

3. See eleven critical articles by Barker, "The Drama," *Democratic Press* (December 18, 1816–February 19, 1817).

4. For a discussion of the varied approaches to nationalism in America see Benjamin T. Spencer, "The Search for National Modes and Principles (1783–1814)," *The Quest for Nationalism* (Syracuse: Syracuse University Press, 1957), chap. 2, pp. 25–72.

5. Quotations from "The American Stage," *Thespian Mirror*, no. 13 (March 22, 1806):104–7.

6. From "*The Gamester* and *Sprigs of Laurel*," *Something* 1 (December 16, 1809):10.

7. "The Theatre," *Stranger* 1 (January 29, 1814):249.

8. "Introduction to the Dramatic Censor," *Mirror of Taste and Dramatic Censor* 1 (January 1810):51.

9. Washington Irving, *The Letters of Jonathan Oldstyle* (1802), "Letter No. V," introduced by Stanley T. Williams (New York: Columbia University Press, 1941), p. 37.

10. George C. D. Odell, *Annals of the New York Stage* (New York: Columbia University Press, 1927), vol. 2, p. 319.

11. Barker described his plays in some detail in a letter written at the request of William Dunlap, who included it in his *History of the American Theatre* (New York: J. and J. Harper, 1832), vol. 2, pp. 308–16. Quotations in this paragraph and in the following paragraph are from that letter.

12. An English play, *Pocahontas; or, The Indian Princess*, produced at Drury

Lane on December 15, 1820, was not a version of Barker's work. See Dunlap, p. 314, and P. H. Earnhart, "The First American Play in England?" *American Literature* 31 (November 1959):326–29.

13. "From the New York Courier—The Critic, No. 1. American Literature," *National Register* 1 (June 22, 1816):258–59.

14. The two plays exist in the Harvard Library in manuscript form, which seems to have been ready for the printer. The title page for the first play reads as follows: "*The Embargo*, A Comedy in Three Acts, written by ME, Philadelphia. Printed for the Amateurs by . . . . . MDCCCVIII." The playscripts are identified at Harvard as MS Am 1097 and MS Am 1097.1.

15. Letter in the Huntington Library, San Marino, California, identified as HM 22382.

16. Reviews appeared in *Dramatic Censor* (January 1810):461–66; *Something* 1 (January 13, 1810):137–40; and *Omnium Catherum* 1 (January 1810):144.

17. White's painting of a scene from the Revolution, *Defense of Ft. Moultrie,* now hangs in the Senate Gallery in Washington, D.C.

18. Two manuscripts, dated 1805 and 1806, are now in the possession of the South Carolina Historical Society.

19. An 1829 manuscript copy bearing the original title is now in the possession of the South Carolina Historical Society.

20. Quoted in Abraham Moise. "A Memoir of His Life," *A Selection from the Miscellaneous History of the Late Isaac Harby, Esq.* (Charleston, 1829). The play was never published.

21. Clipping Collection, Enthoven Collection, Victoria and Albert Museum, Kensington, London.

22. Terminology is frequently a problem in discussing early American drama. For writers at this time, length rather than structure or plot and character development generally determined farce from comedy.

23. Odell, vol. 2, p. 424.

24. Odell, vol. 2, p. 178.

8. Progress and Prejudice: American Drama, 1815–1828

1. "Drama," *National Register* 1 (July 27, 1816):339.

2. Adrienne Koch and William Peden, eds., *The Selected Writings of John and John Quincy Adams* (New York: Alfred Knopf, 1946), pp. 340–41.

3. These comments appear in one of a series of articles which Neal wrote for *Blackwood's Magazine* 16 (October 1824):567; ibid. 17 (January 1825):48.

4. *American Quarterly Review* 1 (June 1827):331–57. The ostensible purpose of the essay was a review of Dunlap's *The Father of an Only Child* and Barker's *Marmion* and *Superstition,* which the writer considered the best America had to offer.

5. "Editor's Cabinet—American Drama," *National Register* 4 (July 12, 1817): 31.

6. *Critic* 1 (November 22, 1828):62.

7. *National Register* 4 (July 12, 1817):30-32.

8. *Boston Weekly Magazine* 1 (January 25, 1817):62.

9. "The Theatre," *Boston Recorder* 11 (October 6, 1826):159.

10. "Morality of the Stage—No. 1," *Correspondent* 1 (March 10, 1827): 100-101.

11. *New York Mirror* 5 (February 16, 1828):255.

12. "For the Portfolio," *Port Folio* 3 (March 19, 1803):91.

13. *Minerva* 1 (May 4, 1822):29-30.

14. "The Drama," *National Register* 7 (April 10, 1819):225-27.

15. Anne Hollingsworth Wharton, *Social Life in the Early Republic* (Philadelphia: J. B. Lippincott, 1902), p. 200.

16. See R. Carlyle Buley, *The Old Northwest Pioneer Period, 1815-1840* (Bloomington: Indiana University Press, 1950), vol. 1, pp. 344-46; and ibid., vol. 2, pp. 573-75.

17. John Bernard, *Retrospections of America 1797-1811* (New York: Harper and Brothers, 1887), pp. 36-7.

18. See Oscar Wegelin, "Micah Hawkins and the Saw-Mill," *The Magazine of History with Notes and Queries* 32, No. 3, extra no. 127 (1927):153-210.

19. The New York *Mirror* (March 27, 1824) gives a brief plot. Another outline of *The Avenger's Vow; or, The Haunt of the Banditti* appears in *Ladies Garland* 1 (May 22, 1824):57. Journeying from Madrid to his castle, a gentleman is slain by bandits who keep his children and a servant prisoners in the castle. When two cavaliers take shelter there for the night, the servant as avenger sees his chance and, with the help of the forces of the Inquisition, frees the children. It was, according to the critic, "a terror to evil doers and a praise to them that do well"; it was also "powerfully filled with incident, variety, and interest."

20. "Dramatic Notes," *Lyceum* 2 (November 1827):247.

21. Odell, vol. 3, pp. 370-71.

22. *Theatrical and Literary Chit-Chat* 14 (January, 1819):80.

23. Odell (vol. 3, p. 181) gives the title as *Briar Cliff; or, A Picture of Former Times*; Quinn (*A History of American Drama from the Civil War to the Present Day* [New York: Appleton-Century-Crofts, 1943], p. 433) lists *Briar Cliff; or, A Tale of the Revolution*. The play was published in *The Magazine of History with Notes and Queries* 49, no. 2, extra no. 194 (1935):22-57, as *Briar Cliff; or, Scenes of the Revolution*.

24. Letter to John Stuart Skinner, March 23, 1827, the Huntington Library (HM 25494), San Marino, California.

25. Ibid.

26. *The North American; or, Weekly Journal of Politics, Science and Literature* 1 (June 28, 1827):47.

27. William Dunlap, *A History of the American Theatre* (New York: J. and J. Harper, 1832), vol. 2, p. 322.

28. Adams read the work aloud and wrote to Judah on June 25, 1822: "I have read your horrible *Odofriede*." Although he found marks of "genius and talent," he did not approve such verse which, to his mind, diminished "human happiness" by showing the horrors in the mind of man. For similar reasons, Adams did not enjoy *Hamlet* or *Macbeth*, and he advised Judah to change his habits. See William Van Lennep, "John Adams to a Young Playwright: An Unpublished Letter to Samuel Judah," *Harvard Library Bulletin* 1 (Winter 1947):117–8.

29. Dunlap, vol. 2, p. 316.

30. "American Drama," *American Quarterly Review* 1 (June 1827):340; James Rees, "Dramatic Authors of America," *Dramatic Mirror and Literary Companion* 1 (August 21, 1841):9.

31. Reviewed in *The Ariel: A Literary and Critical Gazette* 2 (May 17, 1828): 12.

32. Included in Abraham Moise, *A Selection from the Miscellaneous Writing of the Late Isaac Harby, Esq.* (Charleston, 1829), pp. 248–61.

33. Letter to John Pierpont, November 15, 1819. Collection in the Pierpont-Morgan Library, New York City. For further commentary read Neal's autobiography, *Wandering Reflections of a Somewhat Busy Life* (Boston, 1869).

34. *The Yankee,* nos. 11–15 (March 12–June 18, 1828).

35. Letter to John Pierpont, June 29, 1819. Collection in the Pierpont-Morgan Library, New York City.

36. Quoted in Charles Tabb Hazelrigg, *American Literary Pioneer: A Biographical Study of James A. Hillhouse* (New York: Bookman Associates, 1953), p. 237.

37. "The Drama," *Critic* 1 (November 13, 1828):62–64.

38. Odell, vol. 3, p. 151.

39. J. F., "For *The Ariel—The Usurper*," *The Ariel: A Semimonthly Literary and Miscellaneous Gazette* 3 (May 30, 1829):22. McHenry was the object of another ironic review in the *North American Magazine* 4 (May, 1834):53–57.

40. See Frances Wright D'Arusmont, *Biography and Notes* (Boston, 1848).

41. Ibid. A comment by J. Miles, a fellow townsman of Dundee.

42. Quoted in Grace Overmyer, *America's First Hamlet* (New York: New York University Press, 1957), p. 48.

43. Letters in the Houghton Library, Harvard University. Five, dated London, 1818, explore this situation.

44. Years later Payne was still haunted by the charges. See letter to Sumner Lincoln Fairchild, Philadelphia author and journalist, November 7, 1834, Houghton Library, Harvard University.

45. From the *Petersburg Intelligence* (April 20, 1819); *"Brutus; or The Fall of Tarquin,"* *National Register* 7 (April 24, 1819):268.

46. Payne chose his plays well. The popularity of Ducange's play may be recognized in the contemporary doll-puppet version, one scene of which is permanently exhibited in the Folklore Museum of the Citadel, Besançon, France.

47. With particular reference to *Adeline,* Payne's careful attention to the "ensemble" acting, the printing, and the advertising of his work is shown in a

letter to Robert W. Elliston, Theatre Royal, Drury Lane, London from Paris, January 16, 1822. Anxious for success, Payne wrote: "There is nothing, either in writing or acting, so difficult to attain as that finish which seems to work without effort, & which makes every body exclaim 'Bless me! I'm sure I could do it if I should try.'" Letter from the private collection of Professor Peter Coulson, Southwest Texas State University, San Marcos, Texas.

48. Correspondence indicates that Irving was very kind to Payne: he worked with Payne on plays, helped him with London theatre managers, and, for this play, suggested a title change to *Charles & Rochester; or, Waggery at Wapping* (letter, November 26, 1823). By early 1824 (letter, January 31, 1824) Irving stated that he could write no more for the theatre. See Thatcher T. Payne Luquer, "Correspondence of Washington Irving and John Howard Payne," *Scribner's* 48 (October and November, 1910):461–82, 597–616.

49. Pierre M. Irving, *The Life and Letters of Washington Irving*, vol. 2, rev. ed. (New York: G. P. Putnam, 1885), p. 26.

50. The other plays were *Azenda, Married and Single, The Mother's Curse*, and *The Waggoners*.

51. Clipping Collection in Enthoven Collection, Victoria and Albert Museum, Kensington, London.

52. Ibid.

53. Quoted by Gabriel Harrison, *John Howard Payne: Dramatist, Poet, Actor* (Philadelphia: J. B. Lippincott, 1885), p. 134.

9. Wanted: American Dramatists

1. "The New York Stage. The New Tragedy of *Metamora*—A Bird's Eye View of Mr. Forrest's Performance," *Irish Shield and Monthly Hilenan: A Historic, Literary, and Dramatic Journal* 10 (December 1829):467.

2. "The Drama," *Boston Lyceum* (February 1827):103.

3. Clipping Collection in Enthoven Collection, Victoria and Albert Museum, Kensington, London.

4. *The Ariel: A Semimonthly Literary and Miscellaneous Gazette* 4 (May 15, 1830):13.

5. Ibid.

6. Quoted in Curtis Dahl, *Robert Montgomery Bird* (New York: Twayne, 1963), p. 69.

7. "Dramatic Authors of America," *Dramatic Mirror and Literary Companion* 1 (August 28, 1841):17.

8. *The Ariel: A Literary and Critical Gazette* 2 (June 14, 1828):32. The essay begins, "A drama founded on Irving's sketch, *Rip Van Winkle*, has been presented before the honest burgomasters of Albany."

9. See Molly N. Ramshaw, "Jump, Jim Crow! A Biographical Sketch of Thomas D. Rice (1808–1860)," *Theatre Annual* 17 (1960):36–47.

SELECTED BIBLIOGRAPHY

The books, articles, and microforms are listed (a) to provide the reader with the major sources used in preparing this volume and (b) to suggest additional reading material. Not all material cited in the notes is included in the bibliography.

Cultural and Historical Background

Adams, James Truslow. *Revolutionary New England, 1691–1776.* Boston: Atlantic Monthly Press, 1923.

Adams, Henry. *A History of the United States of America During the Administrations of Jefferson and Madison.* 9 vols. New York: Charles Scribner's Sons, 1889–1891.

Bancroft, Hubert H. *History of Arizona and New Mexico.* Works, vol. 17. San Francisco: The History Company, 1889.

Bridenbaugh, Carl and Jessica. *Rebels and Gentlemen Philadelphia in the Age of Franklin.* New York: Reynal and Hitchcock, 1942.

Buley, R. Carlyle. *The Old Northwest Pioneer Period, 1815–1840,* vol. 1. Bloomington: Indiana University Press, 1950.

Dwight, Timothy. *Travels in New England and New York.* 4 vols. London: William Baynes and Son, 1823.

Ewen, David. *Panorama of Popular American Music.* Englewood, N. J.: Prentice-Hall, 1957.

Gummere, Richard M. *The American Mind and the Classical Tradition.* Cambridge, Mass.: Harvard University Press, 1963.

Holliday, Carl. *The Wit and Humor of Colonial Days, 1607–1800.* Philadelphia: J. B. Lippincott, 1912.

Hollingsworth, Anne. *Social Life in the Early Republic.* Philadelphia: J. B. Lippincott, 1902.

Mates, Julian. *The American Musical Stage Before 1800.* New Brunswick, N. J.: Rutgers University Press, 1962.

Mather, Cotton. *A Cloud of Witnesses.* New York, 1700.

————. *Magnalia Christi Americana,* vol. 2, books 5 and 6. 1702. Reprint. Hartford: Silas Andrews, 1820.

Morison, Samuel Eliot. *The Intellectual Life of Colonial New England.* New York: New York University Press, 1956.

Morison, Samuel Eliot and Henry Steele Commager. *The Growth of the American Republic,* vol. 1. New York: Oxford University Press, 1950.

Pattee, Fred L. *The First Century of American Literature, 1770–1870.* New York: D. Appleton-Century, 1935.

Quinn, Arthur Hobson, ed. *The Literature of the American People.* New York: Appleton-Century-Crofts, 1951.

Samuel Sewall's Diary, 1674–1729. Edited by M. Halsey Thomas. New York: Farrar, Straus and Giroux, 1973.

Sonneck, Oscar G. *Early Opera in America.* New York: Schirmer, 1915.

Spencer, Benjamin T. *The Quest for Nationality.* Syracuse, N. Y.: Syracuse University Press, 1957.

Wise, Jennings C. *Ye Kingdome of Accawmacke on the Eastern Shore of Virginia in the Seventeenth Century.* Baltimore: Regional, 1967.

Wright, Louis B. *The Atlantic Frontier.* New York: Alfred A. Knopf, 1947.

Wright, Thomas Goddard. *Literary Culture in Early New England, 1620–1730.* New York: Russell and Russell, 1966.

Theatre History

[Aston, Anthony.] *The Fool's Opera; or, The Taste of Age. Written by Mat Medley. And Performed by his Company in Oxford, to which is Prefix'd a Sketch of the Author's Life. Written by Himself.* London, 1731.

Bernard, John. *Retrospections of America, 1797–1811.* Edited by Mrs. Bayle Bernard. New York, 1887.

Clapp, William W., Jr. *A Record of the Boston Stage.* Boston: James Monroe, 1853.

Culp, Ralph Borden. "Drama—and—Theater in the American Revolution." *Speech Monographs* 32 (March 1965):79–86.

Dunlap, William. *History of the American Theatre.* 2 vols. New York: J. and J. Harper, 1832.

Hill, George H. *Scenes from the Life of an Actor.* New York, 1853.

Hornblow, Arthur. *A History of the Theatre in America from Its Beginnings to the Present Time.* 2 vols. Philadelphia: J. B. Lippincott, 1919.

Mathews, Mrs. *Memoirs of Charles Mathews Comedian,* vol. 3. London, 1839.

Moreland, James. "The Theatre in Portland in the 18th Century." *New England Quarterly* 11 (June 1938):331–42.

Odell, George C. D. *Annals of the New York Stage,* vols. 1, 2, and 3. New York: Columbia University Press, 1927.

Pollock. John Clark. *The Philadelphia Theatre in the Eighteenth Century.* Philadelphia: University of Pennsylvania Press, 1933.

Rankin, Hugh F. *The Theatre of Colonial America.* Chapel Hill: University of North Carolina Press, 1965.

Wemyss, Francis Courtney. *Chronology of the American Stage from 1752–1852.* New York: W. Taylor, 1852.

Willis, Eola. *The Charleston Stage in the XVIII Century.* Columbia, S. C.: State, 1924.

Wright, Richardson. *Revels in Jamaica 1682–1838.* New York: Dodd, Mead, 1937.

Drama: Bibliography, History, and Criticism

Several of the historical and critical volumes on individual dramatists have helpful bibliographies. For further bibliography see Walter J. Meserve, *American Drama to 1900: A Guide to Information Sources* (Detroit: Gale Research, forthcoming).

Blair, John. *The New Creature Delineated in a Sermon.* Philadelphia, 1767.

Cairns, W. B. "American Drama of the 18th Century," *Dial* 59 (July 15, 1915): 60–62.

Colby, Elbridge. "Early American Comedy." *Bulletin of the New York Public Library* 23 (July 1919):3–11.

Cutspear, W. *Dramatic Rights: of Private Theatricals and Pic-nic Suppers Justified by Fair Argument.* London: T. Burton, 1902.

Edwards, John. *Warning to Sinners; or an address to all Play-actors, Play-hunters, Legislators, Governors, Magistrates, Clergy, Churchmen, Deists, and the World at Large.* New York, 1812.

Ellis, Milton. "Puritans and the Drama." *American Notes & Queries* 2 (July 1942):64.

Ewing, Robert. *The Theatrical Contributions of "Jacques" to the United States Gazette.* Philadelphia, 1826.

Ford, Paul Leicester. "The Beginnings of American Dramatic Literature." *New England Magazine*, n.s. 9 (February 1894):673–87.

Gafford, Lucile. "The Boston Stage and the War of 1812." *New England Quarterly* 7 (1934):327–35.

Gallagher, Kent G. *The Foreigner in Early American Drama.* The Hague: Mouton, 1966.

Gay, F. L. "The First American Play." *Nation* 88 (February 11, 1909):136.

Havens, Daniel F. *The Columbian Muse of Comedy: The Development of a Native Tradition in Early American Social Comedy, 1787–1845.* Carbondale and Edwardsville: Southern Illinois University Press, 1973.

Henry, T. Charlton. *An Inquiry into the Consistency of Popular Amusements with a Profession of Christianity.* Charleston, S. C., 1825.

Hill, Frank Pierce. *American Plays, Printed 1714–1830:A Bibliographical Record.* Stanford. Calif.: Stanford University Press, 1934.

Hill, Richard. *An Address to Persons of Fashion, containing some particulars relating to Balls; and a Few Occasional Hints Concerning Playhouses.* Boston, 1770.

Hodge, Francis. *Yankee Theatre: The Image of America on Stage, 1825–1850.* Austin: University of Texas Press, 1964.

Keach, Benjamin. *War with the Devil.* New York, 1707.

Law, Robert A. "Notes on Some Early American Dramas." *University of Texas Studies in English* 5 (1925):96–100.

Mayorga, Margaret G. *A Short History of the American Drama.* New York: Dodd, Mead, 1932.

Meserve, Walter J. *An Outline History of American Drama.* Totowa, N. J.: Littlefield, Adams, 1965.

Moses, Montrose J. *The American Dramatist.* Boston: Little, Brown, 1925.

Porter, Jane. *A Defence of the Profession of an Actor.* London, 1800.

Quinn, Arthur Hobson. *A History of the American Drama from the Beginning to the Civil War.* New York: Appleton-Century-Crofts, 1943.

Rees, James. *The Dramatic Authors of America.* Philadelphia: G. B. Zieber, 1845.

Ridpath, George. *The Stage Condemn'd.* N.p., 1698.

Theatrical Comicallities, Whimsicalities, Oddities and Drolleries. N.p., 1828.

The Thespian Preceptor; or, A Full Display of the Scenic Art. Boston, 1810.

Tisdale, Joseph. *Speech . . . Against the Bill then before the House of Representatives for Presenting Stage Plays, and Other Theatrical Entertainments.* Boston, 1767.

Watson, Charles S. *Antebellum Charleston Dramatists.* University, Ala.: University of Alabama Press, 1976.

Wegelin, Oscar. *Early American Plays, 1714–1830.* New York: Dunlap Society, 1900.

Selected Works on Particular Dramatists

Barker, James Nelson

Kuhn, John G. "James Nelson Barker's Play of Ideas in 1812 and 1824." Ph.D. dissertation, University of Pennsylvania, 1970.

Muser, Paul H. *James Nelson Barker.* Philadelphia: University of Pennsylvania Press, 1919.

"The Drama." 11 essays. *Dramatic Press* (December 18, 1816–February 19, 1817).

Bird, Robert Montgomery

Dahl, Curtis. *Robert Montgomery Bird.* New York: Twayne, 1963.

Foust, Clement E. *The Life and Dramatic Works of Robert Montgomery Bird.* New York: Knickerbocker Press, 1919.

Brackenridge, Hugh Henry

Newlin, C. M. *The Life and Writings of Hugh Henry Brackenridge.* Princeton, N. J.: Princeton University Press, 1932.

Burk, John Daly

Campbell, Charles, ed. *Some Materials to Serve for a Brief Memoir of John Daly Burk.* Albany, N. Y., 1868.

Shulin, Joseph I. "John Daly Burk: Playwright of Libertarianism." *Bulletin of the New York Public Library* 65 (September 1961):451–63.

Wyatt, Edward A. "John Daly Burk: Patriot-Playwright-Historian." *Southern Sketches,* no. 7, first series. Charlottesville, Va.: Historical, 1936.

Doddridge, Joseph

Doddridge, Joseph. *Notes of the Settlement and Indian Wars, of the Western Parts of Virginia and Pennsylvania, from the Year 1763 until the year 1783 inclusive.* 1824. Reprint. Alfred Williams, ed., with a memoir of the author by his daughter. New York: B. Franklin, 1973.

Dunlap, William

Canary, Robert H. *William Dunlap.* New York: Twayne, 1970.

Coad, Oral S. *William Dunlap: A Study of His Life and Works and of His Place in Contemporary Culture.* New York: Dunlap Society, 1917.

Moramarco, Fred. "The Early Drama Criticism of William Dunlap." *American Literature* 40 (1968):9–14.

Godfrey, Thomas

Carlson, C. L. "Thomas Godfrey in England." *American Literature* 7 (November 1935):302–9.

Carlson, C. L. "A Further Note on Thomas Godfrey in England." *American Literature* 9 (March 1937):73–76.

Henderson, Archibald. "Thomas Godfrey: Carolina Days." *Everywoman's Magazine* 1 (1917):19–24.

Wolf, H. B. "Thomas Godfrey: Eighteenth-Century Chaucerian." *American Literature* 12 (January 1941):486–90.

Harby, Isaac

Moise, Abraham. "A Memoir of His Life." *A Selection from the Miscellaneous History of the Late Isaac Harby, Esq.* Charleston, S. C., 1829.

Moise, Lucius Clifton. *Biography of Isaac Harby.* Columbia: University of South Carolina Press, 1931.

Hawkins, Micah

Wegelin, Oscar. "Micah Hawkins and the Saw-Mill." *Magazine of History with Notes and Queries* 33, no. 3, extra no. 127 (1927):153–210.

Hillhouse, James

Hazelrigg, Charles Tabb. *American Literary Pioneer: A Biographical Study of James A. Hillhouse.* New York: Bookman, 1953.

"Review of James A. Hillhouse's *Dramas, Discourses, and Other Pieces.*" *Englander* 16 (November 1858):705–41.

Hopkinson, Francis

Hastings, George. *The Life and Works of Francis Hopkinson.* Chicago: University of Chicago Press, 1926.

Sonneck, Oscar G. *Francis Hopkinson and John Lyon.* Washington, D. C., 1905.

Humphreys, David

Humphreys, F. L. *The Life and Times of David Humphreys.* 2 vols. New York: G. P. Putnam's Sons, 1917.

Hunter, Robert

Leder, Lawrence H. "Robert Hunter's *Androboros.*" *Bulletin of the New York Public Library* 68 (March 1964):153–60.

Ingersoll, Charles Jared

Meigs, W. M. *The Life of Charles Jared Ingersoll.* 1897. Reprint. New York: Da Capo Press, 1970.

Ioor, William

Simms, William Gilmore. "Our Early Authors and Artists." *Century* 1 (1867): 779–80.

Watson, Charles S. "Jeffersonian Republicanism in William Ioor's *Independence,* the First Play of South Carolina." *South Carolina Historical Magazine* 69 (1968):194–203.

Judah, S. B. H.

Judah, S. B. H. *Gotham and its Gothamites.* New York, 1823.

Leacock, John

Dallett, Francis James, Jr. "John Leacock and *The Fall of British Tyranny.*"

Pennsylvania Magazine of History and Biography 78 (October 1954):456–75.

Lescarbot, Marc

    Lescarbot, Marc. *The Theatre of Neptune in New France.* Translated with Introduction by Harriette Taber Richardson. Boston: Houghton Mifflin, 1927.

Linn, John Blair

    Linn, John Blair. *Miscellaneous Works, Prose and Political.* New York, 1795.

    Linn, John Blair. *Valerian, A Narrative Poem intended, in part, to describe the Early Persecutions of Christians and to Illustrate the Influence of Christianity on the Manners of Nations.* With a Sketch of the Life and Character of the Author (by Charles Brockden Brown). Philadelphia, 1805.

McHenry, James

    Blanc, Robert E. "James McHenry (1785–1845), Playwright and Novelist." Ph.D. dissertation, University of Pennsylvania, 1939.

Munford, Robert

    Baine, Rodney M. *Robert Munford, America's First Comic Dramatist.* Athens: University of Georgia Press, 1967.

    Munford, Robert. *A Collection of Plays and Poems by the Late Colonel Robert Munford of Macklenburg, in the State of Virginia.* Petersburg, Va., 1796.

Murray, Judith S.

    Murray, Judith S. [Constantia]. "Observations of Female Abilities," no. 88, "The Equality of the Sexes," no. 88, and "Panegyric on the Drama," no. 24. *The Gleaner.* Boston: I. Thomas and E. T. Andrews, 1798.

Neal, John

    Neal, John. *Blackwood's Magazine* 16 (October 1824):427; ibid. 16 (November 1824):567; and ibid. 17 (January 1825):48.

    Neal, John. *Wandering Reflections.* Boston: 1869.

Noah, Mordecai M.

    Goldberg, Isaac. *Major Noah: American Jewish Pioneer.* New York: Alfred A. Knopf, 1936.

    Wolf, Simon. *Mordecai Manuel Noah.* Philadelphia: American Jewish Society, 1897.

Payne, John Howard

    Harrison, Gabriel. *John Howard Payne, Dramatist, Poet, Actor, and Author of Home, Sweet Home! His Life and Writings.* Rev. ed. Philadelphia: J. B. Lippincott, 1885.

    Irving, Pierre M. *The Life and Letters of Washington Irving,* vol. 2. Rev. ed. 1883. Reprint. Detroit: Gale Research, 1967.

    Overmeyer, Grace. *America's First Hamlet.* New York: New York University Press, 1957.

    Saxon, A. H. "John Howard Payne, Playwright with a System." *Theatre Notes* 24 (Winter 1969–70):79–84.

Rowson, Susanna Haswell

    Rowson, Susanna. *Mentoria; or, The Young Lady's Friend.* London, 1791.

    Vail, R. W. G. *Susanna Haswell Rowson: The Author of Charlotte Temple: A Bibliographical Study.* Worcester, Mass.: The Society, 1933.

Sawyer, Lemuel

> *Blackbeard.* Facsimile ed. Introduced by Richard Walser. Raleigh, N. C.: State Dept. of Archives and History, 1952.
>
> Sawyer, Lemuel. *The Autobiography of Lemuel Sawyer.* New York, 1844.

Smith, Elihu Hubbard

> Bailey, Marcia E. *A Lesser Hartford Wit: Dr. Elihu Hubbard Smith.* Orono: University of Maine Press, 1928.
>
> Cronin, James E., ed. *The Diary of Elihu Hubbard Smith.* Philadelphia: American Philosophical Society, 1973.

Tucker, St. George

> Laughlin, Haller. "St. George Tucker's *The Wheel of Fortune.*" M.A. thesis, College of William and Mary, 1960.

Tyler, Royall

> Peladeau, Marius B., coll. and ed. *The Prose of Royall Tyler.* Rutland: Vermont Historical Society and Charles E. Tuttle, 1972.
>
> Tanselle, G. Thomas. *Royall Tyler.* Cambridge, Mass.: Harvard University Press, 1967.
>
> Tyler, Mary Palmer. *Grandmother Tyler's Book: The Recollections of Mary Palmer Tyler.* Edited by Helen Tyler Brown and Frederich Tupper. New York: G. P. Putnam's Sons, 1925.

Warren, Mercy Otis

> Anthony, Katherine. *First Lady of the Revolution: The Life of Mercy Otis Warren.* 1958. Reprint. Port Washington, N. Y.: Kennikat Press, 1972.
>
> Brown, Alice. *Mercy Warren.* New York: Charles Scribner's Sons, 1896.
>
> Hutchinson, Maud M. "Mercy Warren, A Study of Her Life and Works." Ph.D. dissertation, American University, 1951.

White, John Blake

> Partridge, Paul W., Jr. "John Blake White: Southern Romantic Painter and Playwright." Ph.D. dissertation, University of Pennsylvania, 1951.
>
> Weidner, Paul R., ed. "The Journal of John Blake White." *South Carolina Historical and Genealogical Magazine* 42 (April 1941):61; and ibid. (July 1941):99, 109.

Woodworth, Samuel

> Coad, Oral S. "The Plays of Samuel Woodworth." *Sewanee Review* 27 (1919): 163–75.

Workman, James

> Watson, Charles S. "A Denunciation on the Stage of Spanish Rule: James Workman's *Liberty in Louisiana* (1804)." *Louisiana History* 2 (Summer 1970):245–58.

Wright (D'Arusmont), Frances

> Perkins, Alice J. *Frances Wright: Free Enquirer.* Philadelphia: Porcupine Press, 1972.
>
> Waterman, W. R. *Frances Wright.* N.p., 1924.
>
> Wright, Frances. *Biography and Notes.* Boston: 1848.
>
> ————. *Views of Society and Manners in America.* 1821. Reprint. Edited by Paul Baker. Cambridge, Mass.: Harvard University Press, 1963.

Collections of Plays

Most of the plays used in this study are available on microprint through Henry W. Wells, ed., *Three Centuries of Drama: American (1714–1830)* (New York: Readex Microprints). William G. Bergquist has provided *Checklist* (New York: Hafner, 1963). Other plays have been obtained through Charles Evans' *American Bibliography*, which was completed to the year 1799. Clifford K. Shipton carried this work through 1800, and Ralph R. Shaw and Richard H. Shoemaker have continued it in *American Imprints*. Many of these listed items are on microprint; others may be obtained from the repository libraries indicated by the compilers. Anthologies containing plays of this early period include the works listed below.

Clark, Barrett H., ed. *America's Lost Plays*. 20 vols. 1941. Reprint (20 vols. in 10). Bloomington: Indiana University Press, 1963–1965. See volumes 2, 5, 6, 12, 14, 15; and Meserve, Walter J. and William R. Reardon, eds., vol. 21, 1969.

Moody, Richard, ed. *Dramas from the American Theatre 1762–1909*. New York: The World Publishing Company, 1966.

Philbrick, Norman, ed. *Trumpets Sounding Propaganda Plays of the American Revolution*. New York: Benjamin Blom, 1972.

Quinn, Arthur Hobson, ed. *Representative American Plays*. 7th ed. New York: Appleton-Century-Crofts, 1953.

Current Periodicals and Newspapers, 1714–1828

With the exception of some New York newspapers, all of the material listed below may be found either in the microprint reproductions of materials listed in Charles Evans, *American Bibliography* and in the yearly checklists of Ralph R. Shaw and Richard H. Shoemaker, eds., *American Imprints* or in the microfilm reproductions of the American Periodical Series (I, II) made available by University Microfilms, Inc. The annually revised *Guide to Microforms in Print* (Washington, D. C.: Microcards Eds.) and *Newspapers on Microfilm* (Washington, D. C.: Library of Congress) may be consulted. Carl J. C. S. V. Stratman, *American Theatrical Periodicals, 1798–1967: A Bibliographical Guide* (Durham, N. C.: Duke University Press, 1970) provides a slight and incomplete list for the period 1798–1828; Vincent L. Angotti, *American Dramatic Criticism, 1800–1830* (Ph.D. dissertation, University of Kansas, 1967) adds to the list.

The selected periodicals and newspapers listed below contain commentary on American drama and theatre during the years covered in this volume.

The Albion, or British, Colonial, and Foreign Weekly Gazette
American and Commercial Daily Advertiser
American Minerva; A Literary, Entertaining, Scientific Journal
American Monthly Magazine and Critical Review
American Quarterly Review
The Ariel: A Literary and Critical Gazette
The Boston Lyceum
The Boston Magazine

The Boston Weekly Magazine, Devoted to Polite Literature, Useful Science, Biography, and Dramatic and General Criticism
The Boston News-Letter and City Record
The Boston Recorder
The Companion and Weekly Miscellany
The Correspondent
The Critic, A Weekly Review of Literature, Fine Arts, and the Drama
Dramatic Censor
Dramatic Mirror
Dramatic Mirror and Literary Companion
The Emerald
The Gleaner
The Hopkinsian Magazine
The Irish Shield and Literary Panorama
The Irish Shield and Monthly Hilenan: A Historic, Literary, and Dramatic Journal
Ladies Afternoon Visitor
The Ladies' Garland
The Ladies' Literary Cabinet
The Ladies' Literary Port Folio
The Ladies' Monitor
The Lyceum
Maryland Gazette
Merrimack Magazine and Ladies' Literary Cabinet
The Mirror of Taste and Dramatic Censor
The Monthly Register and Review
The National Register
The New York Daily Advertiser
The New York Evening Post
The New York Gazette
The New York Gazette and Weekly Mercury
The New York Mercury
The New York Mirror
North American, or Weekly Journal of Politics, Science and Literature
The North American Magazine
North American Review
Omnium Gatherum
The Ordeal
The Opera Glass
Pennsylvania Gazette
The Pennsylvania Journal
Philadelphia Repository and Weekly Register
The Port Folio
The Rambler's Magazine and New York Theatrical Register
Salmagundi
Something

South Carolina Gazette and Country Journal
The Stranger
The Theatrical Budget
The Theatrical Censor
The Theatrical Censor and Musical Review
The Theatrical Register
Thespian Mirror
Thespian Monitor
The Thistle
Virginia Gazette
The Visitor, or Ladies' Miscellany
Weekly Magazine and Ladies Miscellany
The Yankee, and Boston Literary Gazette

Manuscripts and Theatre Collections

Letters by James Kirk Paulding, David Humphreys, and G. W. Parke Custis at the Huntington Library.

Letters by John Howard Payne and manuscript of Payne's play *Mazeppa; or, The Wild Horse of Tartary* (1825) in the Harvard University Library.

Plays by James Puglia, *The Complete Disappointment; or, A Touch at Modern Times* and *The Embargo*, manuscripts in the Harvard University Library.

Play by St. George Tucker, *The Wheel of Fortune,* manuscript owned by Colonial Williamsburg, Virginia.

Letters by John Neal at the Pierpont Morgan Library.

For reference to particular collections consult Joseph Jones, et al., *American Literary Manuscripts, A Checklist of Holdings in Academic, Historical and Public Libraries in the United States* (Austin: University of Texas Press, 1960); William C. Young, *American Theatrical Arts: A Guide to Manuscript and Special Collections in the United States and Canada* (Chicago: American Library Association, 1971); and Ted Perry, ed., *Performing Arts Resources,* vol. 1 (New York: Drama Book Specialists/Publishers, 1975). In addition to microform collections in the Early American Imprint Series and the American Periodical Series, major collections consulted in the preparation of this volume include those listed below.

Bloomington, Indiana. Indiana University. Lilly Library.
Boston Public Library. Rare Book Section.
Cambridge, Massachusetts. Harvard University. Houghton Library, Theatre Collection.
Chicago. University of Chicago. Rare Book Division.
Lawrence, Kansas. University of Kansas. Spencer Library.
London. Public Record Office.
London. Victoria and Albert Museum. Enthoven Collection.
New York. Lincoln Center. NYPL.
New York. Pierpont Morgan Library.

San Marino, California. Huntington Library.
Washington, D. C. Library of Congress. Rare Book Division.

Dissertations

A primary source for dissertations dealing with American drama is Frederic M. Litto, *American Dissertations on the Drama and Theatre: A Bibliography* (Kent, O.: Kent State University Press, 1969); the "Key-Word-in-Context Index" and the "Subject Index" are particularly useful. It is possible to secure titles through "Key-word" computations from University Microfilms, Inc. One must also consult *Dissertation Abstracts*; James Woodress, *Dissertations in American Literature*; and yearly listings in the *Educational Theatre Journal* and in *American Literature*. The dissertations listed below are particularly relevant to the present volume.

Angotti, Vincent L. "American Dramatic Criticism, 1800–1820." Ph.D. dissertation, University of Kansas, 1967.

Blandford, Lucy. "The Production History of Royall Tyler's *The Contrast*." M.A. thesis, University of Virginia, 1970.

Culp, Ralph Borden. "Drama and Theater As a Source of Colonial American Attitudes Toward Independence, 1758–1776." Ph.D. dissertation, Cornell University, 1962.

Elfenbein, Josef Aaron. "American Drama, 1782–1812, As an Index to Social Political Thought." Ph.D. dissertation, New York University, 1951.

Falk, Armand Elroy. "Theatrical Criticism in the New York Evening Post, 1801–1830." Ph.D. dissertation, Michigan State University, 1968.

Lown, Charles R., Jr. "Business and the Businessman in American Drama Prior to the Civil War." Ph.D. dissertation, Stanford University, 1957.

Menelly, John Henry. "A Study of American Drama Prior to 1801." Ph.D. dissertation, New York University, 1911.

Pagel, Carol Ann Ryan. "A History and Analysis of Representative American Dramatizations from American Novels, 1800–1860." Ph.D. dissertation, University of Denver, 1970.

Robinson, Alice Jean McDonnell. "The Developing Ideas of Individual Freedom and National Unity as Reflected in American Plays and Theatre, 1772–1819." Ph.D. dissertation, Stanford University, 1965.

Schoenberger, Harrold William. "American Adaptations of French Plays on the New York and Philadelphia Stages for 1790 to 1833." Ph.D. dissertation, University of Pennsylvania, 1924.

Sederholm, Frederick L. "The Development of Theories of Dramatic Comedy in America through 1830." Ph.D. dissertation, State University of Iowa, 1961.

Sitton, Fred. "The Indian Play in America, 1750–1900." Ph.D. dissertation, Northwestern University, 1962.

Watson, Charles Sullivan. "Early Dramatic Writing in the South: Virginia and South Carolina Plays, 1798–1830." Ph.D. dissertation, Vanderbilt University, 1966.

INDEX OF PLAYS